Global
Environment
of Business

Global Environment of Business

NorthCoast
Publishers, Inc.

Garfield Heights,
Ohio

Vern Terpstra
University of Michigan

Ravi Sarathy
Northeastern University
Lloyd Russow
Philadelphia University

Published by:
Northcoast Publishers, Inc.
5063 Turney Road, Garfield Heights, OH 44125
(866) 537-0323   •   (216) 332.0324 (Fax)
cservice1@northcoastpub.com

Printed in the United States of America   B C D E F G E

ISBN 1-933583-185

This publication is designed to provide accurate and authoritative information
with regard to the subject matter involved. It is sold with the understanding that
the publisher is not engaged in rendering legal, accounting or other professional
advice. If legal advice or other expert assistance is required, the services of a
qualified professional person should be sought.

–From: **A Declaration of Principles**, jointly adopted by a Committee of the
American Bar Association and a Committee of Publishers and Associations.

Visit our home page at: http://www.northcoastpub.com

CONTENTS

PREFACE

The world of the 21st century is the new world of globalization. We are neighbors internationally in a way that was not true before. Television, the Internet, multinational corporations, increasing immigration\emigration are some of the factors creating the new "global village." Since we can't escape from or separate ourselves from this global neighborhood (example 9/11) we must get acquainted with it and learn to live in it peacefully and profitably.

There is no group for which getting acquainted with our global neighbors is more important than business people – and students of business. For businesses in Europe, North America, and Japan that were used to selling to, and competing with each other, with modest involvement with the other two-thirds of the world's population, this growing global village requires serious learning and adjustment. This two thirds of the world, often called the "Bottom of the Pyramid," is now part of our neighborhood. Thus, the audience for this book is undergraduate and graduate programs in business, study abroad programs in business, international executive programs, and any program with an international business module. The text will be available both in print and electronic form.

How do we get to know our neighbors? Study abroad and foreign exchange students in America are one useful way to gain familiarity with these neighbors. For college students, having "foreign" students together in class is helpful, but having an international experience is even more valuable. Indeed, a new goal at Harvard is to "strengthen undergraduate education by providing more international experiences" for their students. Another example is the University of Michigan's MBA program, which was voted Number 1 in 2004 by the Wall Street Journal. The primary reason was its "Action Based Learning" approach which involves a required two month consulting project with a corporation, government organization, or NGO, and many of these are international with contacts in dozens of countries on every continent. As we say, "experience is the best teacher."

Furthermore, colleges and universities (in the United States and elsewhere) that seek accreditation from AACSB International must internationalize the core business curriculum. This book is written to help faculty who teach marketing, finance, management, accounting, and other business disciplines by providing a resource that focuses on the global business environment. The subjects covered provide examples of how professionals carry out their responsibilities around the world. For example, certification, which began in Europe by the International Standards Organization, has set standards firms must meet to remain competitive, whether European or of another nationality. Accountants, through adoption of ethical standards in one country, also provide a basis for accounting standards in other nations; so while professionals must consider the global business environment when developing strategies, they also affect how their counterparts in other countries do business. Business people are interconnected, whether they realize it or not. We demonstrate how these relationships develop and are how they are manifested.

Multinational corporations and domestic businesses are learning by experience. Formerly neglected global neighbors are becoming major customers, suppliers, and **competitors**. India and China, with one-third of the world's population, especially have caught the eyes of world business. The world's largest steel producer is an Indian firm; and India is also a leader in Information Technology. China is coming on strong in many areas, even buying the PC division of IBM. Established firms are responding to the new global business village by forming various relations with these new "neighbors," such as outsourcing, licensing, joint-ventures, strategic alliances, or acquisitions. These are all part of their learning process.

For students also, experience is the best teacher, but it is always good to "look before you leap." That is the purpose of this book, to introduce the variables which distinguish various neighborhoods of the global village from each other, their forms of government, their economies, their social and cultural patterns, and their political-legal practices.

The book begins with an international business overview, setting out the managerial agenda for firms doing global business. Examples of companies such as Nintendo, Lego and others show the myriad ways in which companies can participate in the global marketplace - by marketing and manufacturing overseas, scouring the world for resources and ideas, finding managerial and scientific talent all over the world. We then review the economic environment of global business, paying attention to major developed countries and markets such as the US, Japan, and Europe; we also focus on developing country markets, such as the key markets of China, India, Brazil and others. We also stress the growing importance of regional economic blocs, such as the EU, NAFTA and Asia-Pacific union.

Beyond markets and economics, cultural differences are one of the most important and bewildering variables influencing the success of international business efforts. The chapter on culture discusses how culture differs along multiple dimensions such as family structure, importance of hierarchy and authority, attitudes to risk-taking, to material goods and accumulating wealth, to sharing and focusing on community, clan and nation versus focusing on individual achievement. We draw on the studies of other scholars to underline approaches to achieving cultural understanding.

Countries and markets vary not only along cultural lines, but also along legal and political dimensions. Therefore, the next chapter frames such differences, explaining the relevance of non-market approaches to development, the role of the State in influencing economic growth and managerial actions, and the impact of different legal systems on doing business around the world.

Managing global business is easier with the development of information technology networks which allow for nearly instantaneous communication, coordination and control of far-flung international operations. The chapter devoted to information technology illustrates how companies such as Benetton, Mast and others use information technology to plan and control global business operations. It also discusses the critical tasks that a company's global information network must accomplish.

The sixth chapter discusses how companies should organize for global operations. Planning is useless without implementation, and people are critical to implementing global strategy. Organization of the company, the assignment of tasks, and the performance rewards, all are elements of a company's global organization.

In the aftermath of the Enron debacle – and similar examples of questionable behavior within a goodly number of other international organizations, leading to SEC-related legislation (Sarbanes-Oxley) – we have added a seventh chapter: "Ethics and International Business" to the usual coverage of the Global Environment of Business. Further, we have captured the essence of the Corporate Social Responsibility reformation literature since the mid-1980's, by introducing the concept of "Managing Beyond Compliance." We trust this will add a bit of contemporary flavor to in-class discussions of this oft-omitted dimension of international business.

Taken together, the seven chapters provide a brief but comprehensive look at the scope of managing global businesses. We trust that the book will serve as a useful introduction and review of one of the central challenges facing the business student and the global business manager.

CHAPTER 1

Introduction
The Concept of Global Business

Learning Objectives

Global business has become important to companies around the world for three reasons: (1) Foreign markets constitute an increasing portion of the total world market. (2) Foreign competitors are increasing their market share in one another's markets. (3) Foreign markets can be essential sources of low-cost products, technology, and financial and human capital. In a word, the United States and other major economies are more interdependent with world markets.

The main goals of this chapter are to

1. Show how interdependent nations have become.

2. Distinguish between international and domestic business.

3. Describe the global environment in which business takes place.

4. Show a variety of ways in which a firm may practice global business.

5. Illustrate how the Internet has played a role in reshaping global business.

6. Emphasize that global business is a matter of perspective in which firms consider the whole world as their market, making few distinctions between domestic and foreign markets.

" The world is too much with us," said Wordsworth. In a different sense, that could be the complaint of many domestic firms that are threatened by the loss of market share from imported goods. Import competition has been increasing. For example, imports were only 1 percent of U.S. gross domestic product (GDP) in 1954; they were 6 percent of GDP in 1964, 10 percent in 1984, and 13.4 percent in 2002. Exports and imports, as a proportion of GDP, have been increasing in similar fashion in most of the world's major economies. In the last 25 years, the amount of total world output accounted for by trade in goods and services rose over 20 percent, to 54 percent in 2002.[1] This means that over half of what is produced every year is to be sold in a foreign country. This book deals with the significance of this international interdependence for the business firm.

As data in Table 1-1 indicate, U.S. imports have been steadily growing, contributing to a worsening balance of trade. Although U.S. interdependence with the world economy is still less than that of many other nations listed in Table 1-1, that interdependence is likely to increase. Many more U.S. firms, whether they like it or not, will be forced to become part of world markets and global competition. At the same time, countries such as China are becoming a major force in the world economy. Meanwhile, nations such as South Korea and Germany have had open economies for some time; their firms are more accustomed to selling in international markets. Hence, some U.S. firms may have to catch up to compete effectively and to gain market share in world markets.

Global Business

Global business is defined as "the collection of activities undertaken by a firm in order to assess and satisfy customer needs, wants, and desires, regardless of location of the customers, manufacturing facilities, suppliers, or intermediaries." This broad definition of business encompasses both for-profit and not-for-profit organizations, whether public or private. When discussing products, this textbook refers not only to manufactured goods, but also to services, ideas, and people (as in political campaigns or movies). A firm's ultimate success depends primarily on how well it performs in the marketplace, requiring knowledge of the market. This involves many responsibilities, including the following:

1. A firm must identify and study its consumers: Who are they? Where are they? Who are prospective buyers? Are they similar to or different from current consumers? What factors are important in consumers' decisions to purchase (or not purchase) the product?
2. The firm must develop the products that satisfy customer needs and wants.
3. The company must set prices and terms on the products so they seem reasonable to buyers and return a fair profit to the company.
4. The company must distribute the products so they are conveniently available to buyers.
5. The firm must inform the market about its wares. With the Internet, distance and time have become less important, while delivery and service have become more important.
6. There is an implied warranty of satisfaction with the product, which differs from country to country. Firms must reassure customers and may need to perform a variety of after-sale services. The firm's responsibility does not end with the sale.
7. Firms must monitor the activities of their domestic and international competitors and develop appropriate organizational structure and long-term strategies and competitive responses.

TABLE 1-1   International Trade Profiles, Selected Countries

Country	1998 ($US Billions)	2002 ($US Billions)	Comments
United States			Major trading partners: Canada, Mexico, Japan, and EU.
GDP	7,921.3	10,207.0	Major exports: capital goods and industrial supplies.
Exports	922.5	966.5	Major imports: capital goods, industrial supplies, consumer goods,
Imports	1,108.5	1,408.0	and automobiles.
Germany			Major trading partners: U.S., EU, and China.
GDP	2,122.7	1,876.3	Major exports: machinery and automobiles.
Exports	621.7	712.7	Major imports: machinery, minerals and fuels, and food.
Imports	595.7	642.8	
Japan			Major trading partners: EU, Central Europe, and U.S.
GDP	4,089.9	4,323.9	Major exports: machinery and vehicles.
Exports	449.7	481.6	Major imports: vehicles, aircraft, and chemicals.
Imports	391.2	443.8	
(South) Korea, Rep.			Major trading partners: U.S., China, and Japan.
GDP	369.9	473.0	Major exports: electrical/electronic products, automobiles, and
Exports	156.2	190.0	semiconductors.
Imports	116.8	187.3	Major imports: machinery and transport equipment, petroleum, and chemicals.
China			Major trading partners: U.S., Argentina, and Europe.
GDP	928.9	1,234.2	Major exports: commodities.
Exports	207.8	365.0	Major imports: fuel, machinery, and chemicals.
Imports	169.0	341.3	

Sources: World Bank, *World Development Report* 1999/2000, Table 1, pages 230–231; *World Development Report,* 2000/2001, Table 20, pages 312–313; *World Development Indicators,* 2004, Table 1.1, pages 15–16; Table 4.5, pages 198–200; Table 4.6, pages 202–204; Table 4.7, pages 206–208; and Table 4.8, pages 210–212. Economist Intelligence Unit, Country Reports, various issues.

Note: Exports and imports data are trade in goods and services combined. GDP is calculated using World Bank Atlas method.

Global business management, therefore, is the planning and coordinating of all of these activities to achieve successfully integrated strategies.

Global business is, by definition, the act of conducting business across national boundaries. One difference between domestic and global business is that the latter includes the task of conducting business between countries, as well as within each country, as shown in Figure 1-1. That is, the global business manager has an additional responsibility—moving products across national boundaries—in addition to moving products within each of the markets the company serves.

FIGURE 1-1 Domestic versus Global Business

Global business includes "between" country distribution

Arrows indicate product distribution

Global Business: A Closer Look

Global business consists of identifying, understanding, and satisfying global customer needs better than the competition (both domestic and international) does and of coordinating activities within the constraints of the global environment. Table 1-2 examines this definition in greater detail and breaks down the main components of global business into five objectives:
- Identifying and understanding global customer needs
- Satisfying customer needs
- Being better than the competition (domestic and international)
- Coordinating strategies
- Recognizing the constraints of the global environment

Identifying and Understanding Global Customer Needs

Customer needs can be identified by carrying out international research. Such research helps a firm understand customer needs in different markets and determine whether those needs are different from those of the customers it currently serves. For example, a U.S. company seeking to sell washing machines in Europe must know that Europeans often wash their clothes with hot water (at a temperature of 60 degrees Centigrade—140 degrees Fahrenheit), whereas most washing in the United States is done at lower water temperatures. Companies also need to analyze market segments across countries in order to position their products appropriately for entry into international markets.

Satisfying Customer Needs

If needs differ across countries and regions, a company must consider how to adapt its products to best satisfy customers. If a company needs to lower prices, it should consider how to cut manufacturing costs and whether to shift manufacturing to a country where manufacturing costs are lower. A well-articulated distribution and logistics system is needed to make sufficient quantities of goods and services available at the point of sale (POS). Ideally, firms also should develop global customer databases and information systems in order to understand and respond to customer needs and purchasing decisions.

Being Better Than the Competition

Firms must contend with both domestic and global competitors. Global competitors may include large multinationals and state-owned enterprises that are not profit-oriented, as well as small local firms. Multinational enterprises have operations in more than one country. Whether large or small, they have a more extensive set of experiences to draw upon and generally have access to resources a domestic firm may not, including labor, financing sources, and managers with a broader perspective. Long-term success comes, in part, from assessing, monitoring, and responding to actions by global competitors, especially in the understanding of competitive and comparative advantages that competitors enjoy.

Coordinating Global Activities

Global business creates a new level of complexity because firms must coordinate their activities across countries. This may involve staffing and allocating responsibilities across units in

TABLE 1-2 Global Business: The Essentials	
Objective	**Corresponding Action**
Identifying and understanding global customer needs	Carrying out global research and analyzing market segments; seeking to understand similarities and differences in customer groups across countries.
Satisfying customer needs	Adapting manufactured goods and services to satisfy different customer needs across countries and regions. Including in manufacturing and technology decisions the implications of costs and prices, development of global customer information databases, and distribution channel and logistics information.
Being better than the competition	Assessing, monitoring, and responding to global competition by offering better value and developing superior brand image and product positioning; broader product range; low prices; high quality; good performance; and superior distribution, advertising, and service. Recognizing that competitors may include state-owned enterprises, other multinationals, and domestic firms, each having different goals, such as market share over profits.
Coordinating strategies	Coordinating business strategies and implementing them across countries, regions, and the global market, which involves centralization, delegation, standardization, and local responsiveness.
Recognizing the constraints of the global environment	Recognizing that the global environment includes: • Complex variation due to governmental, protectionist, and industrial policies. • Cultural and economic differences. • Differences in infrastructure. • Financial constraints due to exchange-rate variation and differences in inflation rates.

different countries and deciding which decisions to decentralize and which to control from headquarters, whether to develop standardized strategies and plans, and how much local responsiveness is appropriate.

Recognizing the Constraints of the Global Environment

The global environment is complex, and this complexity increases as the number of markets served by a firm increases. As firms engage in the international arena, they must cope with cultural and economic differences that exist in the global infrastructure. These costs include factors such as the structure and sophistication of the distribution system (people who prefer or have time to purchase food daily tend to rely less on refrigeration and purchase smaller quantities of products than people who purchase on a weekly basis), the financial constraints imposed by exchange-rate changes and varying inflation rates (which, in turn, depend largely on the state of a nation's economy), and the impact of government policies (especially protectionist and other policies that unfairly benefit competitors and create difficulties in market entry).

At its simplest, global business involves exporting products to a few countries. A firm becomes more of a global player as it increases its direct involvement in overseas markets by controlling more of the decisions regarding pricing, promotion, distribution, and product design.

Manufacturing abroad may be a strategy undertaken to enlarge the customer base. A company may begin manufacturing overseas to lower its costs so it can match the lower prices of strong international competition. Sometimes a company manufactures and sells in the same market. However, a firm may not find it feasible to enter foreign markets alone, instead seeking a partner to share some of the risks, to contribute capital, to add new products (to broaden a product line, for example), or to provide a new distribution channel. The local government may prohibit the foreign company from operating in its country unless the firm has a local partner.

Companies unwilling to commit capital and management resources in foreign countries might be happy to settle for less risk, less involvement, and lower returns by licensing their product or technology to a foreign company. The goal of these companies is still to earn profits from foreign demand, but the approach is indirect. Management is saying, "We'll take fewer headaches in return for lower profits." A firm may seek to license its products or enter into a franchise agreement. These approaches, where someone pays a firm to use its patents and to sell its products, allow firms such as McDonald's to open more outlets and gain access to more customers than they could if they were to rely solely on their own capital to build new stores.

Foreign customers can force a company to change the ways it does business. A foreign buyer may insist that the selling firm accept payment in kind: orange juice or wine or chickens in return for machinery. If the firm accepts the offer, it then finds itself peddling orange juice and chickens around the world, a consequence of the growing trend toward countertrade in global business.

Thus, for a company entering foreign markets, activities may include exporting and importing (foreign sourcing), manufacturing overseas (with or without partners), countertrade, licensing, and franchising.

Global Business Management

The complexity of global business is due largely to two factors: global competition and the global environment. Customer needs vary across countries. Competitors with different strengths now come from all over the world. Likewise, the global environment presents a bewildering variety of national governments, cultures, and income levels. Strategic management is often portrayed as the task of responding to the uncontrollable factors in the firm's environment while manipulating the controllable factors.

As depicted in Figure 1-2, the global environment is multifaceted. The controllable elements of the global environment include the product, place, promotion, and physical distribution. The uncontrollable elements are those things firms cannot control, such as the legal environment. However, firms can exert pressure on and affect change in these "uncontrollable" elements. For example, by introducing products such as computers and the Internet, marketers change how people communicate (a part of culture). The so-called "controllable" elements are not always totally under the firms' influence. Governments place price floors on products such as cigarettes (or add to the price of the product through taxes). Global business management has the same task as that of a domestic manager, but must view the environment in broader terms. Thus, product, accounting principles, and financing may vary across, say, France, Brazil, India, and the United States. While managers must consider the laws of a nation when doing business domestically, in the global environment, they must take into account the laws of many nations. Furthermore, they must contend with the possibility that the laws of one country may conflict with those of another.

An added dimension of global business strategic management is the need for a firm to coordinate and integrate its many national programs into an effective multinational program. Indeed, a principal rationale of multinational business operations (as opposed to the alternative

FIGURE 1-2 Global Environment

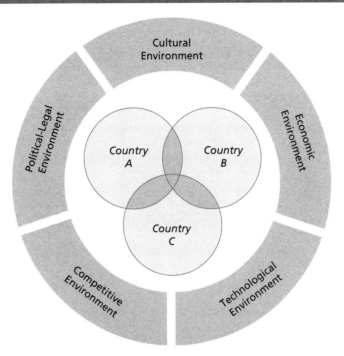

of independent national companies) is that the division of labor and the transfer of know-how in international operations enable the whole to be greater than the sum of its parts.

A practical result of these differences is that a global manager needs broader competence than domestic managers or managers dealing with a specific foreign country. In other words, the global business manager has a dual responsibility: **foreign business management** (the act of doing business within foreign countries) and **global business management** (the act of coordinating business activities in multiple markets in the face of global competition).

Of particular interest is what global business managers think are the most important aspects of their duties and responsibilities. Professor Kashani at IMD, Switzerland, conducted a survey of marketing and general managers.[2] The sample was predominantly European (72 percent) and split among industrial products (45 percent), consumer goods (21 percent), pharmaceuticals (14 percent), and services (20 percent). Their main concerns are presented in Table 1-3.

The Global Marketplace

To get a sense of the range of activities that constitute global businesss, consider some examples of companies operating in the global marketplace. It is helpful to see how different companies make decisions regarding products, prices charged, distribution channels, countries sold to, and partners chosen—all in an attempt to increase sales and profits.

TABLE 1-3 Managers' Major Concerns	
Concern	**Contributing Factors and Explanation**
Developing new products	The pace of innovation is so high that every firm must be capable of launching new products in a timely fashion. Time-to-market is a critical variable in determining competitive advantage.
Developing relationships with suppliers, distributors, and customers	The complexity of technology and markets demands that companies develop long-term partnership relations with suppliers to jointly develop products and processes, with distributors to launch detailed marketing campaigns in many countries, and with customers to learn about the utility of their products and to cooperatively develop product modifications and new products.
Fewer but stronger global competitors	The resource and scale needs of global markets are leading to mergers, acquisitions, and greater industry concentration. Larger competitors have greater resources and the ability to implement global strategies over a longer time horizon; this places pressure on firms to grow, seek alliances, and constantly seek partners and acquisition candidates. The alternative is to become a takeover candidate of other companies.
Growing price competition	Products become commodities more rapidly. This, coupled with scale economies, leads to severe price competition. Firms must either reduce costs or innovate constantly to compete on the basis of differentiated products rather than price.
Greater regional integration and government regulation	Increasing regionalization, examples of which include the European Union, NAFTA, and ASEAN trading blocs. Other important influences on strategy include government regulations, such as local content laws and trade barriers (tariff and non-tariff barriers).
Developing a marketing culture	Listening to the customer is paramount; enhancing and using communication capabilities are essential to successful global business, as is recognition of other important constituencies, such as the environmental lobby.

Source: K. Kashani, "Marketing Futures: Priorities for a Turbulent Environment," *Long-Range Planning* 28(4), 1995, 87–98.

Nintendo in the Global Video Game Market

Is there a teenager in America who has not played a Nintendo game? This 100-year-old Japanese company of the same name, which originally sold playing cards, began marketing the Nintendo game machine as Famicom, a family computer, in Japan in 1983. Meanwhile, in the United States, Atari was leading the computer game industry. Despite waning interest in Atari games, Nintendo was aware of the huge potential in the United States and test-marketed its computer in New York in 1984. By 1991, the product had achieved greater penetration than any other home computer or personal computer: 30 million Nintendo machines had been sold to U.S. consumers.

The Nintendo machine was simple and was designed to be connected to the home TV set. Despite having similar capabilities to early computers, Nintendo called it a "game" rather than a "computer." (The unit had no keyboard and no functions other than to play games.) The units were sold through toy stores and were priced at just under $100, much less than the price of computers at that time.

Nintendo's U.S. sales increased from $800 million in 1987 to $3.3 billion in 1990, with a U.S. market share of nearly 80 percent. Nintendo was able to capture one of every $5 spent on toys in the United States.

Since Nintendo had such a large share of the market, it was slow to introduce new technologies. Meanwhile, in 1991, its competitor, Sega, in an attempt to capture some of this lucrative market, introduced a 16-bit system called Genesis about a year before Nintendo introduced its own machine. (Sega did not achieve much success until it introduced a new game, Sonic the Hedgehog, which was wildly attractive to game players.)

Nintendo followed suit; but because Sega had introduced its machine first, Sega and Nintendo split the emerging market for 16-bit systems, with each firm selling between 5 million and 6 million new systems by 1992.

Competitive pressure is typical for profitable industries: Nintendo, in 1990, earned profits of $350 million on sales of $2.5 billion. Such profits attract competition; therefore, Nintendo later found it difficult to maintain its 80 percent share of the market.[3]

Sony decided to enter the market with an even more advanced technology machine, the Sony PlayStation, which used 32-bit graphics and played games from a CD-ROM. These two features allowed for more complex and faster games with breathtaking graphics, colors, and sound. Again, because Nintendo was slow to introduce a newer-technology machine, Sony was able to gain considerable market share with its Sony PlayStation. This competitive edge continued with Sony's next generation PlayStation 2 (PS2).

Large profits also attracted Microsoft's attention, which saw the video game system as a source of profits as well as an avenue to attract new consumers into a networked gaming world. Microsoft's Xbox was launched at considerable investment—and with the likelihood of large initial losses as it attempted to play catch-up with Sony and Nintendo.

By 2003, video game industry revenues in the United States exceeded revenues from movie ticket sales. Sony had about 60 percent of the video game consoles in the world, with the remaining 40 percent split nearly equally between Microsoft and Nintendo.

The computer gaming business is a fascinating example of how technology and marketing can interact to form a profitable worldwide consumer-oriented industry and how technological and environmental change can threaten market leadership. Evolving customer needs, competition, and technological change led to the successive market leadership of first Atari, then Nintendo, Sega, and Sony, followed by Microsoft, which made a large investment with the next technology cycle of network gaming.[4]

Disney with a Foreign Accent

With Disney characters such as Mickey Mouse having been shown in movies and cartoons all over the world for 50 years, Tokyo Disneyland was a logical creation. It began in 1983 as a joint venture between Mitsui Real Estate Development and Keisei Railway companies. The Walt Disney Company, however, had no ownership share; it designed the amusement park and it supplies its managerial expertise, receiving in return royalties of 10 percent of gate and 5 percent of concessions.

With this foreign success, Disney expanded into Europe. Construction of Euro Disneyland began in the summer of 1989, 20 miles east of Paris, at a cost of $2.8 billion for the first phase. The Paris location was chosen, in part, because 109 million people lived within a six-hour drive and because, as part of the deal, France agreed to build a high-speed train between the theme park and Paris (with travel time estimates of just 30 minutes each way). Unlike its stake in Tokyo Disneyland, Disney owns 49 percent, the maximum permitted by the French government.

Disney began promoting the Disney characters with French corporate partners such as Renault and Banque Nationale de Paris. Disney also started a Disney Channel on European television in a joint venture with media entrepreneur Rupert Murdoch and aired Disney entertainment specials in Europe. Disney even adapted the park to reflect European culture. Fantasyland focused on the Grimm Brothers' fairy tales and Lewis Carroll's *Alice in Wonderland*. Discoveryland focused attention on European greats such as Jules Verne, Leonardo da Vinci, and H. G. Wells.

Signs are in multiple languages, and employees are expected to speak at least two languages.

In its first year of operation, attendance at Euro Disney was about 20 percent lower than targeted. High European admission prices (about 30 percent higher than at Walt Disney World in Orlando), recession in Europe, and roads blocked by protesting farmers have been cited as some reasons for lower-than-planned attendance. Disney also encountered some labor problems because French workers were less willing to comply with stringent Disney standards pertaining to dress, hairstyle, and general appearance.

Euro Disney opened to high hopes in April 1992, but it incurred continual losses for the next three years prior to registering a minuscule profit of 2 million French francs before extraordinary gains on a debt restructuring.

Why did this park perform poorly when Disneyland operations in the United States and Japan were so successful? Reasons include (1) location—a 20-minute train ride from Paris with little else in the area to hold tourists' interest and cold weather much of the year; (2) relatively high prices; (3) a limited number of rides, allowing tourists to go through the park in a day and providing them with little incentive to stay overnight at Disney-owned hotels; (4) little cultural adaptation to familiar childhood characters (Goofy in the United States versus Asterix in France) and a ban on wine sales (later rescinded); and (5) a European recession that resulted in a decrease in the number of visitors (attendance dropped from around 9.8 million in the first year to 8.8 million from 1993 to 1994, with about 9 million in the third year of operation). The Disney Corporation also learned that tourists preferred to bring their meals as picnic lunches rather than purchase fast food and that few customers bought souvenirs. This meant that attendees spent less per person at Euro Disney than at the firm's other parks. Competitors also emerged, such as Blackpool Pleasure Beach, Tivoli Gardens in Copenhagen, and Anheuser-Busch's Port Aventura in the sunnier climate near Barcelona, Spain.[5]

For all of these reasons, the highly leveraged amusement park, with over $3.4 billion in debt, incurred over $750 million in losses its first three years and was forced to restructure its operations. Disney had spent heavily on creating a hotel complex around the park outside of Paris. However, since the park was only a short train ride away from the center of Paris, many tourists avoided staying at park hotels, opting instead to combine a day trip to the park with a hotel stay in Paris. This is quite unlike Orlando, where Disney is the major attraction and tourists, principally Americans, seem to enjoy planning their holidays around entertainment provided by Disney.

Walt Disney, the parent company of Euro Disney, attempted a variety of cost-cutting strategies in the 1990s and early part of this century, including postponing expansions, deferring royalty payments, lowering admission prices, reducing hotel rates, and cutting costs. Yet French labor laws made it difficult to reduce costs by cutting the work force. (Plans were to reduce the number of workers from 17,000 to about 12,000.)

In 2002, the $600 million Walt Disney Studio Park opened; but as with the original theme park, attendance figures and profits were much lower than expected. Among other things, Disney had incorrectly forecasted that a high number of Germans would vacation at the park. Moreover, the timing of the grand opening took place just six months after the September 11, 2001, terrorist attacks, which discouraged travel from other European locations. Losses through mid-2004 increased to $134 million, and the firm accumulated $2.7 million in debt. As part of a refinancing deal by Euro Disney creditors, Disney initiated a second round of restructuring in 2004.

The European market has been tough on the theme park industry. Besides Disney, Universal Studios and Six Flags have encountered similar difficulties.[6]

Profiting from the Newly Rich

To succeed in global business, one must form as well as understand consumers' tastes in different countries. Dickson Poon of Hong Kong has made a fortune estimated at over $1 billion by selling luxury brand-name goods to the newly rich from Japan and the fast-growing countries of Southeast Asia; namely, Hong Kong, Malaysia, Singapore, South Korea, and Taiwan. While working as an apprentice in Geneva at Chopard, a jeweler and maker of fine watches, Poon absorbed the ambience of high-fashion, high-price retailing. Stores were understated, refined, and luxurious; and there was no hard sell. Poon took this style back to Hong Kong, opening a European-type store in Hong Kong's most upscale shopping center. He emphasized attentive service and carefully selected merchandise, concentrating on brands such as Chopard, Rolex, Hermes, and Audemars Piguet. The concept worked. Poon then obtained the Charles Jourdan fashion franchise (adding names such as Polo/Ralph Lauren and Guy Laroche) and, in some cases, obtained licensing rights to manufacture and distribute franchise products in the Far East (and worldwide). Poon's signature is an elegant shop in a prime location; he now operates over 70 such stores. But his winning insight is the appeal of famous brand names to newly rich customers. About one-third of Poon's sales are to traveling Japanese businesspeople and tourists. In November 1987, he purchased S. T. Dupont, which makes luxury lighters and pens. Poon's aim was to use the Dupont name to introduce new lines of menswear, luggage, and watches. His business is vanity, making a profit from it wherever it can be found.[7]

The Asian economic crisis that began in June 1997 hurt retail sales all across Asia, and Dickson Poon was no exception. Sales dropped sharply as the newly rich lost their assets in the stock market and were threatened with job losses and recession. Even so, Poon continued to expand in Asia, developing larger stores, focusing on major brands such as Tommy Hilfiger and Ferrari, and selling off a portion of his ownership in major European luxury goods firms such as Austin Nichols (U.K.) and DuPont (France). These equity sales allowed Poon to raise capital for further expansion in Asia at a time when the economy was reeling and competitors were running for cover. What Poon was banking on was the long-term continued growth of Asia as the recession wound down and incomes started rising again and new fortunes were made. Poon continues to expand rapidly across Asia and to look for additional acquisitions, even an investment in Harrods, the famed up-market U.K. retailer.[8]

Korean Furs (for Less)

Similar thinking drives the world's largest fur manufacturer, Jindo Fur Company of South Korea. Jindo's goal is to develop a chain of stores selling furs worldwide. It targets the low end of the market—furs selling under $2,000. This figure was chosen because approximately 60 percent of all fur sales are at or below that price. To sell profitably at this price, Jindo uses Korean labor and vertical integration. It buys pelts at auctions in North America, Scandinavia, and Russia. Jindo then treats and assembles the pelts in its Seoul factories before selling them in its worldwide outlets. Forty-five Jindo fur salons are located in South Korea, Hong Kong, Europe, North America, Hawaii, and Guam. Although tropical islands may seem like odd locations, Jindo markets furs to tourists on vacation.[9]

Jindo began its worldwide operations by selling in duty-free shops to Japanese tourists and advertising in in-flight magazines. Jindo's discounted prices were appealing to Japanese tourists when compared with the high prices charged at home, as Dickson Poon also discovered. Recently, a joint venture, Jindorus, was established with Interlink of Russia. The first store opened in

Dolls for Chinese Children

China has over one billion people, of whom about one-third are between the ages of 3 and 16, totaling about 375 million. Because population-control practices in China typically restrict families to one child, parents and grandparents lavish much love and attention on their only child or grandchild. Among other things, this means they are willing to splurge on toys, despite the average income of only $1,100 in 2003 (versus $37,600 in the United States). Anthony Chirico, who founded Nanuet Entertainment, had been selling to China such U.S. TV shows as *G.I. Joe* and *Teenage Mutant Ninja Turtles.* He saw an opportunity to increase his markets in China by selling Western toys, teaming up with a client who had been selling the Robotech line of plastic figures in the United States. Chinese children traditionally played with toys made of wood and metal; and the newer colorful plastic figures priced between $1.60 and $30.00, Chirico speculated, might be attractive to the children and their families.

The U.S. toy introduction was accompanied by an 85-episode cartoon series. Chirico began by licensing the TV cartoon show for nominal fees and by persuading the Chinese TV stations to allow his company to insert TV commercials for Robotech toys in the middle of programs. (Chirico also had to overcome the Chinese preference for showing commercials in five-minute blocks at the end of programs). Those negotiations

the Intourist Hotel in Moscow, with additional stores to be opened as the Russian economy improves. Jindo sees a huge untapped market potential for furs, but attention to costs and global expansion is essential to its long-term success.

Where the Buyers Are

Sometimes foreign markets may be the only markets in which a company's products can be sold. Consider water desalination, for instance. About two-thirds of the world's water desalination plants used to convert saltw ater into freshwater are in Saudi Arabia. These plants use considerable energy and are expensive to run. Saudi Arabia has plentiful energy and high incomes; it is also a country where salt water is plentiful, while freshwater is scarce. Ionics, Inc., of Watertown, Massachusetts, has built its business around water desalination, with considerable sales coming from North Africa and the Middle East, not the United States.

Where the Ideas Are

Overseas markets can also be a source of new product ideas. Environmentalists in the United States and Europe have been pushing for cleaner, less-polluting electric cars to replace gasoline-powered vehicles in order to reduce dependence on imported oil. California has even mandated that 2 percent of cars sold in 1998 and after be emission-free. The practical problem is that electric-car batteries retain only enough energy to be driven about 60 miles before requiring a recharge. A battery that promises extended ranges—180 to 250 miles—and that can be recharged in minutes rather than hours is understandably generating much excitement. One such producer is Electric Fuel, which conducted a two-year field test in Germany with the German phone and postal services, car companies Mercedes-Benz and Opel, and Siemens to help took three years. The programs also were dubbed in Mandarin Chinese and were attractive to Chinese stations because their themes—family values and world cooperation against aliens—were not in conflict with Chinese values. A Hong Kong–based toy company supervised production of the toys in China and distributed them. Chirico was able to convince the Chinese TV stations to start showing the Robotech cartoon series shortly after the toys went on sale in department stores.

The toys were first introduced into Shanghai and Guangdong, the most prosperous areas of China, then into other provinces. As children in Guangdong became exposed to Hong Kong TV, however, their tastes evolved to the likes of Batman. As a result, Robotech toys began to sell better in the distant provinces in northeast China, where newer fads such as Batman had yet to catch on.

Chinese parents' preoccupation with their only child is not limited to buying toys. Chinese parents play English language tapes to their unborn child, hoping to give the child a head start. Later, the child might hear Tang dynasty poetry, music, and the Roman alphabet and numbers, all of which could provide Western marketers with new global opportunities. As China becomes more affluent, Chinese scholars have begun to worry about the possible impact of such lavish attention on their children. A study by Kara Chan notes, with relief, that even young children are not overtly affected by materialism.

Sources: Andrew Tanzer, "China's Dolls," *Forbes*, December 21, 1992; "Study This, Baby: Chinese Fetuses Bear Heavy Course Loads," *Wall Street Journal*, February 8, 1994; Kara Chan, "Materialism among Chinese Children in Hong Kong", *International Journal of Advertising & Marketing to Children*, July 2003, Volume 4, Issue 4, pages 47–62.

Data Query: http://devdata.worldbank.org/data-query; accessed January 27, 2004.

decide whether 40,000 phone and postal services delivery vehicles could switch to electric batteries. Recharging is quickly accomplished by removing spent fuel cassettes and replacing them with new ones, the used fuel cells being reprocessed chemically at regeneration plants. These batteries are also safe; Electric Fuel's zinc-air batteries, for example, operate at ambient temperatures and use a combination of zinc, zinc oxide, and air instead of dangerous molten chemicals used in batteries from other developmental efforts.[10] Together with DaimlerChrysler, Electric Fuel successfully completed a multiyear government-funded program to demonstrate the viability of zinc-air fuel cells in an all-electric passenger taxi hybrid van.

How the World Would Like to Smell

Gillette wanted to create an "intentionally global" fragrance—that is, a line of deodorants, shaving gels, aftershave, and related products that would appeal to men in the United States and Europe. However, Carl Klumpp, Gillette's chief perfumer, knew that European men were heavier users of fragrances, starting with shower gel, then using a deodorant body spray, and perhaps finishing off with eau de toilette (similar to a light cologne). American men own cologne and aftershave but don't wear them routinely—"less than one-quarter had a killer cologne for attracting women," and most thought that the subject was too personal to discuss with friends.[11] Klumpp, who might begin the day spending 30 minutes smelling different substances for practice, decided on a citrusy chypre family of fragrances for starters; then he asked four of the world's major fragrance supply houses to come up with a formula using his preferred smell. After much testing, Gillette launched the Cool Wave line of deodorants in 1992. It and the similarly conceived and launched Wild Rain line were enormous successes in both the United States and Europe. And while Klumpp swears by his nose, he also uses a gas chromatograph to analyze the

Global Business: Planning Upstream and Downstream Linkages

Tate & Lyle (T&L), a UK-based food multinational that specializes in ingredients such as sugar, starches, proteins, and animal feed, is constantly scouring the world for new sources of supply. T&L had experience in sugar manufacturing around the world and had worked with joint ventures in Thailand and China. When the firm identified Vietnam as a new Asian source for sugarcane and saw the potential for increasing local demand (for growing consumption of products such as soft drinks), management agreed that it would be a good place to expand its sugar operations. Another factor was the Vietnamese government's interest in expanding domestic sugar operations so the nation would become self-sufficient in sugar, rather than rely on imports.

T&L placed great importance on careful site selection for its sugar refinery, with the goal of locating plants close to local cane growers. It chose a remote location inside Vietnam, the central Nghe An province,

aroma molecules in different substances, making it easier to combine fragrances and to copy specific smells. Givaudan, a Swiss chemical company, undertakes regular expeditions to the rain forest in search of rare and unusual flavors and exotic aromas. Givaudan scientists visited Madagascar and came back with 150 samples, including the scent of the previously unknown rara flower, whose aroma is combination of natural strawberry, floral, jasmine, and honeysuckle.[12]

Risks and Differences of Foreign Markets: Russia

Getting the product to the consumer can be quite a feat in emerging markets. Ben & Jerry's, the manufacturers of superpremium ice cream in unusual flavors, began a 70 percent joint venture with the company Iceverks, manufacturing and selling ice cream in Karelia, Russia, 700 miles north of Moscow. The companies deliberately waited two years before expanding into Moscow, as they did not want quality to suffer because of poor logistics and supply problems. There were shortages of refrigerated trucks, which had to be imported. Franchisees lacked freezers, and Iceverks had to sell or lease equipment to them so that ice cream could be kept frozen. Franchisees and their employees had to be taught to be polite to customers and to restock inventory before completely running out of certain flavors. Franchisees were selected based on personal contacts and trust. Iceverks chose a small Moscow distributor, Vessco, because key managers at the two companies had been classmates. Despite these efforts, continued Russian economic difficulties made profitable operation a distant dream, ultimately leading Ben & Jerry's to divest from their Russian venture and consider U.S. expansion instead.[13]

A somewhat different tack was taken by Mary Kay in selling cosmetics in Russia. With economic liberalization, Russian women began to seek Western cosmetics. At the same time, several Russian state-owned enterprises privatized and Russian women were often getting laid off in downsizings. These women were seeking new jobs and stable income sources. Mary Kay thus found a ready-made environment for its products—reasonably priced American cosmetics—as well as for its sales approach of multilayered marketing. Relying on women acting as independent representatives, buying cosmetics for themselves at 40 percent off retail and then because of suitable soil and large-acreage farms. But Nghe An had few good roads, and few farmers had experience growing sugarcane. The farmers were reluctant to plant sugarcane until T&L had built its factory, then waited until other farmers planted the new crop. Despite these difficulties, T&L was able to convince enough farmers to plant sugarcane. However, a drought in the initial year of production lowered yields and meant another setback, resulting in the factory operating at just over 5 percent of capacity (65,000 tons compared to a target of 1.1 million tons).

T&L obtained a loan from the International Finance Corporation (IFC) of $50 million. It designed a highly automated refinery, with quality and throughput in mind. The firm had to continuously work on developing relationships with farmers, who wanted cash on delivery, not staggered payments as was T&L's custom. T&L adapted, though, and paid cash on delivery of the sugarcane. It also developed software to help farmers decide when crops should be harvested, when fields should be fertilized, and where to plant improved seedlings. The farmers had to be persuaded to accept such advice. In running its operations, it used few expatriates, preferring to train local management.

Source: "Tate & Lyle Is Well Placed in Vietnam," *Wall Street Journal*, May 5, 2004.

selling them in small groups of friends and acquaintances, Mary Kay found Russian women avid to take on the job of selling its products. This was particularly true since a Mary Kay representative could earn $300 to $400 a month compared to an average salary for Russian women of a little over $100 a month. Mary Kay has had to train its representatives, of course, with more experienced representatives training new recruits in areas such as understanding the quality and use of products, being well groomed, being polite and complimentary to potential clients, and doing basic bookkeeping. Representatives from more distant locales face further difficulties, having to come to Moscow to replenish their cosmetics supplies. Sales continue to grow, from US $90 million in 2000 to nearly $150 million by 2003—a whopping 40 percent increase![14]

Timken in China
Timken entered China in 1996, planning to manufacture automotive bearings in a joint venture in China and sell the output to local Chinese firms. But the company had difficulty collecting receivables from Chinese state-owned firms. Timken then attempted to sell products to foreign auto firms, which were beginning to locate and manufacture in China. But the 1997 Asian financial crisis and low volumes led Timken to re-examine its strategy.

The company decided to begin manufacturing in China for export, sending 70 percent of output to Europe. The goal was eventually to export 100 percent of production. At the same time, Chinese economic growth and equipment needs in manufacturing allowed Timken to begin importing newer technology products for sale in China, with the potential for after-sales service and revenues. Strategic flexibility in response to performance shortfalls and the changing environment were key to Timken's gradual success.

Piracy Lives On!
William Tay, owner of the Hye Mieko, saw his ship leave Singapore, headed for Cambodia with photographic supplies and general cargo. He lost contact with the ship when it was about 180 nautical miles from Cambodia. Already having had another ship hijacked and $2 million of

cargo stolen, he hired a Lear jet to search for his ship. Searching in international waters off the coast of China, he found the ship 60 miles from Vietnam. The ship, which seemed to have a naval vessel in its wake, did not respond to signals; so Tay took pictures and flew to Shanwei, 120 kilometers from Hong Kong, where the ship was expected to land. The hope was that the Chinese authorities would help recover the ship and its cargo. China launched a campaign against sea pirates and in 1994 alone, investigated 209 cases of piracy, recovering 22 ships.[15] The problem is a continued headache for shippers, with the International Maritime Bureau reporting a 37 percent increase to 234 pirate attacks worldwide in the first six months of 2003, compared to 171 in the corresponding period in 2002.[16]

Learning from the Examples

Companies market their products internationally for several reasons:

1. They want to take advantage of the potential of world markets. Nintendo, Disney, the Japanese motorcycle industry, and Jindo Furs have all benefited from expanding their foreign market potential.
2. They want to diversify geographically.
3. They want to use excess production capacity and take advantage of a low-cost position due to experience-curve economies and economies of scale. The Japanese motorcycle industry's thrust into the United States was aided greatly by its superior low-cost position.
4. A product can be near the end of its life cycle in the domestic market while just beginning to generate growth abroad. Dickson Poon's export of brand-name luxury goods to the Far East is an example of taking advantage of the general rise in conspicuous consumption that accompanies prosperity. Selling Robotech toys to China is an example of responding to lagging product cycles in developing countries.
5. Sometimes overseas markets are a source of new products and ideas. Companies in foreign markets can become joint-venture partners, providing capital and market access.
6. Tested market entry methods can work in emerging markets, as shown by Mary Kay in Russia. Emerging markets, however, require patience and sometimes innovative market entry modes, as in the case of Ben & Jerry's in Russia. Global business activities can bring expected risks, such as international currency risk, but also unexpected risks, such as piracy in the China Sea.
7. One of the most difficult aspects of global business is developing products with universal appeal, as illustrated by Disney. Success in one country does not always translate to success in another country, as Euro Disney illustrates. In the face of competition from video games, LEGO is faced with trying to make its bricks appealing to children in the Far East.
8. Any successful global business effort will attract competition. Nintendo has seen its 90 percent video game market share erode as competitors innovate with new products, price cutting, alliances, and persistence.
9. There are many ways to enter foreign markets, as the examples suggest, ranging from simple exporting to more complex and risky investments involving manufacturing, marketing, and top management.

The U.S. Firm in the Global Marketplace

Although the global market is attractive, U.S. firms have been slow to take advantage of it. The United States has always been one of the world's largest markets. It is also a self-contained, continent-sized market. For about 30 years after World War II, little foreign competition existed in the United States. Today, however, foreign firms from all over the world vie for a piece of the U.S. market. At the same time, other countries have grown so fast and become so prosperous that their markets have become more attractive than the U.S. market. An example is the fax machine, which grew rapidly in Japan before becoming popular in the United States as the Japanese market was reaching saturation. Likewise, the market for railroad cars is small in the United States as compared to Europe, where train transportation is more popular. Also, the building of nuclear power plants in the United States has become strictly regulated, even though foreign countries readily accept them as a source of energy.

Ignoring foreign markets and foreign competition presents two risks for U.S. companies: losing market share at home and not profiting from higher growth in overseas markets.

Export Sales and Sales from Foreign Subsidiaries

Larger U.S. firms have generally been able to participate in global business due to their superior financial and managerial resources. Table 1-4 lists multinational companies with significant foreign sales from their overseas operations. For the purposes of this text, a **multinational corporation** (MNC) is one in which the company manufactures and markets its products or services in several countries. Almost every company on the list find it more efficient to sell from their foreign manufacturing subsidiaries than through exports. In addition, exports may have no chance to succeed because they are too highly priced in relation to local competition or they are kept out by government barriers. Most of the firms on the list could not maintain their market share in foreign markets without establishing a foreign subsidiary.

The question of how much a firm should obtain from foreign revenues and how much it should export is unresolved. As market conditions and the product life cycle change, companies may find that effective selling overseas requires foreign subsidiaries and that such foreign subsidiary sales may replace exports over time.

Importance of Foreign Direct Investment (FDI)

Companies can generate international sales from exporting or by selling goods made by their subsidiaries in foreign countries. As a method of market entry, foreign sales subsidiaries or foreign manufacturing facilities are preferred over other alternatives for a variety of reasons:

• To lower costs, such as manufacturing expenses, by using cheaper inputs such as labor (*outsourcing* is a familiar term for this strategy); to lower distribution costs by shortening the number of channels; and to reduce transportation costs by shortening the distance that products or components need to be shipped

• To get around trade barriers, such as tariffs, by manufacturing locally or bypassing government disincentives, such as *buy local* or *buy member* legislation (as one might see among members of NAFTA [North American Free Trade Agreement] and the EU [European Union])

• To serve customers better by learning about local needs through closer contact

TABLE 1-4 Foreign Sales of Major MNCs, 2003			
Company	Total Sales ($ billions)	Foreign Sales ($ billions)	Foreign Sales as a % of Total Sales (%)
Wal-Mart Stores	256.3	47.6	18.6
BP (U.K.)	232.6	184.7	79.4
General Motors	185.5	51.6	27.8
DaimlerChrysler (Germany)	171.9	142.0	82.6
Ford Motor	138.4	54.8	39.6
General Electric	134.2	60.8	45.0
Total (France)	131.6	105.6	80.2
Toyota Motor (Japan)	129.0	73.9	57.3
ChevronTexaco	120.0	64.2	53.5
Carrefour Group (France)	96.9	47.5	49.0
Allianz Worldwide (Germany)	96.9	67.8	70.0
ING Group (Netherlands)	94.7	71.0	75.0

Source: Forbes 2000—The World's Leading Companies, 2004; company web sites and annual reports (for complete list, see Instructor materials).

- To forgo at least some foreign exchange risk by offsetting foreign income with foreign liabilities (for example, using local sales to purchase local supplies)

Table 1-5 shows foreign direct investment (FDI) flows, which provide some indication of the level of firm market entry activity via FDI. Note that most of the FDI goes to rich or developed nations, which number fewer than 50 countries, rather than the 150 developing nations. When looking at the FDI inflow among the top ten host nations, note the figures on China, which is considered a developing nation.

The Role of the Internet in Reshaping Global Business

The Internet impacts strategic business decisions about promotion and distribution, as well as all communication among a firm's employees, its customers, its suppliers, and other stakeholders. For example, with respect to physical distribution, web sites provide firms with a nonstore retail outlet and provide retailers with a wholesale outlet. The Internet can also be a means of product delivery in the case of electronic or digitized products such as music, video, and software. Strategic decisions about promotion are also affected by the Internet. When promoting products, firms need to decide when to place advertisements. (Why do windshield wiper ads air on the radio only when it is raining?) Advertising—information about products, services, etc.—is available all of the time. Geography is no longer a problem. (Compare Internet advertising to billboards; for example, a billboard on Route 76 is not seen by people on Route 23.) As long as a server is running and connected to the Internet, anyone can view the material on a web page, regardless of location. Promotion via the Internet can act as mass personal selling, where the communication is tailored to the individual. The technology exists to personalize information for each viewer (My MSN page, for example).

Internet advertising is more interactive than other avenues, with consumers and nonconsumers having the power and control to select what they see; to compare product, price, and delivery offerings among competitors quickly and easily; and to have access to a broader set of

TABLE 1-5 Foreign Direct Investment Inflows		
Country	1998 ($ billions)	2001 ($ billions)
World	694.5	735.1
Developed Nations	484.2	503.1
United States	103.4	124.4
United Kingdom	33.2	53.8
France	23.2	52.6
Netherlands	11.1	50.5
Germany	12.2	31.8
Developing Nations	187.6	204.8
China, PRC	44.2	46.8
Mexico	14.0	24.7
China, Hong Kong	11.4	22.8
Brazil	19.0	22.5
Poland	4.9	8.8

Sources: Foreign Direct Investment Inflows in Country Groups (http://www.unctad.org/Templates/WebFlyer.asp?intItemID=2111&lang=1); accessed July 22, 2004; Top Ten Foreign Direct Investment Host Economies in 2001 (http://www.unctad.org/Templates/WebFlyer.asp?intItemID=2087&lang=1); accessed July 22, 2004; United Nations Conference on Trade and Development (UNCTAD).

alternatives in nearly every product category. (Firms must put a lot of information on the Web and make it easily accessible, allowing consumers to pick and choose.) Consumers rely on the Internet as a search tool in large part because it is cheaper, it is less time-consuming, and it offers a broader assortment than conducting a search by driving around or calling or writing companies with questions. Consumers can become better informed (or ill-informed depending on the source) quicker. Consumer power comes from the ability to direct the message received.

Segmentation may be more difficult, but that is changing as technologies allow computer users to determine who is accessing information on their computer.

The Internet can be used to collect and disseminate vast amounts of information. Collection of information on people who are connected to the Internet is under constant scrutiny for ethical and moral reasons. Controls and guidelines are being developed and refined regularly.

Companies must incorporate their domain name, which is a firm's URL (Internet address), into their branding strategy. No one wants to key in an address such as http://www.getabetter-mousetrapforlessmoney.com. Consumers must also be able to find a company's web site easily, using search engines, which is partly a function of design (meta tags, for instance). Locating a site easily also has to do with how useful people find the site—the more a site is referenced, the more likely it is to be near the top of search engine results.

Despite the claim that promotion via the Internet is relatively cheap compared with other methods, it is costly to design, upgrade, and maintain a web presence. Small companies do compete more directly with larger firms. However, with their limited resources, smaller companies must spend the necessary time, energy, and money to design an effective web site that is easy to navigate, that is stimulating, and that provides the content consumers are seeking. Bulk e-mail may be cheaper to send than bulk land-based mail, but carefully designing the message and harvesting or purchasing e-mail addresses is not cost-free.

Consumers can also use the Internet as a tool to extol or vilify a company, the company's products, or the company's actions. People are able to gain access to a broad population almost instantaneously. This complicates the public relations aspect of marketers' responsibilities. The

LEGO and Strategic Adaptation

LEGO comes from the Danish words *leg godt,* or "play nicely." LEGO toys seem out of place in today's world of video games, where putting together colorful little plastic bricks to build castles appears childish. But LEGO, founded in 1949, thrives, perhaps, because young children use their imagination and build pirate ships, bridges, and fortresses. Parents also like LEGOs, finding the toy wholesome and considering it something they might have played with when they were children. In fact, LEGO found that about 13 percent of LEGO sets in the Netherlands were bought for use by adults! About 80 percent of all children who play with LEGOs are boys. The company has been experimenting with pastel colors and themes that appeal more to girls, such as dollhouses and nurseries. (See http://www.lego.com/scala.) Its recent line, Clickits, is aimed squarely at girls. As explained by Raymond Hastings, LEGO's marketing research manager: "Clikits fits into girls' interests and their desire to control their immediate surroundings. It is open-ended, process-oriented and consistent with **Lego's** principles of appealing to people's creativity."

The newer Mindstorm line incorporates motors and batteries and computer chips inside the familiar LEGO bricks so that creations can be programmed and made to spring into action. Robots are the logical and latest evolution of these trends.

Internet allows people to test the boundaries of freedom of speech and good taste, whether they are posting their opinions about vendors or DVDs.

Market research opportunities go beyond sending e-mail to customers, asking about new features or products. Virtual malls and stores can be created to simulate certain live conditions and to perform experiments while controlling many exogenous variables not possible in a real-world setting. Marketers can use white boards, discussion groups, and chat rooms to elicit opinions and advice from people around the globe, making it as anonymous as people like (which tends to affect the types of responses market researchers get).

The Internet permits businesses to expand consignment-like models, which means they can offer a broader product line to consumers. For example, Amazon.com sells books and DVDs that it carries in its own inventory, but it also allows others to advertise and sell books and DVDs. (Amazon collects and forwards the charges for the merchandise, shipping, and handling and provides a measure of warranty about the other sellers.) While the Internet allows consumers to "shop the world," it also allows businesses to form vast geographic areas in which to combine resources in a synergistic manner. Amazon.com quickly expanded from being a seller of books to a company in the entertainment business to a firm that fulfills a variety of shopping needs.

Global Business: The Trade Barrier of the Mind

As its trade deficit shows, the United States lags behind other nations in the general level of international trade activity. This poses a question: How does a U.S. firm approach overseas markets? The answer is, in many cases, reluctantly.

LEGO, which is a privately owned and secretive company, is enormously profitable. Its Danish-registered companies alone show profits after taxes of around $70 million on sales of about $900 million. LEGO has another 23 companies registered outside Denmark, about which information is scant. However, LEGO is finding that markets in Europe and the United States are mature. A lower-priced U.S. competitor, K'NEX, in partnership with Hasbro, had gained share. LEGO has naturally turned to the East, with sales in Japan growing 14 percent and sales in Korea growing 50 percent (though from a small base). As families in India and China reach middle class, LEGO hopes they, too, will buy the bricks. Counterfeiting is a problem, though, as the bricks are easy to copy and lower prices appeal to the generally lower-income consumers in Asia.

LEGO's LEGOLAND theme park near its Billund, Denmark, headquarters opened in 1968 and attracts a million visitors a year. The park features miniature versions of famous landmarks, such as the Statue of Liberty, as well as animals and rides—all built from LEGO bricks. More recently, LEGO built a theme park near Windsor Castle in London, called LEGOLAND Windsor, which is entirely made of LEGO bricks. The park is aimed at children 2 to 13 years old and stresses that learning is fun. For example, guests "ride" in cars built out of LEGO bricks and focus on learning responsible driving. A similar theme park opened in 1999 in California.

Sources: C. Darwent, "Lego's Billion-Dollar Brickworks," *Management Today,* September 1995; "LEGO Interlocks Toy Bricks, Theme Parks," *Wall Street Journal,* December 27, 1994; "Playing Well with Others," *Technology Review,* May 15, 1998; Greg Johnson, "Legoland Contented to Build Slowly; New Theme Park Not Billing Itself as Rival to Bigger Neighbors," *Los Angeles Times,* December 17, 1998; Ruth Mortimer, "Building a brand out of bricks," *Brand Strategy,* April 2003; Ravi Chandiramani, "Lego Moves In on The Girls' Market," *Marketing* (UK), February 13, 2003.

A statement made nearly two decades ago by Kenneth Butterworth, chair of Loctite Corporation, still holds true for far too many U.S. managers. Mr. Butterworth said that "the problem really lies in the mind. That is the greatest trade barrier in America."[17] In other words, long insularity and overdependence on the American market have made American firms unsure about their ability to capture markets overseas. Culture, language, and environmental differences are sometimes intimidating. Firms from other countries, however, have overcome such differences, and many U.S. companies are following suit.

Due to continued U.S. trade deficits, small- and medium-sized businesses are being urged, both at the federal and state levels, to export. They can get help by signing up for trade missions sponsored by the U.S. Department of Commerce and other organizations. Export finance is available to carry export receivables for longer periods and to offer favorable interest rate financing. The large number of foreigners and immigrants hired by these companies helps them learn about opportunities in foreign markets, as well as efficient ways to approach the markets. A weaker dollar also makes exporting easier. From its peak in 1985, the dollar declined by 60 percent in 1995 against currencies such as the yen, the German mark, and the Swiss franc before appreciating once again through 1997. Dollar depreciation makes U.S. products more competitive and allows U.S. firms to raise prices while offering goods and services priced lower than those of foreign competitors. The dollar began depreciating again by the end of 2001, losing about one-third of its value in relation to the yen and the euro by October 2003.

Ultimately, global business is a matter of perspective. The term *global business* best captures this perspective of the world as a market, with individual countries being submarkets. For those companies that hold such a view, the distinction between domestic and international marketing disappears and the focus is on market opportunities, wherever they may be.

The Approach of This Book

The sources of the differences between international and domestic business are to be found not in the functions themselves, but in the parameters that determine how the functions are performed. Therefore, students of international business should be able to identify the relevant parameters and understand how they affect business strategy. This book assumes that readers have that ability from their background in other business courses. This text presents the world environment in which global business is practiced.

Summary

As foreign economies continue to grow and account for a larger portion of the total world market and as foreign competitors actively seek market share in the United States, many U.S. firms are being forced into some form of international business. This may extend to manufacturing, carrying out joint ventures with local partners, licensing, importing, and taking part in counter-trade transactions. The varied strengths of foreign competitors, the ramifications of dealing with different national governments, and economic and cultural differences in foreign markets contribute to the complexity of global business.

Companies compete globally because (1) strong market potential exists overseas; (2) international sales allow them to enhance their long-run profitability; (3) low-cost production and quality are critical to competing successfully in global markets; and (4) they can achieve success by carefully choosing certain market segments, as witnessed by Dickson Poon's success in the Far East.

Large multinationals are more likely to get more of their foreign revenues from sales of their foreign subsidiaries than through exports. This can be a key element of strategic success in global business. More important, though, is a global perspective of the world as one market, with individual countries treated as submarkets and a focus on exploiting opportunities wherever they may occur.

Questions and Research

1.1   What is global business? How does it differ from domestic business?

1.2   Why is global business important to most firms?

1.3   Consider the examples described in the section "The Global Marketplace." Compare and contrast the global business actions of the firms discussed. Focus on their choices in the areas of products, market segments, the sequential choice of countries to sell to, pricing, the growth of and response to competition, and the use of licensing and joint ventures.

1.4   How do large U.S. multinationals compete in the global marketplace? Why do most of them sell more from their foreign subsidiaries than through exports?

1.5   "The greatest trade barrier to exporting lies in the mind." Explain that statement.

1.6   "Global business is a shift in perspective." Explain that statement.

1.7   Choose a prominent publicly held company in your geographic area. Find out what its total foreign revenues have been for the past five years and how much of its foreign sales come from overseas operations and how much come from exporting from the home market. Also study the comments about international markets made by the chair of the company in its annual report. How important is international marketing to this firm?

Endnotes

1 The World Bank, 2004 *World Development Indicators,* NY, 2004, page 303.

2 Kashani, K. "Marketing Futures: Priorities for a Turbulent Environment," *Long-Range Planning,* Volume 28, Issue 4, 1995, pages 87–98.

3 "Just Like the Computer Games It Sells, Nintendo Defies Persistent Challengers," *Wall Street Journal,* June 27, 1989; "Atari Tests Technology's Antitrust Aspect," *Wall Street Journal,* December 14, 1988.

4 See Wilson, Johnny. "Bad Moon Rising: A Primer on PC Game Industry Myopia," *Computer Gaming,* January 1999; "Nintendo Unveils 64-bit Game Player in Bid to Top Sony, Sega CD Machines," *Wall Street Journal,* November 27, 1995; "Older Machines Win Video-Game Crowd," *Wall Street Journal,* December 26, 1995; "3-D Video Games: The Next Generation," *Business Week,* October 16, 1995; "Nightmare in the Fun House," *Financial World,* February 21, 1995; "Sega," *Business Week,* February 21, 1994; "Sony's Big Bazooka," *Fortune,* December 30, 2002; "A Grown-up's Guide to Games," *Wall Street Journal,* November 21, 2002; Dean Takahashi, *Inside the Xbox, Prima,* 2002.

5 "Step Right Up, Monsieur," *New York Times,* August 23, 1995.

6 See "Euro Disney's Fiscal Loss to Spur Study of Woes by U.S. Concern," *Wall Street Journal,* July 9, 1993; "Euro Disney's Loss Narrowed in Fiscal 1994," *Wall Street Journal,* November 4, 1994; "Euro Disney's Prince Charming?" *Business Week*, June 13, 1994; "A Faint Squeak from Euro-Mickey," *The Economist,* July 29, 1995; "Euro Disney Posts First Annual Profit," *Wall Street Journal,* November 16, 1995; "California; For Struggling Euro Disney, Help from Abroad," *Los Angeles Times,* June 10, 2004; "Disney Gives Plans to Aid European Parks," *New York Times*, July 1, 2004.

7 Tanzer, Andrew. "Keep the Calculators Out of Sight," *Forbes,* March 20, 1989; Lucas, Louise, "Dickson Concepts Faces Loss As Recession Bites," *Financial Times,* December 11, 1998.

8 "Dickson on Lookout after Big Profit Rise," *Hong Kong IMail,* June 24, 2003; "Dickson in $100m Expansion," *Hong Kong IMail,* August 27, 2003.

9 "Jindo to Set its Export Goal," *Korea Economic Daily*, December 8, 1994.

10 "Electric Fuel of Israel Poised to Draw Two More European Concerns to Project," *Wall Street Journal,* May 30, 1995.

11 "Thank Carl Klumpp for the Swell Smell of Right Guard," *Wall Street Journal,* May 11, 1995.

12 Black, Jane. "It's All in the Nose (and Tongue)," Businessweekonline.com, July 8, 2003.

13 "Ben & Jerry's Is Trying to Smooth out Distribution in Russia As It Expands," *Wall Street Journal,* September 9, 1995; The History of Ben & Jerry's Ice Cream (http://www.benjerry.com/our_company/about_us/our_history/timeline/index.cfm); Unilever Company History (http://www.unilever.com/company/unilevertoday).

14 "For Mary Kay Sales Reps in Russia, Hottest Shade Is the Color of Money," *Wall Street Journal,* August 30, 1995; "Mary Kay's Eastern Front," Forbes.com, September 13, 2003; Mary Kay, Russia (http://www.marykay.ru).

15 "Owner Hires Plane for Search and Spots Vessel," *Straits Times* (Singapore), June 27, 1995.

16 Marine Watch Keeps Straits Safe," *New Straits Times-Management Times,* August 5, 2003; Hodge, Neil. "Attacks by Sea Pirates Up Markedly This Year," *Business Insurance,* July 28, 2003, Volume 37, Issue 30.

17 "You Don't Have to Be a Giant to Score Overseas," *Business Week,* April 13, 1987.

Further Readings

Ball, Donald, Wendell H. McCulloch, Michael Geringer, Paul L. Frantz, and Michael S. Minor. *International Business: The Challenge of Global Competition*, 9th Edition. Boston: McGraw-Hill/Irwin, 2003.

Bell, Jim. "The International Business Environment: Diversity and the Global Economy," *International Small Business Journal*, February 2004, Volume 22, Issue 1, pages 107–109.

Daniels, John D., Lee H. Radebaugh, and Daniel P. Sullivan. *International Business: Environments and Operations*, 10th Edition. Upper Saddle River, NJ: Prentice Hall, 2004.

Eaker, Mark R. and Faith J. Rubenstein. *Managing in the Global Business Environment: Issues, Organization, and Limitations.* Mansfield, OH: South-Western College Publishing, 1997.

Meier, Gerald M. *The International Environment of Business: Competition and Governance in the Global Economy.* New York: Oxford University Press, 1998.

Phatak, Arvind V., Rabi S. Bhagat, and Roger J. Kashlak. *International Management: Managing in a Diverse and Dynamic Global Environment.* Boston: McGraw-Hill Irwin, 2005.

Teegan, Hildy, Jonathan P. Doh, and Sushil Vachani. "The Importance of Nongovernmental Organizations (NGOs) in Global Governance and Value Creation: An International Business Research Agenda," *Journal of International Business Studies,* Volume 35, Issue 6, pages 463–483.

Case 1.1

Agro Industria Exportadora S.A. (AI)

Agro Industria Exportadora S.A. (AI) was founded in 1973. Its original owners were from Zamora and Michoacan, in Mexico; and they planned to buy agricultural produce and process it for sale, using labor-intensive processes. AI's operations, employing as many as 450 people, lasted until 1982. During this early period, the founding partners invited Mr. Gonzalez, from Guadalajara, to join the company as manager. Over time, he received an ownership interest; and in 1978, he decided to buy out the original owners, a process that was completed in 1982. At this point, however, the Mexican economy was in a perilous state, with the peso heavily devalued after a long period of being tied to the dollar at a fixed parity of 12.5 per dollar. The difficult economic situation led Mr. Gonzalez to cease operations.

However, given Mexico's potential in agriculture and agribusiness, IFC, which is a division of the World Bank, decided to make agribusiness investments in Mexico. IFC invited a Mexican national, Mr. Ojeda, who was also a director of Banamex, to become involved in such a venture. He, in turn, contacted Mr. Gonzalez to restart operations, with a greater focus on exporting.

The reborn company slowly progressed; and in 1986, Mr. Ojeda quit Banamex to become a partner in the company, with additional investment from the venture capital arm of Banamex. The company decided to focus on exporting frozen vegetables and sought another partner, Mr. Polari, a big grower of vegetables. Mr. Polari's association with the company lasted three years, until 1989, when he sold his share in the company. By then, AI had its ownership divided as follows: Mr. Gonzalez held 25 percent, Mr. Ojeda had 35 percent, and an investor from Mexico City held the balance. IFC, which had held an ownership stake in the company during its difficult years, sold out, as was its custom once the company stabilized and did not require continued IFC capital or support.

Initially, the company had canned Anaheim chilies for export to the United States. Once the United States opened its market to the import of fresh Mexican chilies, however, prices shot up and selling canned chilies was no longer viable. Hence, AI had to find another product line for its canning plant, which had started initial operations in 1987.

Mr. Gonzalez had been invited to Japan; and when scouting business opportunities there, he noticed that the Japanese were heavy users of grapefruit segments in jellies, cakes, pies, etc. He returned to Mexico, thinking that this represented a potential opportunity for AI. However, some practical problems immediately arose. Whereas chilies are high in acidity, fruit is generally low in acid and high in sugar content. As a result, cans are likely to explode easily. Hence, AI had to experiment with new canning methods and processes. However, Japanese canning technology as applied to grapefruit was not useful to AI because of differences in weather, altitude (Guadalajara is about 3,000 feet above sea level), and humidity. Further, fresh fruit is soft and has a different texture than frozen produce. Therefore, AI had to adapt its production processes. Its initial exports to Japan were of poor quality, and shipments suffered from spoilage. Consequently, AI had to request time from its Japanese clients to solve its production problems.

In 1990, AI decided to begin importing U.S. cans. The cans needed a special enamel coating to accommodate citrus products. Further, the Mexican cans oxidized easily (even before use) and were not of uniform quality, as different kinds of steel imported from Spain and Venezuela were used in production. Consequently, AI decided to import cans from Florida, even though this meant paying for transporting empty cans to be shipped to the AI plants. But the U.S. cans were of superior quality, and soon AI stopped experiencing problems with exploding cans and other problems of uneven quality. AI had learned that the Japanese were continually seeking quality improvements at continually lower prices.

At first, AI exported on an exclusive basis to the Marubeni Corporation. However, when Marubeni began lowering the quantities it purchased, AI began to seek additional Japanese distributors, including the Japanese trading companies Mitsui and Toshoku. Because AI had established a good name in Japan, it had actually been approached by Marubeni about becoming a distributor. AI's competition came from Mexico, Israel, and South Africa. AI had the best quality (or so it claimed), though its prices were slightly higher. AI thought it was too difficult to sell directly to the final Japanese consumer firms, who numbered about 50 in all: major grocery chains, food processors, and others.

AI typically processed the fruit in Mexico, packed it in cans without labels, and used a Mexican shipping line for transportation to Japan. It shipped about one container every ten days to Japan, with the final customer price about double the FOB Manzanillo price.

A critical point in export success is the quality of the produce. AI took care in its purchasing. Japanese customers wanted the grapefruit segments to be all of the same size. Hence, AI had two people permanently stationed at the growers' sites, where they made commitments to purchase fruit at the bloom stage, picking producers based on taste, freshness, and fruit size. Once fruits were ready to pick, picking was done every day, with AI's two people supervising. Once the fruit was received, it was graded by size, with the smaller units sold off to juice firms. Only fruit of the requisite size was exported to Japan. On average, for fruit with a value of 100 pesos, transportation costs added another 120 pesos. Since the cans were destined for re-export, imported cans were stored in-bond to avoid duties. Most of the fruit exports to Japan were in #10 cans, containing 2 kilograms of product and 1 kilogram of syrup. As was to be expected, AI faced seasonal cycles and had to develop multiple fruit lines to remain busy year round. For example, in the 1992 fiscal year, AI exported the following:

Grapefruit	August–December	1.575 million pounds
Valencia oranges	January–March	1.470 million pounds
Lemons	May–August	.4 million "cell sacks"[a]

a Lemon juice in lemon-shaped containers

AI believed that it had to pick produce lines that were not chosen by its competitors. Its most recent produce addition was strawberries, with a target of 7 million pounds annually. To enter this line, AI made an agreement with Congeladora de Samora, whereby it took over operations of its factory in return for a 50-50 split of the profits. Strawberries are generally sold in 30-pound plastic pails, in Pure-Pak cartons, or in 425-pound drums for use by jam manufacturers.

Foreign Markets

AI has a U.S. food broker, World Food Sales, which it owns. World Food's sales director, a former partner of AI in its earlier incarnation, has over 30 years of experience in the frozen produce industry. AI pays a 6 percent sales commission to World Food. World Food also represents other Mexican food produce companies, such as growers of broccoli and cauliflower. Sometimes the U.S. broker served as an alternative export conduit to Japan, enabling AI to export incremental quantities if demand from its (then) exclusive distribution arrangement in Japan was low. As part of operating procedures, all sales are made on letters of credit and quotes to all international customers are priced in U.S. dollars.

In addition to Japan and the United States, AI also sells to Europe, principally to Germany. Like Japan, Germany requires quality and is willing to pay a higher price if necessary. Mr. Gonzalez's wife is German and was instrumental in helping AI break into the German market, achieved gradually by repeated visits to the World Food Fair, held every third year in Cologne. German exports are to IC Frozen Foods, the German distributor, who also exports to Sweden and Denmark, where it has representatives.

The United Kingdom is a more difficult market, as lower-quality, highly discounted products compete with AI's produce. AI has also considered Korea as a market, though a 1991 visit indicated that while AI quality was considered superior, its prices were considered high.

New Directions

AI's goal is to diversify its export markets. In 1990, its export sales were 70 percent to the United States and Canada, 25 percent to Japan, and 5 percent to Europe. In 1992, the respective percentages were 60, 30, and 10. In 1993, targeted percentages were 50, 40, and 10, respectively. AI notes that each market has peculiarities and presents a different set of challenges. For the U.S. market, AI is experimenting with new lines such as broccoli, cauliflower, romanesco (a hybrid of cauliflower and broccoli), brussel sprouts, and cucumbers (pickled and fresh). Cucumbers represent its latest success, which it buys from 92 growers who devote 205 hectares to the crop, with exports totaling 4.4 million pounds. AI is renting a plant to process cucumbers. It houses three grading machines, where the cucumbers are first sorted by size. They are then hydro-cooled; loaded onto 40-ton trailers in green plastic bags (along with 2 tons of ice); and exported at a temperature of 38 degrees to the United States, with more ice added after the trucks cross the border. The cucumbers continue on to Colorado, where they are washed, packed, and sold as fresh produce. The entire cycle averages 17 hours from receipt of cucumbers to the crossing of the border, with a total elapsed time of 24 hours to Colorado. The central, critical element is freshness.

Role of Logistics

Logistics are extremely important. AI uses the Mexican carrier Aguilas de Oro, with a handoff at the border to Middleton Trucking, which has a fleet of 110 trucks. The crossing point is Laredo, Texas, which is extremely hot. Therefore, the produce has a high risk of perishing. Success is partly a matter of minimizing transportation costs. In July and August, at the height of the cucumber pickling season, trucking rates are seasonally low due to excess capacity. Therefore, AI is able to negotiate rates averaging 1 cent per pound for ordinary cargo to Laredo and 2 cents for cooled cargo—a savings of almost 33 percent over normal tariffs. AI negotiated directly with trucking companies, choosing Middleton over competitive bids from Freymiller and Prime.

Another bottleneck is the availability of containers, but major clients such as Vlasic guarantee the availability of containers at the border. In general, it is important for AI to arrange the U.S. transportation leg with Middleton first, before closing the link by entering into a contract with its Mexican partner. An alternative is to sell cucumbers in a brine solution for pickling, with cucumbers in brine sent to the United States for further processing: washing, slicing, and then selling to clients such as McDonald's or to major pickling companies such as Vlasic Foods. In 1992, AI cucumber sales reached 2.75 million pounds of brine pickles.

For shipment to Europe, the company contracts for a certain number of containers each month to transport its products (currently 10 to 12 containers a month) on terms typically set out separately as FOB plant, plus freight, in-bound expenses, transloading, and ocean freight. In 1993, shipping estimates were for 150 containers of produce, split 70 percent broccoli and 30 percent romanesco, which is gaining a market. Three hundred tons of romanesco were shipped in 1992, with an estimated 1,000 tons shipped in 1993. Romanesco is costlier to grow, however, with a pound of seed costing $2,500, versus $200 for a pound of broccoli seed; but the potential return is greater.

Costs and Regulations

AI's food processing is labor-intensive though seasonal. For example, the grapefruit segment preparation requires an assembly line of about 2,250 workers who cut, peel, segment, and can the grapefruit. A key is intelligent buying of raw materials, signing contracts with growers in advance, and never growing its own produce. In 1992, AI sales were $16 million, yielding a profit of $1.5 million. In 1993, sales were $27 million, with a net profit of about 8.5 percent.

Because AI is a Mexican company, capitalization is also critical, especially in export markets where working capital requirements are high. To enable AI to take a longer-term perspective on export markets, AI's partners contributed an additional $1.5 million in capital in order to reduce borrowing costs (over 30 percent on an annual basis on peso-denominated debt in Mexico).

A complication is divergent agricultural standards in different export markets. Regulations differ among countries about permissible levels of chemical additives and fertilizers. Hence, the two supervisors assigned to grower relations must monitor the farming process. AI often supplies chemicals and fertilizers to facilitate certification of additive levels in the exported produce. In addition, AI carries out the necessary inspections prior to export, as in the case of strawberries destined for the U.S. market, where permissible chemical parts per million have been lowered from .5 to .05.

Duties are a concern, as most advanced nations protect agricultural products. For example, U.S. duties have averaged 17 percent on vegetables and 14 percent on strawberries—on average, about 13 percent of shipment value. With the passage of NAFTA, these tariffs will be lowered but will not disappear. In comparison, Central America enjoys duty-free access to Europe and the United States, a considerable advantage over AI produce. Similarly, in Japan, there is a 17 percent duty on products in a sugarcane-based syrup, but syrup with a corn base can enter duty-free. At the same time, quality standards are such that exports to Japan must meet higher quality standards than exports for the U.S. market.

The Future

AI is serious about expanding its export business. Its owners believe that in international business, once they make a deal, they must honor it. In one case, they bought lemons out of season at six times the regular price and air-freighted the cell-sack product to meet a commitment to a customer. The customer's satisfaction led to a large order the next year. The partners are convinced that AI can succeed only by building long-term relationships in export markets. Timely delivery is also a must, given the perishable and seasonal nature of the products. AI knows that it must deliver the best-quality products, both to win customers and to get repeat orders.

Questions and Research

1   How did AI first enter export markets? What factors enabled it to compete in the U.S. market?

2   How did AI enter the Japanese market? What were the challenges in exporting to Japan?

3   Trace the evolution of AI's expansion into international markets in terms of product lines and geographic market scope.

4   Do you think that AI has been successful in entering international markets? Discuss the factors critical to AI's success.

5   What are the challenges facing AI as it seeks to continue expanding internationally? What recommendations would you give AI in terms of products, markets, and the way it conducts international business?

CHAPTER 2

Global Economic Environment
The World, Regional, and National Economies

Learning Objectives
When a firm leaves its home market to market internationally, it must deal with the challenges of the larger, more complex world economy. Chapter 2 introduces the various dimensions of that environment.

The main goals of this chapter are to

1 Present an overview of world trade to re-emphasize the economic linkages among nations.

2 Describe how the World Trade Organization (WTO), the United Nations Conference on Trade and Development (UNCTAD), and other global organizations influence trade.

3 Explore the developments in regional trading blocs and other areas such as Eastern Europe.

4 Discuss the national role in global trade and identify some key countries for business in the coming decade.

5 Present information on population, urbanization, income, natural physical endowments, and infrastructure; then provide an overview of how those characteristics impact global business.

Business is an economic activity affected by the economic environment in which it is conducted. International business has an impact on two interrelated economic environments: (1) the global, or world, economy and (2) the economy of individual countries.

It is reasonable to speak of the "world economy" because the nations of the world affect one another economically. Nations, of course, also relate to each other politically, diplomatically, militarily, and culturally. Many of these other elements of international relations are intertwined with economic considerations. For example, Marco Polo's travels and the Crusades had significant economic impacts. The great voyages of discovery and the building of colonial empires were motivated by economic as well as political aspirations. More recently, economic considerations have played a role in regional cooperative movements such as the **EU**, the economic amalgamation of 25 European nations. International economic concerns are also frequent items on the agenda of the United Nations (UN) and its affiliated agencies.

The existence of this world economy is critical for the business firm. Because nations relate to each other economically, international business operations are possible. Today, in fact, international companies are major participants in international economic relations. For that reason, it is necessary to examine the world economy to see how it aids and constrains international business. This chapter begins with a discussion on international trade, a major element in international economic relations.

A Picture of World Trade

The interrelated nature of the world economy is most easily seen in examining trade among nations and in closely scrutinizing the nature of the trade taking place.

Global Volume

Total world trade in 2002 exceeded $13.0 trillion in merchandise ($6.5 trillion in exports and $6.7 trillion in imports) and $3.1 trillion in commercial services ($1.6 trillion in exports and $1.5 trillion in imports). Gross world product was approximately $32.3 trillion in 2002; thus, the world's nations exported about 25 percent ($8.1 trillion) of what they produced in 2002. (See Table 2-1.)

According to the World Bank, global interdependence, fostered by increasing trade and the associated relationships among nations, has played a significant role in the decline in world poverty over the past 15 years.[1]

Internationalism is increasing as a way of life. Nations moving in the direction of trade expansion can raise their standard of living, while countries that restrict trade increase their political separation and isolation and slow economic progress. Firms, like nations, must recognize that they are in the world marketplace when considering opportunities for growth and when facing new competition. The isolationist position is difficult for firms as well as nations to maintain. One can't just say, "Stop the world—I want to get off."

Foreign Trade of Individual Nations

The United States is the world leader in trade. In 2002, U.S. trade in merchandise totaled $1.84 trillion ($640 billion in exports and $1,202 billion in imports) and trade in commercial servic-

TABLE 2-1   Foreign Trade of Individual Nations

Area or Nation	Gross National/World Income (current)[a]	2002 $US billion and (percent)	
		Exports (percent of world total)	Imports (percent of world total)
World	$32,312.2 (100.0)		
Manufactured Goods[b]		6,455.0 (100.0)	6,693.0 (100.0)
Commercial Services		1,570.0 (100.0)	1,545.0 (100.0)
Brazil	$452.4 (1.4)		
Manufactured Goods		60.4 (0.9)	49.7 (0.7)
Commercial Services		8.8 (0.6)	13.6 (0.9)
China	$1,266.1 (3.9)		
Manufactured Goods		295.2 (4.4)	325.6 (5.0)
Commercial Services		39.4 (2.5)	46.1 (3.0)
Germany	$1,984.1 (6.1)		
Manufactured Goods		613.1 (9.5)	493.7 (7.4)
Commercial Services		99.6 (6.3)	149.1 (9.6)
Mexico	$637.2 (2.0)		
Manufactured Goods		160.7 (2.5)	173.1 (2.6)
Commercial Services		12.5 (0.8)	17.0 (1.1)\
Russian Federation	$346.5 (1.1)		
Manufactured Goods		106.9 (1.7)	60.5 (0.9)
Commercial Services		12.9 (0.8)	21.5 (1.4)
United States	$10,383.1 (32.1)		
Manufactured Goods		639.9 (10.7)	1,202.4 (18.0)
Commercial Services		272.6 (17.4)	205.6 (13.3)

[a]The World Bank currently uses gross national income (GNI) rather than gross national product (GNP) as a measure of wealth.

[b]These contain significant reexports; for example, total exports of Singapore and Hong Kong in 2002 totaled $326.3 billion, but $240.3 billion (74%) were reexported.

Sources: GNI data: World Bank Group; Data Query performed on July 16, 2004 (http://devdata.worldbank.org/data-query); Trade data: World Trade Organization, *International Trade Statistics*, 2003 (http://www.wto.org/english/res_e/statis_e/its2003_e/its03_bysubject_e.htm) (files: i05.xls [merchandise]; i07.xls [commercial services]).

es totaled $478 billion ($273 billion in exports and $206 billion in imports). This translated into a $496 billion trade deficit in 2002. Trade balances are calculated by subtracting that which is purchased abroad (imports) from that which is sold (exports). A trade deficit exists when imports exceed exports and a surplus exists when exports exceed imports in the time period being measured.

Germany was second in trade volume with $1.11 trillion in merchandise trade ($613 billion in exports and $494 billion in imports) and trade in commercial services of $249 billion ($100 billion in exports and $149 billion in imports). Japan traded $754 billion in manufactured goods ($417 billion in exports and $337 billion in imports) and $172 billion in services ($65 billion in exports and $107 billion in imports). Note also that in China, with a population of over 1.2 billion (20 percent of the world's population), trade has been growing rapidly and now accounts for approximately 5 percent of world trade in manufactured goods and 3 percent in commercial services. What surprises many people is that China is experiencing a trade

Ford–Made in Japan (and Spain and England and Mexico and even the United States)

Most people would say that a Ford is an American car company and might assume that most of the parts that go into making a Ford car or truck are American-made. An analogous case could be made for Volvo (a Swedish company), Jaguar (English), and Mazda (Japanese).

Surprisingly to some people, all of those auto brands are owned and managed in part or whole by the Ford Motor Company, as are Aston Martin, Land Rover, Mercury, and Lincoln. Ford and other companies account for much of the world's trade as they ship parts and supplies between partners and subsidiaries for their products all over the globe. Companies pay less attention to national borders as they seek to cut costs in an increasingly competitive and interdependent global economy.

Mazda and Ford announced a new "Global Engine Family Strategy," which will rely on plants in Hiroshima (Japan), Dearborn (the United States), Chihuahua (Mexico), and Valencia (Spain) to produce inline engines for passenger cars and light trucks for its assembly facilities around the world. Ford will also

deficit in both goods and services. Many attribute growing demand to enormous infrastructure projects (for example, the Three Gorges Dam), increasing imports of oil and other fuels to run new factories, and the rapid increase in consumerism that is taking place. Table 2-1 highlights trade among the world trade leaders and other selected nations.

Top products traded in 2002 were in the machinery and transportation equipment category, which accounted for about 41 percent of world trade ($2.5 trillion). Office and telecommunications equipment (one of the product categories within machinery and transportation equipment) accounted for over 13 percent of trade ($838 million), while other major merchandise categories such as chemicals (11 percent, or $660 billion) and fuels (10 percent, or $615 billion) remain on the "top traded merchandise" list. Services show a trend toward declining importance of travel and transportation relative to other commercial services (for example, accounting, advertising, and consulting). In 1995, travel and transportation accounted for nearly 60 percent of all services traded; in 2002, those categories accounted for just over 50 percent.[2]

Some nations are more dependent on trade. That is, rather than earning most of their income from national sales to domestic consumers, some countries earn 10, 20, even more than 50 percent of national income by selling what they produce to foreigners. For example, Japan exported $482 billion worth of goods and services in 2002, which accounted for 12 percent of its gross national product (GNP). Germany depends on trade for 36 percent of its GNP; Belgium exports over 70 percent of what it produces every year. (A large proportion of Belgian trade, two-thirds, occurs with other EU nations.) By contrast, the United States exports only about 9 percent of what it produces.[3]

Foreign Trade of Individual Firms

Foreign trade is just as important to a firm as it is to a nation. In fact, much of international business involves international trade—the cross-border movement of goods and services. In relation get about 20,000 engines per year for its Ikon, a midsize car model that uses a 1.3- and 1.6-liter gasoline-powered engine, from Hindustan motors (India), with parts coming from Ford plants in South Africa and Spain. This plan is consistent with Ford's strategy to increase its reliance on India as a sourcing hub. Some Mazda models manufactured in the United States will be built with engines from a Ford plant in Mexico, but will get transmissions from a Ford plant in the United States. Other Mazda models, also made in the United States, get engines from Mazda plants located in Japan, the United States, and Spain.

How do companies keep all of this straight and the supplies running smoothly? Ford uses Vastera, Inc., a U.S. company in Dulles, Virginia, to provide logistics services. Third-party logistic companies (3PLs), such as United Parcel Service, Deutsche Post, and APL Logistics, and 4PLs (those that select and manage 3PLs), such as Vastera and Kuehne & Nagel, can ship, store, truck, and provide whatever logistical network services are needed to ensure that components and supplies move efficiently from plant to plant worldwide.

Sources: Ford Motor Company web site (http://www.ford.com/en/ourVehicles/allVehicles/default.htm); "Mazda Announces Sourcing for New Global Engine Family" (http://www.mazda.com/mnl//200002/engine_e.html); "Ford Enters Sourcing Deal with India's Hindustan Motor," January 15, 2002, *Asia Pulse*, New Delhi, Northern Territory Regional; "Ford Seeks to Make India Sourcing Hub," November 18, 2001, Indian Express Online Media, Financial Express; "Year of the 3PLs," February 18, 2002; *Journal of Commerce*, Logistics, page 12.

to this subject, "Global Environment: Ford—Made in Japan (and Spain and England and Mexico and Even the United States)" shows how one company, Ford, sources the products they make.

Composition of World Trade

A study of the commodity composition of world trade gives further insight into international economic relations. Considering just four commodity categories—food, fuel, other primary commodities, and manufactured goods—long-run shifts in market share are seen.

Agricultural/Food Products

In 2002, trade in agricultural products accounted for 9 percent of total world trade. Yet at $583 billion that year, agricultural exports accounted for 43 percent of total world exports of primary products. Of the $583 billion, $189 billion, or over 32 percent, was accounted for by intra-Western European trade; nearly $65 billion (11 percent) was traded among Asian nations; and $34 billion (6 percent) was accounted for by intra-North American trade. Conversely, in 2002, agricultural products accounted for 11 percent of all North American exports, nearly 20 percent of exports from Latin America, and 16 percent of African exports. Despite some recent declines, the value of agricultural trade increased by 6 percent between 2000 and 2002.

Fuel

The WTO categorizes fuel as a mining product. While mined products also include ores, minerals, and metals, 78 percent ($615 billion) of trade in mined products was attributed to fuels in 2002. Ten percent of total world trade is accounted for by fuel, which is expected to increase primarily because of high demand in the large Chinese market.

Trading Services

According to the WTO, trade in services accounted for nearly 24 percent of world trade in 2002, up nearly 4 percent in the last two years. Four trends will drive the proportion of trade in services to manufactured goods still higher—cross-border mergers and consolidations, increased online usage of services, reduction of barriers to trade in services, and better measurement of service trade. Each of these is explained below.

1. Continuing mergers and consolidations in key service areas such as accounting (Deloitte Touche Tohmatsu), banking (Credit Suisse First Boston), entertainment (AOL and Time Warner), and travel (Carnival and Princess Cruise lines). These mergers will create global companies that serve their clients and customers wherever they may be.

2. Increased service usage among consumers, particularly among Internet users of e-business. All estimates predict phenomenal growth for business-to-consumer (B2C) service e-commerce in the next few years. Business-to-business (B2B) service, while attracting less attention, will continue to dominate Internet activity.

3. WTO and others' efforts to reduce trade barriers for services. The goal of the General Agreement on Trade in Services (GATS) is freer trade in services—accountancy, advertising, architectural and engineering services, education, postal and courier services, sporting services, telecommunications, and tourism.

4. Better measurement. Advances in hardware, software, and data analysis techniques, as well as adoption of standards such as the Harmonized System of product classification, will make it easier to measure the flow of services from nation to nation.

On the importing side, the EU (15 nations) led the way with $190 billion (30 percent of total trade in fuels in 2002), followed by the United States with $122 billion (20 percent), and Japan with $66 billion (10 percent). China imported only $19.3 billion in fuels in 2002, but this was up from $1.3 billion in 1990; fuel now constitutes 6.5 percent of total imports by China.

Middle Eastern nations are highly dependent on fuel (70 percent of merchandise exports); this is followed by African nations (50 percent) and Central European, Baltic, and Commonwealth of Independent States (CIS) nations (25 percent of exports come from fuels). Nearly 30 percent of the world's fuel comes from the Middle East. Twenty percent comes from Western Europe, followed by Africa, Asia, and Central Europe, each accounting for approximately 11 percent of the annual trade in fuels.

Manufactured Goods

This large category includes iron, steel, chemicals, machinery and transport equipment, textiles, and other consumer goods. Trade in manufactured goods grew at an annual rate of 7 percent from 1990 to 2000, but has leveled out since 2000, accounting for 75 percent ($4.7 trillion) of all merchandise exports in 2002. The largest subcategory, machinery and transport equipment, accounted for $2.5 trillion of exported manufactured goods. Within that subcategory, office and telecommunications equipment accounted for $838 billion while automotive products totaled

Using financial services as an example, the following are a few noteworthy headlines and statistics that relate to the worldwide increase in trading in the services sector:

- The Check Clearing for the 21st Century Act allows American banks to use electronic facsimiles of checks rather than physically send checks around the nation. This is another factor leading to rapidly declining use of checks as a payment method in the United States, where check use is declining by 3 to 5 percent per year. ("Banking Law Mints Tech Windfall," *CNET News.com*, July 16, 2004)
- Oracle is focusing on China, where the information technology (IT) market is growing by 20 percent annually. The driving forces are telecommunications, financial services, and high-tech manufacturing (in that order). ("Oracle Counts on Success in China," *Reuters*, July 18, 2004; ZDNet.com)
- By 2007, online banking accounts in Germany are expected to reach 32.6 million, an annual growth rate of 11 percent. Online trading accounts will increase from 2.7 million in 2002 to 4.8 million by 2008. ("Online Banking on the Rise in Germany," *IDC Research*, March 14, 2003)
- In the United States, 17 percent of Americans were using online banking services by the end of 2002. Forecasts indicate that 67 million, or 30 percent, of U.S. citizens will be using online banking by the end of 2007. ("Online Banking Goes Mainstream in U.S.," *Gartner Group*, March 10, 2003)

Certain legal factors will negatively affect trade in services. Antitrust laws aimed at curtailing the formation of huge companies that dominate an industry will rise as a result of megamerger trends. Antitrade laws designed to protect industries that play an important role in the nation's economy or industries that are considered vital to defense will continue to be enacted. Consumer protection laws are likely to become more elaborate and labyrinthine as countries within the EU and other regional groups attempt to coordinate these laws. Finally, intellectual property protection (IPP) is an important topic in most trade negotiations. With respect to piracy of entertainment, movies, software, and music are at the top of stolen intellectual property (IP) lists in nearly every country of the world.

$621 million in exports in 2002. Trade in office and telecom equipment was led by Asian nations, accounting for 50 percent of the world's exports in this subcategory ($422 billion) and 35 percent of imports in 2002. Western Europe imported nearly the same amount as Asia, but only exported 28 percent of total world exports for 2002. North America accounted for approximately 15 percent of the exports and 21 percent of the imports.

One trend worth noting is the decline in exports from the EU (36 percent of world share in 1980 but 28 percent in 2002), Japan (21 percent in 1980 but 10 percent in 2002), and the United States (20 percent in 1980 but 13 percent in 2002). On the importing side, the overall trend is for increased imports in developing nations and for decreased imports in developed nations. (The United States is an exception. In 1980, this market accounted for 16 percent of world imports; and in 2002, it accounted for 20 percent of imports.)

Commercial Services

Tracking of service trade is still in its infancy, and this is reflected in the poorly defined categories used by the WTO. Commercial services are classified into three categories: transportation, travel, and other commercial services. Other commercial services accounted for 47 percent of total commercial service exports in 2002 ($740 billion of the $1.57 trillion total). The second largest category, travel services, accounted for $480 billion, or 31 percent, of service exports in 2002. The largest exporting regions were Western Europe with a 43 percent share, followed by North America with 20 percent and Asia with 19 percent. The United States had $85 billion in travel service exports in 2002, more than the next two largest exporters, France ($34 billion) and Spain ($33 billion), combined. The largest importers that year were the United States ($61 billion), Germany ($53 billion), and the United Kingdom ($42 billion). Transportation services accounted for 22 percent ($350 billion) of exports of services in 2002. The largest exporters included the United States ($46 billion), Germany ($26 billion), and Japan ($24 billion). The largest importers of travel services in 2002 were the United States ($59 billion), Japan ($32 billion), and Germany ($30 billion). As the statistics show, trade in services is dominated by industrialized nations; but China and Thailand are now on the list of top 15 importers with 3 percent and 2 percent, respectively, of world import share in 2002.[4]

For international firms, a detailed study of the composition of world trade reveals what is being traded as well as who is buying and selling. Trend analysis shows which products are growing and which are fading, indicating potential threats and opportunities. The interest of less developed countries in industrialization may also create investment opportunities for firms in manufacturing or processing. Ventures such as these could help less developed countries increase manufactured exports by adding items to their export line or by refining or processing their primary commodities.

Patterns of World Trade

Which countries are the major players—and winners—in the game of international trade? Trade statistics show that in any given year, 50 of the world's nations account for between 90 and 95 percent of merchandise trade and only 40 of the more than 200 nations in the world account for over 90 percent of the trade in services. As shown in Table 2-1, the three top traders (the United States, Germany, and Japan) supply nearly 30 percent of the total exports of goods and services while the top ten account for more than 55 percent of trade in both merchandise and services.

Historically, the industrial nations supply three-quarters of all exports and nearly 80 percent of the services traded annually. (See Table 2-2.) The low-income nations, by contrast, supply a mere 3 percent of the world's trade in goods and services. Considering there are approximately 200 nations, those figures show the lopsided nature of trade. Poorer nations get a small percentage of their income from few products and few sources. A poorly diversified economy makes the economy more vulnerable to downturns in the industry it depends upon on most. Accepting the argument that trade leads to higher gross national income (GNI), the historical trends in trade, if they continue, will lead to a wider economic gap between rich and poor nations. For the purposes of this text, GNI will be defined as: "GNP, plus net primary imcome from nonresident sources." [Jeannet, J. and Hennessey, Global Marketing Strategies, 6th ed. Houghton-Mifflin, Boston, MA. (2004), p. 164].

After rapid growth in the 1990s, world trade actually declined in 2001. (Merchandise trade declined by 4 percent in value, while trade in services merely stagnated.) In 2002, world trade grew again in nearly all regions and sectors, enough to offset the loss from the previous year. Observers noted that growth was coming not so much from the wealthy nations, but from China, other developing nations, and the transition economies in Europe.

TABLE 2-2 World Trade Export Shares 2002				
	Merchandise Exports ($US billion)	Merchandise (percent)	Service Exports ($US billion)	Service (percent)
World	6,454.9	100.0	1,511.2	100.0
Economic Development				
Low	211.2	3.3	41.0	2.7
Middle	1,447.0	22.4	225.6	14.9
High	4,796.7	74.3	1,244.6	82.3
Geographic Area				
Africa	140.0	2.2	31.0	2.0
Asia	1,620.0	25.8	322.0	20.5
Central & Eastern Europe	314.0	5.0	60.0	3.8
Western Europe	2,657.0	42.4	763.0	48.6
Middle East	244.0	4.0	29.0	1.8
Latin America	350.0	5.6	56.0	3.6
North America	946.0	15.1	309.0	19.7

Sources: Economic development category data: World Bank, *World Development Indicators,* 2004, Table 4.5, pages 198–200; Table 4.7, pages 206–208; Geographic area and individual nation data: World Trade Organization, *International Trade Statistics,* 2003, Tables 1.3 and 1.4, page 20; Table 1.5, page 21; Table 1.7, page 23.

Note: WTO data includes Mexico in Latin America, not North America.

In reporting the geographic area data, the WTO *excluded* reexports; therefore, the merchandise trade total of $6,272 and service trade of $1,570 is different from the WTO-reported world totals in other tables. The trade shares shown in the geographic areas above are calculated on the basis of these lower total figures.

The overall picture of world trade patterns shown in Table 2-2 provides necessary background for understanding world trade. However, it is often more important to identify the trading patterns of the particular nations. For example, Table 2-3 shows the major trading partners of the United States. Of particular importance is that China replaced Mexico as the second most important supplier of the United States in 2003. (China also moved from ninth to sixth place on the export side between 2001 and 2003.) France, historically one of the largest trading partners of the United States, may soon fall off the list of top ten traders. To complement this information, a firm might use a product breakdown by country to provide a more complete profile of a nation's trade.

The statement that most trade is with industrial countries is borne out by the figures for the United States, but the importance of other factors becomes evident as well. For example, the role of Canada and Mexico as trading partners of the United States cannot be explained very well in terms of their size or degree of industrialization. **Geographic proximity** is an important consideration. In general, countries that are neighbors are better trading partners than countries that are distant from each other. The lower transportation costs are accompanied by greater familiarity and ease of communication and control.

Surprisingly, recent research suggests that the Internet may not have a major impact on trading patterns of manufactured goods and that geographic proximity will continue as a major factor in explaining trading patterns. This is borne out by some recent surveys and statistics showing that Europeans prefer to purchase from local merchants and to make purchases offline, as do many other consumers, because of lack of trust and the desire to see or touch the mer-

TABLE 2-3　Major Trading Partners of the United States in 2003

Top 10 Purchasers	U.S. Exports ($US billions)	Top 10 Suppliers	U.S. Imports ($US billions)
Canada	169.5	Canada	224.2
Mexico	97.5	China	152.4
Japan	52.1	Mexico	138.1
United Kingdom	33.9	Japan	118.0
Germany	28.8	Germany	68.0
China	28.4	United Kingdom	42.7
Korea, Republic	24.1	Korea, Republic	37.0
Netherlands	20.7	Taiwan	31.6
Taiwan	17.5	France	29.2
France	17.1	Ireland	25.8

Note: Merchandise exports only.

Sources: *Top Trading Partners:* Total Trade, Exports, Imports; U.S. Census Bureau, Foreign Trade Statistics (http://www.census.gov/foreign-trade/statistics/highlights/top-partners.html); accessed July 26, 2004; Trade Stats Express, Office of Trade and Economic Analysis (OTEA), Trade Development, International Trade Administration, U.S. Department of Commerce (http://ese.export.gov); accessed July 26, 2004.

chandise. This requires a trip to the local store. Recent reports also show that, with the exception of the United States and Europe, Internet traffic is highest among nations within the same region. While far from conclusive, these findings show that the role of geographic proximity explains a lot about trading patterns.[5]

Political influences continue to be a critical factor in trade relations and may be borne out by reviewing trade statistics such as those presented in the previous tables. One explanation for the declining trade between the United States and France over the 2000–2003 period is that France did not support the United States in the war on Iraq. Another long-standing example is U.S. trade with Cuba. Although Cuba is a close neighbor of the United States, practically no trade exists between the two countries. This controverts the statement about geographic proximity made earlier. While speaking in Miami to an audience of mostly Cuban-Americans on May 20, 2002, President Bush announced that the United States would not lift trade sanctions that were first imposed in 1962.[6] These sanctions constitute a near complete embargo, allowing Americans to sell only agricultural goods and then for cash only. Even attempts to allow travel and imports of medicine were quashed in Congress. These decisions put the United States in a lonely position. Other nations expanded travel and trade with Cuba as Fidel Castro neared his eightieth birthday. The point here is that an analysis of trade patterns both on an aggregate and national basis can be useful to a firm when it is planning its global logistics systems. Examination of the causes of trade patterns suggests possible approaches to adapting to the patterns or to modifying them.

International Trade Theory

Domestic firms recognize the importance of buyer behavior and motivation. For the international businessman, knowledge of the basic causes and nature of international trade is important. It is easier for a firm to work with the underlying economic forces than against them. To work with them, however, the firm must first understand them.

Essentially, international trade theory seeks the answers to a few basic questions: Why do nations trade? What goods do they trade? Nations trade for economic, political, and cultural reasons. But the principal economic basis for international trade is difference in price; that is, a nation can buy some goods more cheaply from other nations than it can make them. In a sense, the nation faces the same "make-or-buy" decision as the firm does. Just as most firms do not seek complete vertical integration, but buy many materials and supplies from outside firms, so most nations decide against complete self-sufficiency (or **autarky**) in favor of buying cheaper goods from other countries.

An example given by Adam Smith helps illustrate this point: When discussing the advantages to England in trading manufactured goods for Portugal's wine, he noted that grapes could be grown "under glass" (in greenhouses) in England but to do so would lead to England's having both less wine and fewer manufacturers than if it specialized in manufacturers. (Nations—and, in fact, people—have an **absolute advantage** when it comes to making or doing certain things. Florida has a climate that is better suited for growing oranges than Alaska does and, therefore, can grow oranges less expensively. Japan has a more skilled workforce than the Philippines does for producing highly sophisticated robots. And while a physician may be able to install a new light fixture, a licensed electrician is likely to be able to do it better and faster.) In fact, Smith's major conclusion was that the wealth of nations is derived from the division of labor and specialization. Applied to the international picture, this means trade rather than self-sufficiency.

Comparative Advantage (CA)

It has been said that price differences are the immediate basis of international trade. The firm that decides whether to make or buy also considers price as a principal variable. But why do nations have different prices on goods? Prices differ because countries producing the goods have different costs. And why do countries have different costs? The Swedish economist Bertil Ohlin came up with an explanation generally held to be valid: Different countries have dissimilar prices and costs on goods because different goods require a different mix of factors in their production and because countries differ in their supply of these factors. Thus, in Smith's example, Portugal's wine would be cheaper than England's wine because Portugal has a relatively better endowment of wine-making factors (for example, land and climate) than England does.

This discussion has dealt with the principle of **comparative advantage**; namely, that a country tends to produce and export those goods in which it has the greatest comparative advantage and import those goods in which it has the least comparative advantage. As Smith suggested, the nation maximizes its supply of goods by concentrating production where it is most efficient and trading some of those products for imported products where it is least efficient. An examination of the exports and imports of most nations tends to support this theory.

Product Life Cycle

A refinement in trade theory is related to the **product life cycle**, which in business refers to the consumption pattern or sales trend for a product. When applied to international trade theory, it refers primarily to international trade and production patterns. According to this concept, many products go through a trade cycle wherein one nation is initially an exporter, then loses its export markets, and finally may become an importer of the product. Empirical studies have demonstrated the validity of the model for some kinds of manufactured goods.

Outlined below are the four phases in the production and trade cycle, with the United States as an example. Assume that a U.S. firm has come up with a high-tech product. What follows is:

Phase 1: The United States exports the product.
Phase 2: Foreign production starts.
Phase 3: Foreign production becomes competitive in export markets.
Phase 4: Import competition begins.

In Phase 1, product innovation is likely to be related to the needs of the home market. The firm usually serves its home market first. The new product is produced in the home market because, as the firm moves down the production learning curve, it needs to communicate with both suppliers and customers. As the firm begins to fill home-market needs, it starts to export the new product, seizing on its first-mover advantages, and to increase sales (assuming the U.S. firm is exporting to Europe).

In Phase 2, importing countries gain familiarity with the new product. Gradually, producers in wealthy countries begin producing the product for their own markets. (Most product innovations begin in one rich country and then move to other rich countries.) Foreign production will reduce the exports of the innovating firm. (Assume that the U.S. firm's exports to Europe are replaced by production within Europe.)

In Phase 3, foreign firms gain production experience and move down the cost curve. If they have lower costs than the innovating firm, which is frequently the case, they export to third-country markets, replacing the innovator's exports there. (Assume that European firms are now exporting to Latin America, taking away the U.S. firm's export markets there.)

In Phase 4, the foreign producers now have sufficient production experience and economies of scale to allow them to export back to the innovator's home country. (Assume that the European producers have now taken away the home market of the original U.S. innovator.)

In Phase 1, the product is "new." In Phase 2, it is "maturing." In Phases 3 and 4, it is "standardized." The product may become so standardized by Phase 4 that it almost becomes a commodity. This modification of the theory of comparative advantage provides further insight into patterns of international trade and production and helps the international company plan logistics, such as when it will need to produce—or source—abroad.

Technological advances have changed many aspects of global business, and the impact on the product life cycle is the speed at which products move through these stages. Information is more readily available, and ideas are exchanged more rapidly; so the time between product introduction in one country and its introduction in other nations has grown much shorter. Competitors are also entering industries more quickly—which means that firms must seek lower production alternatives more quickly—so movement to Stage 4 occurs more rapidly as well.

Balance of Payments

In the study of international trade, the principal source of information is the **balance-of-payments** (BoP) statement of the trading nations. These are summary statements of all of the economic transactions between one country and all other countries over a period of time, usually one year. As an accounting of all transactions between one nation and the rest of the world, the BoP is a double-entry report in which the total of all payment and receipts are equal. Deficits (spending exceeds earnings) or surpluses (earnings exceed deficits) occur in specific BoP accounts. The accounts most often discussed are the current account and the capital account.

The current account includes a list of trade transactions in manufactured goods and services, as well as a list of unilateral transfers. Unilateral transfers, as the term suggests, are one-way transfers. Assume that a firm exports a manufactured good, such as a book, and in exchange gets the value of that book in some currency. Those actions are offsetting parts of the transaction (outflow: book; inflow: money). But when someone earns money during the year, purchases a gift, and sends it to a relative in another country, the transaction is only one-way. (The gift is shipped or exported, but no money flows back into the country.) Where there are large numbers of foreign workers, as in Germany and Saudi Arabia, these transfers can be substantial.

The capital account includes flows such as direct and portfolio investments, private placements, and bank and government loans. Again, in countries that receive a lot of investment funds (such as those in Eastern Europe and China) or in countries that supply a lot of funds (such as the United States, the Netherlands, and the United Kingdom), the capital account can be a significant component in the total BoP accounting statement.

Managers of global firms usually are more interested in the details of current account transactions; that is, in the nature of the goods being traded and their origin and destination. Careful examination of the current account can identify the source of competing products as well as potential markets. A more detailed explanation of the usefulness of balance of payments is provided below.

Strategic Business Decisions

The BoP is an indicator of the international economic health of a country. These data help government policy makers plan monetary, fiscal, foreign exchange, and commercial policies. The data can also provide information for strategic global business decisions. By reviewing import data, marketers can determine the major sources of foreign-made products and, from this, gain some idea of *competitors'* locations. Export data, on the other hand, can be used to identify where a nation's products are being shipped and thereby divulge some information about *consumers'* locations.

For those companies facing severe import competition, another useful aspect of the data in the BoP records is that they may aid a firm in arguing for protection of its industry. This would be the case if imports are rising rapidly and displacing workers or if imports are threatening strategic industries. Companies supplying products to a foreign nation should also review the BoP statistics for warning signs of impending trade legislation. For example, rapidly rising imports might presage government regulation of trade for that particular product. This means that watching trends in the BoP data for a few years is also critical.

Data in Table 2-4 (pages 44–45) presents a snapshot of current account information for one U.S. product. The data are taken from the *World Trade Annual*, a comprehensive five-volume pub-

TABLE 2-4   Examples of Import/Export Statistics from Balance-of-Payments Data, 1998–2000

Imports (partial table at four-digit product code level)

SITC Number / Importer / Provenance	Quantity Units	Value Thousands of U.S. Dollars	SITC Number / Importer / Provenance	Quantity Units	Value Thousands of U.S. Dollars
751.1 Typewriters, Cheque Writers			**751.1 Typewriters, Cheque Writers (Cont.)**		
Canada..................Tot	N	25102	2770	Ireland..................Tot	W	41	1041
USA	N	16058	1861	USA	W	1	53
Mexico	N	2123	141	Japan	W	4	181
Japan	N	824	128	Asia, other, NS	W	1	55
Indonesia	N	1331	241	United Kingdom	W	27	624
Germany	N	3838	270				
United Kingdom	N	358	67	Italy......................Tot	W	494	6596
			USA	W	–	165
USA......................Tot	N	570723	46063	Bermuda	W	7	80
S.Africa Cus. Union	N	710	277	Mexico	W	299	3276
Mexico	N	389103	25723	Japan	W	5	149
Japan	N	19634	4673	China	W	23	359
China	N	82595	4499	India	W	38	339
Indonesia	N	36883	6636	France	W	5	126
Korea Republic	N	3490	175	Germany	W	56	1290
India	N	1222	540	United Kingdom	W	49	604
Germany	N	5400	128	Switzerland	W	5	93
Italy	N	794	235				
United Kingdom	N	8133	2551	Netherlands...........Tot	W	59659	9541
Bulgaria	N	21600	501	USA	N	6260	708
			Japan	N	7477	2992
Israel....................Tot		–	117	China HK SAR	N	1953	173
			Indonesia	N	2538	324
Japan....................Tot		–	48636	Korea Republic	N	1532	446
USA		–	679	Philippines	N	7197	1345
Mexico		–	65	Belgium-Lux	N	4571	842
China		–	25441	France	N	8727	760
Malaysia		–	201	Germany	N	2752	616
Asia, other, NS		–	2172	Sweden	N	253	55
Germany		–	65	United Kingdom	N	15470	1397
Italy		–	64				
United Kingdom		–	192	Portugal.................Tot	W	56	904
			Mexico	W	10	157
Austria..................Tot	W	241	3797	Japan	W	4	89
USA	W	4	171	India	W	6	77
Mexico	W	37	598	Singapore	W	3	52
Japan	W	2	98	Germany	W	3	59
China	W	15	197	Italy	W	4	108
Indonesia	W	4	54	Spain	W	15	204
Germany	W	19	298	United Kingdom	W	6	97
Italy	W	10	259				
United Kingdom	W	148	2045	Spain ....Tot	W	490	7540
			USA	W	1	112
Belgium-Lux...........Tot	W	152	3191	Mexico	W	320	4680
USA	W	12	449	China	W	78	988
Mexico	W	32	643	Indonesia	W	23	293
France	W	3	110	Asia, other, NES	W	5	219
Germany	W	10	331	Thailand	W	11	434
Italy	W	29	419	Germany	W	5	99
Netherlands	W	16	330	Italy	W	10	204
United Kingdom	W	37	774	United Kingdom	W	25	323
			Slovenia	W	5	55

W: weight, metric tons; N: number; "-" indicates the data are not available; this is a partial list of statistics for this product category.

Source: United Nations, *World Trade Annual* 1998, 2000, Volume 5, New York: Walker & Company, pages 267, 997, 998.

TABLE 2-4   Examples of Import/Export Statistics from Balance-of-Payments Data (continued)

Exports (partial table at four-digit product code level)

SITC Number Exporter Destination	Quantity Units		Value Thousands of U.S. Dollars	SITC Number Exporter Destination	Quantity Units		Value Thousands of U.S. Dollars
751.1 Typewriters, Cheque Writers				**751.1 Typewriters, Cheque Writers (Cont.)**			
Canada.................Tot	N	1878	160	Germany (Continued)			
USA	N	1783	157	Austria	W	23	777
				Belgium-Lux	W	14	538
USA......................Tot	N	161749	32401	Denmark	W	4	211
S.Africa Cus. Union	N	1070	496	Finland	W	4	184
Canada	N	6188	1829	France	W	29	1017
Brazil	N	387	192	Greece	W	19	574
Chile	N	11038	1408	Italy	W	16	565
Colombia	N	3393	1388	Netherlands	W	26	1264
Ecuador	N	1055	117	Portugal	W	2	79
Mexico	N	71435	6849	Spain	W	16	699
Peru	N	97	108	Sweden	W	6	331
Uruguay	N	6580	593	United Kingdom	W	24	778
Venezuela	N	6773	1152	Switzerland	W	6	246
Costa Rica	N	309	99	Bulgaria	W	3	238
El Salvador	N	1365	350	Czech Republic	W	48	753
Guatemala	N	3593	1125	Hungary	W	3	87
Honduras	N	572	286	Poland	W	82	1864
Dominican Repub.	N	718	277	Romania	W	8	190
Trinidad & Tobago	N	819	283	Slovak	W	8	181
Panama	N	8488	1047	Belarus	W	5	100
Japan	N	685	395	Latvia	W	2	64
United Arab Emir.	N	377	175	Lithuania	W	6	142
China	N	658	668	Russian Federation	W	84	1878
China, HK SAR	N	104	113	Ukraine	W	51	850
Korea Republic	N	165	270	Croatia	W	6	110
Malaysia	N	43	67	Slovenia	W	2	88
Asia, other, NS	N	466	196				
Mongolia	N	282	99	Italy ....Tot	W	400	9174
Philippines	N	1304	451	S.Africa Cus. Union	W	13	317
India	N	2683	604	Algeria	W	9	114
Singapore	N	748	290	Libya	W	55	1625
Thailand	N	121	69	Morocco	W	11	162
Austria	N	203	86	Cote D'Ivoire	W	3	67
Belgium-Lux	N	1331	442	USA	W	17	451
Denmark	N	830	290	Brazil	W	20	512
France	N	11024	3552	Chile	W	10	252
Germany	N	1429	661	Venezuela	W	2	62
Ireland	N	236	80	Israel	W	8	53
Italy	N	41	169	United Arab Emir.	W	4	120
Netherlands	N	1435	198	Turkey	W	6	109
Spain	N	85	407	Korean Republic	W	2	105
Sweden	N	645	379	Austria	W	10	212
United Kingdom	N	9530	3773	Belgium-Lux	W	11	269
Norway	N	11	72	Denmark	W	17	315
Switzerland	N	12	59	France	W	11	243
Australia	N	816	350	Germany	W	17	320
New Zealand	N	1556	382	Portugal	W	1	78
				Spain	W	30	733
				United Kingdom	W	10	243
				Czech Republic	W	5	129
				Romania	W	10	243
				Russian Federation	W	68	1584
				Bosnia Herzegov.	W	4	73
				Australia	W	3	202

W: weight, metric tons; N: number; "-" indicates the data are not available; this is a partial list of statistics for this product category.

Source: United Nations, *World Trade Annual* 1998, 2000, Volume 5, New York: Walker & Company, pages 267, 997, 998.

lication of the UN. The publication provides details of exports and imports by Standard International Trade Classification (SITC) category. (Partial data are provided for illustrative purposes.)

The first part of the table lists some of the major *importing countries* for typewriters (yes, people still buy them) and the countries that supplied them. The second part of the table shows a similar list of the *exporters* and the markets to which they exported.

Financial Considerations

Up to this point, the text has dealt primarily with the current account in the BoP, especially the movement of goods reflected in that account. A look at the capital account is also useful.

A nation's international solvency can be evaluated by checking its capital account over several years. If the nation is steadily losing its gold and foreign exchange reserves, there is a strong likelihood of a currency devaluation or some kind of exchange control, meaning that the government restricts the amount of money sent out of the country as well as the uses to which it can be put. With exchange control, a firm may have difficulty obtaining foreign exchange to **repatriate** (send home) profits or import supplies needed to manufacture its products. If the firm is importing products that are not considered necessary, the scarce foreign exchange will go instead to goods on which the nation places a higher priority.

The firm's pricing policies, too, are affected by the balance-of-payments problems of the host country. If the firm cannot repatriate profits from a country, it tries to use its transfer pricing to minimize the profits earned in that country, gaining its profits elsewhere where it can repatriate them. If the exporting firm fears devaluation of a currency, it hesitates to quote prices in that currency, preferring to give terms in its home currency or another "safe" currency. Thus, the BoP is an important information source, particularly for international marketing and international finance decision makers.

Commercial Policy

One reason international trade is different from domestic trade is that it is carried on between different political units, each one a sovereign nation exercising control over its own trade. Although all nations control their foreign trade, they vary in the degree of such control. Each nation invariably establishes laws that favor its nationals and discriminates against traders from other countries. This means, for example, that a U.S. firm trying to sell in the French market faces certain handicaps from the French government's control over its trade. These handicaps to the U.S. firm are in addition to any disadvantages resulting from distance or cultural differences. By the same token, a French firm trying to sell in the United States faces similar restrictions when competing with U.S. firms selling in their home market.

Commercial policy is the term used to refer to government regulations bearing on foreign trade. The principal tools of commercial policy are tariffs, quotas, exchange control, and administrative regulation (the "invisible tariff"). Each of these terms will be discussed as it relates to the task of international business. Governments often use trade barriers to protect domestic industries and the jobs they provide. (This is the reason some individuals refer to this intervention as *protectionism*.) For instance, if a government places a tax (tariff) on all foreign-made cars, making the cars more expensive, simple rules of supply and demand will show people buying more domestic-made cars than foreign-made cars. People with jobs are happier than people without work because they can provide for themselves and their families. When people are happy, they tend to support the government and the officials who impose the protection.

Tariffs

A **tariff** is a tax on products imported from other countries. The tax may be levied on the quantity—such as 10 cents per pound, gallon, or yard—or on the value of the imported goods—such as 10 or 20 percent *ad valorem*. A tariff levied on quantity is called a *specific duty* and is used especially for primary commodities. *Ad valorem* duties are generally levied on manufactured products.

Governments may have two purposes in imposing tariffs: They may want to earn revenue and/or make foreign goods more expensive in order to protect national producers. When the United States was a new nation, most government revenues came from tariffs. Many less developed countries today earn a large amount of their revenue from tariffs because they are among the easiest taxes to collect. Today, however, the protective purpose generally prevails. One could argue that with a tariff, a country penalizes its consumers by making them pay higher prices on imported goods; it penalizes producers that import raw materials or components. The rationale is that a policy that is too liberal with imports may hurt employment in that country's own industries.

Tariffs affect international business pricing, product, and distribution policies as well as foreign investment decisions. If a firm is supplying a market by means of exports, the tariff increases the price of its product and reduces competitiveness in that market. This necessitates a price structure that minimizes the tariff barrier. A greater emphasis on marginal cost pricing could result. This examination of price is accompanied by a review of other aspects of the firm's approach to the market. The product may be modified or stripped down to lower the price or to get a more favorable tariff classification. For example, watches could be taxed as timepieces at one rate or as jewelry at a higher rate. The manufacturer might be able to adapt its product to meet the lower tariff.

Another way the manufacturer can minimize the tariff burden is to ship products completely knocked down (CKD) for assembly in the local market. The tariff on unassembled products or ingredients is usually lower than that on completely finished goods in order to promote the use of local labor. This establishment of local assembly operations is a form of the phenomenon known as **tariff factory**, the term used when the primary reason a local plant exists is to get behind the tariff barriers of protected markets that it can no longer serve with direct exports. The assembly operations may eventually lead to completely manufacturing the product in the host market. This generally requires the use of additional local labor, the goal of the government in imposing a tariff.

All trade barriers raise prices of targeted goods and services. *Ad valorem* tariffs are more effective against high- and low-priced products, while specific tariffs are more effective at keeping low-priced goods out. Nations wanting to keep out low-priced vehicles could impose a specific duty of $2,500 on every auto. This amount is relatively large for a car that costs $25,000 versus a car that costs $250,000. An *ad valorem duty* of 10 percent, however, would raise the *relative* price of all imported cars by the same amount.

There is another aspect to the debate about using different trade barriers. The tariff collected goes back into the coffers of the nation that imposed the duty. This money can be distributed to consumers and others in the home country. *Non-tariff barriers* (NTBs) raise prices for consumers, but the additional money does not go to the government or other home national parties. Instead, the money flows out of the country and may even go to the exporter in the form of higher profits.

Tariffs used to be the most effective and easiest tool for countries to use in reducing or eliminating foreign-made goods. Over the past 50 years, though, the WTO, bilateral trade agreements, and agreements among nations (such as NAFTA) have significantly reduced and even eliminated tariffs. Tariffs are easily identifiable as trade barriers and, therefore, are one of the main targets of free-trade proponents. Protecting local industries remains a goal of many government leaders, though; so innovative ways were—and still are—being invented to stem the tide of imports. Increasingly, as governments agreed to reduce tariff barriers, they turned to NTBs, such as quotas, to affect changes in the flow of trade.

Quotas

Quantitative restrictions, or **quotas**, are barriers to imports. They set absolute limits on the amount of goods that may enter a country. An import quota can be a more serious restriction than a tariff because a firm has less flexibility in responding to it. Price or product modifications do not get around quotas the way they might get around tariffs. The government's goal in establishing quotas on imports is obviously not revenue. Rather, government's goal is the conservation of scarce foreign exchange and/or the protection of local production. About the only response a firm can make to a quota is to assure itself a share of the quota or to set up local production if the market size warrants doing so. Since the latter is in accord with the wishes of government, the firm might be regarded favorably for taking such action.

In April 2002, U.S. President Bush unveiled a plan to protect the steel industry that included tariffs of up to 30 percent on imported steel. Since the WTO now prohibits the use of so-called voluntary restraints that were used to protect the industry, quick-acting tariffs were imposed.[7] For political reasons, including the desire for support for the war in Iraq and WTO pressure, the United States lifted these tariffs in December 2003, 18 months after imposing them.

Fallout from the steel tariffs imposed by the United States includes finding other markets for the products barred from entry. In an effort to find new markets, these producers compete more heavily in markets with fewer trade barriers. In an effort to prevent potential dumping of diverted U.S. imports, the EU imposed quotas on imported steel to protect its market. Furthermore, the EU threatened to impose retaliatory restrictions on American-made goods such as Harley Davidson motorcycles and Tropicana orange juice. Clearly, imposing trade barriers in one country can and often does have negative global repercussions.[8]

Exchange Control

The most complete tool for regulation of foreign trade is **exchange control**, a government monopoly of all dealings in foreign exchange. Exchange control means that foreign exchange is scarce and that the government is rationing it out according to its own priorities. A national company earning foreign exchange from its exports must sell this foreign exchange to the control agency, usually the central bank. In turn, a company wanting to buy goods from abroad must buy its foreign exchange from the control agency.

Firms in the country must be on the government's favored list in order to obtain exchange for imported supplies. Alternatively, they may try to develop local suppliers, running the risk of higher costs and indifferent quality control. The firms exporting to that nation must also be on the government's favored list. Otherwise, they will lose their market if importers can get no foreign exchange to pay them. Generally, exchange-control countries favor the import of capital goods and necessary consumer goods but not luxuries. While the definition of "luxuries" varies from country to country, it usually includes cars, appliances, and cosmetics. If the exporter does lose its market through exchange control, the only option may be to produce within the country if the market is large enough for this to be profitable.

Another implication for a firm when foreign exchange is limited is that the government is likely to restrict companies' profit remittances as another way of keeping the country's scarce foreign earnings within its borders. In this situation, the firm tries to use transfer pricing to get earnings out of the host country or to avoid accumulating earnings there. It accomplishes this by charging high transfer prices on supplies sold to the subsidiary and low transfer prices on goods sold by that subsidiary to affiliates of the company in other markets. The firm's ability to do this depends on the plan's acceptance by tax officials of the country.

Invisible Tariff and Other Government Barriers

There are other government barriers to international trade that are hard to classify; for example, administrative protection, the invisible tariff, and **NTBs**. As traditional trade barriers have declined since World War II, the NTBs have taken on added significance. They include customs documentation requirements, marks of origin, food and drug laws, labeling laws, antidumping laws, "buy national" policies, subsidies, and many other means. For example, nations can make goods more expensive simply by adding the requirement that all incoming products must have additional forms or paperwork. This documentation takes time and costs money for the exporter. Another example of an NTB is subsidies. (See "Global Environment: Subsidies and Retaliation.") There are many types of NTBs. Because these barriers are so diverse, their impact cannot be covered in a brief discussion. But some idea of what nations are doing to impede trade can be gained by reading the disputes under consideration by the WTO (http://www.wto.org).

Other Dimensions and Institutions in the World Economy

The global business environment is complex and includes many players—national, regional, and local governments; private and publicly held firms; and innumerable international organizations, special interest groups, and individuals. The following discussion includes some of the more widely known institutions and, in some respects, most important institutions and other aspects that have an impact on the global business environment.

World Trade Organization (WTO)

Because each nation is sovereign in determining its own commercial policy, the danger is that arbitrary national actions will minimize international trade. This was the situation in the 1930s, when international trade was at a low ebb and each nation tried to maintain domestic employment while restricting imports that could help foreign rather than domestic employment. The economic reality of tariffs is that if one nation erects trade barriers, other nations are likely to follow suit by erecting their own barriers, most typically retaliating by imposing duties on products it purchases from the other nation. The bankruptcy of these "beggar my neighbor" policies was evident in the worldwide depression to which they contributed. This unhappy experience

Subsidies and Retaliation

After September 11, 2001, travelers were understandably shaken and reluctant to get back in airplanes. Airlines, already facing poor earnings in a highly competitive industry, faced collapse. In hindsight, the number of passengers actually declined very little. Yet airlines slashed prices dramatically in an attempt to regain customers in the months following the attacks on New York and Washington.

Drastically lower revenues produced global industry losses of $2.5 billion in 2001, and losses in subsequent years dwarfed this amount. To support the hard-hit airline industry, the U.S. government provided over $15 billion in aid, including subsidies and loan guarantees, to the U.S. airline companies. Even though the EU provided similar, although smaller, subsidies to its industry, it filed a charge with the WTO, stating that U.S. companies were abusing the government aid to unfairly lower prices in Europe to make up for lost revenue at home.

In response, the EU proposed that a surcharge be placed on foreign airline tickets for non-EU companies that were using subsidies to unfairly lower their prices. This action, referred to as a countervailing duty or tariff, caused a reaction among affected firms. The United States threatened to counter the EU surcharge with surcharges on European-carrier tickets. Just like two children fighting, this sort of behavior can easily escalate. Given the number of jobs at stake in the global airline industry, these subsidies and related issues were important agenda items at future WTO GATS talks.

Sources: "EU Ponders Duty on Foreign Airlines," March 13, 2002, *Financial Post,* World, page FP14; "Airlines Face More Heavy Losses," May 28, 2002, *South China Morning Post,* Section: Business Post, page 5; "U.S. Carriers Could Incur Large Costs From EC Tariff Plan," March 25, 2002, *Airline Financial News,* Volume 20, Number 12.

Note: The reference to EC is the European Commission.

Documents on Air Transport Services, World Trade Organization, Air Transport Services (http://www.wto.org/english/tratop_e/serv_e/transport_e/transport_air_e.htm), December 22, 2004.

led the major trading nations to seek better solutions after World War II. One outcome of their efforts was the General Agreement on Tariffs and Trade (GATT), now called the **WTO**.

Although GATT's initial membership consisted of only 23 countries, it included the major trading nations of the Western world. Today WTO is more than ever the world's trading club, accounting for over 90 percent of world trade. It has approximately 150 members with two dozen applicants currently negotiating membership. The WTO has contributed to the expansion of world trade. Since 1947, it has sponsored eight major multilateral trade negotiations, the latest being the Uruguay Round, which lasted from 1986 to 1994. As a result of these conferences, the tariff rates for tens of thousands of items have been reduced and a high proportion of world trade has seen an easing of restrictions on most manufactured goods (apparel, textiles, and agricultural products have traditionally involved difficult negotiations) and many services.[9]

Providing a framework for multilateral trade negotiations is a primary reason for WTO's existence, but there are other WTO principles that further trade expansion. One is the principle of **nondiscrimination**. Each contracting party must grant all others the same rate of import duty; that is, a tariff concession granted to one trading partner must be extended to all WTO members under the most-favored-nation (MFN) clause.

Another WTO principle is the concept of **consultation**. When trade disagreements arise, WTO provides a forum for consultation. In such an atmosphere, disagreeing members are more likely to compromise than to resort to arbitrary trade-restricting actions. All in all, world trade cooperation since World War II has led to a much better trading policy than the world might have expected. WTO has been a major contributor to this.

Some indication of the scope of WTO's activities in this area can be seen in "Global Environment: Disputes Brought Before the WTO." Economic troubles are making further contributions from WTO very difficult. Unemployment in the industrialized nations, large trade deficits in the United States, and heavy debt in many developing countries are causing nations to give more attention to national concerns than to international cooperation.

United Nations Conference on Trade and Development (UNCTAD)

Although WTO has been an important force in world trade expansion, benefits have not been distributed equally. Less developed countries, many of which are members of the WTO, have been dissatisfied with trade arrangements because their share of world trade has been declining and prices of their raw material exports compare unfavorably with prices of their manufactured goods imports. These countries believed that the organization accomplished more to further trade in goods of industrialized nations than it brought about to promote the primary products produced by developing nations. It is true that tariff reductions have been far more important to manufactured goods than to primary products. The result of these countries' dissatisfaction was the formation of **UNCTAD** in 1964. UNCTAD is a permanent organ of the United Nations General Assembly and counts over 190 member countries.

The goal of UNCTAD is to further the development of emerging nations—by trade as well as by other means. Under WTO, trade expanded, especially in manufactured goods, creating a growing trade gap between industrial and developing countries. UNCTAD seeks to improve the prices of primary goods exports through commodity agreements. If the commodity-producing countries could get together to control supply, higher prices and higher returns would result.

UNCTAD has also worked to establish a tariff preference system favoring the export of manufactured goods from less developed countries. Since these countries have not been able to export commodities in a quantity sufficient to maintain their share of trade, they want to expand in the growth area of world trade: industrial exports. They believe they might achieve this if manufactured goods coming from developing countries faced lower tariffs than the same goods coming from developed countries.

UNCTAD has made modest progress. One achievement is its own formation, a new club for world trade matters that is a lobbying group for developing country interests. Former Tanzanian president Julius Nyerere called it "the labor union of the developing countries." Through UNCTAD, developing countries have also received preferential tariff treatment from the EU, Japan, and the United States, as they requested. Overall, UNCTAD has focused world attention on the trade needs of developing countries and has given them a more coherent voice. UNCTAD's committees and studies have also made for a more informed dialogue.

WTO, UNCTAD, and the Firm

WTO's success in reducing barriers to trade has meant that a firm's global logistics can be more efficient. Further, the firm, through its subsidiaries in various markets, can help protect its interest in trade matters through discussions with governments in advance of trade negotiations. In

Disputes Brought Before the WTO

The WTO addressed approximately 300 complaints between 1995 and 2004. All of the member countries are or were involved in some dispute at one point in time; but the most commonly named complainant or respondent is the United States, followed closely by the EU. Disputes are as likely to rise between developing countries as they are between developed and developing nations; and disputes cover every imaginable good, service, and law—from alcohol, apples, and auto parts to grapefruit, macaroni, pet food, and polypropylene, as well as underwear and water. Telecommunication services, patent codes, tariff preferences, and subsidies, as well as film revenue and sound recordings, are the basis of other disputes. The most commonly cited areas, though, remain agricultural, steel, and textile goods. A representative selection follows.

1. Mexico: Measures Affecting Telecommunications (filed by United States); 6 June 2004
2. India: Anti-dumping measure on batteries from Bangladesh (filed by Bangladesh); 2 February 2004

the United States, for example, a committee holds hearings at which business representatives can present their international trading problems. These problems are noted for consideration in WTO negotiations. Firms in the EU usually work with trade associations that channel industry views to the EU negotiators. Brazil also looks to trade associations for industry views.

UNCTAD can have a more direct impact on a firm than WTO. Developing countries have limited experience in exporting manufactured goods. By itself, elimination of tariffs is not sufficient to help those countries. In these cases, the multinational firm can be a decisive factor. If the firm combines its know-how and resources with those of the host country, it can offer competitive exports. Included in the firm's resources is its global distribution network, which could be the critical factor in gaining foreign market access. Also, the firm supplies the foreign business know-how lacked by most developing country producers. For example, if Ford had the choice of importing engines from its plant in Britain or its plant in Brazil, it might choose Brazil if engines from Brazil had a zero tariff and engines from Europe faced a 15 percent duty.

International Financial System

A major goal of business is to make a profit, so firms pay close attention to financial matters. International companies must be even more concerned with financial matters than national firms because international companies deal with many currencies and with many national financial markets where conditions differ. Conducting business across national boundaries involves financial considerations, which will be discussed next.

EXCHANGE RATE INSTABILITY

International payments are one aspect of the financial side of international trade. In most cases, international transactions occur in different currencies. Dealing with multiple currencies is not

3. Dominican Republic: Measures affecting the importation and internal sale of cigarettes (filed by Honduras); 13 October 2003
4. United States: Definitive Safeguard Measures on Imports of Certain Steel Products (filed by Brazil); 23 May 2002
5. Turkey: Import Ban on Pet Food from Hungary (filed by Hungary); 7 May 2002
6. Slovakia: Safeguard Measure on Imports of Sugar (filed by Poland); 17 July 2001
7. Mexico: Measures affecting telecommunications services (filed by the United States); 27 August 2000
8. Trinidad and Tobago: Provisional anti-dumping measure on imports of macaroni and spaghetti from Costa Rica (filed by Costa Rica); 20 January 2000
9. Canada: Measures affecting film distribution services (filed by EU); 22 January 1998
10. Peru: Countervailing duty investigation against imports of buses from Brazil (filed by Brazil); 9 January 1998
11. Turkey: Taxation of foreign film revenues (filed by the United States); 17 June 1996
12. European Union: Import duties on rice (filed by Thailand); 11 October 1995

Source: WTO web site (http://www.wto.org/english/tratop_e/dispu_e/dispu_status_e.htm).

a serious problem in itself, but difficulties arise because currencies frequently change in value with regard to each other and in unpredictable ways.

A foreign exchange rate is the domestic price of a foreign currency. For the United States, this means that there is a dollar rate, or price, for the British pound, the Swiss franc, and the Brazilian real, as well as every other currency. If one country changes the value of its currency, firms selling to or from that country may find that the altered exchange rate is sufficient to wipe out their profit or, on the brighter side, provide a windfall gain. In any case, the firms must be alert for currency variations in order to optimize their financial performance. (See "Global Environment: That Will Cost You a Little More, Sir.")

If you ever traveled abroad and used a foreign currency, you participated in a foreign exchange transaction. You bought or exchanged your currency for another currency. From a tourist's perspective, it's good when your currency is strong and you can purchase a lot for your (domestic) currency; it's bad when your (domestic) currency is weak and you have to spend more for a good meal or a nice jacket. But if you are a manufacturer who depends on exports, when your domestic currency is expensive, demand for your products will likely decrease. Supply and demand for goods and services are affected by the price of currency that people use and by the volatility of that currency. The more a currency changes in value, the more volatile the currency is and the harder it is to predict the cost of whatever people buy with that currency.

Major currency traders include banks and other financial institutions, which trade currencies in the hundreds of billions of dollars every day. Trading is used in business transactions (for example, Dell may need yuan to pay suppliers in China), but also for speculative reasons. Just as traders in stock exchanges seek profits, foreign currency traders gamble on whether the price of a currency will rise or fall.

Currency prices also reflect the overall health of an economy and, in part, explain why people believe a strong currency is good and a weak currency is bad. A nation that has a positive balance of trade, or trade surplus, is exporting more products than it is importing. That means traders need to purchase the nation's currency to pay for those products. The more demand there is for a currency, the higher the price. Countries that are growing or that have a stable economy attract investors. Investors need the local currency to buy property, build factories, etc., which, in turn, increases demand for the currency and raises its price.

Added exchange stability within the EU was a major reason behind the adoption of the *euro* (€). This process involved cooperation and coordination of fiscal and monetary policies among the EU member participants, the creation of a European Central Bank, and the loss of substantial national sovereignty on policies that had a direct impact on employment and economic growth.

The following historical perspective is helpful in understanding the global organizations that formed shortly after World War II, the goals of which included fostering an environment of exchange rate stability.

In the days of the gold standard, exchange rates did not change in value. The stability and certainty of the international gold standard came to an end, however, with the advent of World War I. The international financial system of the 1930s had no certainty, stability, or accepted rules. Instead, there were frequent and arbitrary changes in exchange rates. This chaotic and uncertain situation contributed to the decline in international trade during that period. The worldwide Depression of the 1930s was reinforced by the added risks in international finance.

At the conclusion of World War II, nations met to address some of the problems that were believed to be contributing factors leading up to the war. In 1944, some of the allied nations met at Bretton Woods, New Hampshire, to design a better international economic system for the postwar world. One element of this system dealt with international trade, resulting in the formation of the WTO. Another element concerned with the need for international capital led to the formation of the World Bank. A third aspect involving the international monetary system resulted in the establishment of the International Monetary Fund (IMF).

INTERNATIONAL MONETARY FUND (IMF)

The **IMF** was originally designed to help nations control exchange rate fluctuations by having members agree on a specific exchange rate (U.S. dollars per British pound, for example) and then using vast stores of gold to buy and sell currencies to maintain those exchange rates. (For instance, buying U.S. dollars with gold—taking dollars out of circulation—would make dollars scarce and force the price up; selling dollars for gold—releasing dollars into the world supply—would force the price to decline.) This worked well; and trade increased dramatically after World War II, in part because currency prices were stable, making it less risky to buy and sell products and services denominated in other currencies.

The system failed in the early 1970s because there was too little gold to offset the tremendous amount of foreign currency being used. In essence, the system fell victim to its success. Since then, currencies "float" freely in price relative to one another, with prices being determined by supply and demand, with only occasional intervention by the IMF or central banks of various nations.

In the new millennium, the IMF plays a slightly different role. The organization and some of its members still occasionally intervene in foreign exchange markets; but this intervention, while it does affect currency prices, cannot control prices to the degree that was first established under the Bretton Woods agreement. Most often the IMF acts as a forum for monetary and fiscal discussions that affect the world economy, much as the UN acts as a forum for initiatives designed to promote peace. In addition to providing a forum for discussion, the IMF supplies financial assistance in the form of loans (usually for stabilizing a currency or for dealing with balance-of-payment problems) and technical assistance in the form of economic consultants (who provide advice to governments on designing effective economic and financial policies). All of their initiatives are designed to support the core IMF goals, which have remained the same since its inception: the promotion of worldwide financial stability and economic growth. Financial stability and economic growth lead to more customers for the world's products and remove some of the risks associated with international trade.

The importance of currency prices is that firms must contend with exchange rates that are continuously changing, which complicates strategic decisions such as those surrounding international pricing and logistics.

THE WORLD BANK GROUP

The **World Bank** is another institution conceived at Bretton Woods. Originally called the International Bank for Reconstruction and Development (IBRD), its primary mission was to assist war-torn countries of World War II in rebuilding their cities and infrastructure through loans with very favorable terms. Like the IMF, the World Bank plays a different role today. The goal of promoting economic growth remains, and the World Bank still provides many loans for infrastructure development. However, instead of helping countries such as England and other developed nations, assistance goes primarily to developing nations. Today the World Bank Group includes the IBRD, the International Development Association (IDA), the IFC, and the Multilateral Investment Guarantee Agency (MIGA). The activities of these organizations support the main goal of the World Bank Group, which is to improve the living conditions of the world's population, especially among the poorest countries. Loans for schools, roads, and telecommunication projects create potential consumers and an environment better able to support the needs of businesses.

Regional Economies

Nations have agreed to work together to pursue common economic goals. Formal agreements have been signed among nations that are similar in terms of culture and religion (such as ALADIA), among neighbors (ECOWAS), and among countries that are similar in terms of relative wealth and economic development (CARICOM). When discussing these agreements or groups of nations, the term *regional economic integration* is used. While the countries invariably sign these agreements because of the potential or perceived economic benefits, they are not always comprised of nations from a specific region. For instance, in late 2004, the EU began accession talks with Turkey that may eventually lead to EU membership. Many believe that the culture of Turkey is too different from that of other EU members and that because Turkey is an Asian, not a European, nation, it is not an appropriate EU candidate. The next section highlights some of these regional groups.

Regional Economic Integration

As stated previously, another major development since World War II has been the growth of regional groupings. The EU is best known and most successful, but it is only one of many.

That Will Cost You a Little More, Sir

Imagine that the $300 stereo equipment you are looking at suddenly goes up in price to $500. When buying products that are made abroad (and so many things *are* made abroad), you don't usually think about the exchange rate between your currency and that of the manufacturer. Do you own a Toyota or a Volkswagen? Did you look up the exchange rate between the U.S. dollar and the Japanese yen or German euro? Probably not. If you ever traveled to a country that uses a different currency, you undoubtedly watched the exchange rate, which probably changed a few cents or more between the time you planned your trip and the time you returned. So whether buying a hamburger in Paris or a jacket in Hong Kong, you are likely to calculate the cost in dollars or some other home currency.

When companies manufacture something in another country, even if the item consists of only one of the components of a product, the firm must consider the cost of doing so in the local currency because that is how the locals expect to be paid. Or if a firm makes something in one country and sells it in another country, the exchange rate is important because the price must be stated in a foreign currency (like the stereo sold in the United States and the hamburger sold in Paris). When the exchange rate changes, costs and prices change, too. Sometimes currency prices relative to one another are very stable and change little over time; sometimes, though, the change can be substantial and sudden. Consider the following:

Change in Price Relative to $US

Country/ Area	Currency	Change over 3 Months (%)	Change over 1 Year (%)	Country/ Area	Currency	Change over 3 Months (%)	Change over 1 Year (%)
Euro-zone	Euro	-2.82	-10.72	Switzerland	Franc	-2.77	-11.36
Mexico	Peso	-1.80	+4.69	United Kingdom	Pound	-2.17	-13.96
South Africa	Rand	-2.10	-11.03				

August 20, 2004, was used as end date. Source: http://www.uta.fi/~ktmatu/rate-datamenu.html (University of Tampere).

Regional groupings result from agreements between nations in the same region; their goal is to cooperate in various economic matters. There may also be political ties between these nations, but it is the economic aspect that is important. **Regionalism**, or economic cooperation within regions, is an attempt by nations to attain goals they cannot achieve in isolation. The North Atlantic Treaty Organization (NATO) is a counterpart in the military field. Some major regional groupings are shown in Table 2-5.

There are costs to a nation in joining a regional group, the chief one being that it must give up some **national sovereignty**, which is a nation's right to govern itself without outside interference. Nations do this only because they hope the benefits will be greater than the costs. The major benefit sought through economic integration is faster economic growth. By joining together, member nations gain additional resources, larger markets, and economies of scale for their industries. Another objective of regional groupings is countervailing power. For example, the EU seeks a stronger position against the economic power of the United States and Japan.

To put this in perspective, imagine that firms making the following products decided to pass along to the consumer the entire 10 or 15 percent increase in their prices.

			Change in Price ($US)				
Item	Original Price	10% Increase	15% Increase	Item	Original Price	10% Increase	15% Increase
Jeans	$50.00	$55.00	$57.50	Computer	$1,500.00	$1,650.00	$1,725.00
Textbook	$110.00	$121.00	$126.50	Car	$18,000.00	$19,800.00	$20,700.00

Sometimes that "little bit more" can be a lot.

Whether a currency increases or decreases in value relative to another currency is important. When the Canadian dollar is strong or strengthens relative to other currencies, you can buy more euros for each Canadian dollar, for example. That is good for tourists traveling to the Euro-zone. It is not good for Canadian manufacturers, though, because Canadians will buy foreign-made goods and services instead of those produced in Canada. When the Canadian dollar is weak or weakens, you can purchase fewer units of foreign currency. That generally means that tourists will spend less time abroad and purchase fewer souvenirs. Businesses that use foreign suppliers also have to pay more Canadian dollars for the foreign currency used to pay for their foreign-made components and supplies.

The reduction of trade barriers within the group adds dynamism to member economies by increasing competition. Sluggish national firms and monopolies lose their protective walls and are forced to change in a more competitive direction. Furthermore, the group of countries together may be able to afford an industry that is too large for any individual member country. Thus, industrialization can be aided by regional integration. All of this may mean greater wealth, progress, and self-sufficiency for the region. Various forms and degrees of economic integration are possible.

Forms of Economic Integration

Economic integration takes many forms. Among the most common types is the free-trade area. Distinguishing characteristics and examples of various types of economic integration is presented in the following section.

FREE-TRADE AREA

Although all regional groupings have economic goals, the various groups differ in organization and motivation. There are three basic kinds of organization for economic integration. The simplest is a free-trade area, in which the member countries agree to have free movement of goods among themselves; that is, no tariffs or quotas are imposed against goods coming from other members. The European Free Trade Association (EFTA) is a major example. The EFTA agreement was signed on January 4, 1960, and included Austria, Denmark, Norway, Portugal, Sweden, Switzerland, and the United Kingdom. Today EFTA is an international organization that includes Iceland, Liechtenstein, Norway, and Switzerland. The original EFTA members, except for Switzerland, decided to take more comprehensive steps to unify trading and other policies by forming what was to become the EU or by joining the EU at a later date. Because of the benefits to members in cooperating, in 1992, EFTA and the EU agreed to form an even larger country grouping called the European Economic Area (EEA); it contains all of the EU and EFTA members except Switzerland. Signing these agreements requires that nations give some of their national sovereignty to the parent organization or group. Switzerland and the other EFTA members do not agree with all of the EU policies and clearly demonstrated their desire to maintain their independence by not joining the EU.[10]

In the 1960s, Latin Americans responded to European integration moves by forming regional groupings of their own. In Central America, they formed the Central American Common Market (CACM); in South America, they formed the Latin American Free Trade Area (LAFTA). The Andean countries broke away from LAFTA to form the Andean Common Market. Unfortunately, none of those groups has made rapid progress. In the early 1990s, the Southern Cone countries (Argentina, Brazil, Paraguay, and Uruguay) formed Mercosur, which has made some progress.

During the Vietnam War, a number of Southeast Asian nations formed the Association of Southeast Asian Nations (ASEAN). ASEAN includes over 500 million people, with a collective GNI of more than US$750 billion. In 1992, ASEAN launched the ASEAN Free Trade Area (AFTA), the strategic objective of which is to increase the ASEAN region's competitive advantage as a single production unit. The elimination of tariffs and NTBs among the member countries is expected to promote greater economic efficiency, productivity, and competitiveness.[11]

The United States is a member of two free-trade areas, one with Israel and one with Canada and Mexico as NAFTA. NAFTA is very important because it creates a free-trade area of 410 million consumers—as large as the EU-EFTA grouping. As with any regional grouping, NAFTA has encountered some rough spots; but its importance can be seen in the fact that the three member countries are each other's largest customers and suppliers. (The United States also has agreements on free trade with many other nations, including Chile, Jordan, and Australia; but these are not the same as free-trade areas.)

In December 1994, Canada, the United States, and Mexico, as well as other nations in the Americas, established the Free Trade Agreement of the Americas (FTAA). FTAA has 34 members (800 million people), stretching from Alaska to Tierra del Fuego. The goal was to complete negotiations for the agreement by December 2005.[12]

CUSTOMS UNION

Though similar to a free-trade area in that it has no tariffs on trade among members, a **customs union** has the more ambitious requirement that members also have a uniform tariff on trade with nonmembers. Thus, a customs union is like a single nation not only in having internal trade, but also in presenting a united front to the rest of the world with its common external tariff. A customs union is more difficult to achieve than a free-trade area because each member must yield its sovereignty in commercial policy matters—not just with member nations, but with the whole world. Its advantage lies in making the economic integration stronger and avoiding the administrative problems of a free-trade area. For example, in a free-trade area, imports of a particular good would always enter the member country with the lowest tariff, regardless of the country of destination. To avoid this perversion of trade patterns, special regulations are necessary.

The leading example of a customs union is the EU. Although the EU is often referred to as the Common Market, it has successfully achieved customs union status. As it continues to put

TABLE 2-5   Selected Regional Economic Groupings

ALADIA: La Asociación Latinoamericana de Integración (Latin American Integration Association [LAIA])
   Argentina, Bolivia, Brazil, Chile, Columbia, Cuba, Ecuador, Mexico, Paraguay, Peru, Uruguay, and Venezuela

ASEAN: Association of Southeast Asian Nations
   Brunei, Cambodia, Indonesia, Laos, Malaysia, Myanmar, Philippines, Singapore, Thailand, and Vietnam

CAN: Comunidad Andina (Andean Community)
   Bolivia, Columbia, Ecuador, Peru, and Venezuela

CARICOM: Caribbean Community
   Antigua and Barbuda, Bahamas, the Barbados, Belize, Dominica, Grenada, Guyana, Haiti, Jamaica, Montserrat, St. Kitts and Nevis, St. Lucia, St. Vincent and the Grenadines, Suriname, Trinidad, and Tobago

ECOWAS: Economic Community of West African States
   Benin, Burkina Faso, Cape Verde, Ivory Coast, Gambia, Ghana, Guinea, Guinea Bissau, Liberia, Mali, Niger, Nigeria, Senegal, Sierra Leone, and Togo

EU: European Union
   Austria, Belgium, Cyprus, the Czech Republic, Denmark, Estonia, Finland, France, Germany, Greece, Hungary, Ireland, Italy, Latvia, Lithuania, Luxembourg, Malta, the Netherlands, Poland, Portugal, Slovakia, Slovenia, Spain, Sweden, and the United Kingdom

Mercosur
   Argentina, Brazil, Paraguay, and Uruguay

NAFTA: North American Free Trade Agreement
   Canada, Mexico, and the United States

into practice the 1992 Maastricht Treaty directives, the EU will possess many common market characteristics. Furthermore, with the implementation of a common currency in 12 member states and the formation of a European Union Central Bank, the EU has begun to adopt properties of an economic union. Though this has taken longer than EFTA, it represents a more ambitious endeavor because it includes not only a free-trade area among members, but also a common external tariff. In addition, it covers agricultural products, which were omitted by EFTA.

COMMON MARKET

A true **common market** includes a customs union but goes significantly beyond it because it seeks to standardize or harmonize all government regulations affecting trade. These include all aspects of government policy that pertain to business; for example, corporation and excise taxes, labor laws, fringe benefits and social security programs, incorporation laws, and antitrust laws. In such an economic union, business and trade decisions would be unaffected by the national laws of different members because the laws would be uniform. The United States is the closest example of a common market. Even in the United States, however, the example is not perfect because different states have different laws and taxes pertaining to business. U.S. business decisions, therefore, are somewhat influenced by differing state laws.

   As mentioned earlier, the EU is the best contemporary example of a common market in formation; but there are added dimensions that go beyond even a common market classification. The diverse cultures make it difficult to implement some initiatives; it took nearly ten years to implement an EU passport because, among other things, there was disagreement over the color and emblem to use on the cover. On the other hand, the implementation of the currency switch in 2002, from national to European euro, took less than the six months originally expected because of careful planning and intense marketing. In the years and months leading up to the conversion, companies and consumers were exposed to television and radio advertisements, information sessions at their workplaces, prices printed in both national and euro denominations, web sites, brochures, and billboards, all explaining the seemingly mundane. On January 1, 2002, the first day the new currency was available, people were so anxious to get it that many ATMs ran out of euros.

There is still a good deal of work to accomplish. Not all members of the EU wanted to give up their national currency (Denmark, Sweden, and the United Kingdom). This makes expansion of the Euro-zone more difficult because initiatives, particularly those related to monetary and fiscal policy, cannot be applied throughout the entire EU until all members join the monetary union. Enlargement is another issue; and in some respects, it is the most important one the EU faces. On May 1, 2004, ten nations were admitted to the EU (Cyprus, the Czech Republic, Estonia, Hungary, Latvia, Lithuania, Malta, Poland, Slovakia, and Slovenia); and other nations, such as Bulgaria and Romania, are awaiting admittance into the union. One major concern is that some of these nations will require extraordinary assistance because they are not as well off economically as many of the current members. In addition, some of these countries have considerable infrastructure needs. This means that the richer nations will have to underwrite or support some of their poorer neighbors. German unification in the early 1990s was an example of this phenomenon on a smaller scale. Former West Germans complain about the high taxes they continue to pay for integrating the former East Germans into the economy. On the other hand, the former East Germans did not automatically become rich overnight; nor did they have the ability to purchase everything they wanted. Goods in the former West Germany were not subject to the price controls the people had come to expect under the Communist regime. While more goods were available, they were also relatively expensive. Few people are completely happy.[13] A summary of differences among various forms of integration is presented in Table 2-6.

OTHER GROUPINGS

Economic unions among nations are characterized by a common currency. Underlying this obvious aspect is the coordination of fiscal and monetary policies (establishment of prime lending rates of interest, size of reserves banks must retain, etc.). This form of integration is uncommon because of the impact on inflation and unemployment rates. A review of the discussions surrounding the adoption of the euro among EU members highlights some of these issues and the difficulties in obtaining Euro-zone consensus. The requirement that members of an economic union adopt harmonized fiscal and monetary policies is a major reason behind some EU members opting out of the Euro-zone. (For an overview of some of the issues involved, see "The Euro, Our Currency" at http://europa.eu.int/comm/economy_finance/euro/our_currency_en.htm.)

As shown in Table 2-6, political unions require adoption of the principles behind the other forms of integration, as well as the adoption of a governing structure that supercedes individual national or state interests. One characteristic that indicates a group is moving in this direction is when the members of the union agree to the jurisdiction of the same governing body. Other characteristics include a common army and common foreign policy related to

TABLE 2-6   Forms of Economic Integration

Stage of Integration	Elimination of Trade Barriers among Members	Common Trade Barriers among Members	Free Factor Mobility	Coordination of Economic Policies	Coordination of Political Policies
Free-Trade Area	Yes	No	No	No	No
Customs Union	Yes	Yes	No	No	No
Common Market	Yes	Yes	Yes	No	No
Economic Union	Yes	Yes	Yes	Yes	No
Political Union	Yes	Yes	Yes	Yes	Yes

international issues. Political unions are actually more common than many people realize. Many nations in the world today are federations of smaller geographic areas that at one time or another believed they would be better off if they cooperated. Germany, a federation of 16 states, is a good example. The United States is a grouping of what were once independent states, some of which minted their own currency, manned their own militias, and collected tolls or duties at their borders. Vestiges of this state independence in the United States include drivers' licenses and driving laws that differ from state to state and licensing requirements for lawyers, doctors, and other professions, which are regulated at the state, not the federal, level of government.

There are also a number of examples of looser forms of economic cooperation. Many of these are of interest because they can affect the operations of a firm. Many nations of Africa are associate members of the EU and enjoy preferential entry of their goods into EU countries. EU producers, in turn, have an advantage over non-EU producers in selling to the associated states. Association agreements exist between the EU and other nations, including Algeria, Egypt, Israel, Jordan, Lebanon, Morocco, Syria, Tunisia, Turkey, and the Palestinian Authority.

The appearance of regional economic groupings is a promising development both for the regions and for multinational firms. For example, in August 2004, Russian President Vladimir Putin announced plans for a "Unified Economic Space" that included Russia, Ukraine, Belarus, and Kazakhstan. The unfortunate reality is that, except for the EU and Mercosur, these groupings have made very little progress. (See "Global Environment: African Unity.")

While NAFTA has its problems, it should be a solid performer. Efforts elsewhere have done little, though ASEAN holds promise for the future. Where integration is successful, it offers opportunities for firms that can operate within the group, but challenges for those on the outside.

Devolution, the decomposition of national and regional groupings, is a reflection of diverse points of view and counteracts some of the regional and global cooperation sought by the EU, NAFTA, and organizations such as the WTO, the IMF, and others. Consider the breakup of the Soviet Union into a multitude of new nations, the creation of new countries from the former Czechoslovakia and Yugoslavia, the continuing call by separatists for more autonomy for Corsicans from France, and the near-national division of the Flemish and Walloons in Belgium. Those examples should serve as a reminder to managers to consider the diversity of needs within regional groups and to proceed with caution when developing regional strategies.

African Unity

In the early 1960s, a number of African nations established the Organization of African Unity (OAU). The OAU did not meet many of its economic goals in the ensuing 40 years. As a result, in July 2000, 53 African nations agreed to disband the OAU and replace it with a new organization, the African Union (AU). The AU is based on the "New Partnership for Africa's Development" and the EU model. Fifty-three nations have agreed on the general terms of the agreement, which include good governance, free press, and fiscal transparency. Their goals include creating an environment in which the nations of the African continent can enter the mainstream of worldwide economic development. Through establishment of peacekeeping forces, a security council, and a legislature, the focus in the immediate future is to mediate wars and internal strife and to begin to address the abject poverty common to many nations by seeking debt relief so the nations can use funds to feed and meet other needs of their people. The ultimate goal is to create an EU-like structure, including monetary union under one currency and a central bank.

REGIONALISM AND THE MULTINATIONAL COMPANY

The rise of regional groupings means that fewer but larger economic entities are gradually replacing the multitude of national markets. When a firm is considering an investment decision, the relevant market area may include up to 25 countries rather than just one national market. For example, the "United States of Europe" and "Euro-land" are expressions used to describe the new Europe. An indication of the importance of the EU to American investors is provided by the following statistic: Over 65 percent of all capital flowing out of the United States in 2003 ($99 of $152 billion) went to Europe. Analysts attribute the amount and the growth in foreign investment flowing into the EU to harmonization of product specifications, lower foreign exchange risk, and other steps taken in the economic integration of the nations that make up the EU.[14]

A firm's logistics will be modified by regional groupings. There will be pressures to supply a region from within rather than to export to it. A firm will have the added incentive of the larger market; but it will also benefit by getting behind the tariff barrier, where it will be able to compete better with local producers and be protected from outside competition. At the same time, these local producers will become stronger competitors due to economies of scale in the larger market, the alliances they are forming, and the stronger competition in the free-trade area. A firm's operations within a regional group will tend to be more uniform and self-contained than they would be in ungrouped national markets.

In response to global forces and economic integration, a firm's strategies will be modified over time. As the differences in markets diminish, greater uniformity will occur in how business is conducted among the member countries. A firm will gain economies of scale in product development, distribution, and promotion. For example, as member nations harmonize their food, drug, and labeling laws, a firm can eliminate product and packaging differences that were required by different national laws. Similar modifications will occur in the other functional areas. The first of the following examples illustrates how firms reacted to the formation of the

While the announcement was accompanied by dancing in the streets (literally), the obstacles to success seem almost insurmountable. These 53 nations have highly diverse ethnic groups within their national boundaries. The differences are sharp enough to be at the center of the warfare and genocide that has been all too common throughout Africa over the past few decades. Furthermore, independence is fiercely guarded after a history of colonial rule. Those factors will make it difficult for the AU to reach any agreements by which all can abide. With few financial resources and crushing levels of debt, there is not enough money to build schools, roads, and other infrastructure. In turn, economic development will be difficult if firms do not have a ready resource of skilled local labor and if they cannot get their products to market. More importantly, without the funds needed to supply basic health care, food, and housing, large numbers of people will continue to die and there will be little hope of focusing much beyond survival. It is vital that the AU succeed in reducing strife and debt levels if economic development and global integration is to occur, and it is a wise leadership that realizes this.

Sources: Jon Jeter, "New Organization Replaces African Post-Colonial Relic," Tuesday, January 9, 2002, *Washington Post*, page A15; see also NEPAD, the document upon which AU is founded (http://www.nepad.com).

EU; the second is a success story of a firm that increased its marketing because of lower trade barriers among NAFTA members.

The New Eastern Europe

One of the major developments in recent history was the fall of the Berlin Wall and the decline of Communism. The fragmentation of the Communist bloc reduced the threat of war between East and West and significantly improved economic relations between the two groups. Each side considered the other to be the enemy until about 1990. Today they share friendly relations, and Western nations are providing substantial financial assistance to Eastern European nations. On May 1, 2004, eight former Communist nations were admitted into the EU.

FDI into these former Communist nations is soaring as well, averaging $25 billion annually between 1998 and 2002. Given these nations' rich oil and natural gas reserves, large investments continue to be made in their petroleum industries.[15]

The countries of Eastern Europe provide a very attractive potential market of 400 million people, which is more than that of all of Western Europe. Generally, there is also a familiarity with and a desire for Western goods and a Western standard of living. And the people in these countries are relatively rich compared to markets in developing nations. (See summary profile in Table 2-7.)

Although the markets look attractive, potential problems in Eastern Europe suggest caution. After years of Communist rule, Eastern European countries need to establish a legal system that can deal properly with a market economy and property rights. In addition, they lack hard currencies and stable monetary systems. After decades of a command economy, people and institutions lack a commercial or market mentality. Problems in adjusting to a market economy have caused political instability. The Russian crisis of 1998, corruption, and other difficulties in the petroleum and banking industries are examples. Another legacy of the command economy is a weak distribution infrastructure. In other words, reaping the Eastern Europe potential is as much a challenge as it is an opportunity.

Despite these problems, many Western firms have entered Eastern European markets. They believe that the potential is too great to ignore and that there are first-mover advantages: The first firm to become well established as the market is developing could be difficult to compete with later.

The U.S. government has recognized the potential promise of Eastern Europe and has established a service to encourage and assist American firms in doing business there. Its acronym, appropriately, is BISNIS. (See "Global Environment: Commerce Promotes Business with Business Information Services for the Newly Independent States [BISNIS].")

National Economies

Some nations bear special consideration because of their population or the amount or growth rate of their trade. Economic-related characteristics also affect what is marketed and how it is marketed. National data about population, income, infrastructure, and natural endowments are presented in the following passages to illustrate their impact on foreign sales.

The United States

Although the international environment of a firm is important, the global influence of its home base cannot be ignored. In ways varying from country to country, the home government affects the international operations of a firm, both positively and negatively. A Swedish or Dutch multinational company operates under a set of advantages and constraints different from those that affect a U.S. or a Japanese firm or a firm from one of the former colonial powers of England or France. Using the United States as an example, the text will discuss the advantages and constraints peculiar to a U.S. multinational company. The pattern can be applied to international firms domiciled in other nations.

One impact on a firm's international operations is its home government's policies toward such business. Most governments encourage exports. The United States is no different: U.S. government assistance is offered through the information and promotional services of the Department of Commerce. Furthermore, the Export-Import Bank helps finance American exports and offers a government-assisted program of export credit insurance and political-risk insurance.

The U.S. foreign aid program has helped U.S. companies export to markets that otherwise would have been closed because of their lack of foreign exchange. Those foreign aid programs that have a favorable effect on recipient nations' attitudes toward the United States improve the environment for the firms. A critical determinant of a firm's ability to export is, of course, the resource endowment of its home country. Furthermore, the business environment at home may have taught the firm skills that aid its performance abroad. Each state in the United States also maintains economic development agencies, the goals of which are to promote state exports and attract foreign investors. The type and level of assistance varies but generally includes market

TABLE 2-7 Central Europe and Former Soviet Union (USSR) Nations, 2002				
Area/Nation	Population (millions)	GNI (billions $US)	GNI Growth (annual %)	GNI per Capita ($US)
Central Europe				
Albania	3.2	4.8	4.7	1,450
Bosnia & Herzegovina	4.1	5.6	3.9	1,310
Bulgaria	7.9	15.5	4.8	1,770
Croatia	4.5	22.4	5.2	4,540
Czech Republic	10.2	69.5	2.0	5,480
Hungary	10.2	65.8	3.3	5,290
Macedonia, FYR	2.0	3.8	0.7	1,710
Poland	38.2	189.0	1.4	4,570
Romania	22.3	45.7	4.3	1,870
Serbia and Montenegro	5.4	23.7	4.7	3,970
Slovak Republic	8.2	15.7	4.0	1,400
Slovenia	2.0	22.0	3.0	10,370
Total	**118.0**	**483.6**		
Average			**3.5**	**$3,644**
Former USSR				
Armenia	3.1	2.4	12.9	790
Azerbaijan	8.2	6.1	10.6	710
Belarus	9.9	14.3	4.7	1,360
Estonia	1.4	6.5	6.0	4,190
Georgia	5.2	3.4	5.6	650
Kazakhstan	14.9	24.6	9.8	1,520
Kyrgyz Republic	5.0	1.6	-0.5	290
Latvia	2.3	8.4	6.1	3,480
Lithuania	3.5	13.8	7.2	3,670
Moldova	4.3	1.6	7.2	460
Russian Fed.	144.1	346.5	4.3	2,130
Tajikistan	6.3	1.2	9.1	180
Turkmenistan	4.8	7.7	14.9	1,090
Ukraine	48.7	41.5	4.8	780
Uzbekistan	25.3	7.9	4.2	310
Total	**286.7**	**487.5**		
Average			**7.1**	**$1,441**
Total of All Nations	**404.7**	**971.1**		
Average of All			**5.5**	**$2,420**

Note: GNI is calculated in current $US; GNI per capita is calculated using World Bank Atlas method in current US$. As defined by the World Bank, Gross National Income (GNI) is the sum of value added by all resident producers plus any product taxes (less subsidies) not included in the valuation of output; plus net receipts of primary income (compensation of employees and property income) from abroad.

Source: World Bank, *2003 World Development Indicators,* Data Query (http://devdata.worldbank.org/data-query); accessed July 27, 2004.

Commerce Promotes Business with Business Information Services for the Newly Independent States (BISNIS)

Since the nations of the former Soviet Union hold a lot of potential, Business Information Services for the Newly Independent States (BISNIS) was established in 1992 as a separate and special entity of the U.S. Department of Commerce's International Trade Administration. BISNIS is charged with promoting and facilitating trade and investment between the United States and the former Soviet Union states of Armenia, Azerbaijan, Belarus, Georgia, Kazakhstan, the Kyrgyz Republic, Moldova, the Russian Federation, Tajik-

assessment, identification of trade leads, and trade missions to other nations.

Other U.S. policies relate to international business. The government has encouraged investment in less developed countries by its investment-guarantee program. Although not as favorable as in the past and undergoing changes, government tax policy is favorable to business in foreign countries.

The government's commercial policy can help or hinder a firm internationally. As was previously stated, when a nation adopts free-trade policies rather than a protectionist stance with other nations, firms of that nation generally find it easier to conduct business in foreign countries. Firms are not completely helpless; they may be able to influence their nation's commercial policy by lobbying the appropriate government officials.

Other government actions and national achievements can affect a firm internationally. U.S. antitrust policy has constrained U.S. companies abroad. American technological and space achievements aid U.S. companies in sales of high-technology products. In part, these technological advances are supported by government funds for research and development (R&D). On the other hand, foreign dissatisfaction with the U.S. role in the world can threaten foreign operations of U.S. firms. Dissatisfaction over some U.S. action may lead to a march on the U.S. Embassy abroad—or the local Goodyear plant or the local Coca-Cola bottler.

The size and wealth of the U.S. economy are a source of both envy and resentment. They affect the image of U.S. companies abroad, often considered to have an unfair advantage over local companies. The United States is the world's leading exporter and importer. This lends weight to U.S. commercial policy negotiations, which favor foreign sales by U.S. firms. Since the U.S. market is so attractive, other countries must open up their markets if they want to sell to the United States. In those and other ways, a company's nationality affects its international sales.

Markets to Watch

Rising personal fortunes from Internet and high-technology ventures in the 1990s was followed by the "dot-com bubble burst," a general decline in economic well-being, and negative economic growth rates in the industrialized world. Not every nation followed this trend, however; and there are some bright areas on the horizon with regard to trade and economic development. Besides those already mentioned—the so-called Triad (the United States, the EU, and Japan), the transition economies in central and Eastern Europe, and the developed nations that are members istan, Turkmenistan, Ukraine, and Uzbekistan. (The United States classifies Estonia, Latvia, and Lithuania as the Baltic States and does not include them in this initiative.) BISNIS has ten offices in Russia and one in each of the other nations. Services offered include market information, counseling, electronic market updates and trade lead information, the monthly newsletter (*BUSINESS Bulletin*), and postings on its English- and Russian-language web pages. BISNIS Expolink Eurasia, an electronic exhibition area for U.S. companies, was recently added. While they are free to post, American firms must have their company information translated into Russian. BISNIS efforts resulted in over $3 billion in U.S. exports and investment between 1992 and 2002.

Source: http://www.bisnis.doc.gov.

of the Organization for Economic Cooperation and Development (OECD)—potential markets can be found in almost every corner of the globe. Table 2-8 identifies a few of those potential markets. Depending on the types of products and the goal (whether to increase a firm's sales or identify markets for sourcing the firm's goods), some of these markets are better than others. However, all are already major trading powers or hold a good deal of promise for the near future.

The second dimension of the economic environment of global business includes the domestic economy of every nation in which a firm is selling. Thus, a global firm faces the traditional task of economic analysis, but in a context that may include 100 countries or more. The investigation will be directed toward answering two broad questions: How big is the market, and what is the market like? Answers to the first question help determine the firm's market potential and priorities abroad. Answers to the second question help determine the nature of the marketing task.

Size of the Market

A firm's concern in examining world markets is the potential the markets offer for the firm's products. The international marketer must determine market size not only for present markets, but also for potential markets. This helps to allocate effort among present markets and to determine which markets to enter next. **Market size** for any given product is a function of particular variables, and its determination requires analysis. Certain general indicators are relevant for many goods. This section will discuss how world markets are described by the following two general indicators: (1) population—growth rates and distribution and (2) income—distribution, income per capita, and GNI.

Population

People are needed to make a market; and other things being equal, the larger the population in a country, the better the market. Of course, other things are never equal; so population figures in themselves are not usually a sufficient guide to market size. Nevertheless, the consumption of many products is correlated with population figures. For many "necessary" goods, such as ethical drugs, health-care items, some food products, and educational supplies, population figures may be a good first indicator of market potential. For other products that are low in price or that meet particular needs, population also may be a useful market indicator. Products in these second categories include soft drinks, ballpoint pens, bicycles, and sewing machines.

Population figures are one of the first considerations in analyzing foreign economies. One striking fact is the tremendous differences in size of the nations of the world. The largest nation in the world has about 10,000 times the population of the smallest countries. Well over half the people of the world live in the ten countries that have populations of more than 100 million. On the other hand, as many as one-half of the countries have populations of less than 10 million and more than 50 have fewer than 1 million people. (See "Global Environment: New Markets in China.")

A company is concerned primarily with individual markets, but regional patterns can also be important for regional logistics. For example, Asia contains six of the ten most populous markets. By contrast, Africa, the Middle East, and Latin America are rather thinly populated. Nigeria is the largest African nation with over 125 million people; but the Democratic Republic of Congo, Egypt, and Ethiopia all have populations that exceed 50 million. Latin America has only two relatively populous countries: Brazil with 175 million and Mexico with 100 million. Europe, much smaller in land area but more densely populated, has three countries with populations over 60 million. The five most populous nations will account for nearly 50 percent of the world's population by 2015. (See Table 2-9.)

Population Growth Rates

Global companies must be concerned with population trends as well as the current population in a market. This is because many strategic decisions will be affected by future developments. Although most countries experience some population growth, the rates among the world's richest nations are typically low.

The World Bank projects that global population will exceed 7 billion people by 2015 even though population growth rates are expected to decline further, to an average of 1 percent per year. The populations of high-income nations are expected to grow by an average of 0.3 percent annually, while low-income nations are expected to grow by approximately 1.5 percent. As the most populous nations, China and India are expected to grow at a slower rate, but will still add almost 300 million people to their combined populations. (Population growth rates are provided in Table 2-9).[16] The data in the table reflect the strong correlation between level of economic development and population growth. The richer countries have more stable populations; the poorer countries are growing rapidly.

Distribution of Population

Understanding population figures involves more than counting heads. The population figures should be classified by age group, gender, education, or occupation, for example, or in other ways that show the relevant segments of the market. Religious, tribal, educational, and other attributes will be discussed later. Here, such population characteristics as age and density are considered.

AGE

People in different stages of life have different needs and present different opportunities. In the U.S. market, many firms recognize different market segments related to age groupings. Each country has a somewhat different profile as to age groupings. Generally, however, there are two major patterns—one for developing countries and one for industrialized countries.

TABLE 2-8   20 Markets to Watch

Nation	Population (millions)	GNI (millions $US)	2002 Trade (billions $US)	FDI Inflows (millions $US)	Investment Climate
Chile	16	64.2	43.6	1,603	143.3
China	1,280	1,266.1	706.2	52,700	138.8
Czech Republic	10	69.5	92.5	9,319	143.9
Greece	11	132.8	72.1	50	156.7
Hong Kong	7	161.5	111.9	13,718	162.6
India	1,049	510.2	151.2	3,449	123.9
Italy	58	1,184.3	614.8	14,545	166.9
Korea, Republic	48	476.7	376.8	1,972	148.5
Malaysia	24	94.9	204.1	3,203	137.4
Mexico	101	637.2	363.3	13,627	132.6
Philippines	80	78.0	78.7	1,111	120.6
Poland	38	189.0	115.1	4,119	139.0
Portugal	10	121.6	80.4	4,276	162.8
Russian Federation	144	346.5	201.7	2,421	124.0
Singapore	4	87.0	230.8	7,655	176.6
South Africa	45	104.2	68.6	754	129.2
Spain	41	653.1	373.6	21,193	167.2
Thailand	62	126.9	231.6	1,068	136.0
Turkey	70	183.7	105.2	1,037	108.0
Vietnam	80	35.1	41.7	1,200	117.6
United States	288	10,383.1	2,374,500	30,030	172.4
World	**6,199**	**32,312.2**	**16,263,600**	**651,189**	**108.5**

Notes: Criteria used in selecting these markets included those shown as well as GNI growth rate, trade in goods and trade in services (exports and imports evaluated separately), and business environment—three separate variables. Most statistics were also compared to world totals. Of the criteria shown, GNI is reported in current $US; trade is the total of all merchandise and service imports and exports (Hong Kong and Singapore trade data do not include reexport or reimport data, which is substantial) and is reported in current $US; and investment climate is calculated by using the 2003 *Composite International Country Risk Guide* (ICRG) and the Euromoney country creditworthiness rating ranks as reported in the *2004 World Development Indicators*. The score can range from 0 to 200.

GNI growth rates in some countries (Italy and Portugal) were below 1 percent over the previous year but over the long run, showed better-than-average growth. China and Turkey had GNI growth rates of 8 percent in 2001–2002; many others were in the 4 to 7 percent range.

One criteria used was "time to enforce a contract" measured in days. The time period measures the number of days from filing a lawsuit until payment or settlement. Poland was exceptionally poor in this respect, with the number of days reported to be 1,000! Time to enforce contracts in Italy also requires a substantial amount of time, 645 days. Most countries' enforcement takes less than 12 months. (As a basis of comparison, the United States is listed as taking 365 days.)

The data for the United States and the world are included for comparative purposes.

Sources: World Bank Data Query (http://devdata.worldbank.org/data-query); World Bank, *2003 World Development Indicators;* accessed July 24, 2004; Investment climate: World Bank, *2003 World Development Indicators*, Table 5.2, pages 258–261; Trade data: World Trade Organization, *International Trade Statistics 2003* (http://www.wto.org/english/res_e/statis_e/its2003_e/its03_toc_e.htm) (Appendix Tables A4–A7); FDI data: UNCTAD—*Handbook of Statistics* (Part Six, International finance, Table 6.2 Foreign direct investment: inward and outward flows) (http://www.unctad.org/Templates/webflyer.asp?docid=4324&intItemID=1397&lang=1&mode=toc).

Developing countries are experiencing population growth and have relatively short life expectancies. This means that nearly 35 percent of their population is in the 0–14 age group and approximately 60 percent is in the productive 15–64 age group (only 4.4 percent is in the 65+ category). Contrast that with the rich industrialized countries, which have less than 20 percent in the 0–14 group, 67 percent in the 15–64 group, and over 15 percent in the over-65 category. The large senior markets are important in the high-income countries, but also in some

New Markets in China

Many people would argue that China, with a per capita income of less than $4,000 per year, is not a good market for high-technology merchandise. Like many other nations, though, China's income is not evenly divided among its people; and one recent Chinese report states that the country will displace Japan as the world's largest personal computer market by 2006. This is good news for Mr. Sim, the CEO of Creative Technology of Singapore. His firm has developed Prodikeys, which combines a special keyboard and software that allows people to learn to play music at the computer. The plan is to introduce the product in China first, then Japan, South Korea, Taiwan, Hong Kong, and Singapore. Priced at $175 per unit, the Prodikey also requires that the user have a computer with a high-end sound board and speakers. Again,

developing markets such as China, even though the proportion of elderly is somewhat smaller, with over 85 million citizens in that group. By 2050, 20 percent of the world's population is expected to be over the age of eighty. Even in poorer nations, people are living longer due to better health care and better living conditions than in years past. In Angola, the life expectancy is now 47, which is low compared to developed nations; but it is nearly twice what it was a half century ago, when life expectancy was only 25 years.

DENSITY

The concentration of population is important to a firm in evaluating distribution and communication problems. The United States, for example, had a population density of 31 people per square kilometer in 2002, which was only a small fraction of the population density in the Netherlands (477 people per square kilometer) or in Singapore (6,826 people per square kilometer). Even with a modern transportation network, distribution costs in the United States are likely to be higher than in the Netherlands. Promotion is facilitated where population is concentrated; but land prices, and consequently rent for office space, will be higher in denser markets.

Even when the density figure for a given country is used, careful interpretation is necessary. For example, Egypt is listed as having 64 people per square kilometer. That is very misleading because Egypt's population is among the world's most concentrated, located almost entirely along the Nile River. The rest of the country is desert. Canada provides a similar example. It has a density of three people per square kilometer; but most of the population is concentrated in a narrow band along the U.S. border, leaving the major portion of the landmass unoccupied. In such cases, the population is much more concentrated and reachable than the statistics indicate.[17]

When evaluating a particular country, a firm is interested in the figures not only for that country, but also for a potential regional market that could be served by common production facilities.

Density is often closely linked with **urbanization**, the number of people living in cities rather than rural locations. Numerous cultural and economic differences exist between people given the per capita income, trying to sell this product may not seem to be the best strategy. Yet Mr. Sim is relying on the projections for computer sales and the overall size of the Chinese market. He is also relying on acceptance because Creative Technology developed the product in China for the Chinese, and he expects the high value placed on education to carry over into learning to play music.

The market for wireless communication is increasing in China, too. With China Unicom recently launching a cellular network based on the U.S. standard and the Chinese purchasing 5,000 cellular phones a month in 2003, the market looks terrific, particularly for U.S. companies. Since China joined the WTO, it has also agreed to open its borders to service providers for Internet data service, call centers, mobile service, and a host of other wired and wireless services. Time and persistence are still necessary to break into the market, but many predict that China will be a leading market for the foreseeable future because of its vast population and economic growth rate.

Sources: "Creative to Pitch Keyboard Combo at China Market," Monday, April 29, 2002, *Business Times*, Singapore; "A Lucrative New Market Is Calling: TELE-COMS," Friday, March 15, 2002, *Financial Times*, page 4.

in cities and people in villages or rural areas. Those differences are reflected in the attitudes of the people. Modern transportation and communication have greatly reduced the differences between urban and rural populations in the United States; but in much of the world, the urban-rural differences persist. Because these differences are important determinants of consumer behavior, global business managers need to be aware of each market's particular situation.

People living in rural communities tend to be more self-sufficient (since trading is often difficult and time-consuming). They also tend to rely more heavily on agriculture for income, rather than on manufactured goods or services.

Several reasons exist for the contrasting behavior of urban and rural populations. Research shows that products aimed at rural markets in developing countries required more adaptation than products sold in urban markets.[18]

Cities are the places in an economy where communications media are most developed. Cities also offer more possibilities for formal and informal education, which affect the literacy, skills, and attitudes of their inhabitants. Urbanites, therefore, tend to be less conservative and less tradition-oriented than rural dwellers. There is a stronger demonstration effect of new products and consumption patterns in urban areas, which leads to stronger markets in those locations.

It helps to assess the relationship of urbanization to the consumption of a firm's product. Several factors may favor the urban markets: income and consumption patterns, distribution facilities, and communications possibilities. Cities such as Bangkok, Istanbul, and Jakarta, for example, possess a highly disproportionate share of their countries' consumption of many consumer goods.

There is a strong correlation between degree of urbanization and the level of economic development. A relationship between the level of economic development of a nation and the agrarian nature of its economy also exists. Poorer nations tend to earn more income from agriculture than rich nations.

Developing countries are generally less urbanized, especially the low-income nations. Combined with low incomes in these regions, the lack of urbanization makes these markets unattractive to firms that manufacture consumer goods. Not only are these poor markets small, they are also difficult to reach when most of the population is rural. Thus, the degree of urbanization is an indicator of the size of the market and the nature of the distribution requirements. Though this kind of data is especially significant for firms that manufacture consumer goods, even companies that produce industrial goods find a correlation between their market potential and urbanization.

Parallels also exist between economic development and pollution. Increased crop yield can be had, but it generally results from the use of modern powered equipment and the use of pesticides and fungicides with associated risk factors. Increased income leads to more purchases of appliances, automobiles, and other pollution-generating devices. Developed countries call for restraint and the use of more energy-efficient and environmentally friendly products within their own borders and by developing nations. The poorer countries counter that the expense associated with these product attributes are high. Why should they be conservative when they have had to endure the results of a century or more of developed nations' pollution?

The rise in gasoline prices in 2004 was due in part to the war in Iraq, terrorism, and uncertainties surrounding the Russian oil industry; but there was a longer-term reason as well. With falling prices for autos and rising affluence in China, sales of autos rose 76 percent in 2003; and this growth is expected to continue at double-digit rates for the next several years.[19] With rising demand for autos, as well as electric appliances and other products requiring power, China is the second largest oil-consuming nation behind the United States. More power means more pollution. China is getting larger amounts of oil from Chad and exchanging arms to get the oil they need to supply the burgeoning energy needs. Some people question the ethical nature of this arrangement and cite numerous human rights concerns associated with this trading relationship.[20]

The watchword is **sustainable economic development**. Perhaps the most visible of initiatives are those undertaken by the UN (e.g., United Nations Conference on Environment and Development in 1992 and the World Summit on Sustainable Development held in South Africa in August 2002). Yet other global organizations, such as the World Bank, as well as developed nations and multinationals are coming to the realization that they must help developing countries by paying or subsidizing the use of environmentally sound practices to reach their economic goals. Some nations, such as Costa Rica, are on the front lines of this battle. While supporting the practice of establishing national parks for their burgeoning tourism industry, the government is countering that support with the desire to build large hydroelectric dams for energy exports. Doing so would flood large tracts of land that support the wildlife that tourists come to see, thus exemplifying the "growth versus protection of the environment" dilemma.

Income

Income is also a factor that firms use when selecting markets. Wages and wealth are not related to the size of a market (Hong Kong, Switzerland, and Qatar are wealthy but small nations), yet firms want to identify markets or segments of markets that are willing and able to buy their goods or services. Firms use measures of income to select potentially good markets, as well as to develop strategies to meet the needs of people with different incomes.

DISTRIBUTION OF INCOME

One way of understanding the size of a market is to look at distribution of income. Per capita income figures are averages; and they are meaningful, especially when most of the population is near the average. Frequently, however, this is not the case. Few nations have an equal distribu-

TABLE 2-9 Population and Life Expectancy (2002), Annual Average Population Growth Rates (2002–2015), and Projected Population (2015)

Nation or Income Group	Population (2002)	Life Expectancy (born in 2002)	Population Growth Rate (%)	Population (2015)
Low-Income	2,494.6	58.9	1.5	3,040.0
Lower-Middle Income	2,408.5	69.3	0.8	2,658.4
Upper-Middle Income	329.3	73.4	1.1	380.6
High Income	966.2	78.2	0.3	1,007.7
China	1,280.4	70.7	0.6	1,389.5
India	1,048.6	63.4	1.2	1,231.6
United States	288.4	77.3	0.8	319.9
Indonesia	211.7	66.7	1.1	245.5
Brazil	174.5	68.5	1.1	201.0
World	6,198.5	66.7	1.0	7,090.7

Sources: World Bank, *2004 World Development Indicators,* Table 2.1 Population Dynamics, pages 38–41; Table 2.19 Mortality, pages 108–111.

tion of income among their people, but the high-income economies are somewhat better in this respect than the other country categories. Managers must be attentive to differences in income levels if their product is at all income-sensitive.

Most countries have an uneven distribution of income. For example, the poorest 40 percent of the people in the Russian Federation account for less than 15 percent of the income generated. The richest 20 percent generate over 50 percent of the income. In Sierra Leone, the poorest 40 percent of the population account for 3 percent of the income; the richest 20 percent account for 63 percent. In developed nations in general, the amount of assets income held by the poorest 20 percent of the population ranges from 5 to 10 percent and the amount held by the wealthiest 20 percent ranges from 35 to 45 percent. Nevertheless, income distribution is not equal in any nation. According to the World Bank's Gini index, Sweden, Norway, and Belgium are among the nations with the most unequal income distribution in the world.[21]

The more skewed the distribution of income, the less meaningful the per capita income figure. When most people are below the per capita income figure and there is a small wealthy group above it, the country has a **bimodal income distribution** but no middle class.

A bimodal income distribution means that the economy has two distinct income groups—a dual economy. The poor group must be studied separately from the wealthy group. One might find, for example, that the two groups are not different segments of the same market, but are actually different markets. Brazil, India, and Mexico are examples of countries with sizable groups of affluent consumers living alongside a majority of the population who live in poverty. As was already mentioned, income is not evenly distributed in industrial markets either. Products designed for affluent consumers in developing nations can be marketed to these upper-income groups as well as to industrial nations. This characteristic is a major reason why firms should pay less attention to national or geographic borders and more attention to consumers' needs and desires. (And it's one of the reasons the Tiffany Company has been successful in expanding beyond New York City.)

TABLE 2-10 Total and Per Capita Income in 2002				
Income Group	Number of Countries	GNI ($U.S. billions)	Population (millions)	GNI per Capita ($U.S.)
Low-Income	61	1,070	2,495	430
Lower-Middle Income	56	3,372	2,408	1,400
Upper-Middle Income	37	1,682	329	5,110
High Income	54	25,596	966	26,490
World	208	31,720	6,199	5,120

Source: World Bank, *2004 World Development Indicators*, Table 1.1 Size of the Economy, pages 14-17.

Note: Data are in current U.S. dollars converted using the World Bank Atlas method; World Bank, *2002 World Development Indicators*, page 21.

Number and names of countries in each income group: World Bank Data. Statistics for country groups (http://www.worldbank.org/data/countryclass/classgroups.htm); accessed August 5, 2004.

PER CAPITA INCOME

GNI has earlier been defined in the text (p.65) as "The sum of value added by all resident producers….plus net receipts of primary income from abroad (absent tax considerations)". The statistic most frequently used to describe a country economically is its **per capita income**. This figure is used as a shorthand expression for a country's level of economic development. Partial justification for using this figure in evaluating a foreign economy lies in the fact that it is commonly available and widely accepted. A more pertinent justification is that it is, in fact, a good indicator of the size or quality of a market.

The per capita income figures vary widely among the countries of the world. Many nations of the world have an average annual per capita income below $500, the poorest of which are in Africa (Burundi, the Democratic Republic of Congo, and Ethiopia—all with an annual per capita income of only $100 in 2002). To put that in perspective, it takes the average Ethiopian one year to earn what a lawyer who charges $300 per hour earns in 20 minutes. People in high-income countries have average annual per capita income nearly 70 times that of the average person in low-income countries, with European nations being among the richest. (In Norway, per capita income is $38,730; in Switzerland, $36,170.) The people in the World Bank categories of "upper-middle income" and "high income" nations account for 15 percent of the population, but they accounted for 80 percent of the world's GNI in 2002.[22] This emphasizes the need for businesses not only to identify those people who are willing to purchase their products, but also to recognize that potential customers must also have the ability to pay for the products.

Table 2-10 provides a summary of the data for all of the countries tracked by the World Bank. Because per capita income figures are relied on so extensively, however, the following words of caution are in order.

Purchasing Power Not Reflected

Per capita income comparisons are expressed in a common currency—often in U.S. dollars—through an exchange-rate conversion. The dollar figure for a country is derived by dividing its per capita income figure in national currency by its rate of exchange against the dollar. The resulting dollar statistic for a country's per capita income is accurate only if the exchange rate reflects the relative domestic purchasing power of the two currencies. There is often reason for doubting that it does.

Country	GNI per Capita ($U.S.)	PPP^a Adjusted GNI per Capita ($U.S.)	Multiplier^b
Ethiopia	100	780	7.8
Tajikistan	164	930	5.7
Bangladesh	380	1,770	4.7
India	470	2,650	5.6
Belarus	1,360	5,500	4.0
Columbia	1,820	6,150	3.4
China	4,250	9,420	2.2
Hungary	5,290	13,070	2.5
Greece	11,600	18,770	1.6
Australia	19,530	27,440	1.4
World	5,120	7,820	1.5

TABLE 2-11 Per Capita Income in 2002, Measured Two Ways

a Purchasing power parity.

b Column 2 divided by Column 1.

Source: World Bank, *2004 World Development Indicators,* Table 1.1 Size of the Economy, pages 14–17.

As mentioned earlier, exchange rates are determined predominantly by the demand for and supply of a country's imports and exports—plus speculative demand. A country's external supply and demand have quite a different character from supply and demand within the country. Thus, it is not surprising that the external value of a currency (the exchange rate) may be different from the domestic value of that currency. Table 2-11 illustrates the differences between the exchange-rate value of a currency and its real purchasing power. In some cases, the real purchasing power is nearly eight times the exchange-rate value.

The limitations of an exchange rate in indicating relative purchasing power can be illustrated further. Take the experience of tourists, who soon learn that some prices appear high; others low. In other words, the value of their own currency abroad depends on what they purchase.

If tourists want to live in the same style abroad as they do at home, their expenses will probably be higher than if they live like the residents of the host country. For example, the price of white bread in Germany is twice as much as it is in France. Of course, the Germans do not consume as much white bread as the French. This indicates another aspect of prices and purchasing power—that is, people tend to consume more of the things that are inexpensive in their country. However, the exchange rate reflects the *international* goods and services of a country, not its *domestic* consumption. (See "Global Environment: Buying a Burger Abroad: A Basic Lesson in PPP.")

A further example is the case of exchange-rate changes, as with a devaluation or currency appreciation. An extreme case involves Japan. In 1985, the Japanese yen was 240 to the U.S. dollar. In 1988, the yen was 120 to the dollar. This meant that, in dollar terms, the Japanese market was twice as large in 1988 as in 1985. This was obviously not true in real terms, as Americans learned. Their sales to Japan rose only modestly.

Buying a Burger Abroad: A Basic Lesson in PPP

It was 2 PM, and we had just departed our hosts after a wonderful four-course luncheon meeting at La Defénse, a major business district on the outskirts of Paris. A colleague asked us to wait while he made a quick stop in one of the stores before we went back to our hotel. Much to our surprise, he returned with some French fries from McDonald's. Even after a full meal, he wanted a "taste of home" after being on the road for the last ten days.

Since McDonald's operates in nearly every country of the word, the Big Mac Index was devised in the mid-1980s as a humorous way to measure purchasing power. The idea was that if the theory of purchasing power parity was accurate, a Big Mac ought to cost the same in every country. If the price was significantly different, the index could be used to predict changes in exchange rates. A Big Mac that cost more in London, for example, would indicate that the British pound is overvalued and that it would fall in the near future. A substantially lower price would indicate that the currency is undervalued and would likely rise. If the cost of Big Macs was nearly the same—Price McParity—the price of the currency would likely remain the same. The following table shows a partial list of the cost of Big Macs around the world.

Lack of Comparability

Another limitation of the use of per capita income figures is that there is a lack of comparability for two reasons. First, many goods entering into the national income totals of developed economies are only partially accounted for in less developed countries. A large part of a North American's budget, for example, goes for food, clothing, and shelter. In many less developed nations, those items may be largely self-provided and, therefore, not reflected in national income totals. Second, many goods that figure in the national income of developed nations do not figure in the national incomes of poorer countries. For example, a significant amount of U.S. national income is derived from such items as snow removal, heat for buildings and homes, pollution control, military and space expenditures, agricultural support programs, and winter vacations in Florida or other warm states. Many less developed nations are in tropical areas, and their citizens are not necessarily poorer for not having the above-mentioned items of consumption. However, their national income figure is lower because of the absence of these items.

The primary author of this text spent eight years in a rural area of Congo. Although not living entirely in the African manner, he found his food, clothing, and housing expenses to be a fraction of those he incurred while living in the northern part of the United States. This meant that a given income went much further for consumption of basic items.

Sales Not Related to Per Capita Income

A third limitation to using per capita income figures to indicate market potential is that the sales of many goods show little correlation with per capita income. Many consumer goods sales cor-

Country (currency)	Exchange Rate[a]	Big Mac Price ($US)[b]	Implied Purchasing Power[b]	Under/Over Valued[b]
United States ($)	1.0	2.90	...	...
Argentina (Peso)	2.9	1.48	1.50	-49
Australia (A$)	1.5	2.27	1.12	-22
China (Yuan)	8.3	1.26	3.59	-57
Euro Area (€)	0.9	3.28	1.06	13
Hong Kong	7.8	1.54	4.14	-47
Japan (¥)	114.4	2.33	90.3	-20
Russia (Ruble)	29.0	1.45	14.5	-50
Switzerland (SFr)	1.3	4.90	2.17	69
Turkey (Lira)	1,530,000.0	2.58	1,362,069	-11

a Average exchange rate in various markets on May 15, 2004.

b "Food for Thought," *The Economist*, May 29, 2004, pages 71–72.

c Calculated (2.90/price $US), where 2.90 is the price of a Big Mac in the United States.

If there is parity in purchasing power in the country, vis-à-vis the United States, the expected exchange rate and the actual exchange rate should be the same.

Sources: "Food for Thought," *The Economist*, May 29, 2004, pages 71–72; XE.Com; historical rates (http://www.xe.com/ict); accessed, August 6, 2004; see also http://www.economist.com/markets/Bigmac/index.cfm.

With so many currencies undervalued (those with a minus sign), what does that say about the U.S. dollar?

relate more closely with population or household figures than with per capita income. Some examples include Coca-Cola, jeans, bicycles, computers, and stereo equipment. Industrial goods and capital equipment sales generally correlate better with the industrial structure or total national income than with per capita income. For example, the airport and office buildings in Kinshasa, Congo, are equipped in much the same way as similar structures in New York City. Extractive or manufacturing industries tend to use similar equipment wherever they are located. Where governments run health and education programs, per capita income is not necessarily a useful guide to the national potential of goods supplied to the health and education industries.

Gross National Income (GNI)

Another useful way to evaluate foreign markets is to compare their GNPs. **Gross national income (GNI)** measures the total domestic and foreign value added by residents. For certain goods, total GNI is a better indicator of market potential than per capita income. Where this is true, it is useful to rank countries by GNI. Table 2-12 lists the economies with a GNI of at least $250 billion in 2002. The fact that only 17 nations qualify for this list (and that they account for more than 80 percent of total world income) gives further insight into the poverty in the world and the limitations of most economies.

It is helpful to contrast the GNI approach to measuring market potential with the per capita income approach. For example, in 2002, Iceland's per capita income was $27,380 and India's was $2,340. Those figures have been adjusted for purchasing power. Without purchasing power parity adjustment, the actual figures are more distant—$470 for India and $27,960 for Iceland. Using those data alone, Iceland is 100 times as attractive economically as India. However, that same year, India's GNI was more than 60 times as large as Iceland's ($495 billion versus $8 billion); and India's population is over 3,000 times as large (1.05 billion versus 284,000).[23] This is an extreme example, but it illustrates the need for proper comparisons.

At this point, consider another view of the per capita income approach. For goods that require high consumer income, it may be true that a small country such as Belgium (about 10 million people) is a better market than India, even though Belgium's GNI is less than that of India. For example, in 2002, Belgium had more cars and personal computers than India. On the other hand, India consumed four to six times as many trucks, buses, and tons of cement and steel. Obviously, the relevant income figure for evaluating a market depends largely on the product involved.

Nature of the Economy

In addition to their size and market potential, foreign economies have other characteristics, including those produced by the nation's physical endowment, the nature of their economic activity, their infrastructure, and their degree of urbanization—all of which affect many strategic decisions.

Physical Endowment

A nation's resources play a major role in economic development. Countries with large land mass tend to have more natural resources, both in terms of quantity and breadth. Australia, China, Russia, Canada, Mexico, and the United States are among the world's largest in terms of land mass; they also have a wealth of natural resources. However, other smaller nations such as Japan must buy much of the raw materials they consume and must buy much of what goes into the production of goods and services. Although there are exceptions, generally, the richer and more diverse the endowments, the higher the country's potential for favorable economic development.

NATURAL RESOURCES

A nation's **natural resources** include its actual and potential forms of wealth supplied by nature—for example, minerals and waterpower—as well as its land area, topography, and climate. The global businessperson needs to understand the economic geography of a nation in relation to decisions that need to be made, especially those concerning distribution and supply. Land area is not very important, except as it figures in population density and distribution problems. Local natural resources can be important in evaluating a country as a source of raw materials for local production. Merck, for example, built a compounding plant in India and received the Indian government's permission to ship key ingredients from the United States. This permission was later withdrawn, and Merck had to locate a new source of raw materials in India to keep the plant operating.

Another reason for exploring a country's resource base is to evaluate its future economic prospects. Some countries that currently have relatively weak markets might develop more rapidly than other countries because of their richer resource endowment. New technologies and discoveries can revolutionize a nation's economic prospects. Oil changed the outlook for Libya and Nigeria, for example.

By the same token, technological change can also impoverish an economy that is largely dependent on just one export commodity. For example, the development of rayon, nylon, and syn-

TABLE 2-12 Countries with Gross National Income over $250 Billion (2002)

Country	GNI ($US billions)[a]	Percent of World Total	Country	GNI ($US billions)[a]	Percent of World Output
United States	10,207	32.2	Mexico	597	1.9
Japan	4,324	13.6	Spain	597	1.9
Germany	1,876	5.9	India	495	1.6
United Kingdom	1,511	4.8	Korea, Rep.	473	1.5
France	1,362	4.3	Australia	384	1.2
China	1,234	3.9	Netherlands	378	1.2
Italy	1,101	3.5	Russian Federation	304	1.0
Canada	702	2.2	Switzerland	264	.8
Brazil	495	1.6	World	31,720	100.0

a Current $US.

Source: World Bank, *2004 World Development Indicators*, Table 1.1 Size of the Economy, pages 14–17.

thetic rubber did great damage to the countries exporting silk and natural rubber. What would be the impact on Brazil if a good synthetic coffee were developed? A glance through the maps in an atlas will show how the various natural resources are distributed among the nations of the world.

TOPOGRAPHY

The surface features of a country's land, including rivers, lakes, forests, deserts, and mountains, are its **topography**. These features interest a global business manager, for they indicate possible physical distribution problems.

Flat country generally means easy transportation by road or rail. Mountains are a barrier that raises transportation costs. Mountains also may divide a nation into two or more distinct markets. For example, the Andes Mountains divide many South American countries into entirely separate areas. Although these areas are united politically, often they are separate markets culturally and economically. Deserts and tropical forests also separate markets and make transportation difficult. A business manager analyzes data on the topography, population, and transportation situation in order to anticipate marketing and logistical problems.

Navigable rivers are desirable because they enable economical transportation. The Mississippi River and the St. Lawrence Seaway are North American examples. In Europe, river and canal transportation are more important than anywhere else in the world. Even landlocked Switzerland can ship by river barge to Atlantic ports. The accessibility of a market should also be determined by its ports and harbors—contact with sea transportation.

Landlocked countries such as Bolivia, Zambia, and Zimbabwe are more costly to reach than neighboring countries with seaports. These countries have transportation problems other than cost (for instance, customs inspections) if there are political differences with the neighbors whose seaports and railroads they must use. Finally, the existence of lakes, seashores, rivers, and mountains can indicate particular business opportunities. Suppliers to the tourist, recreation, and sporting industries find markets in countries endowed with places for boating, skiing, and other recreational activities.

Infrastructure: Building Bridges to Close the Digital Divide

For the digital divide to shrink, technology must be made available to those people who currently do not have it. There are three requirements for e-commerce to take place, whether B2B or B2C: content, income, and infrastructure. All transactions require that the parties involved be willing and able to participate in the exchange process. **Content** (music, videos, e-mail, telephony, and information, for example) is what drives people to want to have an Internet connection; income and infrastructure are the "capability" components that enable people to participate in e-commerce. With literally billions of web sites and the addition of more every hour, content exists. Its access is limited only by entities that charge for the material or by governments and other interested parties who want to protect consumers from fraud and subversive or obscene information.

Income, as previously discussed, is still very low in some nations, which means that even old technology—three- or four-year-old computers and software that may cost only $100 for a complete PC and the software necessary for an Internet connection—is beyond the reach of many, such as the average Ethiopian, who earns $100 per year.

This is a small part of the picture, however, when one considers the time and money needed to build the infrastructure required to connect to other computers, the financial infrastructure that must be in place to allow people to enter into transactions on the Web (worldwide is a bit premature), and the ability to deliver manufactured goods once they are purchased.

Infrastructure at a basic level requires roads for delivering goods, computers and software, and electricity to power the connecting electronics (even if going wireless, power is needed to recharge power packs).

CLIMATE

Another dimension of a nation's physical endowment is its **climate**, which includes not only the temperature range, but also wind, rain, snow, dryness, and humidity. The United States is very large and has great climatic variations within its borders. Smaller nations have more uniform climatic patterns. Climate is an important determinant of a firm's product offerings. An obvious example is the heater or air conditioner in an automobile. Climate also affects a whole range of consumer goods—from food to clothing and from housing to recreational supplies. Even medical needs in the Tropics are different from those in temperate zones.

Extremes of climate may dictate modifications in product, packaging, or distribution. For example, electric equipment and many packaged goods need special protection in hot, humid climates. There is great international variation in climate; for example, in July, India has 13 inches of rainfall, Guinea has 51 inches, and New York City has 4 inches.

Climate may have another, more subtle effect on the nature of the market. Although insufficient evidence exists to prove cause and effect, most less developed countries are tropical or subtropical. Tropical countries generally have low per capita incomes and a high percentage of the population in agriculture. Managers need to be aware of climate to the extent that it affects people as consumers and workers.

Very often financial institutions are needed to complete a transaction—transferring funds from one account to another and sometimes supplying credit (in the form of a credit card, for example). If the parties live in different countries, banks may also provide the service of exchanging currencies. Without a commercial infrastructure, many transactions would not take place.

Perhaps most important, though, is a connection to the Internet. If the industry standard remains land-connected, using traditional telephone lines, coaxial cable, or fiber optics for DSL or cable connections, large amounts of capital and labor are needed to build the infrastructure to link computers in cities and nations with the rural populations prevalent in so many areas of the world. If the standard becomes wireless, scores of additional satellites and transmission towers must be built. Different compression software would also be needed to send pictures, sound, and gigabytes of other data between wireless components.

There are some encouraging signs of people finding solutions to these problems. In Laos, the head of the Jhai Foundation, Mr. Lee Thorn, is distributing sturdy PCs that have no moving parts and cost around $400, including all of the hardware and wireless capabilities needed to connect to the Internet. Farmers can check the prices they get for their crops before they make a long trek to the nearest sales office. The PCs also help farmers make decisions about future crop allocations.

Even with these encouraging statistics and isolated signs of improvement, much needs to be done in terms of building infrastructure and providing the tools needed to reduce the digital divide.

Sources: "Emerging Market Indicators," *The Economist*, November 3, 2001, Volume 361, Issue 8245, page 106; "High-Speed Internet Access; Broadband Blues," *The Economist*, June 23, 2001, Volume 359, Issue 8227, page 62; Joane E. Oxley and Bernard Yeung, "E-Commerce Readiness: Institutional Environment and International Competitiveness," *Journal of International Business Studies*, 2001, Volume 32, Issue 4, pages 705–723; Srilata Zaheer and Shalini Manrakhan, "Concentration and Dispersion in Global Industries: Remote Electronic Access and the Location of Economic Activities," *Journal of International Business Studies*, 2001, Volume 32, Issue 4, pages 667–686; "Making the Web World-Wide," *The Economist*, September 28, 2002, Volume 364, Issue 8292, page 76.

Infrastructure of the Nation

A manufacturing firm generally divides its activities into two major categories: production and marketing. These operations depend on supporting facilities and services outside the firm. These external facilities and services are called the **infrastructure** of an economy. They include paved roads, railroads, energy supplies, and other communication and transport services. The commercial and financial infrastructure includes advertising agencies and media, distributive organizations, marketing research companies, and credit and banking facilities. The more adequate these services are in a country, the better a firm can perform its production and marketing tasks. Where these facilities and services are not adequate, a firm must adapt its operations (or avoid the market altogether).

When considering the potential profitability of operations in a given country, a firm must evaluate the infrastructure constraints as well as the market potential. As might be expected, tremendous variation exists internationally. Generally, the higher the level of economic development, the better the infrastructure.[24] Case 2.3 at the end of the chapter, "The Lifeblood of the World's Economies—Electricity" provides an indication of the variation in energy supplies available. The feature "Global Environment: Infrastructure: Building Bridges to Close the Digital Divide" highlights the importance of infrastructure and its many components in the development of a *truly* World Wide Web as opposed to a developed-country Web.

ENERGY

The statistics on energy production per capita serve as a guide to market potential and to the adequacy of the local infrastructure. Firms that manufacture electrical machinery and equipment and consumer durables are concerned about the extent of electrification throughout the market. In countries with low energy consumption, power is typically available only in the cities, not in the villages or countryside where most of the population lives. Energy production is also closely related to the overall industrialization of an economy and thus is correlated to the market for industrial goods there. Finally, energy production per capita is probably the best single indicator as to the adequacy of a country's overall infrastructure.

TRANSPORTATION

The importance of transportation for business operations needs no elaboration. Transportation capabilities, infrastructure, and modes vary significantly from country to country depending on the topography and level of economic development. The transportation infrastructure is vital to a firm that must move people, components, services, and finished goods to another country or within a nation's borders. Information on railways (miles and gauge), highways (paved and unpaved), waterways, pipelines, airports, and seaports is available from the U.S. Central Intelligence Agency's *The World Factbook*.[25] The International Institute for Management Development (IMD) publishes a competitiveness ranking for 60 nations that includes a comparison of the basic infrastructure as well as scientific and technological infrastructures across nations.[26] Transportation companies and associations are other good resources for such data.

COMMUNICATIONS

In addition to being able to move its goods, a firm must be able to communicate with various audiences, especially workers, suppliers, and customers. Communications with those outside the firm depend on the communications infrastructure of the country. Intracompany communications between subsidiaries or with headquarters depend on local facilities. Table 2-13 shows the distribution and availability of several communications media in major regions of the world.

In general, variations in communications infrastructure follow variations in the level of economic development. Thus, Japan and the countries of Western Europe are well supplied with all kinds of media; whereas the developing countries in Africa, Asia, and Latin America are weak in all of the media, except perhaps for radio. Analysis of communication options identifies promotional possibilities in foreign markets.

COMMERCIAL INFRASTRUCTURE

Equally important to a firm as the transportation, communication, and energy capabilities of a nation is the nation's **commercial infrastructure**. Commercial infrastructure refers to the availability and quality of support services such as banks and financial institutions, advertising agencies, distribution channels, and marketing research organizations. Firms accustomed to strong supporting services at home often find great differences in foreign markets. Wherever the commercial infrastructure is weak, a firm must make adjustments in its operations, which affect costs and effectiveness.

No comparable table on commercial infrastructure is available (as with communication and other indicators), and data in this area are more difficult to find. Nevertheless, a firm can

TABLE 2-13 Distribution of Communications Media per 1,000 Persons

Country or Region	Daily Newspapers[a]	Radios[b]	Televisions[c]	Telephone Mainlines[c]	Mobile Telephones[c]	Personal Computers[c]
United States	213	2,117	938	646	488	659
Europe						
France	201	950	632	569	647	347
Germany	305	570	661	651	727	431
Hungary	465	690	475	361	676	108
Italy	104	878	494	481	939	231
Poland	102	523	422	295	363	106
Spain	100	330	564	506	824	196
United Kingdom	329	1,445	950	591	841	406
Latin America						
Argentina	37	681	326	219	178	82
Brazil	43	433	349	223	201	75
Colombia	46	549	303	179	106	50
Mexico	94	330	282	147	255	82
Uruguay	293	603	530	280	193	110
Venezuela	206	294	186	113	256	61
Asia						
China		339	350	167	161	28
India	60	120	83	40	12	7
Indonesia	23	159	153	37	55	12
Japan	578	956	785	558	637	382
Malaysia	158	420	210	190	377	147
Philippines	82	161	182	42	191	28
Thailand	64	235	300	105	260	40
Africa, Mideast						
Algeria	27	244	114	61	13	8
Egypt	31	339	229	110	67	17
Israel	290	526	330	467	955	243
South Africa	32	336	177	107	304	73
Syrian, Arab Rep	20	276	182	123	23	19
Turkey	111	470	423	281	347	45

a 2000; b 2001; c 2002.

Source: World Bank, *2004 World Development Indicators;* Table 5.10 Power and Communications, pages 290–293; Table 5.11 The Information Age, pages 294–297; except for newspapers and radios, the data comes from the *International Telecommunication Development Report, 2003;* the number of personal computers does not include those located in educational facilities.

get reasonably good information about the commercial infrastructure of a country. The best sources are commercial attachés in embassies and domestic service organizations with foreign operations; for example, banks, accounting firms, and advertising agencies.

Other Characteristics of Foreign Economies

The previous survey of foreign economies has been introductory rather than exhaustive. It should be helpful, however, in giving the market analyst a feel for the relevant dimensions of national economies. The last section of this chapter will cover one other characteristic of economies that can be important in operations in foreign markets, inflation.

INFLATION

Each country has its own monetary system and monetary policy—except for the 12 European countries in the Euro group. The result is differing financial environments and rates of inflation among countries. In general, inflation rates declined in the last ten years, in part because of the bursting of the dot-com bubble as well as the financial and ethical business crises. Yet of all of the nations analyzed by the World Bank, more than one-half had single-digit annual inflation rates in 2002, which means that the other countries had more serious challenges with double- or triple-digit rates. As with most statistics, inflation rates ought to be viewed over time in order to gain a better perspective. The inflation rates for the period covering 1990–2002 ranged from -0.3 (prices actually declined at a rate of 0.3 percent per year) in Japan to triple-digit rates of 121 in the Russian Federation and 139.8 in Brazil (average annual percent growth).[27] In general, inflation rates turned much lower between 1999 and 2004.

Some interesting regional patterns appeared in the inflation picture in 2002. The United States and Canada had low inflation during this period, as did Western Europe, thanks in part to the adoption of the euro, which lowered transaction costs. Hungary, with an inflation rate of 11 percent, and Romania, with inflation at 24 percent, were more similar to the former Soviet Union economies than to the other European nations. Many of the former Soviet economies were experiencing double-digit inflation rates in 2002, the worst of which was Uzbekistan with a 46 percent rate of inflation.

Latin American and the Caribbean nations were generally in the single digits, with some exceptions: Ecuador reported 12 percent; Paraguay reported 15 percent; Uruguay reported 18 percent; and Argentina, Suriname, and Venezuela faced inflation rates over 30 percent in 2002. This was quite a change from the beginning of the 1990s, when Brazil was experiencing more than 2,000 percent inflation at one point and many other nations in the area had double- and triple-digit inflation rates for sustained periods of time.

The Asian nations had low rates, with Papua New Guinea being the only nation with inflation in the double digits (12 percent). As was already mentioned, Japan is one nation where prices actually declined through 2004.

In Africa, as in years past, a number of countries experienced double-digit inflation rates in 2002. Yet there were exceptions. Angola's inflation rate in 2002 was only 103 percent, which is one of the lowest in a decade, coming off an inflation rate of 150 percent in 2001 and over 4,000 percent in 1996. Zimbabwe also had a triple-digit inflation rate of 107 percent in 2002. More than a dozen nations in Africa had inflation rates in double and triple digits in 2002, but the rates were down dramatically from previous years. For example, the Democratic Republic of Congo had an inflation rate of 299 percent in 2001, better than earlier rates of 500 and 600 percent and the unimaginable 23,760 percent in 1994! In 2002, the inflation rate was a relatively modest 23 percent. To put this in context, imagine paying a monthly rent of $1,500, then the landlord increases the rent to $2,250 for the coming year. That's an example of a 50 percent inflation rate.

The Central and Eastern European nations and former Soviet countries continue to substantially reduce inflation rates, too. In some places, double-digit rates are still found (Turkmenistan, 12 percent; Russian Federation, 15 percent; Tajikistan, 22 percent; Romania and Serbia and Montenegro, 25 percent; Belarus, 42 percent; and Uzbekistan, 45 percent); but none of the countries are showing signs of triple-digit or greater inflation rates experienced in the early to mid-1990s.

Of particular note is the fact that inflation means a further complication for operating in foreign markets. High rates of inflation complicate cost control and pricing. Differential rates of inflation also influence how a firm moves funds and goods among its various markets. Firms must also address the consumers' perception of price gouging or unfair profit taking, which often occurs when rising costs force a company to raise product prices.

Summary

International trade, the economic link between nations, is one of the largest and fastest-growing aspects of the world economy. A study of the subject should include the composition of trade—that is, the shifting shares of manufactured goods and services versus various other commodities—and the patterns of trade, both globally and within individual countries, to help a firm's international logistics planning.

The theory of international trade helps in understanding a nation's comparative advantage and is useful for locating supply or production sources. The international product life cycle theory can help a firm know when to source, or produce, abroad.

The BoP is a summary statement of a nation's economic transactions that can be analyzed to determine market potential and competition in a country.

All countries have regulations on their international trade (commercial policy), usually to protect employment in home industries. Tariffs and quotas are the major tools used by industrial countries to control their trade. These affect a firm's pricing, product, and logistics decisions. Exchange control is a more comprehensive and rigid form of trade control.

WTO, as the world's trading club, works to liberalize the exchange of goods and services between countries. To the degree it is successful, WTO facilitates a firm's global sales. UNCTAD is the lobby for developing countries' interests in trade. Its efforts, too, can affect a firm's operations and influence the firm's logistics.

After the decline of Communism and the fragmentation of the Communist bloc, the countries of Eastern Europe offered a large potential market. However, some economic, cultural, legal, and political problems may need to be solved before that potential is fully realized.

In the growing interdependence of the world economy, many nations are finding economic integration with their neighbors desirable. This offers more resources, larger markets, and economies of scale to help the countries compete in the world economy. The EU is the major successful integration story. Efforts elsewhere have made little progress, although NAFTA is a bright spot. Where integration is successful, it offers opportunities for firms that can operate within the group, but challenges for those on the outside.

The major world currencies have been floating since 1973. The resulting instability and uncertainty disrupt the sourcing patterns and pricing decisions. The IMF, though no longer able to maintain stable currencies, is still a force for moderation and stability in international finance. By lending to deficit countries, IMF helps to keep the markets viable and open to international business operations. The World Bank, through its development loans, provides resources to help poor countries strengthen their economies and become more prosperous, thus providing more attractive markets for international firms. World Bank projects themselves can provide attractive marketing opportunities.

A firm's home country is an important determinant of its global success. U.S. regulations, for example, can limit a firm's international operations; but the government also supports international business by supplying information, insurance, financing, and other kinds of assistance. Moreover, the large, competitive U.S. domestic market is a good training ground for global business. The U.S. image in the world, however, can be an advantage or a disadvantage for a firm's foreign business ventures.

The two main areas of investigation for a company evaluating a foreign market are (1) the size of the market and (2) the nature of the economy. Population is one of the primary indicators of market size. Two-thirds of the world's countries have less than 10 million people and represent small markets, especially compared to the United States. Growth rates vary widely and are generally inversely correlated with the attractiveness of a market. The distribution of the population among different age groups with different purchasing power and consumption patterns can have a significant impact on a firm's ability to apply uniform decisions across markets. Population density is important for evaluating distribution and communication problems.

Markets are "people with money," so income figures on a country are necessary for market evaluation. One dimension is the distribution of income among the members of a society. Countries with a bimodal distribution of income represent dual economies with two major market segments, generally one rich and one poor. Countries with a more even distribution of income or a large middle class represent more of a mass market.

Per capita income is the most widely used indicator of market potential. Figures vary widely, with the poorest countries reporting less than 1 percent of the per capita income of the richest countries. World Bank studies show that these figures are often inaccurate, however. Actual purchasing power in many poor countries is three to eight times as high as that indicated by the per capita income figure expressed in dollars. Per capita income figures are a useful indicator of potential for some consumer goods but misleading for other consumer goods and for industrial goods.

Total GNI gives an idea of the total size of a country's market and is a helpful indicator of potential for some kinds of products. The range of GNI figures between the largest and smallest economies is over 10,000 to 1.

A country's physical endowment affects the nature of its economy. Its natural resources are one indicator of its economic potential and raw material availability. Its topography helps determine physical distribution problems and market accessibility. Its climate influences the kinds of products offered and the kinds of packaging needed.

Countries can be grouped according to the nature of their economies or level of economic development. Such groupings can be a useful form of segmentation. For better analysis, countries' economies can be divided into agricultural, manufacturing, and service sectors.

A firm's ability to operate in a country depends on the supporting facilities and services available, collectively called its infrastructure. The transportation and communication facilities in a country affect a firm's ability to get its goods to consumers and to communicate with customers, suppliers, and the home office. Energy availability affects the kinds of products that can be sold to consumer and industrial markets. A country's commercial infrastructure (ad agencies, wholesalers, etc.) may act as constraint in developing nations or as an opportunity in developed nations; but in either case, the financial infrastructure has a significant impact on strategic decisions.

Generally, major differences exist between urban consumers and rural consumers. Countries differ greatly in their degree of urbanization, with the number of city dwellers declining with the level of economic development. The marketing task varies between the city and the countryside.

Inflation complicates global business; and its incidence varies, generally being much higher in developing countries. The role of government as regulator, customer, and partner is another variable affecting a firm's marketing in a country.

Questions and Research

2.1 What can be learned from studying the composition and patterns of world trade?

2.2 How can an understanding of international trade theory help the global business manager?

2.3 What is a BoP? Of what use is it for global business opportunity assessment?

2.4 What is WTO, and what does it do for the international business environment?

2.5 Why might a U.S. exporter feel threatened by the formation of regional economic groupings? How might the firm react?

2.6 What economic characteristics would you look for in an emerging potential market?

2.7 What does the euro mean for U.S. firms already operating in the EU? What impact does the euro have on those countries considering entering the EU?

2.8 What are the potential benefits of World Bank activity for firms involved in foreign markets?

2.9 Discuss the use of population size as an indicator of market potential.

2.10 Why is the international marketer interested in the age distribution of the population in a market?

2.11 Discuss the limitations of per capita income in evaluating market potential.

2.12 How can assessment of a nation's topography help a firm?

2.13 Opportunities and problems in a country vary according to its level of economic development. Explain.

2.14 What differences might be encountered in an agricultural versus an industrialized country?

2.15 Discuss a nation's infrastructure as a business constraint.

Endnotes

1 The World Bank, *World Development Indicators,* 2004, pages 1–2.

2 World Trade Organization, *International Trade Statistics,* 2001, Table IV, Trade by Sector (http://www.wto.org/english/res_e/statis_e/its2003_e/its03_bysubject_e.htm).

3 GNI data: World Bank Group; Data Query performed on July 16, 2004 (http://devdata.worldbank.org/data-query); Trade data: World Trade Organization, *International Trade Statistics,* (2003 (http://www.wto.org/english/res_e/statis_e/its2003_e/its03_bysubject_e.htm) (files: i05.xls [merchandise]; i07.xls [commercial services]).

4 World Trade Organization, *International Trade Statistics,* 2003, Section IV; Table IV.1, page 103; Tables IV.3–IV.5, page 105; and Tables IV.15I–V.19, pages 114–116; Chart IV.9 and Tables IV.43 and IV.45, pages 132–133, 136; Table IV.2, page 104; Charts IV.14 and IV.16, pages 113–114; and Tables IV.74 and IV.77, pages 160–163.

5 Leamer, Edward E. and Michael Storper. "The Economic Geography of the Internet Age," 2001, *Journal of International Business Studies,* Volume 32, Issue 4, pages 641–665.
"Europeans Opt for Local eMerchants," October 4, 1999, *Nau/Jupiter Communications Internet Surveys.*
"Europeans Research Online, but Buy Offline," August 26, 2002, *Forrester Research.*
"Interregional Internet Bandwidth 2000–2001," *TeleGeography Research.*

6 DeYoung, Karen. "Bush: No Lifting of Cuba Policies," Tuesday, May 21, 2002, *Washington Post,* page A01.

7 Barro, Robert J. "Big Steel Doesn't Need Any More Propping Up," *Business Week,* New York, Issue 3776, page 24.
"Europe Responds with Its Own Steel Tariff," April 1, 2002, *Construction Week,* Volume 248, Number 12, page 7.
"Leaders: George Bush, Protectionist; Tariffs on Steel," *The Economist,* London, Volume 362, Issue 8263, page 13.
"Steel in the Melting Pot," April 18, 2002, *Financial Times,* Global News Wire—Asia Africa Intelligence Wire.
"Trade Scene: Steel Yourself—It's a Mess," December 14, 2001, *Journal of Commerce,* JoC Online.

8 "EU Trade Ploy Threat to Recovery," April 18, 2002, *Australian Financial Review*, Section: International News, page 143.

9 "Members and Observers" (http://www.wto.org/english/thewto_e/whatis_e/tif_e/org6_e.htm); "Accessions" (http://www.wto.org/english/thewto_e/acc_e/acc_e.htm); "Trading into the Future: Introduction to the WTO" (http://www.wto.org/english/thewto_e/whatis_e/tif_e/agrm0_e.htm); accessed December 23, 2004.

10 European web site (European Economic Area) (http://europa.eu.int/comm/external_relations/eea/index.htm); The Secretariat of the European Free Trade Association web site (http://secretariat.efta.int/euroeco).

11 Association of Southeast Asian Nations (ASEAN) web site (http://www.asean.or.id/1024x768.html; http://www.us-asean.org/asean.asp).

12 North American Free Trade (NAFTA) web site of the U.S. Department of Commerce, International Trade Association (http://web.ita.doc.gov/ticwebsite/naftaweb.nsf; http://www.nafta-sec-alena.org/english/index.htm); Free Trade Area of the Americas (FTAA) web site (http://www.alca-ftaa.org/alca_e.asp).

13 The Euro (http://europa.eu.int/euro/html/entry.html); Euro Essentials (http://europa.eu.int/comm/economy_finance/euro_en.htm, http://europa.eu.int/comm/enlargement/report2001/, and http://europa.eu.int/comm/enlargement/pas/ocp/ocp_index.htm).
Ms. Harriet Barseghian Marsh of the EU Enlargement Information Centre, personal communication (enlargement@cec.eu.int); January 9, 2003.
With respect to the other three nations, Bulgaria and Romania are not expected to enter the EU before 2007 and Turkey started accession discussions in late 2004.

14 U.S. Bureau of Economic Analysis, U.S. Direct Investment Abroad: Country and Industry Detail for Capital Outflows (http://www.bea.doc.gov/bea/di/usdiacap.htm#2003).

15 NATO web site, "Members" (http://www.nato.int/structur/countries.htm); UNCTAD, NATO (http://www.nato.int/structur/countries.htm); UNCTAD, Foreign Direct Investment inflows (http://www.unctad.org/Templates/WebFlyer.asp?intItemID=2111&lang=1); World Bank, *2003 World Development Indicators*, Data Query (http://devdata.worldbank.org/data-query); accessed July 27, 2004.

16 The World Bank, *2004 World Development Indicators,* Table 2.1 Population Dynamics, pages 38–41.

17 The World Bank, *2004 World Development Indicators,* Table 1.1 Size of the Economy, pages 14–17.

18 See, for example, Hill, John S. and Richard R. Still. "Effects of Urbanization on Multinational Product Planning," Summer 1984, *Columbia Journal of World Business,* 62–67. See also Roth, Martin S. "Effects of Global Market Conditions on Brand Image Customization and Brand Performance," Winter 1995, *Journal of Advertising,* Volume 24, Number 4, pages 55–75.

19 Johnson, Tim. "China's Car Owners Get Crash Course in Driving," *Philadelphia Inquirer,* Wednesday, July 21, 2004; Business section, page 1C.

20 "Fueling Prices? China's Huge Oil Consumption May Add to Soaring Costs," *ABC News,* May 28, 2004; "China Invests Heavily in Sudan's Oil Industry," *Washington Post,* Thursday, December 23, 2004, page A1.

21 The World Bank, *Global Economic Prospects and the Developing Countries 2003* (http://www.worldbank.org/prospects/gep2003/index.htm) and *World Development Indicators, 2004,* Table 2.7 Distribution of Income or Consumption, pages 60–63. The Gini index can be used to measure the distribution equality of an item. In this case, the index measures the extent to which the distribution of income among individuals deviates from a perfectly equal distribution. The lower the value, the more inequitable the distribution. Belgium, Norway, and Sweden all had Gini indexes below 30. Be aware, though, that this is *not* an indication of wealth. Swaziland, with a GNI of $1,240 in 2002, has a Gini index over 60. (The implication is that much of the population earns near or close to the average income.)

22 The World Bank, *2004 World Development Indicators,* Table 1.1 Size of the Economy, pages 14–17.

23 The World Bank, *2004 World Development Indicators,* Table 1.1 Size of the Economy, pages 14–17.

24 See, for example, Mitra, Arup, Aristomene Varoudakis, and Marie-Ange Veganzones-Varoudakis. "Productivity and Technical Efficiency in Indian States' Manufacturing: The Role of Infrastructure," January 2002, *Economic Development and Cultural Change,* Chicago. Volume 50, Issue 2, pages 395–426.

25 *The World Factbook* is published annually and is available in print form as well as online (http://www.odci.gov/cia/publications/factbook/index.html).

26 The competitiveness rankings are available online at the International Institute for Management Development web site (http://www01.imd.ch/wcy/ranking).

27 The World Bank, *2004 World Development Indicators,* Table 4.14 Monetary Indicators and Prices, pages 234–237; The World Bank, *2003 World Development Indicators,* Data Query (http://devdata.worldbank.org/data-query); accessed August 6, 2004.

Further Readings

Altman, Daniel. "Small-Picture Approach to a Big Problem: Poverty," Tuesday, August 20, 2002, *Wall Street Journal,* Section C, page 2.

Baldacci, Emanuele, Luiz de Mello, and Gabriela Inchauste. "Financial Crises, Poverty, and Income Distribution," June 2002, *Finance & Development:* Washington, Volume 39, Issue 2, pages 24–27.

Caplanova, Anetta, Marta Orviska, and John Hudson. "Eastern European Attitudes to Integration with Western Europe," *Journal of Common Market Studies.* Oxford: June 2004. Volume 42, Issue 2, pages 271–288.

De Matteis, Alessandro. "International Trade and Economic Growth in a Global Environment," *Journal of International Development.* Chichester: May 2004. Volume 16, Issue 4, pages 575–588.

Haynal, George. "Building North America," Summer 2002, *Harvard International Review,* Cambridge. Volume 24, Issue 2, pages 88–89.

Lamont, James. "Companies Court Partners Among World's Poor," August 29, 2002, *Financial Times,* page 7.

Moore, Stephen and Julian L. Simon. *It's Getting Better All the Time: 100 Great Trends of the Last 100 Years,* October 2000, Cato Institute (http://www.cato.org).

Pastore, Michael. "At-Home Users Approaching Half Billion," March 6, 2002, *CyberAtlas* (http://cyberatlas. internet.com/big_picture/geographics/article/0,,5911_986431,00.htm).

"PC Market Headed for Geographic Shift," March 11, 2002, *CyberAtlas* (http://cyberatlas. internet.com/big_picture/hardware/article/0,,5921_988841,00.html#table).

Prahalad, C. K. and Allen Hammond. "Serving the World's Poor Profitably," *Harvard Business Review,* September 2002, Volume 80, Issue 9, pages 48–57.

Schaede, Ulrike. "What Happened to the Japanese Model?" *Review of International Economics.* Oxford: May 2004. Volume 12, Issue 2, pages 277–294.

Schiff, Maurice and L. Alan Winters. *Regional Integration and Development,* World Bank, 2003.

"The Americas: Waiting for the IMF to Tango; Argentina's Crisis," March 30, 2002, *The Economist,* Volume 362, Issue 8266, pages 31–32.

Yu, Tyler T., Miranda M. Zhang, Lloyd Southern, Carl Joiner, "An International Comparative Study of Economic Development: The Recent Evidence," *Journal of American Academy of Business,* Cambridge. Hollywood, FL: September 2004. Volume 5, Issues 1/2, pages 1–6.

Recommended Web Sites

Regional Economic Integration:
Association of Southeast Asian Nations (ASEAN): http://www.aseansec.org
Economic Community of West African States (ECOWAS): http://www.ecowas.int
European Union (EU): http://europa.eu.int/index.htm

Global Organizations:
International Monetary Fund (IMF): http://www.imf.org
United Nations (UN): http://www.un.org
The World Bank Group (IBRD): http://www.worldbank.org
World Trade Organization (WTO): http://www.wto.org

Data Sources:
World Bank, *World Development Indicators,* Data Query (http://devdata.worldbank.org/data-query)—selected World Development Indicators (over 200 economic entities and 14 economic country groups; 54 indicators of approximately 550 available with online version or 600 in print edition [for most recent five-year period]).

Strategis, Industry. Create your own comparative reports on commercial policies, foreign investment, geography, government, people, trade, and many other indicators, using a variety of reliable resources; Dynamic Document Creator
(http://strategis.ic.gc.ca/sc_mrkti/ibin/compare.html).

International Data Base (IDB) is an interactive data bank containing statistical tables of demographic and socio-economic data for 227 countries and areas of the world. The population statistics are collected and compiled by the U.S. Census Bureau
(http://www.census.gov/ipc/www/idbnew.html).

Population Reference Bureau (http://www.prb.org), in particular the "Quick Facts" and the "World Population Data Sheet" (data can be accessed online as well as purchased). The data includes population statistics—birthrates, death rates, contraception, life expectancy, and urbanization.

U.S. balance of payments tables are available on the Bureau of Economic Analysis web site (home page: http://www.bea.doc. gov); BoP reports (http://www.bea.doc.gov/bea/di/home/bop.htm) and data (http://www.bea.doc.gov/bea/uguide.htm#_1_22). See also the Library of Economics and Liberty web site (http://www.econlib.org/library/Enc/BalanceofPayments.html).

Case 2.1

Foreign Exchange Rates

Foreign Exchange Rates

Country	Currency	Exchange Rate (per $U.S., August 2, 1999)	Exchange Rate (per $U.S., August 2, 2004)
Argentina	Peso	2.98	2.981
Brazil	Real	3.047	3.04696
Britain	Pound	0.619819	0.547261
Canada	Dollar	1.50753	1.33103
China	Renminbi/Yuan	8.2772	8.282
Euro zone	Euro	0.938031	0.831032
India	Rupee	43.2917	46.29
Indonesia	Rupiah	6,804.00	9,135.69
Japan	Yen	114.374	111.079
Mexico	Peso	11.4229	11.4266
Philippines	Peso	38.5483	55.82
Russia	Ruble	24.24	29.14
South Africa	Rand	6.17527	6.31468
Switzerland	Franc	1.4983	1.27834
Turkey	Lira	430,375.00	1,470,742.00

Source: http://www.xe.com/ucc/; http://www.xe.com/ict/; http://www.x-rates.com.

Questions and Research

1 Find the latest quotations for these currencies.

2 Calculate the approximate changes in the value of these currencies. Show the increase or decrease in relation to the U.S. dollar.

3 Why have these changes occurred? (Give a general explanation.)

4 What are some of the implications of changing exchange rates for international business managers?

Case 2.2

U.S. Pharmaceuticals, Inc. (A)

U.S. Pharmaceuticals (USP) is a U.S. firm with about 30 percent of its sales outside the United States. USP concentrates on the ethical drug business but has diversified into animal health products, cosmetics, and some patent medicines. These other lines account for about one-fourth of USP's $800 million sales.

USP's international business is conducted in some 70 countries, mostly through distributors in those markets. In six countries, however, it has manufacturing or compounding operations. (*Compounding* refers to the local mixing, assembling, and packaging of critical ingredients shipped from the United States.) USP's only Latin American manufacturing/compounding operations are in Latinia, a country with a population of about 30 million. Some products are shipped from Latinia to other Latin American markets.

USP's Latinian plant is operated by the pharmaceutical division. It is engaged in producing and compounding USP's ethical drug line. It does no work for other USP divisions (cosmetics, proprietary medicines, and animal health). All of the other divisions, which also sell in Latinia, export their finished products from plants in the United States. The Latinian plant employs 330 people, of whom only two are North Americans—the general manager, Tom Hawley, and the director of quality control, Frixos Massialas.

USP's cosmetics and toiletries business accounts for $150 million in sales and is handled by a separate division—Cosmetics and Toiletries. The division sells in only 38 of USP's 70 foreign markets. One of the division's better foreign markets is Latinia, where it has sales of over $8 million and an acceptable market position. Cosmetics and Toiletries has a marketing subsidiary in Latinia to handle its business there. Jim Richardson, an American, heads the subsidiary. The rest of the staff are Latinians.

Jim Richardson was very disturbed by news received from the Latinian Ministry of International Trade. Tariffs were being increased on many "nonessential products" because of the balance-of-payments pressures the country had been experiencing for the past year and a half. For USP's Cosmetics and Toiletries specifically, this meant a rise in the tariffs it pays—from 20 percent to 50 percent *ad valorem*. The 20 percent duty had posed no particular problem for Cosmetics and Toiletries because of the prestige of the imported product and the consumer franchise it had established, Richardson explained. He believed, however, that the 50 percent duty was likely to be an insurmountable barrier.

Cosmetics and Toiletries' competition in Latinia was about evenly divided between local firms and other international companies from Europe and North America. Jim believed that local firms, which had about 40 percent of the market, stood to benefit greatly from the tariff increase unless the international firms could find a satisfactory response. When Jim received news of the tariff increase, which was to be imposed the first of October—one week away—he called a meeting to consider what Cosmetics and Toiletries could do. Deborah Neale, manager of Cosmetics Marketing, and Emilio Illanes, manager of Toiletries Marketing, met with Jim to discuss the situation.

Several different courses of action were proposed at the hastily called meeting. Deborah suggested, "We could continue importing, pay the high duty, and change the positioning strategy to appeal to a high-price, premium market." Another idea was to import the primary ingredients and assemble (compound) and package them in Latinia. (Duties on the imported ingredients ranged between 10 and 35 percent *ad valorem*.) Emilio suggested asking Cosmetics and Toiletries in the United States for a lower price on the products shipped to Latinia so the duty would have a lesser impact on the final price in the local market. Jim mentioned the alternative that none of them wanted to consider: "If we can't compete at those high prices, we may have to give up the market."

Questions and Research

1 Evaluate the alternatives that were brought up at the meeting.

2 Are there any other possible courses of action? Explain.

3 Propose and defend a course of action.

4 How would your response differ if, instead of a tariff increase, Latinia had imposed a quota, cutting the imports of these products by 75 percent?

Case 2.3

The Lifeblood of the World's Economies—Electricity

Electricity is a critical part of any nation's infrastructure. Without it, people would not have computers, telephones (even wireless need to be recharged), televisions, and (perhaps most importantly) electric lights and refrigeration—all of which are an important part of people's lives. There is also, of course, the electricity needed to run the machines for industries. Businesses need electricity to function, so researching a nation's ability to provide electricity is important.

Consumption of electricity also gives some indication of a nation's wealth. Assuming that the electricity consumed goes toward powering appliances in homes as well as in manufacturing, the higher the consumption, the larger the middle class—those who can afford electric appliances. The following table provides some recent statistics on average energy use around the world. (Consider that an average energy-efficient refrigerator requires approximately 600 kilowatts of energy per year.)

These data tell only part of the story, though. In the United States and other developed nations, on rare occasions, the ability to supply electricity still does not meet local demand. On a particularly hot day, when people are running air conditioners and fans in addition to using electricity for other needs, they may be subject to a brownout (when lightbulbs grow dim because they and other electrical devices are not getting sufficient power to run at designed levels). California, among other places, has experienced rolling blackouts, where power is available only to a specific area at certain times of the day. Total blackouts are also possible when a storm or another unexpected occurrence completely cuts power to a region.

In India, the problem of getting enough power to run trains, manufacturing plants, and home appliances is becoming severe in some areas. Power outages may last only an hour; even more common, though, are power outages that last five or ten hours (sometimes even longer). In the town of

Annual Electric Consumption, 2001

Country or Income Group	(KwH/person)	Country or Income Group	(KwH/person)
Low income	**317**	**Upper middle income**	**2,505**
India	365	Argentina	2,107
Kenya	117	Czech Republic	4,977
Nicaragua	268	Estonia	3,764
Nigeria	82	Gabon	814
Pakistan	358	Mexico	1,643
Lower middle income	**1,304**	**High income**	**8,421**
Brazil	1,729	Canada	15,385
China	893	Germany	6,093
Indonesia	404	Korea, Republic	5,288
South Africa	3,793	Norway	24,881
Thailand	1,508	Spain	4,933
World	2,159	United States	11,714

Source: The World Bank, Data Query, *2004 World Development Indicators*, Table 5.10 Power and Communications, pages 290–293.

Purnea, for instance, power was out on one occasion for 34 days. While the problems in India have existed for decades, they are becoming acute as more people can afford to purchase computers, refrigerators, televisions, and air conditioners. The shortages are blamed not only on the inability of the power companies to generate enough electricity, but also on the theft of electricity. India's Power Minister, Suresh Prabhakar Prabhu, estimates that half of all power generated is subsequently stolen by people who illegally tap overhead power lines. (Do not attempt this at home!)

Comparing populations and power consumption provides intriguing bases for discussions about major environmental issues facing the world. The United States has a large middle class and uses a lot of electricity. America, with a population that is one-fourth that of India, consumes more than 30 times the electricity. Access to electricity may be as high as 40 or 50 percent in urban areas of India, but available only to between 3 and 10 percent of people living in rural locations. Comparing India or China to Norway, with only 5 million people, is even more dramatic.

China, projecting a rapid increase in demand for electricity, is building the second largest dam in the world, the Xiaolangdi Dam. This is just one of ten dams planned for the Hongshui River. Where is the largest dam? The largest dam, the Three Gorges Dam, is also located in China. Behind this dam sits a lake, created by damming the Yangtze River, that will be 400 miles long and nearly 600 feet deep. Once completed, the dam will be capable of generating 18,200 megawatts of power. The average middle-income electric consumption is approximately 1,400 KwH per person. With a population of 1.3 billion, China would need 1,820 gigawatts (billion watts) of power to satisfy the demand of an average middle-income nation. On the bright side, the Chinese also hope that by building the dam, they will be able to control flooding and the associated loss of life—in the last century, approximately 300,000 people died due to floods.

Across the globe in Costa Rica, the government is eager to sell electricity to neighboring countries as a source of income. As a result, it has been studying the feasibility of building a dam in the

Boruca territory. The estimated yield of the plant would be 1,500 megawatts, most of which would be exported to Mexico and the United States (since Costa Rica is already meeting the demands of its population). Preliminary plans call for a dam over 800 feet tall that would result in the flooding of more than 50,000 acres. Local residents would be displaced; and property destined to be flooded is home to flora and fauna that, if not endangered, are certainly rare. Unique wildlife and plants attract tourists; and building this dam would hurt the tourism industry, one of Costa Rica's major "exports."

While hydroelectric power is seen as a cleaner alternative than coal-burning and nuclear plants, it also presents unique problems. Flooding large tracts of land requires that many people and companies move or be displaced. If the land that is flooded contains dangerous chemicals or by-products from industries, waste treatment plants, and abandoned vehicles (with oil and gasoline left inside), the pollutants must be cleaned or cleared; otherwise, the water will be contaminated. New water treatment plants, factories, roads, housing, and other construction must occur to take the place of the submerged properties. There is also the ecological impact on plant and animal life within the flooded region and the impact of support infrastructure (transmission towers, for example).

Whatever the solutions, as nations develop and people want more power-driven products, economic and ecological consequences will result. Companies that provide the plans for these projects and build them, as well as the firms that produce energy-consuming products (from automobiles to refrigerators), have a responsibility to take these important issues into account when they design, build, and market their products.

Questions and Research

1 Why would frequent brownouts or prolonged blackouts have an impact on after-sales service costs for electrically powered products?

2 How much power will India need in five years (consider current population, population growth rates, and current electricity/power consumption)?

3 How would intermittent power access like that in India and other parts of the world affect sales of electrically powered products?

4 There are vast opportunities for many companies in developing markets. What can companies do to help developing nations plan for the infrastructure needs associated with economic development?

Sources: "China Builds Second Biggest Dam," July 1, 2001, BBC News; "China's Three Gorges Dam—Eco-Boon or Cesspool?" November 4, 1997, CNN Interactive, CNN.com, accessed August 14, 2002; "Costa Rica: Indigenous Territory Threatened by Hydroelectric Dam," *World Rainforest Movement* (http://www.wrm.org.uy/bulletin/4/CostaRica.html), accessed July 15, 2002; "Indians Can Only Wait On Government as Blackouts Strike," August 2, 2002, *Philadelphia Inquirer,* page A21; The World Bank, Data Query, *2002 World Development Indicators* (http://devdata.worldbank.org/data-query), accessed August 14, 2002; The World Bank, *2002 World Development Indicators,* page 130.

Case 2.4

Unicola

Unicola is a medium-sized beverage and snack food company based in the United States. Annual sales are $450 million. The firm has developed some special enriched beverage and snack foods that offer high nutritional value as well as convenience and refreshment. Unicola is interested in foreign markets for these new products. (Its present business is confined to the United States and Canada.) The company believes that these products should not be promoted as "health foods," but as traditional soft drinks and snacks because consumers do not like to buy products just because "they are good for you."

Because promotion is so important to the successful introduction of these products, George Horton, Unicola's advertising manager, has been looking at promotional possibilities in various foreign markets. One of these areas is Southeast Asia. His preliminary screening includes four variables: (1) newspaper circulation per capita, (2) radio receivers per capita, (3) television receivers per capita, and (4) population. The markets being investigated have already been screened on the basis of political criteria. After the political screening, the following Southeast Asian nations remain on the list for further screening on the basis of promotional possibilities: Bangladesh, Hong Kong, India, Indonesia, Malaysia, Pakistan, the Philippines, Singapore, South Korea, Sri Lanka, Taiwan, Thailand, and Vietnam.

Questions and Research

1 Prepare a table showing the scoring for these 13 countries on the four criteria suggested.

2 Which five countries would you choose as offering the best possibilities for promoting Unicola's products? Explain and defend your choices.

3 What other information would you need about these countries? How would you get it?

CHAPTER 3

The Cultural Environment
The People of the World

Learning Objectives

Economic factors are important in determining a consumer's ability to purchase a product. Whether a purchase actually occurs, however, depends largely on cultural factors. Therefore, to understand markets abroad, international businesspeople must have an appreciation for the cultural environment of buyer behavior. This chapter presents the major ingredients of that cultural environment.

The main goals of this chapter are to

1 Show how a country's material culture determines whether a firm's products fit in with the way of life for a group of people and, if not, what adaptation may be necessary.

2 Explain the role of a culture's language in shaping international business.

3 Explore the subject of a society's aesthetics—its sense of beauty, proportion, and appropriateness—in connection with a firm's products and communications.

4 Describe how the local educational system can impact a firm's strategies.

5 Discuss the effect of religion on consumer behavior.

6 Distinguish characteristics among different values and among different attitudes that influence purchasing decisions.

7 Explain how the social organization in a given country (family, age group, class, etc.) affects consumer behavior.

Business has always been recognized as an economic activity involving the exchange of goods and services. Only in recent years, however, have sociocultural influences been identified as determinants of buyer behavior, revealing business as a cultural as well as economic phenomenon. Because an understanding of business practices is culture-bound, one must acquire knowledge of diverse cultural environments in order to be successful in business activities. It is necessary to remove one's culturally tinted glasses to study foreign markets.

The growing application of anthropology, sociology, and psychology in studying the business environment is explicit recognition of the noneconomic bases of consumer behavior. It is not enough to say that consumption is a function of income. Consumption is a function of many other cultural influences, as well. Furthermore, only noneconomic factors can explain the different patterns of consumption of two individuals with identical incomes—or, by analogy, of two different countries with similar per capita incomes.

A review of consumer durables ownership in EU countries shows the importance of noneconomic factors in determining consumption behavior. For example, you could compare penetration levels of home appliances (white goods) among EU members. Slovakians, new members of the EU, own the most refrigerators (40 per 1,000 people) but have the fewest microwave ovens (3/1,000) and few dishwashers (3/1,000). Austrians own more refrigerators than most other EU members (31/1,000) and a lot of microwave ovens (36/1,000) but few clothes dryers (5/1,000). Greeks own more refrigerators than their EU counterparts (32/1,000); but purchases of microwave ovens (9/1,000), clothes dryers (2/1,000), and dishwashers (7/1,000) are among the lowest in the EU. There appears to be some relationship between income and the purchase of white goods when looking at higher-order convenience items such as dishwashers and clothes dryers versus items that might be considered more of a necessity, such as refrigerators and ovens.[1]

Nevertheless, it is remarkable that the same countries can be at high-penetration levels for some appliances and at low-penetration levels for other appliances. People in Luxembourg and Denmark have the highest income of EU members ($40,000 and $30,000, respectively) but only moderate levels of consumption of white goods. People living in Latvia, Lithuania, and the Slovak Republic have lower income levels ($3,500, $3,700, and $4,000, respectively); but as mentioned in the case of the Slovakians, they have the highest per capita consumption of refrigerators among other EU members.[2] Differences in consumption patterns for these and other consumer products cannot be explained by different levels of income alone. However, they can be better explained when cultural differences are taken into account.

What Is Culture?

Culture is too complex to define in simple terms. It seems that each anthropologist has a definition. The anthropologist John Bodley succinctly brings together the major points of agreement in his description of the term: "Culture is learned behavior; a way of life for any group of people living together in a single, related and interdependent community."[3] One fundamental aspect is that **culture** is a total pattern of behavior that is consistent and compatible in its components. It is not a collection of random behaviors, but behaviors that are related and integrated. A second fundamental is that culture is learned behavior. It is not biologically transmitted. It depends on environment, not heredity. It can be called the man-made part of the environ-

FIGURE 3-1 Culture Shapes Business

Culture is that which you can sense (hear, see, smell, taste, and touch) as well as that which is hidden (assumptions, attitudes, beliefs, and values).

What you can sense:
music, art, architecture,
fashion, food, dance

What is hidden:
feelings about work,
wealth, religion, future,
family, friends, time

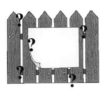

What you *can* see is a manifestation of what you *can't* see. People's reactions to the same marketing campaign, for example, are likely to be different from culture to culture. Businesspeople must recognize this fact if they are to develop effective strategies and accept that they must adapt the movies, watches, cars, insurance, and other products that they market to accommodate the differences among cultures.

ment. The third fundamental is that culture is behavior that is shared by a group of people, a society. It can be considered as the distinctive way of life of a people. The elements of culture will be discussed after the role of cultural analysis in the United States is considered.

Cultural Analysis in the United States

In approaching the cultural environment, it is revealing to see how cultural analysis is used in business. If you scan textbooks in marketing, management, and other disciplines of business, you see that they all have one or more chapters on the contributions of the behavioral sciences. In addition to chapters on consumer behavior, concepts derived from the behavioral sciences occur in chapters on research, promotion, and pricing in marketing. While management texts may present hiring and motivation differences, finance texts may include discussions about savings patterns; and accounting texts may include content about disclosure or privacy as it relates to culture. If managers are to be successful, they must be familiar with the following concepts: (1) reference groups, (2) social class, (3) consumption systems, (4) family structure and decision making, (5) adoption-diffusion, (6) market segmentation, and (7) consumer behavior.

More evidence of the role of cultural analysis is the number of people trained in anthropology or sociology who are working in business. Major companies employ them in human resources, or they may work in advertising agencies and consulting firms, hired by internationally active companies. University consultants to industry come not only from schools of business and engineering, but also from departments of anthropology and sociology. Such attention to cultural analysis is notable. More importance is placed on cultural analysis in foreign markets, where the international businessperson generally knows little about the local culture. (See Figure 3-1.)

Elements of Culture

Varying definitions exist pertaining to the elements of culture, including one that counts 73 "cultural universals." This book uses a simpler list that encompasses eight major areas: (1) technology and material culture, (2) language, (3) aesthetics, (4) education, (5) religion, (6) attitudes and values, (7) social organization, and (8) political life. (The political aspect of culture is reserved for discussion in Chapter 4.) A broad definition of culture would include economics as well; however, the subjects are often treated separately, as is done in this book. The discussion of culture here is not definitive and perhaps would not satisfy the anthropologist. Nonetheless, the material should contribute to an understanding of the cultural environment as it affects a firm.

Aesthetics

Aesthetics refers to the prevalent ideas in a culture concerning beauty and good taste, as expressed in the arts—music, art, drama, and dance—and the appreciation of color and form. International differences abound in aesthetics, but they tend to be regional rather than national. For example, Kabuki theater is exclusively Japanese, but Western theater includes at least all of Western Europe in addition to the United States and Canada in its audience.

Musical tastes, too, tend to be regional rather than national. In the West, many countries enjoy the same classical and popular music. In fact, due to modern communications, popular music has become truly international. Nevertheless, obvious differences exist between Western music and music of the Middle East, Africa, or India. Likewise, the dance styles of African tribal groups or the Balinese are quite removed from Western dance styles. The beauty of India's Taj Mahal is different from that of Notre Dame in Paris or the Chrysler Building in New York City.

Design

The aesthetics of a culture probably do not have a major impact on economic activities. In aesthetics, however, lie some implications for international business. For example, in the design of its plant, product, or package, a firm should be sensitive to local aesthetic preferences. This may run counter to the desire for international uniformity, but the firm must be aware of the positive and negative aspects of its designs. Generally, Asians appreciate complex and decorative styles, particularly when it comes to gift wrapping, for instance.

A historical example of lack of cultural sensitivity is illustrated by early Christian missionaries from Western nations who were often guilty of architectural "imperialism." The Christian churches built in many non-Western nations usually reflected Western rather than indigenous architectural ideas. This was not done with malicious intent, but because the missionaries were culture-bound in their aesthetics; that is, they had their own ideas about what a church should look like.

The U.S. government faces a similar problem in designing its embassies. The U.S. Embassy in India received praise both for its beauty as a building and for the way it blended with Indian architecture. The U.S. Embassy in London, however, has received more than its share of criticism, including comments about the size of the sculpted American eagle on top of the building. Some Britons also took exception to the architecture of the London Hilton. For a firm, the best policy is to design and decorate its buildings and commercial vehicles to reflect local aesthetic preferences. In its thousands of outlets abroad, McDonald's has learned to adapt its facilities to local tastes.

Color

The significance of different colors also varies from culture to culture. In the United States, for instance, people use colors to identify emotional reactions; people "see red," they are "green with envy," and they "feel blue." Black signifies mourning in Western countries, whereas white is often the color of mourning in Eastern nations. Green is popular in Muslim countries, while red and black have a negative connotation in several African countries. Red is an appealing and lucky color in China, blue sometimes suggests evil, and yellow is often associated with authority. Certain colors have particular meanings because of religious, patriotic, or aesthetic reasons. Businesspeople need to know the significance of colors in a culture when planning their company's products and the products' packaging. For any market, the choice of colors should be related to the aesthetic sense of the buyer's culture rather than that of the manager's culture. Generally, the colors of the country's flag are safe colors. Japan has a Study Group for Colors in Public Places. It wages war on "color pollution." Its mission is "to seek out better uses for color, to raise the issue of colors."

Music

There are also cultural differences in music. An understanding of these differences is critical in creating advertising messages that use music. The music of nonliterate cultures is generally functional, or has significance in the people's daily lives; whereas the music of literate cultures tends to be separate from people's other concerns. For example, a Western student has to learn to "understand" a Beethoven symphony, but aborigines assimilate musical culture as an integral part of their existence. Ethnomusicologist William Malm stated that understanding the symbolism in different kinds of music requires considerable cultural conditioning. Therefore, homogeneity in music throughout world cultures is not possible. There are exceptions, of course; but one implication for a firm is that wherever it utilizes music, it should use music of the local culture. Recognizing the importance of music in popular culture, companies such as Coca-Cola, PepsiCo, and Nike are frequent sponsors of events such as MTV Video Music Awards Latin America and WOMAD (Festival of World Music, Arts & Dance).

Paul Anka provides an example of the value of "going native" in music and language. Anka has recorded ten albums that have sold, collectively, 10 million copies, none of which has been heard in the United States. The secret is that the songs in the albums were sung in Japanese, German, French, Spanish, and Italian—songs that Anka composed strictly for those countries in a style indigenous to their musical cultures. Anka isn't fluent in those languages. For months, he worked with native musicians on music and lyrics that would appeal to each nation. He sang in the local language phonetically. Mr. Anka succeeded because of his broad appeal, but also because he recorded his music in so many other languages.

Brand Names

The choice of brand names is also affected by aesthetics. Frequently, the best brand name is one in the local language, pleasing to local taste. This leads to a multiplicity of brand names, which some firms try to avoid by searching out a nonsense word that is pronounceable everywhere but that has no specific meaning anywhere. Kodak is one example. In other cases, local identification is important enough that firms seek local brand names. For example, Procter & Gamble has 20 different brand names for its detergents in foreign markets.

The aesthetics of a culture influence a firm's strategies abroad, often in ways that businesses are unaware of until they make mistakes. A firm needs local input to avoid ineffective or damaging use of aesthetics. This input may come from local marketing research, local nationals working for the firm, and local advertising agencies or distributors.

Material Culture

"What do you do?" If you live in or visit America, you hear that question quite frequently. The question says much about the culture. Instead of "you are what you eat," "you are what you do." The focus of many conversations in the United States is about one's work, not about family, weather, world events, or politics. A person's job title, earnings, car, house, clothes, and other possessions help define that individual in America. While some people view this as overindulgence and self-absorbed behavior, others argue that this behavior reflects a competitive and entrepreneurial spirit. Americans are not alone in the world in terms of material acquisition; they are merely an example. As is discussed next, attitudes toward material wealth differ markedly across cultures.

Technology and Material Culture

Material culture includes the tools and artifacts—the material or physical things—in a society, excluding those physical things found in nature unless they undergo some technological transformation. For example, a tree as such is not part of a culture, but the Christmas tree is. **Technology** refers to the techniques or methods of making and using that which surrounds us. Technology and material culture are related to the way a society organizes its economic activities. The term *technology gap* refers to differences in the ability of two societies to create, design, and use that which exists in nature or to use that which has been transformed in some way.

When referring to industrialized nations, developing nations, the nuclear age, or the space age, one is referring to different technologies and material cultures. One can also speak of societies being in the age of the automobile, the bicycle, or foot transportation—or in the age of the computer, the abacus, or pencil-and-paper calculation. The relationships between technology, material culture, and the other aspects of life are profound but not easily recognized because people are the products of their own culture. It is primarily as people travel abroad that they perceive such relationships.

When discussing this topic, Karl Marx went so far as to say that the economic organization of a society shapes and determines its political, legal, and social organization. His view was termed "economic determinism," his materialistic interpretation of history. Few people today would take such a strong position, but they may recognize many examples of the impact of tools, techniques, and economic organization on the nature of life in society. For example, people's behavior as workers and consumers is greatly influenced by the technology and material culture.

The way people work (and how effectively they work) is determined in large part by their technology and material culture. Henry Ford's assembly line revolutionized U.S. productivity and, ultimately, the standard of living. The U.S. farmers' use of equipment and technology has made them the world's most productive agriculturalists. Ironically, agriculture is one of the most capital-intensive and technology-intensive industries in the United States. The R&D is not done by the farmer, however, but by land-grant universities, equipment manufacturers, and seed and chemical companies. The computer, as one of the newer artifacts, affects the way people work, the kind of work they can do, and even where they work. If you consider the nature of the factory and agricultural methods and the role of the computer in an African nation, you can see technology and material culture as a constraint on work and productivity in a culture. In developed economies, tractors are able to cultivate many acres every day; while in developing countries, where farmers may have only hand tools, it takes days (even weeks) to plant or tend an acre of land.

How people consume and what people consume are also heavily influenced by the technology and material culture. For example, the car has helped to create the conditions that made suburban living possible, with the accompanying lifestyle and consumption patterns. The car has also shaped dating behavior. Television has a wide-ranging impact on consumer and voter behavior. The microwave oven influences not only the preparation of food, but also the nature of the food consumed. Considering artifacts such as the digital camera and the cellular telephone, you can imagine further ramifications of each new product on the life of the consumer. Knowing the impact of these products in the U.S. culture, you can conjecture how consumer behavior might be different in countries with much lighter penetration of such products. For example, the number of cars in use in 2002 ranges from 486 per 1,000 people in the United States to 110 in Mexico, 23 in Egypt, 8 in Nigeria, 5 in India, 5 in China, and 2 in Vietnam.[4]

Material Culture as a Constraint

Managers need to develop insight into how material culture in foreign markets affects their operations abroad. In manufacturing, foreign production by a firm may represent an attempt to introduce a new material culture into the host economy. This is usually the case when a firm builds a plant in a less developed country. The firm generally checks carefully on the necessary economic prerequisites for such a plant; for example, raw-material supply, power, transportation, and financing. Frequently overlooked, however, are the other cultural preconditions for the plant.

Prior to making foreign production decisions, a firm must evaluate the material culture in the host country. One aspect is the economic infrastructure; that is, transportation, power, and communications. Other questions are these: Do production processes need to be adapted to fit the local economy? Will the plant be more labor-intensive than plants at home? The manager discovers that production of the same goods may require a different production function in different countries.

MATERIAL CULTURE AND BUSINESS

It is equally important for businesspeople to understand the material culture in foreign markets. For example, the firm that manufactures industrial products finds it useful to obtain and analyze input-output tables, which show how materials and components are used in making products. Where these tables can be even partially constructed, a firm has a better idea of how its products relate to the material culture and industrial structure of the country. Such information helps identify customers and usage patterns.[5]

Material Culture Matters

The per capita income in Mexico in 2002 was $5,920. Fewer Mexicans own cars, trucks, telephones, and personal computers than people in the United States and other developed nations own. Because of this fact, it's difficult and expensive to ship goods, to travel, and to communicate with customers and suppliers.

Over 11 million cars are on the roads of Mexico. Approximately 33 percent of roads are paved; and although they are expensive to use, the best of these roads are the toll roads (las cuotas). Traveling 200 miles by car between Mexico City and Acapulco costs a little over $40, but the toll for a large truck is $115.

Telephone service was privatized in 1990 and opened to competition in 1997. However, there are still only about 15 telephone lines for every 100 people and installing a new line may take a month or two.

In large diversified markets such as the United States, almost any industrial product can find a market. In developing nations, however, firms that make industrial goods find increasingly limited markets in which they can sell only part of their product line—or perhaps none of it. The better the picture of the material culture in world markets, the better able a firm is to identify the best prospects. The prospects in countries where the principal agricultural implement is the machete differ from those countries in which farmers use tractors.

Firms that manufacture consumer goods are also concerned with the material culture in foreign markets. Such simple considerations as electrical voltages and use of the metric system must be taken into account. Product adaptations may also be necessitated by the material culture of the family. Does the family have a car to transport purchases? Does the family have a stove to prepare foods or a refrigerator in which to store foods? If electrical power is not available, electrical appliances will not be marketable unless they are battery-powered. To those people who wash clothes by a stream or lake, detergents and packaged soaps are not useful; the market is for bar soaps only.

Large multinationals are learning from entrepreneurs in developing countries that the key to success in markets where income is low is to sell products that come in small sizes, are relatively cheap, and are easy to use. Unilever packages its shampoo in single-use sizes, selling it for a few cents in India. Other examples include 3-inch square packages of margarine in Nigeria that don't need refrigeration and an 8-cent tube of Close-Up with enough toothpaste for about 20 brushings. Unilever expects that developing markets will account for 50 percent of all sales by 2010, up from 32 percent in 2005.

There are other examples of firms catering to markets in developing nations, where over half of the world's population is located. Scojo Vision of Brooklyn, New York, provides training and $75 loans to entrepreneurs in Latin America and Asia to purchase kits containing eye charts and glasses. The glasses come in three strengths and sell for only $2. Freeplay Energy in London designed and sold 3 million hand crank radios. Since many people in developing countries have no electricity and cannot afford to purchase batteries, these units are popular for listening to farm and health reports. Phillips Electronics of the Netherlands has developed its own version, which

Mobile phone usage is considerably higher, with 25 cellular phones for every 100 people. Local telephone service is still unreliable in some areas; and in general, the cost of making calls is expensive because of high government taxes on phone services.

Independent messenger services should be used to deliver important correspondence since mail service is slow and, at times, unreliable. Sending mail electronically is an option in some areas, but it reaches only the relatively wealthy segment of the population who own computers. Only 5 million computers are in use in Mexico, or an average of 20 people for every computer. Ten percent of the population of 101 million people were classified as Internet users in 2002. In 2003, the ISP and connection charges were $23 for one month of service.

Sources: World Bank, *2004 World Development Indicators*, Tables 1.1, 5.9, 5.10, 5.11, and Data Query (http://devdata.worldbank.org/data-query); *Mexico Country Commercial Guide, 2004;* U.S. Department of Commerce, International Trade Administration (http://www.buyusa.gov/mexico/en/22.html); Autotransport Administration of Mexico, Division of Secretary of Transportation and Communication (http://www.sct.gob.mx/autotransporte/index.htm).

the firm is now selling in India for around $20. Indian firms located in Madras and Bangalore are developing wireless kiosks that allow users to access the Internet for as little as 3 cents an hour and computers with voice recognition software, which is aimed at users who cannot read.[6]

Marketing strategy is influenced by the material culture. For instance, the promotional program is constrained by the kinds of media available. The advertiser wants to know the availability of television, radio, magazines, and newspapers. How good is the reproduction process in newspapers and magazines? Are there advertising and research agencies to support the advertising program? The size of retail outlets affects the use of point-of-purchase displays. The nature of travel and the highway system affects the use of outdoor advertising.

Modifications in distribution may also be necessary. These changes must be made on the basis of the alternatives offered by the country's commercial infrastructure. What wholesale and retail patterns exist? What warehouse or storage facilities are available? Is refrigerated storage possible? What is the nature of the transport system—road, rail, river, or air? What area does it cover? Firms that use direct channels in the United States, with large-scale retailers and chain-store operations, may have to use indirect channels with a multitude of small independent retailers. These small retailers may be relatively inaccessible if they are widely dispersed and transportation is inadequate.

If local storage facilities are insufficient, a firm may have to supply its own packaging or provide special packaging to offer extra protection. Whereas highways and railroads are most important in moving goods in the United States, river transport is a major means in other countries. And in still other countries, air is the principal means of transport. Thus, in numerous ways, management is concerned with the material culture in foreign markets. (See "Global Environment: Material Culture Matters.")

IMPERIALISM?

Perhaps the most subtle role of international business is that of agent of cultural change. When a firm introduces new products into a market, it is, in effect, seeking to change the country's material culture. The change may be modest—a new food product—or it may be more dramatic—a machine that revolutionizes agricultural or industrial technology in the host country. The product of the international firm is alien in the sense that it did not originate in the host country. The firm must consider carefully the legitimacy of its role as an agent of change. It must be sure that changes it introduces are in accordance with the interests of the host country. When the product is coming from a developed nation and sold in a developing country without modification, people may resent the firm's product as a form of "neo-colonialism," "westernization," or "imperialism." Along this line, someone coined the term *Cocacolonization* in regard to U.S. cocoa business abroad. More recently, the use of *Mc* as a prefix to words or expressions (usually with a negative connotation) refers to McDonald's as an institution that represents American cultural influence.

In Canada, foreign sources—especially American—account for 95 percent of movies shown and 83 percent of magazines sold, as well as books and records.[7] Partly because of this fact, there is a Ministry of Canadian Heritage, whose director is pushing legislation to limit the share of U.S. movies and magazines. There are also regulations requiring TV stations to offer 60 percent "Canadian content" and radio stations to include 35 percent "Canadian content" in their popular music broadcast.

Language

Language is perhaps the most obvious difference between cultures. Inextricably linked with all other aspects of a culture, language reflects the nature and values of that culture. For example, the English language has a rich vocabulary for commercial and industrial activities, reflecting the nature of the English and U.S. societies. Many less industrialized societies have only limited vocabularies for those activities but richer vocabularies for matters important to their culture.

An Indian civil servant, Nabagopal Das, commented on the important role of the English language in India's development. He said it would be a serious error for India to replace English with Hindi or other Indian languages because none of them gives adequate expression to the modern commercial or technical activities necessary for India's development. On the other hand, these other languages are more than adequate, indeed rich, for describing the traditional culture. Similarly, Eskimo has many words to describe snow, whereas English has one general term. This is reasonable because the difference in forms of snow plays a vital role in the lives of Eskimos. The kinds of activities they can engage in depend on the specific snow conditions. Of course, in the United States, the subculture of skiers has a richer vocabulary for snow than that of nonskiers.

Because language is such an obvious cultural difference, everyone recognizes that it must be dealt with. It is said that anyone planning a career in international business should learn a foreign language. Certainly, if a person's career involves dealing with a particular country, he or she will find learning the country's language to be very useful. However, learning German or Japanese is not a great help to those people whose careers do not involve Germany or Japan. Because it is usually impossible to predict to which countries a career will lead, it is best to study a language spoken by many people (Mandarin) or a language that is commonly used as a first or second language in many nations (English, French, and Spanish). Whether or not it is a primary language of the parties involved, English is frequently used in negotiations, legal docu-

TABLE 3-1   Major World Languages

Language	Speakers (millions)	Language	Speakers (millions)
Chinese, Mandarin	874	Russian	167
Hindi	366	Japanese	125
English	341	German	100
Spanish	322	Korean	78
Bengali	207	French	77
Portuguese	176	Chinese, Wu	77

Source: *World Almanac 2003*; World Education Corporation, page 633.

ments, and business transactions. Table 3-1 shows the number of speakers of the major world languages. (The figures for English are misleading because for almost every country, English is the first choice as a second language.)

Americans should not be too complacent, however. More than 340 million of the estimated 566 million Internet users in 2002 (or approximately 60 percent) speak a language other than English. While English-speaking users are the largest group (228 million), Chinese Internet users are the second largest group with 56 million, followed closely by Japanese-speaking users at slightly more than 52 million. Other important languages are Spanish (41 million users), German (39 million), and French and Italian (each with about 20 million users).[8] Despite the large number of European users, the majority of web sites of the largest companies are still available only in the English language.[9]

Language as a Cultural Mirror

A country's language is the key to its culture. Thus, if an individual is to work extensively with any one culture, he or she must learn the language. Learning a language well means learning the culture because the words of the language are merely concepts reflecting the culture. For a firm to communicate well with political leaders, employees, suppliers, and customers, it must assimilate this one aspect of culture more than any other.

Studying the language situation within foreign markets can yield useful information about them. The number of languages in a country is a case in point. In a real sense, a language defines a culture; thus, if a country has several spoken languages, it has several cultures. Belgium has two national languages, French in the South and Flemish in the North. This linguistic division goes back to the days of Julius Caesar, but even today political and social differences exist between the two language groups.

Canada's situation is similar to Belgium's, with Canada having both French and English languages and cultural groups. Many African and Asian nations have a far larger number of languages and cultural groups. Africa has one-tenth of the world's population but one-third of its languages. To communicate in midst this diversity, a *lingua franca* (a hybrid language) must be used for communication between the groups. (The term *lingua franca* was originally coined for the commercial language Sabir, which was used along the Mediterranean during the Middle Ages; it was a mixture of Italian, French, Spanish, and other languages.) There are also language bridges, usually the language spoken by the largest group. In China, it is Mandarin; in India, it is Hindi; in many countries, it is the colonial language.

Language and Translations

According to Worldwatch, 6,800 languages are spoken in the world today—over 1,000 in the Americas, 1,300 in the Pacific and Australia, 230 in Europe, over 2,000 in Africa, and nearly 2,200 in Asia. The most linguistically diverse countries are Papua New Guinea with 832 languages, Indonesia with 731, India with 398, Nigeria with 515, Mexico with 295, Cameroon with 286, and Brazil with 234. Many of these languages are spoken by few people and do not have a written form, which, unfortunately, means they are likely to be extinct within the next generation. However, all reflect the culture of the people speaking them.

Many say that U.S. firms have it easy, but more than 25 languages are spoken in American homes by 125,000 or more people. The fact that there are nearly 7,000 languages coupled with the fact that 5 or more languages may be spoken in any one country makes it difficult for a company to develop an effective marketing campaign. As more firms expand their markets to additional areas of the world, more material will

The Republic of the Congo serves as an example of this situation in many third world countries. Separate tribal languages are spoken by the numerous tribes living there. Some local dialects are *lingua franca* trade languages (Lingala, Monokutuba, and Swahili), but the official national language is again a European one—French. Such situations present real obstacles to learning the "language of the people." The usual approach in these situations is to rely on the European language and the *lingua franca* for business and communications. Unfortunately, they are not the mother tongue of most nationals.

DIVERSITY: LINGUISTIC AND SOCIAL

Other problems accompany language diversity within a nation. Many tribal languages are not written. All intertribal communications are in the *lingua franca*, which is a written language. However, because the *lingua franca* is not everyone's native tongue, it does not communicate as well as the parties' native languages. The European languages used in former colonies have the virtue of covering a wide territory. However, they are foreign to the culture and spoken by only a small part of the population.

Language differences within a country may indicate social as well as communication divisions. In both Canada and Belgium, the two linguistic groups have occasionally clashed to the point of violence. Angola, Nigeria, and India are examples of less developed countries where differing linguistic groups have also engaged in hostilities.

The United States is not exactly a linguistic melting pot either. Spanish accounts for over half of all of the foreign-language speakers, but even several of the other groups can be segmented. While the United States is more homogeneous than the EU, the melting pot is not complete.

Even in China, where 1 billion people "speak Mandarin," more than ten sociolinguistic groups exist. Among the Han Chinese, many Sinitic sublanguages and dialects exist whose speakers are often unable to understand one another. These linguistic variations are related to cultural differences.

need to be translated if customers are to understand advertisements, instruction manuals, and warranties.

Translation is expensive, too. Consider some of the global organizations that include members from all around the world—where ideas rather than products are sold. The WTO spent $16 million, or 22 percent of its operating budget, in 2000 translating the documents it generated. The EU employs more than 4,000 translators and interpreters. In 1999, the EU spent about €600 million of its €85.5 billion budget (0.8 percent) for these services, and that didn't include the paper used to print the documents translated.

Never mind that Coca-Cola has to produce advertisements for its products in over 100 countries. Imagine what it must cost for the translation of technical manuals for medical equipment manufacturers such as Siemens or what SAP and Microsoft spend to produce software in different languages or the training and repair manuals that Airbus and Boeing provide to their customers around the world. It gives new meaning to the phrase *spread the word*.

Sources: Payal Sampat, "Last Words," *Worldwatch*, 2001; U.S. Census Bureau (language usage: http://www.census.gov/population/www/socdemo/lang_use.html); "Tongue-tied" *The Economist*, April 7, 2001, page 83; "Tongue-tied" *The Economist*, October 19, 2002, page 84; Mr. Robert Rowe, Translation Services, European Commission, Brussels e-mail correspondence, September 23, 2002.

Many former colonies have some linguistic unity in the language of the former colonial power, but even this is threatened in certain countries. For example, in India, Hindi is an official language along with English. Hindi has the advantage of being an Indian language but the drawback of belonging to just one segment of India's population. When it was declared an official language, riots broke out, occasioned by the other language groups.

It is said that a language defines a cultural group—that nothing distinguishes one culture from another more than language. But what does it mean when the same language is used in different countries? French, for example, is the mother tongue not only for the French, but also for many Belgians and Swiss. Spanish plays a similar role in Latin America. The anthropologist, however, stresses the spoken language as the cultural distinction. The spoken language changes more quickly than the written language and reflects the culture more directly. Although England, the United States, and Ireland use the same written English, they speak somewhat different dialects. These three cultures are separate yet related, as are the Spanish-speaking cultures of Latin America.

Even where a common language is spoken, different words signifying the same meaning are occasionally used, as are different pronunciations. In Latin America, for example, the word for *tire* is not the same as that used in other Spanish-speaking countries. In England, people say "lorry," "petrol," and "biscuits"; but in the United States, people say "truck," "gasoline," and "cookies." Incidentally, even within one country—for example, the United States, where almost everyone speaks "American" English—there are different cultural groups, or subcultures, among which the spoken language varies.

Language as a Problem

Activities such as advertising, branding, packaging, personal selling, and marketing research are highly dependent upon communication. If management is not speaking the same language as its various audiences, it is not going to enjoy much success. In each of its foreign markets, a

English in Italy

Mr. Silvio Berlusconi, the flamboyant prime minister of Italy, promised a government of three I's: Inglese, Internet, e Imprese (English, Internet, and business). In an attempt to foster two of these, biographies of Italian ministers were posted in English on the government's primary web site (http://www.governo.it). Unfortunately, they were not translated well. The Defense Minister graduated with a maximum of ballots (graduated at the top of his class). The Communication Minister was the former Undersecretary to the Inside (Undersecretary of Internal Affairs). The Technology Minister was born to

company must communicate with several audiences: its workers, its managers, its customers, its suppliers, and the government. Each of these audiences may have a distinctive communication style within the common language. The number of language areas in which a firm operates approximates the number of countries in which it sells. Any advantage gained by the fact that one language may be used in more than one country is partly offset by the fact that in many countries, more than one language is necessary.

Taiwan's garbage trucks blare English phrases as they pass through neighborhoods because the mayor, Mr. Hsu Tain-tsair, is seeking U.S. foreign investors. The mayor believes that "we'll attract more investors if the local population speaks the foreign language."[10] If an employee wants to get promoted at Matsushita Corporation (the makers of Panasonic and other global brands), he or she must pass a proficiency test in English. Toyota Motor Corporation, Komatsu Ltd. (earth-moving equipment), and NEC (computers) have also tied promotions to English-speaking abilities. The reason for this is explained by the director of human resources for Matsushita: "Japanese are insulated by their language and do not have a global mentality because of this language barrier."[11] Other companies can learn from this as well. There is an old international business joke: "What do you call someone who can speak three languages? (Answer: trilingual) What do you call someone who can speak two languages? (Answer: bilingual) What do you call someone who speaks one language? (Answer: American)" (See "Global Environment: English in Italy.")

Language diversity in world markets could be an insuperable problem if managers had to master the languages of all of their markets. Fortunately, that is not the case. To be effective, any person assigned to a foreign operation for a period of a year or more should learn the local language. However, cultural bridges are available in many markets. For example, in countries where a firm is operating through a distributor, the distributor may act as the bridge between the firm and its local market. In advertising, a firm may be able to rely on a local advertising agency. Agency personnel, like the distributor, probably speak the advertising manager's language—especially if the firm communicates principally in English. For example, the Dutch firm Philips uses English as the official company language even though it is domiciled in the Netherlands. Because of its widespread operations, the company finds English to be the most useful language for its markets. In the Chrysler/Daimler-Benz merger, American English was made the corporate language.

Lucera; conjugated; graduated in Economy near the University Mouthfuls of Milan; and in 1994, moved newly to Paris to cover loads with President of IBM Europe (was born in Lucera, is married, earned a degree in economics from the Bocconi University in Milan, and moved to Paris in 1994 to become president of IBM Europe.) All of these mistakes were attributed to the use of a computerized translation program.

There are legions of stories like this. The recommendation from experts is to use parallel translation (have two people translate the same message and compare the differences) or back-translation (translate into the target language, translate back into the original, and compare with the intended message). The advice is to focus on the intent and not to attempt a literal, or exact, word-for-word translation.

Source: Deborah Ball, "Lost in Translation: Italy's First Attempts at English Prove Less Than Meaningful," *Wall Street Journal,* December 17, 2001.

In countries where a firm has subsidiaries, the language requirement becomes even greater. Then a firm has more direct communication with its audiences. Even in this case, however, the burden is lessened because among its national managers, the firm can usually count on people of the "third culture." The expression *third culture* is used to describe nationals who have become so familiar with another culture that they become a bridge between the two. This is the best solution to both the language gap and the culture gap.

As has been suggested, there are ways to circumvent the language problem. However, language is a critical factor. It is the key to understanding and communicating with the local cultures around the world. An international firm needs language capabilities not only among its distributors and other collaborators, but also among its own personnel.

Canada provides an illustration of a situation requiring linguistic sensitivity by international firms. In labor negotiations in Quebec, General Motors helped underwrite the cost of an interpreter to provide documentation in both French and English. GM agreed to recognize the French-language version of the contract as official. Other guidelines recommended to alleviate potential tension between the two groups included (1) bilingual labeling and advertising, (2) bilingual annual reports and press releases (French in Quebec), and (3) bilingual executives for operations in Quebec.

Education

In developed nations, education usually means formal training in school. In this sense, those people without access to schools are not educated; that is, they have never been to school. However, this formal definition is too restrictive. **Education** includes the process of transmitting skills, ideas, and attitudes, as well as training, in particular disciplines. Even so-called "primitive" peoples have been educated in this broader sense. For example, regardless of formal schooling, the Bushmen of South Africa are well educated in relation to the culture in which they live.

One function of education is to transmit the existing culture and traditions to the new generation. (The role of women in Afghan society—particularly their access to formal education under Taliban rule—and the subsequent changes instituted when President Hamid Karzai was elected illustrate the role of education in the process of cultural change.) Education plays an important role in cultural change in the United States, as it does elsewhere. For example, in the past, developing nations' educational campaigns were carried out with the specific intent of improving techniques used in farming and in reducing the population explosion. In Britain, business schools were originally established to improve the performance of the economy. Hall and Petzall attribute the rapid economic development of Singapore to formal apprenticeship programs.[12]

International Differences in Education

When looking at education in foreign markets, the observer is limited primarily to information about the formal process; that is, education in schools. This is the only area for which the United Nations Educational, Scientific and Cultural Organization (UNESCO), the World Bank, and others have been able to gather data. Traditionally, literacy rates have been used to describe educational achievement; recently, however, international agencies have been measuring inputs as well as educational system outputs other than literacy. For example, the World Bank still includes adult and youth illiteracy rates in its reports. (Now it has begun measuring participation in education, which includes enrollment ratios in primary, secondary, and tertiary levels of education, and education efficiency, which includes completion rates at different levels of education and average number of years of school.) The World Bank also reports on inputs such as expenditures per student, teachers' compensation, number of faculty with appropriate qualifications, and pupil-teacher ratios. Perhaps most importantly, the goals of the World Bank have changed—from activities aimed merely at increasing literacy rates to measures designed to ensure that "all children complete a full course of primary education," a target it hopes is achieved by 2015. (See Table 3-2.)

The education information available on world markets refers primarily to national enrollments in the various levels of education—primary, secondary, and college or university. This information can give a global firm insight into the sophistication of consumers in different countries. There is also a strong correlation between educational attainment and economic development. Hanushek and Kimko argue that qualitative measures such as math and science scores on international achievement tests should also be used as indicators of human capital development and long-term economic prospects. Because U.S. students consistently score lower on these exams than students in other countries, Hanushek and Kimko warn that the United States may lose its technological edge in the future.[13]

Because only quantitative data are available, there is a danger that the qualitative aspects of education might be overlooked. Furthermore, in addition to the limitations inherent in international statistics, the problem exists of interpreting them in terms of business needs. For example, a firm's needs for technicians, marketing personnel, managers, distributors, and sales forces must be met largely from the educated population in the local economy. When hiring people, the firm is concerned not only with the level, but also with the nature of applicants' education.

Training in law, literature, or political science is probably not the most suitable education for business needs. Yet in many nations, such studies are emphasized almost to the exclusion of others more relevant to commercial and economic growth. Too often, primary education is preparation for secondary, secondary education is preparation for university, and university education is not designed to meet the needs of the economy. In many nations, university education is largely preparation for the traditional prestige occupations. Although a nation needs lawyers and philosophers, it also needs agricultural experts, engineers, managers, and technicians. The

TABLE 3-2   World Education

Country by Income Group	Primary School Teacher-Pupil Ratio	Secondary School Enrollment (%)	Adult Literacy Rate (%)	
			Male	Female
Low-Income	40	46	72	53
Lower-Middle Income	22	75	92	82
Upper-Middle Income	21	81	95	92
High Income	17	100	99	99
World Average	28	70	84	71

Notes: The teacher-pupil ratio data are for the period 2001–2002; secondary school enrollment is male and female enrollment combined for 2000-2001; literacy rates are for people over age 15 in 2002.

Sources: World Bank, *2004 World Development Indicators;* Table 2.10 Education Inputs, pages 72-75; Table 2.1 Participation in Education, pages 76-79; Table 2.13 Education Outcomes, pages 84-87; UNESCO, Institute for Statistics, July 2004.

degree to which the educational system provides for these needs is a critical determinant of the nation's ability to develop economically.

Education and International Business

The global company must also be something of an educator. The products and techniques a firm brings into a market are generally new to that market. The firm must educate consumers about the uses and benefits. Although a firm may not make use of a formal educational system, its success is constrained by that system because its ability to communicate depends in part on the educational level of its market. A firm is further concerned about the educational situation because it is a key determinant of the nature of the consumer market and the kinds of marketing personnel available. Some implications for businesses include the following:

• When consumers are largely illiterate, existing advertising programs, package labels, instructions, and warranties need to be adapted to include fewer words and more graphics and pictures.

• When women are largely excluded from formal education, advertisements, job postings, etc., may differ from those aimed at female segments in developed nations. When a firm is targeting women audiences with less education, messages need to be simple, perhaps with less text and more graphics.

• Conducting research can be difficult, both in communicating with consumers and in getting qualified researchers. If few people are able to read, written surveys would be an ineffective tool in gathering data. Personal interviews, although more costly, would tend to increase response rates and accuracy.

• Cooperation from the distribution channel depends partly on the educational attainments of members in the channel and of other partners and employees. When overall levels of education are low, finding and hiring local qualified employees for certain service or managerial positions may be difficult and very competitive. Long-term training programs and commitments to employee education may raise local operating costs.

Religion

This chapter is concerned with the cultural environment of business. You have already reviewed several aspects of culture. The material culture, language, and aesthetics are, in effect, outward manifestations of a culture. If you are to gain a full understanding of a culture, however, you must become familiar with the internal behavior that gives rise to the external manifestations. Generally, it is the **religion** of a culture that provides the best insights into this behavior. Therefore, although an international company is interested primarily in knowing *how* people behave as consumers or workers, management's task will be aided by an understanding of *why* people behave as they do.

Numerous religions exist in the world. This section presents brief overviews of animism, Hinduism, Buddhism, Islam, the Japanese following of various faiths (Shinto, Buddhism, and Confucianism), and Christianity. These religions were selected on the basis of their importance in terms of numbers of adherents and their impact on the economic behavior of their followers. Adherents to these religious beliefs account for over three-fourths of the world's population. Estimates for the major religions in 2002 were as follows: Christianity, 2.0 billion; Islam 1.3 billion; Hinduism, 900 million; and Buddhism, 360 million. There are also those people who are described as "secular" (including agnostic, atheist, and nonreligious), which includes approximately 850 million people, and followers of "Chinese Traditional Religion" (a combination of Confucianism, Buddhism, and Taoism), which has approximately 225 million adherents. The number of animists, described as various forms of primal-indigenous religions (tribal, ethnic, etc.), is common but difficult to determine—with the reported number of adherents varying from 100 to 245 million. (Most estimates are in the range of 150 million followers.)[14]

Animism or Nonliterate Religion

Animism is the term used to describe the religion of indigenous peoples. It is often defined as spirit worship, as distinguished from the worship of God or gods. Animistic beliefs have been found in all parts of the world. With the exception of revealed religion, some form of animism has preceded all historical religions. In many less developed parts of the world today, animistic ideas affect cognitive behavior.

Magic, a key element of animism, is the attempt to achieve results through the manipulation of the spirit world. It represents an unscientific approach to the physical world. When cause-and-effect relationships are not known, magic is given credit for the results. The same attitude prevails toward many modern-day products and techniques.

For example, during the senior author's years in Congo, he had an opportunity to see reactions to European products and practices that were often based on a magical interpretation. In one instance, a number of Africans affected the wearing of glasses, believing the glasses would enhance the intelligence of the wearer. Some firms that manufacture consumer goods in Africa have not hesitated to imply that their products have magical qualities. Of course, the same is sometimes true of firms elsewhere.

Other aspects of animism include ancestor worship, taboos, and fatalism. All of them tend to promote a traditionalist, status quo, backward-looking society. Because such societies are more interested in protecting their traditions than in accepting change, companies face problems when introducing new products, ideas, or methods. A firm's success in bringing change depends on how well it understands and relates to the culture and its animistic foundation.

Hinduism

There are over 900 million Hindus in the world, most of them in India. In a broad sense, about 80 percent of India's population is Hindu; but in the sense of strict adherence to the tenets of Hinduism, the number of followers is smaller. A common dictum is that Hinduism is not a religion, but a way of life. Its origins go back approximately 3,500 years. It is an ethnic, noncreedal religion. A Hindu is born, not made; so a person cannot become a Hindu or convert to Hinduism, although he or she may become a Buddhist, for example. Modern Hinduism is a combination of ancient philosophies and customs; animistic beliefs; legends; and more recently, Western influences, including Christianity. A strength of Hinduism has been its ability to absorb ideas from outside; Hinduism tends to assimilate rather than exclude.

Despite this openness, many in India are unhappy about marriages between Christians or Muslims and Hindus because it is viewed as a threat or dilution of Hindutva (Hindu-ness) of the culture. Much violence has occurred between the Hindu and Muslim populations, with one instance of over 500 people killed in Gujarat in early 2002.[15] Because Hinduism is an ethnic religion, many of its doctrines apply only to the Indian situation. However, they are crucial in understanding India and its people.

Sikhism is a religion also practiced in India that represents a combined form of Hinduism and Islam, featuring a much-debated aspect, the **caste** system. While the Indian government officially abolished it over a half century ago and instituted quotas and job-preferment policies, there are still examples of separate *gurdwaras* (houses of worship) for Sikhs and the *Dalit*, or scheduled caste (formerly called "untouchables"), some of whom are converting to Buddhism, Christianity, and Islam to escape the caste system.[16, 17]

Another element—and a strength of Hinduism—is *baradari*, or the "joint family." After marriage, the bride goes to the groom's home. After several marriages in the family, there is a large joint family for which the father or grandfather is chief authority. In turn, the older women have power over the younger. The elders give advice and consent in family council. The Indian grows up thinking and acting in terms of the joint family. If a member goes abroad to a university, the joint family may raise the funds. In turn, that member is expected to remember the family if he or she is successful. *Baradari* is aimed at preserving the family.

Veneration of the cow is perhaps the best-known Hindu custom: Gandhi called this the distinguishing mark of the Hindu. Hindu worship of the cow involves protecting it, but eating the products of the cow is also considered a means for purification. Another element of traditional Hinduism is the restriction of women, following the belief that to be born a woman is a sign of sin in a former life. Some marriages are still arranged by relatives. Traditionally, a man may remarry if widowed, but a woman may not. This attitude toward women makes it all the more remarkable that India placed a woman, Indira Gandhi, in its highest office.

Nirvana is another important concept, one that Hinduism shares with Buddhism. This topic is discussed in the following section.

Buddhism

Buddhism springs from Hinduism, originating about 2,600 years ago. Buddhism has approximately 360 million followers, mostly in South and East Asia from India to Japan. There are, however, small Buddhist societies in Europe and America. Buddhism is, to some extent, a reformation of Hinduism. It did not abolish caste, but declared that Buddhists were released from caste restrictions. This openness to all classes and both sexes was one reason for Buddhism's growth. While accepting the philosophical insights of Hinduism, Buddhism tried to avoid its dogma and ceremony, stressing tolerance and spiritual equality.

At the heart of Buddhism are the Four Noble Truths:

1. The Noble Truth of Suffering states that suffering is omnipresent and part of the very nature of life.

2. The Noble Truth of the Cause of Suffering cites the cause of suffering to be desire; that is, desire for possessions and selfish enjoyment of any kind.

3. The Noble Truth of the Cessation of Suffering states that suffering ceases when desire ceases.

4. The Noble Truth of the Eight-Fold Path that leads to the Cessation of Suffering offers the means to achieve cessation of desire. This is also known as the Middle Way because it avoids the two extremes of self-indulgence and self-mortification. The eight-fold path includes (1) the right views, (2) the right desires, (3) the right speech, (4) the right conduct, (5) the right occupation, (6) the right effort, (7) the right awareness, and (8) the right contemplation. This path, though simple to state, is a demanding ethical system. Nirvana is the reward for those who are able to stay on the path throughout their lifetime or, more probably, lifetimes.

Nirvana is the ultimate goal of the Hindu and Buddhist. It represents the extinction of all cravings and the final release from suffering. To the extent that such an ideal reflects the thinking of the mass of the people, the society's values would be considered antithetical to such goals as acquisition, achievement, and affluence. This is an obvious constraint on business. Of course, not all Buddhists are so nonmaterialistic.

Islam

Islam dates from the seventh century AD. It has over 900 million adherents, mostly in Africa, Asia, and the Middle East. Most of the world of Islam is found across the northern half of Africa, the Middle East, and throughout parts of Asia to the Philippines. Islam is usually associated with Arabs and the Middle East, but non-Arab Muslims outnumber Arab Muslims by almost three to one. The nations with the largest Muslim populations are all outside the Middle East. Indonesia, Pakistan, Bangladesh, and India all have over 100 million Muslims. Although there are two major groups in Islam (Sunni, 85 percent, and Shi'ite, 15 percent), they are similar enough on economic issues to permit identification of the following elements of interest to firms.

Muslim theology, *Tawhid*, defines all that one should *believe*; whereas the law, Shari'a, prescribes everything one should *do*. The *Koran (Qur'an)* is accepted as the ultimate guide. Anything not mentioned in the *Koran* is likely to be rejected by the faithful. Introducing new products and techniques can be difficult in such an environment. An important element of Muslim belief is that everything that happens, good or evil, proceeds directly from the Divine Will and is already irrevocably recorded on the Preserved Tablet. This belief tends to restrict attempts to bring about change in Muslim countries; to attempt change may be a rejection of what Allah has ordained. The name *Islam* is the infinitive of the Arabic verb to *submit*. *Muslim* is the present participle of the same verb; that is, a Muslim is one submitting to the will of Allah.

TABLE 3-3 Islam and Business

Islamic Element	Marketing Implication
1. Daily prayers	Work schedules; hours of peak/off-peak customer traffic; timing of sales calls
2. Prohibition on usury and consumption of pork and alcohol	Prohibition of or difficulty in selling certain products (insurance, banking and financial services); processes used in manufacturing of food and other products for human consumption or use; inappropriateness of layaway and other credit tools
3. Zakat (mandatory alms)	Spending patterns; attitude toward charity; social consciousness; excessive profits used for charitable purposes
4. Religious holidays (e.g., Ramadan) and other religious or sacred periods	Sales and special promotions; lavish gift periods; food distribution and restaurant hours; Muslim "weekend" is Thursday and Friday.
5. Public separation of sexes	Access to female customers; direct marketing to women; mixed-gender focus groups

The Five Pillars of Islam, or the duties of a Muslim, include (1) the recital of the creed, (2) prayer, (3) fasting, (4) almsgiving, and (5) the pilgrimage. The creed is brief: There is no God but God, and Mohammed is the Prophet of God. The Muslim must pray five times daily at stated hours. During the month of Ramadan, Muslims are required to fast from dawn to sunset—no food, no drink, no smoking. Because the Muslim year is lunar, Ramadan sometimes falls in midsummer, when the long days and intense heat make abstinence a severe test. The fast is meant to develop self-control and sympathy for the poor. During Ramadan, work output falls off markedly, which is attributable as much to the Muslim's loss of sleep (from the many late-night feasts and celebrations) as to the rigors of fasting. The average family actually spends more money on the food consumed at night during Ramadan than on the food consumed by day in the other months. Other spending rises also. Spending during Ramadan has been said to equal six months of normal spending, corresponding to the Christmas season elsewhere. Sales increases of 20 to 40 percent of furniture, cars, jewelry and other large or expensive items are common. One firm stated that between 35 and 40 percent of all auto sales take place during Ramadan.[18]

By almsgiving, the Muslim shares with the poor. It is an individual responsibility, and there are both required alms (*zakat*) and freewill gifts. The pilgrimage to Mecca is a well-known aspect of Islam. The thousands who gather in Mecca each year return home with a greater sense of the international solidarity of Islam. Spending for the pilgrimage is a special form of consumption directly associated with religious behavior.

There is a relationship between religion and culture, as is discussed here; but there is also a relationship between culture and laws, which will be discussed later in the text. Behavior deemed acceptable or not acceptable is often reflected in the laws of a nation or group of people. The tie between religion and law is perhaps most clear in Islam. With respect to business, Muslims are not allowed to consume pork or alcohol. Furthermore, people are not allowed to invest in firms whose primary business involves alcohol, defense, entertainment, gambling, or the manufacture of or processes using pork products. Under shariah law, investors are not allowed to hold any stake in conventional banks or insurance companies because these institutions are believed to engage in usurious practices that are illegal. Even the ability to own stock or shares in companies with large amounts of debt or that make annual interest payments is

Shinto in Japan

Shinto rituals play an important role in Japanese culture, as demonstrated by the naming ceremonies attached to the new Princess Aiko born in December 2001, the first child of Prince Naruhito and Princess Masako. Mother and father did not get to name her. Rather, the child was taken to a Shinto shrine, where she was bathed while two scholars played wooden stringed instruments to ward off evil spirits and the household's chief of protocol recited from the eighth-century Chronicles of Japan. Naruhito's father, Akihito, the emperor of Japan, then revealed the child's name—the little girl was to be called Princess Toshi during her youth. The following year was filled with many other ceremonies, including one to ensure that she had enough to eat throughout her lifetime.

Shinto temples contain many shrines devoted to various deities (*kami*) from various religions, such as the Kangiten or Shoten. These shrines are used to intone marital harmony and fruitful marriages, which is believed to have been adapted and adopted from the Hindu deity Ganesha. Thousands of Shinto shrines are

being called into question. While there is some tolerance for investing in these companies, devout Muslims point out that this is a breach of shariah rules against usury. Some implications of Islam are noted in Table 3-3.

Japan: Shinto, Buddhism, and Confucianism

Japan is a homogeneous culture with a composite religious tradition. The original national religion is Shinto, "the way of the gods." In the seventh century, however, Japan came under the influence of China and imported an eclectic Buddhism mingled with Confucianism. In 604, Prince Shotoku issued a moral code based on the teachings of both Confucius and Gautama Buddha. Its 17 articles still form the basis of Japanese behavior. The adoption of the religions from China was only after the authorities decided they would not conflict with Shinto. Traditional Shinto contains elements of ancestor and nature worship; state or modern Shinto added political and patriotic elements. Official estimates of 90 million Japanese Buddhists are somewhat misleading. An old refrain is that Japanese are born as Shinto, get married as Christians, and die as Buddhists.[19] Depending on whom and how you ask, figures on followers of Buddhism in Japan vary widely, from 20 to 90 percent of the total Japanese population of 127 million people. (The high figures are based on birth records and on Buddhism being the "preferred religion" in a response to research questions posed to Japanese; the low figures incorporate the response of up to 75 percent of Japanese who claim to be nonreligious or follow no religion.)

Among the more important aspects of modern Shinto are (1) reverence for the divine origin of the Japanese people and (2) reverence for the Japanese nation and the imperial family as head of that nation. The term *modern* Shinto is used because when the imperial powers were restored in 1868, state Shinto became a patriotic cult, whereas sectarian Shinto was purely religious. Of course, sectarian Shinto, through ancestor worship, also affects Japanese attitudes. In many houses, there is a god-shelf (*kamidana*) on which the spirits of the family ancestors are found throughout Japan. Perhaps the largest and most elaborate ceremonies take place at New Year, when as many as 70 million people seek good health, good fortune, and other blessings for the coming year.

Kirigami are white paper cutouts of cranes and other auspicious forms meant to connect humans with the Shinto gods. Although not as popular an art form as it once was, *kirigami* can still be found in household shrines. One of the more important duties for the imperial family is presiding over the annual *Niiname-sai* (Festival for the New Tasting) Shinto rite in late November. This ceremony involves an offering of rice to ensure a good harvest and has, over the years, become a part of other traditions, including the grand opening of new businesses. Also, many businesses have a shrine to a deity whose customary symbol is a pair of foxes, and Japanese companies generally choose a patron god or goddess.

Other signs reflect the importance of the Shinto religion and the unique way in which the Japanese incorporate other beliefs. The new luxury hotel Nikko Kumamoto in Kyushu, on the southern island of Japan, includes a Northern Italian-style chapel for couples who want to get married under the sun or stars, as well as a Shinto shrine for Shinto-style weddings.

Sources: "Cutting Out a Spiritual Tradition," *Daily Yomiuri*, January 5, 2002; "JAWOC Looks to Cure Transportation Headache," Global Newswire, February 2, 2002; "Princess Aiko Taken to Imperial Palace Buildings," Japan Economic Newswire, March 12, 2002; "Nikko Hotels International to Open Hotel in Kumamoto, Japan," PR Newswire, May 29, 2002.

thought to dwell and watch over the affairs of the family. Reverence is paid to them, and the sense of the ancestors' spirit is a bulwark of the family's authority over the individual. (See "Global Environment: Shinto in Japan.")

The impact of modern Shinto on Japanese life is reflected in an aggressive patriotism. The mobilization of the Japanese of World War II and their behavior during the war are examples. One longtime observer said, "Nationalism is the Japanese religion." More recently, the economic performance of Japan is due, at least in part, to the patriotic attitude of those working in the economic enterprise. The family spirit is carried over to the firm, which has meant greater cooperation and productivity. Some Eastern religions seek virtue through passivity. Shinto, by contrast, stresses the search for progress through creative activity. Japan's economic performance clearly seems to follow the Shinto path. The aggressive Japanese attitude is reflected in the company song of Kyocera, a Japanese firm.

As the sun rises brilliantly in the sky,
revealing the size of the mountain, the market, oh, this is our goal.
With the highest degree of mission in our heart, we serve our industry,
Meeting the strictest degree of customer requirement.
We are the leader in this industry and our future path, Is ever so bright and satisfying.

Christianity

Christianity is a major religion worldwide, and little time will be spent describing its general teachings. The emphasis here is the impact of the different Christian religious groups (Roman Catholic and Protestant) on economic attitudes and behavior. Two studies have dealt with this subject: Max Weber's *The Protestant Ethic and the Spirit of Capitalism* and R. H. Tawney's *Religion and the Rise of Capitalism*. The Eastern Orthodox churches are not discussed in this section, but their impact on economic attitudes is similar to that of Catholicism.

Roman Catholic Christianity traditionally has emphasized the Church and the sacraments as the principal elements of religion and the way to God. The Church and its priests are intermediaries between God and human beings; and apart from the Church, there is no salvation. Another element is the distinction between the members of religious orders and the laity, with different standards of conduct applied to each. An implicit difference exists between the secular and the religious life.

The Protestant Reformation, especially Calvinism, made some critical changes in emphasis but retained agreement with Catholicism on most traditional Christian doctrine. The Protestants, however, stressed that the Church, its sacraments, and its clergy were not essential to salvation: "Salvation is by faith alone." The result of this was a downgrading of the role of the Church and a consequent upgrading of the role of the individual. Salvation became more an individual matter.

Another change by the reformers was the elimination of the distinction between secular and religious life. Luther said that all of life was a *Beruf*, a "calling," and even the performance of tasks considered to be secular was a religious obligation. Calvin carried this further by emphasizing the need to glorify God through one's calling. Whereas works were necessary to salvation in Catholicism, works were evidence of salvation in Calvinism.

Hard work was enjoined to glorify God, achievement was the evidence of hard work, and thrift was necessary because the produced wealth was not to be used selfishly. Accumulation of wealth, capital formation, and the desire for greater production became Christian duty. The Protestant Reformation thus led to greater emphasis on individualism and action (hard work), as contrasted with the more ritualistic and contemplative approach of Catholicism.

Although it is useful to recognize the separate thrust of Roman Catholic and Protestant Christianity, it is also important to note the various roles Christianity generally plays in different nations. Some nations reflect varying mixtures of Catholic and Protestant, and the resulting ethic may be some combination of both doctrines. Of course, within Christianity (as with Buddhism, Hinduism, and Islam), wide variations exist in the degree to which adherents follow the teachings. In all groups, segments range from fundamentalist to conservative to casual.

Religion and the Economy

In discussing various religions, the text suggested some economic implications that are elaborated on here. Religion has a major impact on attitudes toward economic matters. The following section, "Attitudes and Values," will discuss the different attitudes religion may inspire. Besides attitudes, however, religion may affect the economy more directly, as in the following examples.

- Religious holidays vary greatly among countries—not only from Christian to Muslim, but also from one Christian country to another. In general, Sundays are a religious holiday where Christianity is an important religion. In the Muslim world, however, the entire month of Ramadan is a religious holiday for practical purposes. A firm must see that local work schedules and other programs take into account local holidays, just as American firms plan for a big season at Christmas.

- Consumption patterns may be affected by religious requirements or taboos. Fish on Friday for Catholics used to be a classic example. Taboos against beef for Hindus or pork for Muslims and Jews are other examples. The Muslim prohibition against alcohol has been a boon to companies such as Coca-Cola. Heineken and other brewers sell a nonalcoholic beer in Saudi Arabia. On the other hand, dairy products find favor among Hindus, many of whom are vegetarians.

- The economic role of women varies from culture to culture, and religious beliefs are an important cause. Women may be restricted in their capacity as consumers, as workers, or as respondents in a marketing study. These differences may require major adjustments in the approach of a management conditioned in the U.S. market.

  Procter & Gamble's products are used mainly by women. When the company wanted to conduct a focus group in Saudi Arabia, however, it could not induce women to participate. Instead, it used the husbands and brothers of women for the focus group.

- The caste system restricts participation in the economy. A company may feel the effects not only in its staffing practices (especially its sales force), but also in its distribution and promotional programs because it must deal with the market segments set up by the caste system.

- The Hindu joint family has economic effects. Nepotism is characteristic of the family business. Staffing is based more on considerations of family rank than on any other criteria. Furthermore, consumer decision making and consumption in the joint family may differ from those in the U.S. family, requiring an adapted strategy. Pooled income in the joint family may lead to different purchase patterns.

- Religious institutions themselves may play a role in economic matters. The Church, or any organized religious group, may block the introduction of new products or techniques if it sees the innovation as a threat. On the other hand, the same product or technique can be more effectively introduced if the religious organization sees it as a benefit. The United States has seen the growing role of religious groups. "Global Environment: Businesses Get Religion" provides some examples from other countries.

- Religious divisions in a country can pose problems for management. A firm may find that it is dealing with different markets. In Northern Ireland, there is strong Catholic-Protestant hostility. In India, Muslim-Hindu clashes led to the formation of the separate nation of Pakistan; but the animosity continues. In the Netherlands, major Catholic and Protestant groups have their own political parties and newspapers. Such religious divisions can cause difficulty in staffing an operation or in distributing and promoting a product. Religious differences may indicate buyer segments that require separate strategies.

Clearly, an international firm must be sensitive to religious differences in its foreign markets and be willing to make adaptations. To cite one example, a firm that is building a plant abroad might plan the date and method of opening and dedicating the building to reflect the local religious situation. In particular, a firm's advertising, packaging, and personal selling practices need to take local religious sensitivities into account.

Businesses Get Religion

The U.S. Post Office sells stamps for Christmas, Chanukah, Kwanza, and a host of other holidays and events. On September 1, 2001, it released the first Islam-themed American stamp. The new first-class postage EID stamp commemorates the end of Ramadan and the end of the pilgrimage to Mecca.

In Moscow, the Holy Land Exhibition Company is planning a $38 million religious theme park that is expected to open in 2005. Visitors will be able to dine on "Last Supper" meals, visit a replica of the Church of the Nativity in Bethlehem, or see a miniature version of the Red Sea. This park is based on the Scriptorium, a $25 million Christian Foundation theme park that opened in Florida in 2002. Included in the park is a re-creation of ancient Jerusalem, animatronic robots that "talk" about the Bible, and a fiber-optic finger of God that writes the Ten Commandments on a rock.

Coca-Cola and PepsiCo held special promotions for Ramadan in Turkey. PepsiCo offered free 600-milliliter bottles of soda with the purchase of larger 2.5-liter bottles so customers could "get through *iftar* and *sahur* in one purchase." (*Iftar* is the meal at the start of the day before the fast begins, while *sahur* is taken in the evening to end the fast.) Coca-Cola offered special commemorative Ramadan plates for consumers

Attitudes and Values

People's attitudes and values help determine what they think is right or appropriate, what is important, and what is desirable. The attitudes that relate to business will be presented. It is important to consider attitudes and values because, as someone said, "People act on them." Douglas North, the Nobel Prize-winning economist said, "People act on the basis of ideologies and religious views." People have attitudes and values about work, money, time, family, age, men, women, and a host of other topics that have an impact on business. The list is long and goes beyond the scope of this book; only a few will be highlighted here.

Business Activities

Ever since Aristotle, selling activities have failed to gain high social approval. The degree of disapproval, however, varies from country to country. In countries where business is looked upon unfavorably (a wicked or immoral profession), business activities are likely to be neglected and underdeveloped. Capable, talented people are not drawn into business. Often these activities are left to a special class or to expatriates. One is reminded of the medieval banking role filled by Jews or the merchant role of the Chinese in Southeast Asia. In any case, depending on a country's attitude toward business, an international firm may have problems with personnel, distribution channels, and other aspects of its marketing program.

Wealth, Material Gain, and Acquisition

The United States has been called the "affluent society," the "achieving society," and the "acquisitive society." Those somewhat synonymous expressions reflect motivating values in society. In who sent in bottle caps.

McDonald's agreed to pay $12 million to settle a class-action suit filed by Hindus, Sikhs, and Jews for not disclosing that beef flavorings were used in the McDonald's French fry recipe. American Muslims also want a portion of the funds since the use of beef likely violated the halal food code (specifies how the beef is to be prepared).

There are banks, mortgage companies, and other financial institutions in Muslim nations, despite the prohibition on earnings through interest payments (*riba*). If someone wants to purchase a car, a typical deal might go something like this: The person buying the car would go to the local Jaguar dealer and pick out the model and features. Then, through a transaction referred to as *murabaha*, the buyer would ask his bank to purchase the car (for, say, $50,000), which would then resell the car to the buyer for $55,000, paid in monthly installments.

There are many other examples of how businesses have attempted to address religious-based opportunities, as well as many cases where businesses have failed to do so. Further Readings, at the end of this chapter, includes recommendations that will enlighten and entertain.

Sources: "Banking on Allah," *Fortune*, Volume 145, Issue, 12, June 10, 2002, pages 154-164; "Holy Robots Give Bible Buzz in Pond's 8m Theme Park," *Sunday Times*, August 18, 2002, page 18; "Muslims Making Push to Join McDonald's Fries Settlement," *Dallas Morning News*, July 5, 2002; "Sale of Islamic-Themed Stamps Shouldn't Be Affected by September 11 Attacks," *Patriot News*, November 27, 2001; "This Europe: Russia Drops Disney for Biblical Dancers," *The Independent*, July 16, 2002, page 10.

the United States, wealth and acquisition are often considered signs of success and achievement and are given social approval. In a Buddhist or Hindu society, where nirvana or "wantlessness" is an ideal, people may not be so motivated to produce and consume. Businesses obviously prefer to operate in an acquisitive society. However, as a result of rising expectations around the world, national differences in attitudes toward acquisition seem to be lessening. For example, Buddhist Thailand is proving to be a profitable market for many consumer goods firms.

Work may be an end unto itself for some people, and one's position with a particular organization may be an important measure of the person's social status. For others, family, leisure time, and friends take precedence over money and position. German and French workers have gone on strike, even rioted over plans to extend their workweek beyond 35 hours, to cut paid vacation time, or to raise the age that one becomes qualified for retirement benefits.[20]

Change

When a company enters a foreign market, it brings change by introducing new ways of doing things and new products. In general, North Americans accept change easily. The word *new* has a favorable connotation and facilitates change when used to describe techniques and products. Many societies are more tradition-oriented, however, revering their ancestors and traditional ways of consuming.

Business as an agent of change has a different task in traditional societies. Rather than emphasizing what is new and different about a product, the businessperson might relate the product to traditional values, perhaps noting that it is a better way of solving a consumer problem. In seeking acceptance of its new product, a firm might try to get at least a negative clearance—that is, no objection—from local religious leaders or other opinion leaders. Any product must first meet a market need. Beyond that, however, to be accepted, the product must also fit in with the overall value system.

The Campbell Soup Company met this kind of obstacle when it introduced its canned soups into Italy. In conducting research, it received an overwhelmingly negative response to the question, would you marry a user of prepared soups? Campbell had to adjust its questionnaire accordingly.

Risk Taking

Consumers take risks when they try a new product. Will the product do what they expect it to do? Will purchasing or using the product prejudice their standing or image with their peers? Intermediaries handling the untried product may also face risks beyond those associated with their regular line. In a conservative society, there is a greater reluctance to take such risks. There-fore, a firm must seek to reduce the risk perceived by customers or distributors in trying a new product. In part, this can be accomplished through education; guarantees, consignment selling, and other techniques can also be used.

Risk avoidance is a major factor in the low number of online shoppers. While the number of users is growing exponentially, a recent survey found that one-third of Internet users did not shop online because they did not want to risk providing credit card information over the Inter-net. One-quarter of those surveyed believed it was safer to purchase at a retail shop. The number of Internet users who are also online shoppers is highest among developed nations (generally between 15 and 25 percent of users purchase something online) and lowest among developing nations (generally below 5 percent of users shop online).[21] Recent research indicates that this dif-fers from one culture to another[22], but this may also be a reflection of different use patterns (that is, some people use the Internet for entertainment or research, while others use it for shopping).

Consumer Behavior

The attitudes just discussed are relevant to understanding consumer behavior in the markets of the world. International managers must have such an understanding to develop effective pro-grams. Because of the impossibility of gaining intimate knowledge of a great number of mar-kets, they must rely not only on company research, but also on help from others. Those who can assist managers in understanding local attitudes and behavior include personnel in the firm's subsidiary, the distributor, and the advertising agency. Although a firm is interested in changing attitudes, most generally it has to adapt to them. As Confucius said, "It is easier to move moun-tains than to change the minds of men."

Social Organization

The **social organization** of a group of people helps define their roles and the expectations they place upon themselves and others in the group. Concepts such as family vary from group to group, which becomes evident when talking about these concepts to people from other cultures. The nature of people's friendships with others—how quickly the relationships develop, how the friendships are nurtured, and how long they last—also reflect on the social organization within the culture or group. Social organization is formally defined in the government and the laws that

TABLE 3-4	Average Number of Occupants per Household				
Saudi Arabia	8.21	Nigeria	5.23	Czech Rep.	2.71
Gabon	6.87	Mexico	4.43	Japan	2.63
Pakistan	7.59	Turkey	3.97	United States	2.63
India	5.94	Ireland	3.12	Sweden	1.99

Source: *International Marketing Data and Statistics,* 2004; *European Marketing Data and Statistics,* 2003, Euromonitor.

proscribe certain behavior among people. The nature of social organization and the impact on business is discussed next.

Kinship

Kinship includes the social organization or structure of a group—the way people relate to other people. This differs somewhat from society to society. The primary kind of social organization is based on kinship. In the United States, the key unit is the family, which traditionally included only the father, the mother, and the unmarried children in the household. Of course, the definition is changing, as is reflected in each census. The family unit elsewhere is often larger, including more relatives. The large joint family of Hinduism was discussed previously. A large extended family is also common in many other less developed nations. Those who call themselves brothers in Congo, for example, include cousins and uncles.

In developing countries, the extended family fulfills several social and economic roles. The family unit is not prescribed or defined by a specific religious restriction, as does the *baradari* of Hinduism. The extended family provides mutual protection, psychological support, and economic insurance or social security for its members. In a world of tribal warfare and primitive agriculture, this support was invaluable. The extended family, still significant in many parts of the world, means that consumption decision making takes place in a larger unit and in different ways. Pooled resources, for instance, may allow larger purchases. (For this reason, per capita income may be a misleading guide to market potential.) The researcher may find it difficult to determine the relevant consuming unit for some goods. Is it a household or a family? How many members are there?

As Table 3-4 demonstrates, the size of households varies greatly around the world. An interesting comparison is the United States and Japan. The United States has slightly more than twice the population of Japan but 25 times the land mass. (The United States has approximately 293 million people and covers 9.6 million square kilometers, while Japan has 128 million people and covers an area about the size of California—378 thousand square kilometers.) With relatively less land but so many people, it is reasonable to expect that the number of occupants per dwelling is higher in Japan than in the United States.[23]

Common Territory

In the United States, **common territory** can be a neighborhood, a suburb, or a city. In many countries of Asia and Africa, common territory is the tribal grouping. In many countries, the tribe is often the largest effective unit because the various tribes do not voluntarily recognize the central government. Unfortunately, nationalism has not generally replaced tribalism. Tribalism

Teens – Truly Global Consumers

"Cultural convergence continues to transform the marketplace as borrowing among cultures accelerates." This is the opening sentence in a recent article comparing teenagers in the United States and Korea. The authors look at many attitudes of young people in those two nations and come to the same conclusion that many others have. The findings of many cross-cultural studies are that young people, because of their exposure to new ideas and to one another through television and the Internet (as well as their willingness to take risks and try new things), are similar in those respects that are not confined to a particular geographic area or culture. That is, certain characteristics, beliefs, attitudes, and behaviors are common to teenagers; and because of that fact, firms can get teenagers' attention in similar ways. Something else businesses do not miss is the fact that teenagers are more affluent than in the past. Those factors are also highlighted by Parmar,

and religious or ethnic divisions often lead to bloody conflict, shown by such examples as Congo, Ireland, Israel and Palestine, Pakistan, the Philippines, Rwanda, and Sudan. Even in Europe, the Scots and the Welsh are not happy about being under British rule. For businesses, in many countries, groupings based on common territory may be a clue to market segmentation.

Special Interest Group

A third kind of social grouping, the **special interest group** or association, may be religious, occupational, recreational, or political. Special interest groups can also be useful in identifying different market segments. For example, in the United States, the American Association of Retired Persons (AARP), the Sierra Club, and the National Rifle Association (NRA) represent market segments for some firms.

Other Kinds of Social Organization

Some kinds of social organization cut across the three categories just discussed. One is **caste** or **class groupings.** These may be detailed and rigid, as in the Hindu caste system; or they may be loose and flexible, as in U.S. social classes. The United States has a relatively open society, but there is still concern about social standing and status symbols. While social class is more (or less) important and rigid in comparing countries, each country has its own social and ethnic groupings that are important for its society and the economy. These groupings usually mean that some groups are discriminated against and others are favored. A firm needs to know this social organization because it will affect the company's overall strategies. Different groups may require different marketing strategies, for example.

Other groupings based on age occur especially in affluent industrialized nations. Senior citizens usually live as separate economic units with their own needs and motivations. They are a major market segment in industrialized countries. And although teenagers do not commonly live apart from their families, they still compose a significant economic force to be reckoned with. (See "Global Environment: Teens—Truly Global Consumers.")

who refers to a "homogeneous global youth customer segment."

Look in teens' bedrooms in cities around the world—Des Moines, Los Angeles, Jakarta, Mexico City, Paris, Santiago, Singapore, and Tokyo. You will find an amazing similarity of items: Nikes and Reeboks, Levis, MP3 players, PCs, and NBA jackets. Teens everywhere watch MTV and the World Cup, and most of them shop in malls that look amazingly alike.

These are promising developments for international firms making consumer goods. Caution is necessary, however, before firms implement a one-size-fits-all strategy. Many seasoned observers note that cultural differences persist. For example, one survey found that American teenagers prefer to eat on the run, while teens elsewhere prefer meals they can savor. The same survey showed that American teenagers use fewer features on their cell phones than their European and Japanese counterparts. So despite similarities among teenagers around the world, firms are unable to use identical practices to reach teenagers in all markets.

Sources: Mark Mitchell, Barbara Hastings, and Faruk Tanyel, "Generational Comparison: Xers in the United States and Korea," *International Journal of Commerce and Management*, 2001, Volume 11, Number 3/4, pages 35-53; Arundhati Parmar, "Global Youth United; Homogeneous Group Prime Target for U.S. Marketers," *Marketing News*, October 28, 2002, pages 1, 49.

As noted in the discussion of the extended family, much less separation between age groups exists in less developed areas. Generally, strong family integration occurs at all age levels, as well as a preponderant influence of age and seniority, which is in contrast to the youth *motif* prevalent in the United States. Of course, Generation X and baby boomers are important age groupings in the United States.

A final aspect of social organization concerns the role of women in the economy. Women seldom enjoy parity with men as participants in the economy; and their participation is related to the economic development of nations—the poorer the nation, the fewer women seen in jobs outside the home. The extent to which women participate in the money economy affects their role as consumers and consumption influencers. Even developed countries exhibit differences in attitudes toward female employment. For example, significant differences in female employment exist between the United States, several European countries, and Japan. These differences are reflected both in household income levels and in consumption patterns.

In spite of the constraints noted, the economic role of women is undergoing notable change in many countries. Many believe this change is occurring too slowly, however. Some of the differences in women's role in society are highlighted in Case 3.2 at the end of the chapter.

Cultural Variables and Management

Culture is an integrated pattern of behavior shared by people in a society. This chapter has presented several dimensions of culture. These cultural variables are important to international firms. What firms are able to do in selling to a particular society and what they want to do are shaped by these variables. In other words, international business is a function of culture. (See "Global Environment: Culture Is Dynamic—Something Businesses Need to Remember.")

Culture is Dynamic –
Something Businesses Need to Remember

People's behavior changes in response to changes in the environment, which emphasizes the dynamic nature of culture. In certain situations, these statements may seem obvious. Fashion changes from year to year, and popular songs change from week to week. Foods eaten today might have seemed strange a decade or two ago, and the language includes new words to describe new things in the environment. The dynamic nature of culture is not always noticeable, though. If firms fail to recognize these changes, they may lose opportunities—or worse.

Demand for kitchen appliances is changing in Europe; people want larger refrigerators. What's behind this change? Europeans are working longer hours; and they're moving farther from cities and their jobs, which requires a longer commute. With fewer hours in the week for shopping, people are purchasing larger quantities of food. Because Europeans generally have small families and prefer bottled water, they don't need or want in-the-door water and ice dispensers commonly found on American refrigerators. Consequently, appliance manufacturers have to adapt designs, rather than send the large models common in the U.S. market.

Summary

Culture is an integrated pattern of behavior and the distinctive way of life of a people. The various dimensions of culture influence a firm's behavior and strategic plans.

A country's worker behavior and consumer behavior are shaped by the technology and material culture. The kinds of products a firm can sell and its distribution and promotional programs are constrained by the country's infrastructure. This includes not only the country's transportation and communications systems, but also things such as the availability of media and advertising agencies.

Communication is a major part of what a firm does, so it must communicate in the languages of its markets. This may require adaptation in packaging and labeling, advertising and personal selling, and training programs. Fortunately, national employees, distributors, and local agencies can help with the language barrier.

Each society has its own ideas about beauty and good taste—its own aesthetics. When a firm is considering the design and color of its products and packaging, is advertising, and is selecting music and brand names, it must try to appeal to those tastes.

Differences in literacy and consumer skills, as a result of a country's educational system, determine what adjustments in products and communications are necessary. The quality of support services in a country is also affected by the output of the educational system there.

Religion is a major determinant of attitudes and behavior in a society. Each country has its own religious profile; but major world religions such as Buddhism, Christianity, Hinduism, Islam, and secular (agnostic, animism, atheist, and nonreligious) include approximately 85 percent of the world's population. Each of those religions has its own impact on the attitudes and behaviors of consumers who follow the religion. For example, a traditional animist might be

The picture of the aging is also changing, thanks in part to global companies. No longer the toothless, doddering, rocking chair-bound image of yesterday, older citizens are traveling, dancing, rock climbing, and even sky diving. People who retire at sixty or sixty-five can expect to live another quarter century or more. In 2002, more than 23 million Japanese, or 18.5 percent of the population, was over sixty-five. In the United States, Americans over fifty own 75 percent of all financial assets, control over 80 percent of money invested in savings and loan associations, and own 67 percent of all shares sold in the stock market. Because older people are one of the largest, fastest-growing populations that control a lot of wealth, firms are making more adaptations to products to cater to this group. Japan is leading the way with universal design products—goods that are easy to use, not just for older people, but for all age groups. Examples include OXO Good Grips utensils, Fiskars Soft Touch scissors, and the NTT (Nippon Telephone & Telegraph) Raku Raku ("easy easy") cellular phone with large key pad. Ford Motor company has its designers dress in "'third-age suits" that add age to the wearer by stiffening their joints and making their waists bigger; this is done so they can design car seats that are easier to get in and out of.

Sources: "Over 60 and Overlooked," *The Economist,* August 10, 2002, pages 50-51; Allyson Stewart-Allen, "U.S. Kitchen Goods Makers Find Euro Market Worth Courting," *Marketing News,* American Marketing Association, September 24, 2001, page 8.

reluctant to accept new products and a devout Buddhist who is seeking an absence of desire, or a state of wantlessness, is not a strong potential consumer. Other religious impacts on business include religious holidays and product taboos, the role of women in the economy and society, and the caste system. Finally, religious divisions in a country may indicate market segments that require different programs and sales forces. Even Japan's composite religious tradition has affected the economy of that country.

Attitudes and values greatly affect consumer behavior. Attitudes about wealth and acquisition, change, and risk taking are especially important for the global firm that may be introducing innovation to a society in the form of new products—and new lifestyles.

Social organization refers to the way people relate to one another and to the various groups and divisions in a society. The size and nature of the family, tribalism and ethnic divisions, and different roles for women or age groups (such as senior citizens) can all influence a program.

Questions and Research

3.1 What is culture?

3.2 Give examples of cultural concepts used in U.S. business.

3.3 How can a nation's technology and material culture affect a firm's business in that country?

3.4 Discuss the role of the international business as an agent of cultural change. Is this role legitimate? Explain.

3.5 Why are international businesses interested in the linguistic situation in their markets?

3.6 How can an international firm deal with language challenges in its foreign markets?

3.7 How can the aesthetic ideas and values of a society influence a firm's sales in that country?

3.8 How is international business constrained by the educational level in a market?

3.9 What, if anything, does a country's religious situation have to do with a firm's operations in that country?

3.10 Discuss the implications of the following religious phenomena: (a) religious holidays, (b) taboos, (c) religious institutions (church and clergy), and (d) nirvana.

3.11 Identify some constraints in business to a traditional Muslim society.

3.12 What is the significance of these aspects of social organization: (a) the extended family, (b) tribalism, and (c) the role of women in the economy?

3.13 Convenience Foods Corp. has asked you to do a cultural analysis of a South American country in which it is considering operations. How would you go about completing this task?

Endnotes

1 European Marketing Data and Statistics, 2003; 38th Edition, Euromonitor, Tables 13 and 14.

2 World Bank, *2002 World Development Indicators* (http://www.worldbank.org/data/countrydata/countrydata.html), Tables 1.1 and 1.6.

3 Bodley, John H. *Cultural Anthropology: Tribes, States, and the Global System.* Mountain View, CA: Mayfield, 1994.

4 International Marketing Data and Statistics, 2004; 28th Edition, Euromonitor, Table 4.2, pages 167-169.

5 United States input-output tables are available on the Bureau of Economic Analysis web site (http://www.bea.gov/bea/uguide.htm#_1_15).

6 Kirpalani, Manjeet and Pete Engardio. "25 Ideas for a Changing World," *Business Week*, August 26, 2002, Issue 3796, page 112.

7 *Wall Street Journal*, September 24, 1998, B1.

8 "English Is Not the Net's Only Language," *Global Reach*, NAU Internet Surveys, May 24, 2002; "Non-English Speakers Dominant Online," *Global Reach*, October 31, 2002.

9 "Europemedia: Multinationals Fail European Internet Users," NAU Internet Surveys, April 5, 2002.

10 Dean, Jason. "Throwaway Phrases: Taiwan's New Way to Pick Up English," *Wall Street Journal*, September 25, 2002, page 1.

11 Voight, Kevin. "Japanese Firms Want English Competency," *Wall Street Journal*, June 11, 2001.

12 Hall, Kenneth and Stanley Petzall. "The Making of Technicians for a High-Technology Future: The Singapore Apprentice," *Journal of Asian Business*, Volume 16, Number 4, 2000, pages 39-56.

13 Hanushek, Eric A. and Dennis D. Kimko. "Schooling, Labor-Force Quality, and the Growth of Nations," *American Economic Review*, 2000, Volume 90, Issue 5, pages 1184-1208.

14 Adherents.com, Major Religions of the World Ranked by Number of Adherents (http://www.adherents.com/Religions_By_Adherents.html); accessed September 3, 2004.

15 "Religious Violence in India Ebbs After 4 Days of Killing," *Wall Street Journal,* March 4, 2002, Section A, page 12.

16 "Caste in India, Still Untouchable," *The Economist,* June 16, 2001, Volume 359, Issue 8226, page 42.

17 "Quitting Hinduism," *Christianity Today,* December 9, 2002, pages 22-23.

18 "Oman's Auto Distributors Gearing Up for Ramadan," *Times of Oman,* September 1, 2002.

19 "Japan's Mori Adds Religion Card to Hand," *Wall Street Journal,* June 23, 2000, page A16.

20 "Longer Workweeks Likely in Europe," *USA Today,* Tuesday, July 27, 2004, page 4B.

21 "Cyber-Nervous," *Marketing News,* August 19, 2002, page 3.

22 "Information Sensitivity and E-Commerce: A Cross-National Study of Japan, the U.S., and France," *2001 AMA Educators' Proceedings: Enhancing Knowledge Development in Marketing,* Volume 12, pages 255-264.

23 U.S. CIA Factbook, 2004 (http://www.odci.gov/cia/publications/factbook); accessed January 19, 2005.

Further Readings

Ahn, Se Young and Jeon, Bang Nam. "The Association of Individual Attitudes toward Foreign Firms: A Korean Case Study," *Journal of Asian Business,* Volume 17, Number 1, 2001, pages 45-68.

Axtell, Roger E. *Dos and Taboos of Humor Around the World,* 1999, New York: John Wiley & Sons.

Carvalho, Sergio W. "Assessing the Role of Nationalistic Feelings in Consumer Attitudes toward Foreign Products: An Exploratory Study in Brazil," *2002 AMA Educators' Proceedings: Enhancing Knowledge Development in Marketing,* Volume 13, pages 261-262.

Chaney, Lillian H. and Jeanette S. Martin. *Intercultural Business Communication,* 2d Edition, 2000, Upper Saddle River, NJ: Prentice Hall.

Chen, Ming-Jer. *Inside Chinese Business: A Guide for Managers World-Wide,* 2001, Boston, MA: Harvard Business School Press.

Dicle, I. Atilla and Ulku Dicle. "A Cross-Cultural Study of Managerial Work Values in Singapore," *Journal of Asia-Pacific Business,* Volume 3, Issue 1, 2001, pages 63-82.

Doran, Kathleen Brewer. "Lessons Learned in Cross-Cultural Research of Chinese and North American Consumers," *Journal of Business Research,* October 2002, Volume 55, Number 10, pages 823-829.

Ezzell, Carol. "Clocking Cultures," *Scientific American,* September 2002, Volume 287, Issue 3, pages 74-75 (http://proquest.umi.com/pqdweb?Did=000000148764391&Fmt=3&Deli=1&Mtd=1&Idx=1&Sid=1&RQT=309).

"Fast-food Firms Hope to Get More Bucks with Clucks (Chicken Takes Increasing Portion of Menu Space)," *USA Today,* July 28, 2004, page B1.

Ferraro, Gary P. *The Cultural Dimensions of International Business,* 4th Edition, 2002, Upper Saddle River, NJ: Prentice Hall.

Hewlett, Sylvia Ann. *Creating a Life: Professional Women and the Quest for Children,* 2002, New York: Hyperion/Talk Miramax Books.

Hofstede, Geert. *Culture's Consequences: Comparing Values, Behaviors, Institutions, and Organizations Across Nations,* 2d Edition, 2001, Thousand Oaks, CA: Sage Publications.

Luna, David and Susan Forquer Gupia. "An Integrative Framework for Cross-Cultural Consumer Behavior," *International Marketing Review,* Volume 18, Issue 1, 2001, pages 45-69.

Neelankavil, James P., Anil Mathur, and Yong Zhang. "Determinants of Managerial Performance: A Cross-Cultural Comparison of the Perceptions of Middle-Level Managers in Four Countries," *Journal of International Business Studies,* Volume 31, Issue 1, 2000, pages 121-140.

Raymond, Mary Anne, John D. Mittelstaedt, and Christopher D. Hopkins. "Perceptions of Consumer Needs Levels and Implications for Standardization—Adaptation Decisions in Korea," *2002 AMA Educators' Proceedings: Enhancing Knowledge Development in Marketing*, Volume 13, pages 376-377.

Trofimon, Yaroslaw. "Faith at War,", 2005, Henry Holt, New York, NY.

Recommended Web Sites

Women Watch: Information and Resources on Gender Equality and Empowerment of Women (http://www.un.org/womenwatch); for gender-specific statistics, see the UN Statistics Division—statistics and indicators on women and men (http://unstats.un.org/unsd/demographic/products/indwm); United Nations Statistics Division.

What Is Culture? (http://www.wsu.edu:8001/vcwsu/commons/topics/culture/culture-index.html); created by faculty and staff at Washington State University.

Statistical tables and culture indicators (http://www.unesco.org/culture/worldreport/html_eng/tables2.shtml) and Youth and Culture (http://www.unesco.org/culture/youth); United Nations Educational, Scientific and Cultural Organization (UNESCO).

YourDictionary.com (http://www.yourdictionary.com); translate words and phrases, play games (crossword puzzles in English, French, German, and Spanish), write your name in hieroglyphs, and learn about dead and dying languages.

World Religions: Adherents.com (http://www.adherents.com); includes brief explanations of religions and statistics on adherents.

Case 3.1

Bottled Spirits

The Hopi are the westernmost tribe of Pueblo Indians, located in northeastern Arizona. There are fewer than 10,000 of them. They typically live in terraced pueblo structures of stone and adobe and are clustered into a number of small, independent towns. Like all Pueblo Indians, the Hopi are peaceful, monogamous, diligent, self-controlled, and very religious.

The most conservative tribe in the Southwest, the Hopi want no tourists to photograph, sketch, or record their dances. They do, however, allow visitors to observe their ceremonies by watching masked Kachina dancers impersonate Hopi gods. The Hopi also invite tourists into their homes to buy Kachina dolls and Hopi pottery.

Kachinas are the Hopi Indians' holy spirits. They are sometimes personified by masked dancers and sometimes represented by wooden dolls. There are roughly 250 different Kachinas. Although the Hopi will sell Kachina dolls to tourists, they are sensitive to how others may use the Kachina costume or idea. For example, in 1987, Miss New Mexico won the costume competition in the Miss USA competition, wearing a Kachina costume. Hopi religious leaders complained that that use was sacrilegious.

In another incident, the Hopi protested when Kentucky's Ezra Brooks distillery began selling its bourbon in bottles shaped like Kachina dolls. As a Christmas promotion, the Brooks distillery had planned to distribute 5,000 of the Kachina doll bottles in Arizona and the Southwest. It had already shipped 2,000 bottles when it learned of the Hopi complaint.

Reflecting the Hopis' anger, a tribal leader asked, "How would a Catholic feel about putting whiskey in a statue of Mary?" The Hopi not only complained, but also received assistance from the Arizona senator to have production halted.

Questions and Research

1   What should the distillery do? What courses of action might it take?
2   Propose and defend your solution to this problem.

Case 3.2

The Role of Women in Society

Look around the classroom or think about the people in your class. If you are in the United States, approximately half of the students are probably women. Did you ever consider why? People's attitudes and expectations about family and friends are a part of culture. So are their attitudes and expectations about the role of men and women in society. What is of added interest is that these attitudes are not the same from culture to culture, and they change over time.

In the United States, dual-income households and single parenthood are not new or extraordinary; but in other nations, those situations would be unexpected. Consider Japan, where, on average, women are paid less for performing the same jobs as men. In fact, in 2001, women earned only 65 percent of what their male counterparts earned. That may not surprise you, but the expectations of Japanese over the age of forty might. The typical family in Japan consists of a working father, a stay-at-home mother, and one child. One transplanted American working in Japan said that the culture is like the 1950s in the United States—something out of the old television show of that era, *Leave It to Beaver*. Until recently, women were expected to work until they found a husband, then devote their lives to raising a child and overseeing other domestic responsibilities. Once the child was grown, some women would return to the workforce, but only for part-time or temporary work, often cleaning others' homes, caring for children, or teaching.

This is changing, though, in part by decree. In June 1999, the Japanese government enacted a law designed to create an environment in which men and women are treated equally and participate jointly in all aspects of society. Attitudes are changing, but very slowly. Younger men want to participate in the raising of their children and want to spend more time at home than in the past. Younger women want to finish college, have a career, and get married later. Miyuki Yasuo, a public relations and advertising manager for L'Oreal, started using a house cleaning service to reduce the stress associated with caring for her home and child, in addition to pursuing her career. Her housekeeper is paid ¥100,000 per month (approximately $850) to do the shopping, prepare meals, clean the house, and pick up Mr. and Mrs. Yasuo's child from child care every evening.

Men and women over forty hold more traditional Japanese values. In addition, many Japanese businesses are still slow to reward women by promotion or pay; nor do they allow husbands more time off to be with their family and help raise their children. Yet more Japanese households are calling on housekeeping services to help care for their homes and children, creating a whole new industry in Japan. While some see the change as beneficial—leading to equal treatment of women and men, with a side benefit of helping create jobs and improving the economy of Japan—others see this as cause for alarm. As more women work and put off having a family, there will be fewer children to take care of an aging population, which has been the traditional method of caring for the elderly.

The role of women in society and business is important because interactions between men and women are affected by expectations about what is and is not acceptable behavior. From one culture to the next, differences exist about expected gender roles; and people working in these environments must have some appreciation for or understanding of the differences if they are to succeed in relationships with coworkers. Sensitivity to this situation will affect how a person is perceived as a manager, negotiator, business partner, and colleague.

One way of determining how cultures view women and their role in society is to review statistics on education and the distribution of men and women in the workforce. Generally, the more even the distribution between men and women in work and education, the more likely it is that women are treated equally in business. Table 3-5 shows illiteracy rates (the lower the rate, the more educated the group) as well as distribution of the labor force.

Table 3-5   Women in Society

				Percentile, 2002							
	Literacy Rate				Distribution of Labor Force						
Country or Region	Illiterate (ages 15-24)		Illiterate (ages > 24)		Wage & Salaried[a]		Self-Employed[b]		Family Worker[c]		
	W	M	W	M	W	M	W	M	W	M	
Africa											
Benin	73	45	88	67	3	7	64	54	29	32	
Egypt	46	29	79	50	35	55	12	29	36	10	
Kenya	14	8	54	26	12	32	17	19	56	30	
Namibia	10	14	35	27	36	60	20	16	28	10	
South Africa	10	9	…	…	70	78	5	8	…	…	
Latin America											
Brazil	10	15	25	22	64	61	22	29	10	6	
Columbia	4	5	12	11	70	61	28	38	2	1	
Honduras	20	23	43	40	48	46	42	41	11	12	
Mexico	5	4	20	13	58	58	23	32	19	10	
Venezuela	4	5	14	11	70	58	23	34	2	1	

Table 3-5   Women in Society (continued)

	Literacy Rate				Distribution of Labor Force					
					Percentile, 2002					

Country or Region	Illiterate (ages 15-24) W	M	Illiterate (ages > 24) W	M	Wage & Salaried[a] W	M	Self-Employed[b] W	M	Family Worker[c] W	M
North America										
Canada	...	...	...	...	90	88	9	12	1	0
United States	...	...	...	...	93	91	6	10	0	0
Asia										
Bangladesh	62	41	...	...	9	15	8	43	77	17
Indonesia	5	3	34	16	24	32	29	52	45	14
Malaysia	5	4	31	15	72	71	14	25	15	4
Philippines	3	4	9	7	41	42	30	40	19	10
Turkey	12	3	40	13	25	49	8	39	67	12
Europe										
Finland	...	...	...	...	90	81	10	18	1	1
Greece	<1	1	8	3	58	53	19	42	24	5
Ireland	...	...	...	...	91	72	8	27	2	1
Poland	<1	<1	...	...	74	70	20	26	7	4
Portugal	1	1	19	11	73	71	26	28	2	1

Sources: The UN Statistics Division—statistics and indicators on women and men (http://unstats.un.org/unsd/demographic/products/indwm/table5e.htm); World Bank Data Query (http://devdata.worldbank.org/data-query); accessed September 3, 2004.

a Wage and salaried workers are those who work for a private or public entity for which the workers/employees receive a salary.

b Self-employed are those who operate their own business.

c Family workers are those who are unpaid employees of a family-run enterprise of another person in the same household.

... indicates that data is not available; but in all cases, except for illiteracy rates associated with people over twenty-four in South Africa (around 14 percent for men and women over fifteen years old according to the World Bank), all are near zero.

Questions and Research

1 Review the figures on illiteracy rates in Table 3-5 and discuss the disparity between the rates for men and women. The rates seem most different among developing nations. Why?

2 A large disparity in pay still exists between men and women, even in industrialized nations. Countries such as Japan and the United States have laws about equal pay for equal work. What activities can the people of a nation engage in to reduce the inequity more quickly? What roles can schools and companies play?

3 Men and women are depicted differently in advertisements that are shown on television and that appear in magazines. Identify some stereotypes from these ads

Sources: Brian Bremner, "Japan Overlooks the Power of Its Women at Its Own Peril," *Business Week*, November 1, 1999, Business Week Online; William Hall, "The Status of Women in Japan," J@pan.inc, December 2000; "More Working Women Employing Housekeepers," *Financial Times*, June 15, 2002.

Case 3.3

AFLAC

AFLAC became the official name of the American Family Life Assurance Company in 1989. It entered the Japanese market in 1975 and soon became one of the most successful foreign companies in any industry operating in Japan. By 1982, 1 in 20 Japanese households was an AFLAC policyholder. By 1988, the ratio was 1 in 6. And by 1995, about 1 in 4 Japanese households had an AFLAC policy, which is still true today. AFLAC is the second largest insurance company in Japan and the number one foreign life insurance company. It is the second most profitable foreign company operating in an industry in Japan. In 2001, Japan accounted for 78 percent of the total company sales of $9.6 billion.

Founded in the United States in 1955, AFLAC specializes in cancer insurance (about 54 percent of its policies are in this field). Although AFLAC was the second foreign insurance company to enter the Japanese market, it was the first company, either Japanese or foreign, to introduce a policy for cancer protection in Japan. Two Japanese firms also issued independent health insurance coverage, but they had a much smaller number of policies outstanding.

Cancer insurance is a controversial product in the United States because consumer advocates argue that disease-specific policies are an inefficient, costly form of coverage. Bans on the sale of these policies were only lifted in Connecticut and New York in the late 1990s. Attitudes in Japan are somewhat different. When AFLAC hired Nomura Research to see what its customers wanted, the answer was more coverage. On the government side, company president John Amos had developed a strong relationship with the powerful Japanese bureaucracy. Indeed, in 1988, John Amos was named by *Forbes* magazine as the insurance industry's most innovative executive for his success in penetrating the Japanese market. (The company has won many other prestigious awards since then, too.)

Japan is one of the largest insurance markets in the world. About 90 percent of Japanese households carry life insurance with a relative contract value much higher than that in either Europe or the United States. Japan also has rather comprehensive national health insurance; so private company plans supplement the government program in such areas as private rooms, costly major disease, and lost income. AFLAC's cancer insurance sales grew rapidly, in part because cancer is the major cause of death in Japan and because cancer is usually associated with costly treatment and long stays in the hospital. Thus, the Japanese perceive cancer as the most threatening and the most expensive disease they can encounter, wanting to provide for it as best they can.

Most Japanese insurance companies use homemakers as a part-time sales force for door-to-door sales. Amos came up with another idea—use retired Japanese workers to sell to their former colleagues. "Their retirement benefits weren't good enough to last them forever, so AFLAC became a little like their social security," he recalled. AFLAC uses different methods for distributing its products, which also helps to reduce operating costs.

Japanese corporations agreed to encourage their workers to buy the insurance and to deduct the premiums from their monthly paychecks. Retired executives from each corporation are often enlisted to do the actual selling. Over 17,000 such payroll groups have been established. Over 92 percent of the corporations listed on the Tokyo Stock Exchange use AFLAC's payroll deduction plan, although less than half of their employees subscribe to it. Even Nippon Life and Dai-ichi Mutual Life, two of Japan's largest life insurance companies, offer AFLAC's cancer policies to their employees.

Another part of AFLAC's approach is "bank set sales." With this program, a bank automatically deducts the annual premium from the accumulated interest on a policyholder's savings account and transfers it to AFLAC's account. Some 250 banks are participating in this program, serving about 500,000 policyholders. The Japanese have a favorable attitude toward saving, and this program appeals to their orientation to save and to their strong desire for insurance coverage. Because the banks enjoy a good reputation, AFLAC's insurance program gains further credibility by this association with them.

AFLAC has not relied on advertising in Japan, depending instead on its strong sales network and full-time sales force. Because the company innovated cancer insurance and because of the company's different approach, however, it received a lot of publicity in various media.

In 1994, AFLAC expanded its product line with Super Care, a policy for nursing home care, and Super Cancer, an upgrade on its original policy. Super Cancer allows for a cash payment when cancer is first diagnosed. Nursing home costs are another major concern in Japan because the population has a very long life expectancy.

One indicator of AFLAC's success is a first-year renewal rate of 90 percent—and 94 percent after the second year. Both of those figures are higher than in either the Japanese or U.S. life insurance industries. AFLAC views those figures as corroboration of its product and overall strategy.

Some changes are taking place. In 2000, sales of accident/disability policies surpassed those for cancer policies in the United States. As a result of an aggressive program, the CEO, Dan Amos, is on his way to meeting his goal of increasing U.S. sales as a percentage of total sales. (In 2001, 70 percent of the firm's earnings and 80 percent of its assets were Japanese.) Deregulation in the Japanese insurance industry has led AFLAC to form an alliance with the largest Japanese insurer, Dai-ichi Mutual Life; and noncancer products now account for 60 percent of new sales. AFLAC also uses new technologies, such as processing claims on the Internet, to increase profitability. It costs the firm about $72 to write and process new policies, versus a cost of $120 for Japanese insurance firms, giving AFLAC a big advantage over its competitors.

Questions and Research

1 Describe AFLAC's program in Japan—product policy, pricing, promotion, and distribution.
2 Explain how this program relates to the Japanese culture and economy and why it is so successful.

To view the "Duck Campaign" commercials (in English), which are being used to promote the debut of AFLAC's first accident policy in Japan, access http://www.aflac.com/about_us/corp_overview_commercials.asp.

Sources: AFLAC corporate web site (http://www.aflac.com); Hoover's Company Profile Database, 2002; "How AFLAC Laid a Golden Egg in Japan," *Business Week,* November 11, 2002, page 56.

CHAPTER 4

The Political-Legal Environment

Learning Objectives

The political environment of international business has three dimensions: the host country, home country, and international environments. The many laws affecting international business fall into three categories: U.S. law, international law, and foreign law.

The main goals of this chapter are to

1 Discuss concepts critical to nations, such as sovereignty, security, and prestige, in order to understand political risk.

2 Describe the role of firms in the political and legal environment—how firms are shaped by it and how firms shape the laws and politics of a nation.

3 Identify the areas of the home country environment that affect a firm's international business.

4 Explain how U.S. export controls, antitrust laws, and tax laws affect the feasibility and profitability of a U.S. firm's global business.

5 Discuss the effect of international organizations such as the IMF and the WTO and regional groups such as the EU on the international legal environment.

6 Describe international conventions designed to protect intellectual property.

The politics and the laws of a nation obviously influence the global business. This chapter examines the nature of the political-legal environment and its impact on business.

The Political Environment

The **political environment** of international business includes any national or international political factor that can affect its operations. A factor is political when it derives from the government sector. The political environment comprises three dimensions: the host country environment, the international environment, and the home country environment. Surveys have shown that dealing with problems in the political arena is the number one challenge facing international managers and occupies more of their time than any other management function. Yet international managers' concerns are different from those of political scientists. Managers are concerned primarily about political risk—the possibility of any government action adversely (or favorably) affecting their operations.

Host Country Political Environment

By definition, an international firm is a guest, a foreigner in all of its markets abroad. Therefore, international managers are especially concerned with nationalism and dealings with governments in host countries.

HOST COUNTRY NATIONAL INTERESTS

One way to gain an understanding of the situation in a foreign market is to see how compatible a firm's activities are with the interests of the host country. Although each country has its own set of national goals, most countries share many common objectives. Nationalism and patriotism refer to citizens' feelings about their country and its interests. Such feelings exist in every country. The celebration of a major holiday in recognition of a country's birthday and its achievement of independence or nationhood reinforce the sense of national identity and nationalism.

All countries want to maintain and enhance their national sovereignty. Foreign firms, individually or collectively, may be perceived as a threat to that sovereignty. The larger and more numerous the foreign firms, the more likely they are to be perceived as a threat—or at least an irritant. In times of turmoil, foreign firms and foreign embassies may be targets.

Countries want to protect their national security. Although a foreign firm is not a military threat as such, it may be considered as potentially prejudicial to national security. Governments generally prohibit foreign firms from involvement in "sensitive" industries such as defense, communications, and perhaps energy and natural resources. For example, when Libya nationalized the service stations of foreign oil companies, the reason it gave was that this commodity was too important to be in the hands of foreigners. When a firm is from a country deemed unfriendly to the host country, the firm may have difficulty operating or may even be denied admission.

Countries are also concerned about their national prestige. They establish national airlines and send their best athletes to the Olympics as ways of gaining international recognition. Economically, they may foster certain industries for the same reason. Foreign firms may be prevented from entering those industries or from acquiring a national firm in a certain industry. Many countries seek "national solutions" to help troubled companies retain what are perceived to be national champions. International firms need to be sensitive to these issues and must be careful not to be too "foreign." This includes their advertising and branding policies as well as ownership and staffing. Establishing local R&D would be perceived favorably in this context.

All countries want to enhance economic welfare. Generally, this means increasing employment and income in the country. Foreign firms contribute by generating employment. They can contribute further by using local suppliers and having local content in their products. They can contribute further still by exporting from the country and generating foreign exchange. They can contribute in a different way by supplying products, services, and/or training that enhance productivity.

HOST COUNTRY CONTROLS

Host countries don't depend entirely on the goodwill of foreign firms to help them achieve their national goals. To try to ensure desirable behavior by foreign firms—and to prevent undesirable behavior—governments use a variety of tools, some of which are explained here.

Entry restrictions. If allowed to enter a country, a firm may be restricted in terms of industries it can enter. A firm may be prohibited from acquiring a national firm. It may not be allowed 100 percent ownership, instead being required to enter a joint venture with a national firm. It may be restricted as to the products it can sell. For example, the United Kingdom, Australia, Brazil, and Canada are debating whether to reduce foreign ownership restrictions on media, while the post-9/11 United States is not likely to loosen (and may even tighten) current ownership regulations. (A domestically-owned free press is viewed as critical for imparting an unbiased view of local and global events.)

Price controls. Once in a country, a foreign firm may encounter a variety of restrictions. One of the most common is price controls, which, in inflationary economies, can severely limit profitability. Instead of reducing the dosage they are supposed to take or foregoing needed medications altogether, U.S. citizens (particularly seniors) are going to Canada by the busloads for their medications and ordering them from foreign sources via the Internet to take advantage of price-controlled pharmaceuticals. Companies selling drugs in the United States argue that if price controls are imposed in the United States, they would have to reduce R&D budgets for new drugs.

Quotas and tariffs. A country's quotas and tariffs may limit a firm's ability to import equipment, components, and products, forcing a higher level of local procurement than the firm may want.

Exchange control. Many countries run chronic deficits in their balance of payments and are short of foreign exchange. They ration its use according to their priorities. Foreign firms may be low on that priority list and may have difficulty getting foreign exchange for needed imports or profit repatriation. Ballooning foreign debt and an inflation rate of 200 percent in 2002 led Zimbabwe President Mugabe to centralize all foreign exchange transactions and force exporters to surrender all hard foreign currencies in return for the official rate of 55 $Zimbabwe for 1 $US (versus 600 $Z to the $US on parallel black market rates).[1]

(Forced) asset transfer. This can take the form of confiscation (government seizure of assets with no remuneration), expropriation (seizure with some compensation, though typically less than fair market value or a firm's valuation), or nationalization (seizure of entire industries, such as banking and railroad, regardless of nationality). (Other forms of asset transfer typically target non-native firms and owners.) Domestication, another form of asset transfer, generally takes

Terrorism—Taking Its Toll

Terrorism takes a terrible toll, not just because of the death and destruction, which is horrific, but also because of the loss of a sense of security that people everywhere feel. Examples include the killing of the Olympic athletes in Munich in 1972; the embassy bombings and other attacks in Africa in 1998 (nearly 6,000 dead); the attacks on the eastern United States on September 11, 2001, when approximately 3,000 people were killed; the bombing of a Balinese nightclub that resulted in nearly 300 casualties in October 2002; and the hostage taking in a Moscow school in September 2004 that resulted in over 300 deaths, many of whom were children. The locations of these events; the nationalities, ages, and occupations of the victims; and the reasons cited for the attacks clearly show that no one is safe—whether going to work, visiting attractions, sightseeing, or simply relaxing. As horrific as these events were, they provide only some understanding of terrorism.

Unfortunately, acts of terrorism are an everyday occurrence. According to the U.S. State Department, between 1999 and 2003, there were 1,589 separate terrorist attacks, resulting in 15,301 casualties. Most of the attacks took place in Latin America (581, or over 30 percent during the five-year period). Casualties have

place over a longer period of time and is often a planned part of an investment—when a firm wants to transfer ownership to locals to increase their stake, thereby increasing local interest in protecting its assets.

Fortunately, expropriation, confiscation, and nationalization are occurring less often as developing countries begin to see FDI as desirable. From a peak of 83 cases in 1975, the number declined as the 1980s progressed, with only one case in 1985. It is a rare phenomenon today. In fact, many governments are going through privatization of key industries, which is a transfer of state-owned property into private hands.

This decline does not mean that expropriation or nationalization should not be a concern to investors. There are still many examples of government-enforced transfer of assets of both individuals' and companies' investments and holdings. Some experts argue that this downward trend of expropriation can be reversed quickly and easily. (See, for example, Comeaux and Kinsella in "Further Readings" at the end of this chapter.) Reasons provided by governments for these asset transfers include protection of its citizens against terrorism (where assets may be frozen or confiscated), restitution for former human rights violations (farm property seizure and redistribution in Zimbabwe and gold mine ownership in South Africa), and the potential of nationalization to protect vital industries such as banking (Japan) and utilities (England).

Host country controls take many forms. Future regulations will likely focus on the protection of individuals and national security, protection of privacy rights, corporate ethical behavior, and environmental protection. These are complicated issues that will lead to different, often conflicting laws. Mexico's "opt-in" program is one example of a privacy rights law. In Mexico, direct marketers are required to purchase a list of people who have expressed an interest in receiving direct mail. There are also the European Data Protection Directive and the U.S. anti-spam initiatives.[2]

risen sharply in Middle East terrorist attacks (from 31 in 1999 to 1,823 in 2003), but the number of casualties is historically highest in Asia (nearly 5,000 in the last five years). In comparison, over the same five years, North America experienced six attacks; and all 4,465 casualties occurred in 2001. Those numbers don't tell the whole story. The many attacks and few casualties in Latin America are the result of the kidnapping and ransom of business executives, government officials, and others, which is quite different from the embassy bombings in Kenya and the attacks on the United States in 2001.

While most attacks and casualties are a result of bombings, the State Department also tracks hijacking, firebombing, armed attacks, kidnapping, and other forms of terrorism. In spite of heightened security and other antiterrorism efforts, the ability of terrorists to acquire the finances and weapons needed to carry out these tactics is proving to be more sophisticated. This means that the number and severity of attacks in terms of lives and financial impact will not likely abate in the near future.

Why should businesses be concerned? Of the total number of facilities struck by terrorist attacks each year between 1999 and 2003, 62 percent were against business.

Note: The data do not include deaths of soldiers and others involved in fighting terrorism in Afghanistan, Iran, or elsewhere.

Source: U.S. Department of State, *Patterns of Global Terrorism*, 2003 (http://www.state.gov/s/ct/rls/pgtrpt/2003).

Increasingly, individuals are being held liable for their own and for their company's actions. Ignorance is not bliss, and it is no longer accepted as a defense by many courts. As the officers of Enron, Arthur Andersen, Tyco, WorldCom, and a host of others discovered, the penalties can be severe. Prosecution can be long-sought, as in the ongoing case of India versus Warren Andersen (Union Carbide's chair at the time of the Bhopal disaster in 1984); and no one is immune from investigation or above scrutiny, as Martha Stewart (ImClone stock sale) and the President of the United States, George W. Bush, discovered (Harken Energy stock sale).

POLITICAL RISK ASSESSMENT

In a matter of hours, some form of political unrest (Nigeria), a short statement ("We have a viable nuclear weapons program."—North Korea), or an act of terrorism (a bomb exploding in a Bali nightclub) can alter the relationship between nations. Such events underscore the importance of continuous monitoring of host country political environments because they can change rapidly. Terrorism occurs worldwide and, alarmingly, with increasingly devastating results. (See "Global Environment: Terrorism—Taking Its Toll.") A change in leadership, whether through coup, appointment, or election, likely means a change in regulations, many of which have an impact on business.

A firm must develop political and diplomatic skills in-house but may also use consultants who have expertise with particular countries. The U.S. Department of Commerce Commercial Services branch provides useful information and has a staff of country-specific advisers. Some private firms provide evaluations about the political risk environment of specific countries. These services are moderate in cost in some cases, but, depending on coverage, may cost several thousand dollars a year. Firms use different methods and come up with somewhat different ratings of a country's political risk, although many ratings are comparable. Table 4-1 provides information on one firm's country risk service. A recent article questions the accuracy of country risk assessment measures, though.[3]

In its own study of the political environment, a firm can include a preliminary analysis of its political vulnerability in a particular host country. Elements in such an analysis may include external and company factors, which are described in the sections that follow.

External Factors

Political risk is also affected by factors beyond a company's control:

Firm's home country. A firm is usually better accepted in a country that has good relations with the firm's home country.

Product or industry. Sensitivity of the industry is an important consideration. Generally, raw materials, public utilities, communications, pharmaceuticals, and defense-related products are most sensitive.

Size and location of operations. The larger the foreign firm, the more threatening it is perceived to be. This is especially true when the firm has large facilities and is located in a prominent urban area, such as the capital, which serves as a constant reminder of the foreign presence.

Visibility of the firm. The greater the visibility of the foreign firm, the greater its vulnerability. Visibility is a function of several things, including the size and location of the firm's operations in the country and the nature of the firm's products. Consumer goods are more visible than industrial goods. Finished goods are more visible than components or inputs that are hidden in the final product. Heavy advertisers are more visible than nonadvertisers. International brands are more provocative than localized brands.

Host country political situation. The political situation can affect a firm. The company should evaluate a country's political risk.

Company Factors

The risk factors listed here are more controllable, since firms are the decision makers.

Company behavior. Each firm develops some record of corporate citizenship based on its practices. Some firms are more sensitive and responsive to the situation in the host country than others. Goodwill in this area is a valuable asset.

Contributions of the firm to the host country. Many of these contributions are objective and quantifiable. How much employment has been generated? How much tax has been paid? How many exports has the firm generated? What new resources or skills has the firm brought in?

Localization of operations. Generally, the more localized a firm's operations, the more acceptable the firm is to the host country. There are several dimensions to localization, including having local equity, hiring local managers and technical staff, using local content in the products (including local suppliers of goods and services, for example), developing local products, and using local brand names.

Subsidiary dependence. This factor somewhat contradicts the preceding point. The more a firm's local operation depends on the parent company, the less vulnerable it is. If a firm cannot function as a separate, self-contained unit but is dependent on the parent for critical resources and/or for markets, it will be seen as a less rewarding takeover target.

Political monitoring and analysis are continuing tasks for a firm. A firm must use the information that these analyses provide to manage its political relations. Table 4-2 suggests some approaches to managing potential political risk, both before and after entering a country.

TABLE 4-1   The Economic Intelligence Unit (EIU) Country Risk Service

Category of Risk and Description

Political risk—The factors in this category relate to the threat of war, social unrest, disorderly transfers of power, political violence, international disputes, regime changes, and institutional ineffectiveness, but also include the quality of the bureaucracy, the transparency and fairness of the political system, and levels of corruption and crime in the country in question.

Economic policy risk—Open economies with low inflation and low fiscal deficits are rated more favorably. Among the criteria considered are monetary policy, fiscal policy, exchange-rate policy, and trade and regulatory policies.

Economic structure risk—Measures include economic variables central to solvency. Among the subcategories of risk are growth and savings, the current account, and debt structure.

Liquidity risk—This risk measure is indicative of potential imbalances between resources and obligations that could result in disruption of the financial markets. Among the factors considered are the direction of reserves, import cover, M2/reserves, the degree of a country's dependence on portfolio inflows, and the size of a country's direct investment inflows.

Currency risk—A score and ratings are derived to assess the risk of devaluation against the dollar of 20 percent or more in real terms over the forecast period.

Sovereign debt risk—A score and ratings are developed to assess the risk of a buildup in arrears of principal and/or interest on foreign-currency debt that are the direct obligation of the sovereign or are guaranteed by the sovereign.

Banking sector risk—A score and ratings are used to assess the risk of a buildup in arrears of principal and/or interest on foreign-currency debt that are the obligation of the country's private banking institutions.

Notes: EIU assesses four types of general political and macroeconomic risk (political risk, economic policy risk, economic structure risk, and liquidity risk) independently of their association with a particular investment vehicle. Each risk is given a letter grade. These factors are then used to compile an overall score and rating for the country. EIU also evaluates risk exposure associated with investing in particular types of financial instruments; namely, specific investment risk. This includes risk associated with taking on foreign-exchange exposure against the dollar, foreign-currency loans to sovereigns, and foreign-currency loans to banks.

Source: *Country Risk Service, April Handbook, 2002*; Economist Intelligence Unit, Ltd., pages 10–13 (http://www.eiu.com).

TABLE 4-2   Managing Political Risk

Pre-entry Planning

1. Perform research; assess potential risks.

2. Avoid threatening countries.

3. Negotiate with host government. (Include planned domestication.)

4. Purchase insurance—government agencies such as OPIC (Overseas Private Investment Corp.) and MIGA (Multilateral Investment Guarantee Agency), as well as private providers.

5. Adjust entry method.

6. Use local capital.

Post-entry Planning

1. Have a monitoring system.

2. Develop a corporate communications program.

3. Develop local stakeholders (employees, suppliers, customers).

4. Have appropriate national executives and an appropriate advisory board.

5. Change operations over time as perceived host country cost-benefit ratio changes; for example, new products and processes, more local equity and management, new exports, and local R&D.

6. Have contingency plans.

Government: Friend or Foe?

National leaders and lawmakers believe that trade is good for the economy and that exports mean more jobs and a better chance of getting re-elected. The U.S. government has various initiatives and programs to encourage exports, such as the Gold Key Service provided by the Commercial Service of the U.S. Department of Commerce. Trade missions are a common component of trade promotion, and they often lead to positive results. An aerospace trade mission to Vietnam in the fall of 2002 led by the Department of Commerce included Boeing and a dozen other manufacturers. Potential deals from meetings with Vietnamese firms were worth billions over the next few years.

Export-promoting activities are undertaken by state and local development offices as well. Denver, Colorado, opened an office in Shanghai and sponsored a trade mission to China for Denver firms to assist China with security and other aspects of hosting of the 2008 Olympics.

In 1993, the United States created the Advocacy Center, a department within the Department of Commerce's International Trade Administration. Its role is to assist American firms that believe they are facing

International Political Environment

The international political environment involves political relations between two or more countries. This is in contrast to the previous concern for what happens only within a given foreign country. An international firm almost inevitably becomes involved with the host country's international relations, no matter how neutral it may try to be. It does so, first, because it is a foreigner from a specific home country and, second, because its operations in a country are frequently related to operations in other countries, on the supply side, the demand side, or both.

One aspect of a country's international relations is its relationship with a firm's home country. U.S. firms abroad are affected by a host nation's attitude toward the United States. When a host nation dislikes any aspect of U.S. policy, it may be the U.S. firm that is bombed or boycotted along with the U.S. Information Service office. English and French firms operating in the former colonies of those countries are affected by that relationship, favorably or otherwise. In 2002, Arabs continued their call for a boycott of all American goods for policies viewed as pro-Israeli. Coca-Cola, McDonald's, Procter & Gamble, and KFC were among the firms that expected the boycott to negatively impact sales.

A second critical element affecting the political environment is a host country's relations with other nations. If a country is a member of a regional group, such as the EU or ASEAN, that fact influences a firm's evaluation of the country. If a nation has particular friends or enemies among other nations, a firm must modify its international logistics to comply with how that market is supplied and to whom it can sell. For example, the United States limits trade with various countries. Arab nations have boycotted companies dealing with Israel.

Another clue to a nation's behavior is its membership in international organizations. Besides regional groupings, other international organizations also affect a member's behavior. Members of NATO, for example, accept a military agreement that may restrict their military or political action. Membership in WTO reduces the likelihood that a country will impose new unfair competition because of foreign government support. The Advocacy Center investigates such claims and, if well-founded, provides representation for firms on a nation-state level in discussions with other governments and international agencies, such as the WTO.

On the other hand, governments also enact legislation to limit trade to protect consumers against certain products (genetically modified foods, for example), as well as to support specific ideas. American President George Bush supported a continued embargo against Cuba because of the Communist regime in that country. Annual votes in the UN show that most other nations around the world do not support the 40-year-old embargo, and some of them openly trade with Cuba. Embargo critics in the United States and abroad argue that it has failed to lead to the downfall of Communism or its leader, President Castro, and that it hurts the people of Cuba by denying them access to many essentials. It also denies Americans free access to Cuban cigars and cheaper sugar. One recent report indicated that the embargo costs U.S. businesses between $1 billion and $2 billion each year in travel-related industry alone!

Sources: "Denver Mayor to Lead China Trade Mission," *Denver Post*, October 18, 2002; "Lifting Travel Ban to Cuba Would Generate $1.18 Billion to $1.61 Billion for U.S. Economy," PR Newswire, July 15, 2002; "U.S. Aerospace Contingent Flies to Talk to Business," *Vietnam Investment Review*, September 2, 2002; The Advocacy Center web site (http://www.ita.doc.gov/td/advocacy); accessed September 10, 2004.

trade barriers. Membership in the IMF or the World Bank also puts constraints on a country's behavior. Many other international agreements impose rules on their members. These agreements may affect patents, communication, transportation, and other items of interest. As a general rule, the more international organizations a country belongs to, the more regulations it accepts—and the more dependable its behavior.

Home Country Political Environment

A firm's home country political environment can constrain its international as well as domestic operations. The political environment can limit the countries that an international firm will enter. The *U.S. Bureau of Industry and Security* (BIS—formerly the Bureau of Export Administration) provides information on export limits regarding specific products and recipients and destinations of U.S. exports. (The most recent *Export Administration Regulations* [EAR] can be found in the Federal Register.) There are broad trade restrictions for exports to Cuba, Iran, Iraq, Libya, North Korea, Sudan, and Syria. As well, there are export restrictions on certain products, such as those incorporating short-range wireless technologies, open cryptographic interfaces, beta test software, and encryption source code. (See "Global Environment: Government: Friend or Foe?") Governments of nearly every nation have limits on what products they will sell and to whom they will sell them. In the U.S. the guiding principles of the BIS parallel other nations' reasons for these limits, including the following:

- The Bureau's paramount concern is the security of the United States. The Bureau's mission is to protect the security of the United States, which includes its national security, economic security, cybersecurity, and homeland security.
- Protecting U.S. security includes not only supporting U.S. national defense, but also ensuring the health of the U.S. economy and the competitiveness of U.S. industry.[4]

The best-known example of the home country political environment affecting international operations used to be South Africa. Home country political pressures induced more than 200 American firms to leave that country in the latter decades of the 20th century. After U.S. companies left South Africa, the Germans and the Japanese remained as the major foreign presence. German firms did not face the same political pressures at home that U.S. firms did. However, the Japanese government was embarrassed when Japan became South Africa's leading trading partner. As a result, some Japanese companies reduced their South African activity. Matsushita closed an office there; Sanyo and Nissan reduced their exports to South Africa; NEC and Pioneer Electronics agreed to suspend exports.

A more recent example occurred when pressure from American human rights groups induced some U.S. firms to leave Myanmar. PepsiCo, for example, pulled out of a joint venture even though it held 85 percent of the soft drink market there.

One challenge facing multinationals is that they have a legitimate triple-threat political environment. Even if the home country and the host country pose no problem, multinational firms can face threats in third markets. Firms that do not have problems with their home government or the host government, for example, can be bothered or boycotted in third countries.

The Legal Environment

In addition to the political environment in a nation, the **legal environment**—that is, the nation's laws and regulations pertaining to business—also influences the operations of a foreign firm. A firm must know the legal environment in each market because those laws constitute the "rules of the game." At the same time, a firm must know the political environment because it determines how the laws are enforced and indicates the direction of new legislation. The legal environment of international business is complicated, possesssing three dimensions. For a U.S. firm, these are (1) U.S. laws, (2) international law, and (3) domestic laws in each of the firm's foreign markets.

Law and Global Business

U.S. managers are familiar with domestic regulations affecting business, such as the Pure Food and Drug Act and the Robinson-Patman Act. These are not the U.S. laws that affect international business, however. Numerous other laws are relevant to international business and relate to exporting, antitrust, and organization and ownership arrangements.

EXPORT CONTROLS

Export control laws have changed significantly in response to increased concerns over security and personal safety. One clear indication of this is the U.S. government renaming in 2002 one of the main export control offices, from the Bureau of Export Administration to the Bureau of Industry and Security (BIS), which "better reflects the broader scope of the agency to include homeland, economic and cyber security."[5]

There have always been trade regulations about "dealing with the enemy," policies that dictate what and to whom people may sell. As in the past, U.S. businesses may not sell sophisticated aircraft; biological, nuclear, or conventional weapons; computer hardware and software; telecommunications equipment; and a host of other products to people in nations such as Cuba, North

Korea, Iraq, and Sudan. But there are also limits on certain optical equipment, sensing devices, flow control equipment, and advanced textiles (for example, those that can change color to mimic surroundings). While there may be very few U.S. trade restrictions to Canada, the United Kingdom, Sweden, and other nations that are long-term allies, there are always exceptions.

How do exporters know what and to whom they may ship? There are many agencies in the U.S. government with trade oversight responsibilities, as shown in Table 4-3. Three important agencies are the U.S. Department of Commerce and its many agencies (including the BIS, which was mentioned previously); the U.S. Customs Service, the agency responsible for ensuring that imports and exports enter and exit the country in accordance with U.S. regulations; and the U.S. Department of the Treasury, particularly the Office of Foreign Assets Control (OFAC), which provides information on sanction programs and country summaries (restrictions on shipments to specific countries and areas of the world). A relatively small number of U.S. exports require a special license (98 percent of all exports require only a general license for which no application is needed or they must qualify for NLR—no license required—status). BIS relies heavily on exporters to ensure that the products they sell are not dual-use items (items that have both commercial and military applications) going to someone on their "denied persons" or "entity" list. The latter list is composed of end users who have been determined to constitute an unacceptable risk or who are considered unreliable in handling sensitive products. For the transactions that do require an export license, an application for an individually validated license, issued on a case-by-case basis, must be filed.

The BIS also has a list of "red flags"—items that should raise suspicion when being exported (for example, the buyer is willing to pay cash for expensive items normally purchased through some form of financing). When an order is placed by someone on the denied persons list or there is a red flag, exporters are expected to report this fact to the BIS.

There are fines and other penalties for those firms that do not adhere to the export control regulations. A New Jersey firm paid $30,000 because it violated U.S. regulations by shipping chemicals through the United Arab Emirates to Iran. The company also violated Arab antiboycott rules by verifying that the goods did not originate in Israel. In another case, a fine of $52,500 was imposed on a firm for illegally selling to Singapore, Taiwan, and Thailand sophisticated measuring devices used in constructing military hardware. In November 2001, a $2.12 million penalty was imposed on McDonnell Douglas for allegedly exporting machine tools to China, while the Chinese firms that accepted shipment of the tools were slapped with a $1.32 million penalty and a denial of export privileges order. And in August 2002, the Department of Commerce imposed a fine of $30,000 on Hans Wrage & Co. for re-exporting nearly $500,000 worth of shotguns from Germany to Poland. While Hans Wrage is a German firm, the guns originated in the United States and the company shipped them to Poland without the required U.S. authorization. The U.S. Department of Commerce, through the BIS Export Administration Regulations, administers and enforces export controls. Violations of EAR may result in fines, as in the examples provided (typically being settled rather than going to court), but can also lead to criminal penalties and administrative sanctions.[6]

ANTITRUST CONTROLS

It might seem strange that U.S. antitrust laws would affect the foreign business activities of U.S. companies. However, that is a fact. The opinion of the U.S. Justice Department is that even if an act is committed abroad, it falls within the jurisdiction of U.S. courts *if the act produces con-*

sequences within the United States. Many activities of U.S. businesses abroad have repercussions on the U.S. domestic market. The question arises primarily in three situations: (1) when a U.S. firm acquires a foreign firm, (2) when it engages in a joint venture with a foreign firm, or (3) when it enters into an agreement with a foreign firm.

The two agencies in the U.S. government that have jurisdiction over antitrust regulations for most industries are the *Department of Justice* (DOJ) and the *Federal Trade Commission* (FTC). There are many antitrust regulations; but perhaps the most familiar are the Sherman and Clayton acts, both of which were written in the late 1800s. When a U.S. firm expands abroad or when a foreign corporation enters the U.S. market by acquiring an existing company, the DOJ and FTC are concerned about the possible impact on competition in the United States. If it is determined that the activity is anticompetitive, it will not be approved; or if the activity is already underway, it may be halted. As shown in the following examples, there are civil and criminal penalties, including officer liability, for corporate violations. Government action is more likely when the firms are in the same industry.

The acquisition of Princess Cruise Line (United Kingdom) by American rival Carnival had to be brought before the FTC. While the European Commission approved a takeover bid, the FTC had not initially decided how to classify the market in which these firms operate—as a "holiday industry" or "high-end cruise industry." If it had been the latter, approval was unlikely since that classification is more specialized and has fewer firms. Subsequently, the acquisition was approved.

Joint venturing, alliances, and other forms of cooperation among firms can lead to government intervention, too. The reasoning by the government is the same—competition in the U.S. market will be reduced by a particular marriage of a U.S. and foreign firm, regardless of location.

Laws in the United States can reach foreign countries and affect the international operations of U.S. and foreign firms. These laws also affect the global business strategy of foreign firms operating in the United States; foreign firms are also subject to U.S. antitrust regulation.

Three of the world's largest Dynamic Random Access Memory (DRAM) chip makers are part of an industry-wide investigation into anticompetitive predatory pricing. Micron Technology (United States), Samsung Electronics (Korea), and Infineon Technologies (Germany) are suspected of keeping prices artificially low in order to drive smaller competitors out of the industry. The commodity-like price for 128 megabit chips rose from $1 to over $2, but it was still considerably less than the estimated $4 it cost to manufacture them.

Elf Atochem of France is one of the largest chemical firms in the world. An executive of the company, Patrick Stainton, has pled guilty to a DOJ charge of antitrust conspiracy, the penalty being 90 days in jail and a $50,000 criminal penalty. Mr. Stainton had participated in suppressing competition in the sales of an important compound used in making pharmaceuticals, herbicides, and plastics.

The U.S. Department of Commerce imposed a $30,000 fine on Sun Microsystems of California, Ltd., for arranging for shipments of computers to the People's Republic of China that did not adhere to conditions of the export license issued to the firm.

Businesses must contend with U.S. laws that are applied both in the United States and in firms' foreign markets. Companies must also be aware of the counterparts to the FTC and DOJ in other parts of the world, which may have their own perspective on the importance of competition and what might be viewed as anticompetitive behavior. A dramatic example of this was the attempted merger of General Electric (GE) and Honeywell in 2001. The proposed $43 bil-

TABLE 4-3   U.S. Government Departments and Agencies with Export Control Responsibilities

Department of State, Office of Defense Trade Controls (DTC): DTC licenses defense services and defense (munitions) articles.

Department of the Treasury, Office of Foreign Assets Control (OFAC): OFAC administers and enforces economic and trade sanctions against targeted foreign countries, terrorism-sponsoring organizations, and international narcotics traffickers. The OFAC web site provides information on these sanctions as well as the Specially Designated Nationals and Blocked Persons list (SDN list).

Nuclear Regulatory Commission, Office of International Programs: It licenses nuclear material and equipment.

Department of Energy, Office of Arms Controls and Nonproliferation, Export Control Division: It licenses nuclear technology and technical data for nuclear power and special nuclear materials.

Department of Energy, Office of Fuels Programs: It licenses natural gas and electric power.

Defense Threat Reduction Agency—Technology Security: This agency of the Department of Defense (DoD) is responsible for the development and implementation of policies on international transfers of defense-related technology. It also reviews certain dual-use export license applications referred by the Department of Commerce.

Department of the Interior, Division of Management Authority: This agency controls the export of endangered fish and wildlife species.

Drug Enforcement Administration, International Drug Unit: It oversees the export of controlled substances.

Drug Enforcement Administration, International Chemical Control Unit: It controls the import and export of listed chemicals used in the production of controlled substances under the Controlled Substances Act.

Food and Drug Administration, Office of Compliance: This agency licenses medical devices.

Food and Drug Administration, Import/Export: This agency licenses drugs.

Patent and Trademark Office, Licensing and Review: It oversees patent filing data sent abroad.

Environmental Protection Agency, Office of Solid Waste, International and Special Projects Branch: This agency regulates toxic waste exports.

Source: Bureau of Industry and Security (formerly Bureau of Export Administration) (http://www.bxa.doc.gov/about/reslinks.htm).

lion acquisition of Honeywell by GE had been approved by the U.S. government, but it was blocked by the European Commission antitrust division. In other cases, companies face different penalties or requirements in different markets. For example, as part of the settlement in its antitrust cases, in 2005, Microsoft was fined $650 million and had to unbundle its Media Player software and Windows operating systems for the European market, but not in the United States or elsewhere.[7]

ORGANIZATION AND OWNERSHIP ARRANGEMENTS
The organization of a firm can be influenced by specific laws that are designed to promote foreign trade. In general, more restrictive laws may, indeed, allow certain exceptions to firms meeting specified conditions.

Webb-Pomerene Associations and Export Certificates of Review
The Webb-Pomerene Act of 1918 permits competing firms to form Webb-Pomerene Associations in order to cooperate when engaged in export trade. It specifically excludes them from antitrust prosecution in the development of foreign markets; that is, even though the firms

compete domestically, they can collaborate when exporting. Today there are only a handful of Webb-Pomerene Associations still in existence (in chemical, cotton, film, paper, and wood products). A more commonly used vehicle is the Export Trade Certificate of Review (**COR**, or "export certificate" as it is sometimes called). Under the Export Trade Act of 1982 (Title III), Certain American firms, associations, and individuals are granted immunity from federal and state antitrust laws and unfair competition lawsuits for their export activities. COR applications are jointly reviewed and certified by the U.S. Department of Commerce and the DOJ, while the Webb-Pomerene Associations are administered by the FTC.

Foreign Sales Corporation (FSC)

Since the early 1970s, the U.S. government has attempted to provide exporters with some form of tax relief on profits earned from exports. The WTO has ruled that the U.S. FSCs (Tax Reform Act of 1984), which allowed American firms to pay less tax on their profits from exports, is an export subsidy and is not in keeping with WTO goals of reducing trade barriers. The United States responded by enacting the Extraterritoriality Income Exclusion Act (ETI, signed in 2000), which allowed non-U.S. firms the same treatment. In 2002, responding to a complaint filed by the EU, the WTO ruled that the ETI did not eliminate the subsidy and that the U.S. tax law must be changed. Otherwise, the United States faced up to $4 billion in retaliatory tariffs. Barring an unlikely change in the U.S. tax law, these changes will result in higher tax bills for some firms (for example, Boeing and GE would have gained approximately $4 billion in annual tax savings under ETI), but will still provide some beneficial treatment of profits on active business transactions earned abroad by U.S. and non-U.S. firms.[8]

Export Trading Company Act of 1982

This was another effort by the United States to aid exporters. The **export trading company (ETC)** that was to result from this legislation was supposed to emulate Japanese and Korean trading companies. To reach the size and sophistication of Japanese ETCs, the legislation permitted banks to invest in these entities and eased antitrust restrictions on export activities. Participation by banks has not materialized, though. Instead of the huge conglomerates that were supposed to result from this act, most ETCs provide marketing and transportation services for a particular region of the world or focus on a particular set of products. While sophisticated in many respects, these ETC's are unlike the Korean or Japanese counterparts in terms of size and scope of services.

Yet, American firms have benefited from the Export Trading Company Act of 1982. The Office of Export Trading Company Affairs (OETCA) was created by Congress as part of the act. OETCA administers two programs available to all U.S. exporters or potential exporters— the COR program, which was described previously, and the *MyExports program*. The MyExports program gives U.S. exporters and export service providers a convenient way to establish contacts and to market their products and services through postings with the *U.S. Exporters' Yellow Pages* and the *U.S. Trade Assistance Directory*. OETCA also provides export news and information on exporting resources and sponsors special events such as trade missions and export-related conferences.[9]

OTHER CONTROLS

Examples of other controls include U.S. laws against bribery by U.S. firms, antiterrorism initiatives, and laws against the support of Arab boycotts.

Foreign Corrupt Practices Act (FCPA)

As a result of public outcry in the late 1970s about the ethical behavior of firms and bribery, the U.S. government passed the Foreign Corrupt Practices Act (FCPA) to prohibit U.S. firms from using bribery in any business transactions (although "grease payments" are still allowed). At first, the problem for U.S. firms was that their competitors from Japan and Western Europe were not forbidden to use bribes. U.S. firms complained that the act put them at a serious competitive disadvantage because bribery has often been the most effective form of persuasion in business and government markets abroad. Fortunately, in December 1997, the members of the OECD, a group of 30 industrialized nations, and five nonmember countries signed the Convention on Combating Bribery of Foreign Public Officials in International Business Transactions. All participants have ratified the agreement, and all except Turkey adopted legislation to implement enforcement of the conventions' articles.

This does not mean the end of bribery or similar behavior, though. Transparency International publishes the *Bribe Payers Index*, which provides information about business sectors and nations in which businesses are prone to instances of corruption, as well as suggested solutions to bribery. (See "Global Environment: Bribery around the World.")

Antiterrorism Regulation

After September 11, 2001, the United States and other governments became aware of the need to monitor and halt financing of terrorism. An example of an initiative to address this growing problem is the Uniting and Strengthening America by Providing Appropriate Tools Required to Intercept and Obstruct Terrorism Act of 200" (USA PATRIOT Act). It expands reporting requirements by financial institutions and those businesses that conduct financial transactions with clients that might attract criminals or terrorists (a broad spectrum that includes banks, casinos, and mutual fund investment houses, but may soon include others, such as precious metal dealers, pawnbrokers, and travel agencies). Activities that are illegal or suspicious (for example, transferring large funds or purchasing many money orders in small amounts) must be reported to the government. This means that smaller transactions and more kinds of transactions will come under scrutiny and will require customers to give up privacy that many associate with firms in financial industries. Failure by businesses to comply with reporting these transactions can result in million dollar fines and other penalties.[10] Yet disclosure requirements where one nation (for example, the United States) requests information on transactions that took place in another nation (for example, Switzerland) is a challenge to national sovereignty (Swiss in this example) and would undoubtedly raise issues of extraterritoriality.

Antiboycott Rules

Antiboycott laws were enacted to prohibit U.S. firms from participating in foreign boycotts that the United States did not sanction. While the Arab League boycott of Israel is the principal foreign economic boycott that U.S. companies must be concerned with today, the laws apply to all boycotts imposed by foreign countries that are unsanctioned by the United States.

The oil wealth of the Arab states has given them power that they use in several ways. One way is to try to force companies that sell to lucrative markets not to have any dealings with Israel. In other words, the Arabs boycott firms that sell to Israel. Because the Arab markets are much larger collectively than the Israeli market, many firms are tempted to drop the Israeli market and sell to the Arabs. This is counter to U.S. foreign policy. An example of a request to vio-

Bribery around the World

Which nations and business sectors are most prone to bribery?

Most Likely Nations	Most Likely Sectors
Russia	Public works/construction
China (PRC)	Arms and defense
Taiwan	Oil and gas
South Korea	Real estate/property
Italy	Telecommunications
Hong Kong and Malaysia	Power generation/transmission
Japan and **the United States**	Mining
France	Transportation/storage
Spain	Pharmaceutical/medical
Germany and **Singapore**	Heavy manufacturing
United Kingdom	Banking and finance
Belgium and **the Netherlands**	Civilian aerospace
Canada	Forestry
Austria	Information technology (IT)
Switzerland and **Sweden**	Fishery
Australia	Light manufacturing

Most Likely Nations: In response to "How likely are companies from the following countries to pay or offer bribes to win or retain business?" Nations in bold print have ratified the OECD convention against bribery; the others have not. Countries listed together are perceived to be approximately equal in terms of bribery potential.

Most Likely Sectors: In response to "How likely is it that senior public officials would demand or accept bribes in the following business sectors?"

Notes: Interestingly, according to perceptions of "well-informed" people (*Corruptions Perception Index, 2003*), Finland, Iceland, and Denmark are the least corrupt nations; while Bangladesh, Nigeria, and Haiti are most corrupt. The Corruption Perceptions Index (CPI) is a composite of data from 17 organizations (including the World Economic Forum and the Economist Intelligence Unit) and 13 indexes over three years (2001–2003) and includes more than bribery. For more information on the CPI, including when and how it was developed, see the Internet Center for Corruption Research (http://www.icgg.org).

Sources: *Global Corruption Report, 2004*, Transparency International (http://www.globalcorruptionreport.org); *Bribe Payers Index 2002*, Transparency International (http://www.transparency.org/cpi/2002/bpi2002.en.html); accessed, September 10, 2004.

late the antiboycott rules is provided by the BIS: "Importation of goods from Israel is strictly prohibited by Kuwait import regulations; therefore, certificate of origin covering goods originating in Israel is not acceptable."

Companies found violating the antiboycott regulations must desist and may be subject to civil penalties, but these penalties are often less than $10,000. There are some exceptions. Two subsidiaries of L'Oreal were fined nearly $1.5 million in 1995; and in 1993, Baxter International (medical equipment) agreed to pay a civil suit that exceeded $6 million for violating the anti-Arab boycott rules.

International Law and International Business

No international lawmaking body corresponds to the legislatures of sovereign nations. What then is international law? For this discussion, it is defined as "the collection of treaties, conventions, and agreements between nations that carry, more or less, the force of law." International law in this sense is quite different from national laws that have international implications, such as the U.S. antitrust laws. The international extension of U.S. law is on a unilateral basis. International law involves some mutuality, with two or more countries participating in the drafting and execution of laws or agreements.

Discussion of the impact of international law begins here with those international agreements having a general effect on international business and then addresses those dealing with more specific questions. Then the legal implications of regional groupings will be presented.

FCN, TAX, AND OTHER U.S. TREATIES

The United States also has many multilateral and bilateral treaties and agreements with other nations. Among them are the *Treaty of Friendship, Commerce and Navigation* (FCN Treaty) that the United States has entered into with approximately three dozen other nations. FCN treaties cover commercial relations between two nations. They commonly identify the nature of the rights of U.S. companies to do business in those nations with which the United States has such a treaty, and vice versa. FCN treaties usually guarantee "national treatment" to the foreign subsidiary; that is, it will not be discriminated against by the nation's laws or judiciary.

Tax treaties that the United States has signed with a number of nations are also generally bilateral. The purpose of such treaties is to avoid double taxation; that is, if a company has paid income tax on its operations in a treaty nation, the United States will tax the firm's income only to the extent that the foreign tax rate is less than the U.S. rate. Thus, if the corporate income tax rates are equal in the two countries, there is no tax to pay in the United States on income earned in the other country. Obviously, tax treaty nations are, in general, better places for a subsidiary than countries that do not have such a treaty.

The Wassenaar Arrangement on Export Controls for Conventional Arms and Dual-Use Goods and Technologies is a multilateral treaty that the United States and 32 other nations have signed. The purpose of the agreement is to deny transfer of goods that could be used for military purposes and that might threaten the security of the participating nations.

Many other treaties exist between the United States and other nations. The examples provided here emphasize the need for careful evaluation of opportunities and the recognition that home rules as well as foreign regulations may have an impact on how, what, and where business is conducted.

IMF AND WTO

The IMF and the WTO were discussed in Chapter 2, but both agreements are part of the limited body of effective international law. Both agreements identify acceptable and unacceptable behavior for member nations. Their effectiveness lies in their power to apply sanctions. The IMF can withhold its services from members that act "illegally"; that is, contrary to the agreement. WTO allows injured nations to retaliate against members that have broken its rules.

International business managers are interested in the IMF and WTO because of a shared concern in the maintenance of a stable environment conducive to international trade. These firms are concerned about the IMF's ability to reduce restrictions on international finance, and they support WTO's efforts to free the international movement of goods.

The legal reach of WTO and IMF does not extend to issues about business, but rather to the behavior of the nations within which the firm is operating. The environment for international business is more dependable and less capricious because of these two organizations.

UNITED NATIONS COMMISSION ON INTERNATIONAL TRADE LAW (UNCITRAL), OECD, WORLD HEALTH ORGANIZATION (WHO), INTERNATIONAL LABOR ORGANIZATION (ILO), AND OTHER INTERNATIONAL ORGANIZATIONS

The UN, the OECD, the WHO, the ILO, and other international organizations do not have legislative rights or responsibilities over nations; but they are concerned about the behavior of firms and the impact their activities have on the economic and social well-being of the world. They also recognize that multinational businesses make a large contribution economically and socially and that an environment conducive to conducting international business is essential. To address those concerns, these bodies have developed *codes of conduct,* or guidelines, for ethically and socially responsible corporate behavior that promote the fair treatment of corporate entities. While these international bodies do not formally coordinate or consult with one another in developing these guidelines, it is safe to assume that the people in each organization do review one another's work. Emphasis should be on the word *guidelines,* since these do not constitute any form of international law.

Two organizations described previously focus on specific aspects of world economics—trade (the WTO) and financial stability (the IMF). The UN and the OECD take a more general perspective in the guidelines they have developed.

The UN established the United Nations Commission on International Trade Law (UNCITRAL) with a goal to "promote the adoption of new international conventions and model laws and the wider acceptance of uniform international trade terms, provisions, customs and practices."[11] With respect to the conduct of firms, UNCITRAL is concerned with the following main areas:

- International Commercial Arbitration and Conciliation
- International Sale of Goods and Related Transactions
- Cross-Border Insolvency (where the debtor has assets in more than one state)
- International Payments
- International Transport of Goods
- Electronic Commerce
- Public Procurement and Infrastructure Development

The OECD has only 30 members, but they are the home countries to nearly all of the largest multinationals and constitute the largest markets for firms' products. *The Corporate Governance Principles* were adopted by the OECD in 1999. The principles are now used as a benchmark by international financial institutions and are the focus of roundtable discussions taking place around the globe. The World Bank Group and OECD, using these principles as a framework, established the Corporate Governance Forum, the mission of which is to "assist nations to improve the standards of governance for their corporations, by fostering the spirit of enterprise and accountability, promoting fairness, transparency and responsibility."[12]

Other global bodies focus on specific topics and occasionally propose codes. Often they hold discussions on topics that, if or when legislation is adopted on a national level, have an impact on business transactions. For example, the WHO has adopted a code of conduct surrounding the selling of infant formula that, in essence, serves as international law on the subject. The ILO has developed international labor standards, being especially mindful of how children in the workforce are treated. The Financial Action Task Force (FATF) of the OECD has developed the FATF Forty Recommendations as the international definition of money-laundering enforcement procedures, which are designed to curtail criminal and terrorist activities.[13]

Still supportive of the concept of a code of conduct, the World Bank launched a somewhat different program in 2000 called Corporate Social Responsibility and Sustainable Competitiveness, under which is the CSR for Future Leaders Program, which is aimed at young future entrepreneurs. The goal of these World Bank programs is to promote the idea that corporate social responsibility is a vital component of an effective corporate strategy.

STANDARDS ORGANIZATIONS

Numerous other international organizations have a semilegal influence on international business. One group of special interest is the *International Standards Organization* (ISO). The ISO is a nongovernmental organization (NGO) that is a network of the national standards institutes of nearly 150 countries. ISO specifications are system standards about materials, products, processes, and services used in manufacturing products and supplying services. Industry groups in most of the major industrial countries participate in the work of ISO, and many firms require that their partners be ISO-certified.

Perhaps because foreign markets are relatively small compared to the domestic market, U.S. industries have been less active in the ISO than other nations. This lack of interest may be costly in the long run; the United States may find itself closed out of many markets because its products do not meet more widely accepted standards.

Other standards organizations include the International Electrotechnical Commission (IEC), which develops standards for all electrical, electronic, and related technologies. The International Telecommunications Union (ITU), which is part of the United Nations System, is the international body that assists with coordination of global telecommunications networks and services.

Differing national standards are a major hindrance to international trade. The standards developed by these organizations, while not binding, serve as a basis for national standardization and as references when drafting international tenders and contracts. It is important that firms be aware of these organizations and their standards and that firms participate in designing these standards, rather than merely reacting to regulations that eventually result.

It would also be appropriate for firms to conduct business in a manner that is consistent

GIs: Consumer Protection or Trade Barrier?

You may want to hurry and buy some domestic Swiss cheese, Budweiser beer, and Kraft Grated Parmesan cheese. If the WTO gets agreement among its members to adopt all of the recommended GIs, the only Swiss cheese you will be able to buy is the cheese imported from Switzerland; Budweiser will be an expensive Czech beer; and the only Parmesan cheese will come from Parma, Italy.

GIs are signs used on products that have a geographically distinctive characteristic or association and may be used by all producers in the designated area. This is different from a trademark, which only a single producer may use. Generally, GIs are applied to food or agricultural products. Examples include champagne, which comes only from the Champagne region of France; Roquefort, which is made in Roquefort, France (the rest is blue cheese); feta, which comes from certain areas in Greece; and, of course, the one and only Tuscany olive oil. Yet GIs may also be used when selling Swiss watches, for example. Support for GIs is based in part on the belief that consumers should know where the products are produced so they are better informed and better protected from false or misleading business practices. A counterargument is that many of these terms have become synonymous with an entire product class and should be available to all. If GIs were to become regulations, they would act as trade barriers and limit competition. According to GI proponents, if a wine is referred to as "champagne," customers should be assured that it comes from the region of

with the *Universal Declaration of Human Rights,* which was adopted by the UN shortly after the organization was formed. In essence, the General Assembly of the UN proposed that all must recognize that "the inherent dignity and equal and inalienable rights of all members of the human family is the foundation of freedom, justice and peace in the world."[14]

INTELLECTUAL PROPERTY (IP)

Intellectual property (IP) is created in the human mind. It includes thoughts and ideas that are turned into paintings, music, software, and architectural designs and the processes used to create products. It may be debatable whether someone "owns" an idea, and the protection of IP takes on ethical dimensions when questions such as how much an idea is worth and how long it should be protected are considered. Clearly, IP is a complicated topic that one could devote an entire semester discussing. Here, however, the concerns associated with IP are what it is, why it's important, and how to protect it.

IP usually brings to mind "inventions," which are defined as "products or processes that provide a new way of doing something or that offer a solution to a problem, and which require a patent to have some protection from theft."[15] IP does include inventions, but it also refers to trademarks (branding, which includes names, marks, and characters used in identifying products and companies), industrial designs (ornamentation and aesthetic aspects of something), and geographical indications (GIs). (See "Global Environment: GIs: Consumer Protection or Trade Barrier?")

IP is important, but it is difficult to state how much is created each year. Not only is it challenging to assign a value to IP, it is difficult to count the number of IP creations since so much of

Champagne in France. Opponents argue that common use of the term *champagne* should allow its use for all sparkling wines; and if not allowed, customers would be confused by the different terms.

The use and adherence to GIs is voluntary among WTO members, at least for now. The EU is pushing hardest for acceptance of GIs and is seeking more formal protection under the WTO Agreement on Trade-Related Aspects of Intellectual Property Rights (TRIPS).

Examples of GIs that are protected in selected countries include the following:
- Bulgaria: Bulgarian yoghurt and Merlou from Sakar (wine)
- Canada: Canadian Rye Whisky, Canadian Whisky, and Vancouver Island
- Czech Republic: Pilsen and Budweis (beers)
- EU: Champagne, Sherry, Porto, Chianti, and Moselle Luxembourgeoise (wines)
- Hungary: Eger (wine) and Szatmar (plum)
- Slovak Republic: Modranská majolika (hand-painted pottery)
- United States: Idaho (potatoes and onions), Real California Cheese, and Napa Valley Reserve (still and sparkling wines)
- Other products: Newcastle brown ale, Kentish ale, Scottish beef, Scotch Whisky, Irish Whiskey, Jersey Royal potatoes, Cornish clotted cream, Roquefort, Gorgonzola, Olive de Kalamata, Opperdoezer Ronde, Danablu, Lübecker Marzipan, and Coquille Saint-Jacques des Côtes-d'Amour

Sources: The World Intellectual Property Organization (WIPO), "What is a geographical indication?" (http://www.wipo.int/about-ip/en/about _geographical_ind.html); accessed, November 27, 2002; "What are Geographical Indications?" Slide Show (http://www.wto.org/english/thewto_e/whatis_e/eol/e/wto07/wto7_19.htm); "Discussion develops on geographical indication" WTO News Release, TRIPS Council 1–2 December 1998 (http://www.wto.org/english/news_e/news98_e/pu_e.htm).

what is created is not reported or registered. Statistics on the number of applications for patents, copyrights, and other forms of protection are often used to provide an indication of the number of new inventions and other IP created each year. The International Intellectual Property Alliance, which tracks computer software, films, television programs, music, and books, conducted a study that showed that the aforementioned IP products contributed about 8 percent ($800 billion) to the U.S. GDP in 2001; they represent the fastest-growing sectors in the economy.

Why is IP protection necessary? One problem is that rather than purchase a product from the producer, many consumers merely copy the product (for example, downloading music from the Internet or copying software) or buy the product, sometimes unknowingly, from individuals who have copied the product without the permission of the IP owner and are selling unlicensed, counterfeited, or pirated copies. Lost revenue for the companies owning the IP is substantial. Estimates vary considerably, but the projected loss to businesses because of piracy is between $25 billion and $50 billion worldwide.[16] One study found that 92 percent of all software in China is unlicensed—with little or no enforcement of IP laws and relatively small fines and no jail time for those caught making counterfeit products![17] This is despite China's membership in the WTO.

Illegal as the practice may be, people have no reservations about copying a song or an article or piece of software. From a business perspective, this is not just lost revenue because it does not take into account the added liability and other costs, such as losing future sales. If someone copies a pair of designer jeans and sells them to you and they fall apart in the washing machine, who gets the returned merchandise? Not the pirate. If a pair of brakes fail on your car or the medication you take does not work, the pirate cannot be held liable because that individual is not identified. But the person making the repairs to your car, the pharmacist, and the owner of the IP can be, and often are, held liable. Consumers may also lose confidence in (or blame) the IP holder for shoddy products and not return to make purchases in the future.

Perhaps most serious of all is that when the owners of IP are not paid for their inventions and other creations, they have little incentive to invest more time, effort, and money into creating and commercializing other new ideas. In the end, the consumer has fewer choices. That may not be so important when it comes to the latest video games or style of automobile; but it may be an issue for, say, the development of a cure for a deadly disease.

INTELLECTUAL PROPERTY PROTECTION (IPP)

IP without **intellectual property protection (IPP)** is not worth much because others could take and use a product and there would be no need to compensate the inventor. Registration of trademarks and patents are common methods used to protect a firm's IP. The U.S. Patent and Trademark Office (USPTO) tracks information on applications filed in the United States and makes this information available, as do other national agencies in other countries. The USPTO granted its six millionth patent in 1999 (granted to 3Com Corporation for its HotSync Technology) and in 2003 received over 350,000 patent and nearly 270,000 trademark applications.[18] The *World Intellectual Property Organization* (WIPO) and other international organizations provide similar data. Most patents, trademarks, and copyrights are granted to companies and individuals in developed countries. For example, of the 9.4 million patent applications recorded in 2000, the five countries with the most applications were Japan (486,000), the United States (332,000), Germany (263,000), the United Kingdom (233,000), and Sweden (205,000), accounting for 16 percent of all patent applications.[19] The importance of protection can be seen in "Global Environment: Pirates at Large."

Patent and Trademark Protection Systems

Many firms have patented and trademarked products to sell. When selling outside their home market, they want to protect their intellectual rights in those markets as well. Generally, applications for patents and trademarks must be filed separately in whatever country the firm wants protection. This can be a time-consuming and expensive process.

Because of the expense and inconvenience of applying for patents and trademarks in multiple countries, various efforts have been made to develop a multilateral approach. The main feature is a simplified application system, which can be a major convenience for firms wanting protection in many countries, although individual national filing fees generally must still be paid. The benefit is the elimination of duplicate procedures. Developing countries will tend to accept the preliminary search and evaluation findings of industrialized countries.

Several efforts include global and regional agreements and conventions that are designed to eliminate some duplication in applying for IPP. There are also some multinational bodies whose mission encompasses IPP.

The most significant of the conventions is the Paris Union (officially called the Paris Convention for the Protection of Industrial Property) because of the broad scope of protection and the number of contracting member nations. The Paris Union includes 164 nations and allows a six-month protection period in the case of trademarks and a one-year period for patents. That is, registration of a trademark in one member country gives the firm six months in which to register in other member countries before it loses its protection in those countries. There are many other conventions, such as the Berne Convention that focuses on Literary and Artistic Works and currently has 149 members.

Another important convention is the Madrid Agreement Concerning the International Registration of Marks, or simply the Madrid Agreement (not to be confused with the Madrid Agreement for the Repression of False or Deceptive Indications of Source on Goods, which was signed in 1994). This treaty, originally signed in Madrid in 1891, focuses on trademark registration and protection among the 70 member nations.

In addition, the Patent Cooperation Treaty (or International Patent Cooperation Union) signed in Washington, D.C., in 1970 is a cooperative union for the filing of applications for the protection of inventions among 120 member nations. WIPO reported that over 100,000 patent applications were filed under the Patent Cooperation Treaty in 2003—39,250 applications (or 36 percent) coming from the United States, 16,774 (15.2 percent) coming from Japan, and 13,979 (12.7 percent) coming from Germany. The number of patents filed under this treaty indicates its popularity and nations' belief in the enforcement of IPP when disputes arise, as specified in the treaty. International protection of IP is critical for the expansion of world trade and investment.

There are many other conventions and agreements, the goal of which is to bring some order to IPP. WIPO is an agency of the UN, which coordinates the protection of IP on a global scale through information services and administration of many of the international IPP conventions. The mission of WIPO is "the maintenance and further development of the respect of intellectual property throughout the world" and "that the acquisition of the protection and its enforcement should be simpler, cheaper, and more secure."[20] This must be balanced with the needs of developing nations, though. Because the vast majority of patents originate in industrialized countries, less developed nations argue that for them, patents mean high prices for products, import monopolies rather than local manufacturing, and high royalty payments for the use of patents. Those nations are expected to attempt to change the patent system to give them less expensive access to technology.

The WTO, within its TRIPs agreement, contains an MFN ("most favored nation") clause regarding trademark registration. This agreement includes WTO members, some of which are not Paris Union members, thereby extending protection to other nations.

Regional counterparts provide similar protection, registration, and information. The European Patent Office (which includes the EU members and other European nations) and the Office for Harmonization in the Internal Market (which provides a single system for trademark registration throughout the EU, called Community Trade Mark—CTM) are European examples. The Inter-American Convention for Trademarks and Commercial Protection (also known as the Pan-American Convention) and the Buenos Aries Convention for the Protection of Trade Marks and Commercial Names are examples in the Western Hemisphere.

When selling products abroad, firms must pay attention to IPP and the agencies and conventions that provide assistance and information. The most interesting question in brand and trademark protection concerns the countries that are not members of one of these arrangements.

REGIONAL GROUPINGS AND INTERNATIONAL LAW

Many nations have felt the need for larger market groupings to accelerate their economic growth. Such regional groupings have developed on all continents. What each grouping has found, however, is that economic integration alone is not sufficient without some internation-

Pirates at Large

Piracy on the high seas still takes place, as indicated by the International Chamber of Commerce (ICC) headlines "Pirates Attacks Against Ships Increase" and "Shipping Warned to Steer Clear of Pirated-Infested Somali Coast." This type of piracy, which involves boarding a vessel, stealing the multimillion-dollar cargo, and sometimes killing the crew, is a serious commercial risk. However, another type of piracy involves the illegal copying of trademarks and the manufacturing of fake products for resale.

Many companies fall victim to piracy of IP and counterfeiting of their products. With over 1 billion people, China is an attractive market for companies, but it is also a market in which a large percentage of trademarked goods are counterfeited. Procter & Gamble estimates that 15 percent of its soaps and detergents bearing the brand names Tide, Head & Shoulders, and Vidal Sassoon that are sold in China are fake (cost: $150 million per year). For Gillette, the situation is even worse—as many as 25 percent of all Gillette razors, Duracell batteries, and Parker pens are bogus. One raid in the Chinese district of Yiwu netted 4 million fake razors. The following week the distributors were back selling more. Anheuser-Busch representatives walked into a store to make an initial sales call only to find their beer on the shelves—identical in package, but not in taste. Converse shoes had millions of loyal followers in Brazil; the problem was that Footwear

al legal agreement. Initially, this takes the form of a treaty that establishes the regional grouping. Inevitably, however, as integration proceeds, further legal agreements are necessary. In this way, the body of international (regional) law grows. Because these groupings are primarily economic alliances, the international law that develops relates primarily to economic and business questions. Therefore, regional groupings provide a development of international law that is of interest to multinational companies.

The EU Example

The basic laws of the EU are contained in the Treaty of Rome. Under this international law, the member countries succeeded in forming a customs union and harmonizing certain economic regulations. The Single European Act (SEA) of 1985 and the Treaty on European Union (or Maastricht Treaty) in 1992 considerably expanded the EU's law-making ability. Adoption of a common currency among most EU members in 2002 makes foreign exchange easier and less risky in Europe. But it also has far-reaching monetary and fiscal policy implications. This, in turn, has an impact on laws governing the banking industry. Furthermore, the ten new members that joined the EU in 2004 will adopt EU laws. Business in the EU will largely be governed by the new international laws rather than by national laws of the member countries.

An example of the impact of European law is when Japanese video games maker Nintendo and seven of its distributors were fined €167.8 million for colluding in an attempt to control prices of video games. The rejection of GE's bid to merge with Honeywell in 2001 is another instance of the substantial impact of EU laws. Note that references in both cases are to laws and a court with jurisdiction across EU member nations.

Acquisition (the owner of the Converse name and shoe style) wasn't selling the shoes—they were all fakes. Pirates of Microsoft software have become so sophisticated that even experts have a difficult time telling what is real from what is fake. (The counterfeiters use a million-dollar machine to copy the CDs and have figured out how to duplicate the holograms used as an antitheft device.)

Yamaha, recognizing the enormous potential in the Chinese market, entered into a joint venture with a state-owned motorbike manufacturer, investing $93 million to update three plants. Not only was the excess plant capacity used to produce copies of the Yamaha motorbikes, the latest engine technology used in new products quickly showed up in the products of Yamaha's competitors. Yamaha suspected that its Chinese partners were selling the technology. It is believed that as many as five of every six "Yamaha" motorbikes in China is a fake.

There are thousands of examples of piracy. All one needs to do is walk down a crowded city block in any part of the world, where he or she is likely to see peddlers selling "Rolex" watches, "Kate Spade" handbags, and videos or DVDs of new movie releases. Piracy is a serious problem with potentially serious consequences beyond lost income. The ICC has reported on fake eyedrops that contained untreated tap water rather than sterile solution and contraceptive pills made from flour. According to the WHO, 10 percent of all pharmaceuticals are fake and may contain harmful ingredients or little or no medication at all.

Sources: "New Service Will Help Firms Fight Fake Drugs," International Chamber of Commerce (http://www.iccwbo.org/home/news_archives/2002/stories/drugs.asp); accessed November 26, 2002; International Chamber of Commerce web site (http://www.iccwbo.org/); "China's Piracy Plague," *Business Week*, June 5, 2000, pages 44–48; "In Wooing Brazil's Teens, Converse Has Big Shoes to Fill," *Wall Street Journal*, July 18, 2002, pages B1–B2.

Reinforcing the strength of international law in the EU is the European Court of Justice, which is more effective in dealing with supranational legal questions than the famous World Court in The Hague.

Experience Elsewhere

The EU has, by far, made the most progress of all of the regional groupings. This is especially true in the area of regional law. The CACM made great strides in its early years, even proposing a monetary union similar to the EU adoption of the euro. CACM was unable to achieve many of its goals because of disagreements among members and became stagnant between 1969 and 1990. Since 1991, CACM has discussed the possibility of joining other economic groups in the area, including the North American free trade area. The idea is to enlarge the community into a more effective, more economically diverse group. None of these initiatives has gotten much further the discussion stage, however.

Mercosur and the Andean Community are examples of other regional groupings in the Western Hemisphere. While they, too, made progress in their early years, the members had difficulty achieving the groups' economic and trade goals.

NAFTA continues to make hesitant strides to freer trade. Proposed changes in U.S. laws are always underway to strengthen, or at times counteract, NAFTA goals. One initiative would allow Mexican trucks on American roads, which have been banned because of safety and pollution concerns (shipments had to be transferred to U.S. carriers at the border). Another recent proposal was the elimination of all tariffs on imported manufactured goods by the year 2015. Those changes will have an impact on laws in the other member nations as well.

In Asia, ASEAN has also made halting steps toward freer trade and harmonization of laws. The Asian crisis in the mid-1990s hit ASEAN heavily, of course, but it continued to add new members (Vietnam in 1995, Myanmar and Laos in 1997, and Cambodia in 1999). Members are also cooperating in the building of a trans-ASEAN transportation network for road, air, and sea traffic; the coordination of telecommunication networks to increase compatibility; and the beginning stages of trans-ASEAN power grid and gas pipeline projects.

Coordination of economic and social goals among nations means that the laws of the members will overlap. In some cases (as within the EU), they may be administered by a central body. Similar laws, coordination, and cooperation across national boundaries have an impact on how business is conducted in every part of the world.

THE WORLD OF INTERNATIONAL LAW

The body of international law is small compared to domestic law. Nevertheless, examples of international law and the ways it can impinge on international business have been presented. International law, whether regional or global, is the growth area in the legal environment of global business.

Because agreement is easier to obtain with a small number of countries, regional law grows faster than other international law. International law generally facilitates international trade. When a change in law is unfavorable, however, firms want to be informed about the change so they can optimize performance within the new constraints.

International managers need to scrutinize two other areas of international law. One is the codes of conduct developed by international groups already mentioned. While these guidelines are not binding and cannot be strictly considered international law, they are often used to steer national and, in the case of the EU, regional legislative activities.

The second development affecting the internationalization of law is the increasing cooperation between countries with regard to legal matters. As one example, Britain and the United States have a treaty spelling out situations in which judgments of the courts of one country are enforced in the courts of the other country. Most commercial disputes will be covered. Broader than that treaty is the informal cooperation between regulators in different countries. Regulators visit various countries and exchange information in the formulation of new regulations concerning business. In the antitrust area, there have been exchanges of personnel between the United States and the EU.

Legal cooperation exists among industrialized countries. Nations work together in UNCITRAL, WIPO, OECD, and the World Bank, where mechanisms exist for the exchange of information about multinationals. The rapid transplantation of regulatory initiatives from one country to another means that companies can no longer deal with regulations on a country-by-country basis, but must devise coordinated strategies.

Foreign Laws and Global Business

U.S. laws play a ubiquitous role in U.S. business practices. The laws of other nations play a similar role with regard to the activities of businesses within their boundaries. The importance of foreign laws to a business lies primarily in the domestic laws in each foreign market. Problems arise when the laws in each market are somewhat different from those in every other market.

DIFFERING LEGAL SYSTEMS

Before considering national peculiarities in laws relating to business, a brief discussion of the predominant legal systems that underlie individual national law is in order. Legal systems are most often based on common law, civil or code law, or Islamic traditions. When categorizing nations, one must exercise care because many nations are best classified as a mixture of one or more types of legal systems. For example, Quebec province uses both civil and common law traditions, while in Nigeria, Islamic law is applied in the northern, predominantly Muslim areas, but common law is used in other parts of the country.

Common law is English in origin and is found in the United States and other countries that have had a strong English influence, usually a previous colonial tie (about 40 nations). Common law, often called "case law," is tradition-oriented; that is, the interpretation of what the law means on a given subject is heavily influenced by previous court decisions as well as by usage and custom. If there is no specific legal precedent or statute, common law requires a court decision. To understand the law in a common law country, one must study the previous court decisions in matters of similar circumstance, as well as the statutes.

Civil or **code law** is based on an extensive and, presumably, comprehensive set of laws organized by subject matter into a code. The intention in civil law countries is to spell out the law on all possible legal questions rather than rely on precedent or court interpretation. The "letter of the law" is very important in code law countries. However, this need to be all-inclusive may lead to some rather general and elastic provisions, permitting application to many sets of facts and circumstances. Because code law countries do not rely on previous court decisions, various applications of the same law may yield different interpretations. This can lead to some uncertainty for a manager.

Code law is a legacy of Roman law. It is predominant in Europe and in nations of the world that have not had close ties to England. Thus, code law nations are more numerous than common law nations. Many civil code systems are influenced by the French, German, and Spanish systems because of previous colonial or other relationships. For example, the German code has had an influence on the Teutonic and Scandinavian countries. There are about 90 civil law countries.

Islamic law represents the third major legal system. About 35 countries follow Islamic law in varying degrees, usually mixed with civil, common, and/or indigenous law. The Islamic resurgence in recent years has led many countries to give Islamic law, Shari'a, a more prominent role. Shari'a governs all aspects of life in areas where it is the dominant legal system, as in Saudi Arabia. Rules not defined by Shari'a are decided by government regulations and Islamic judges. Although it has harsh penalties for adultery and theft, Islamic law is not dramatically different from other legal systems with regard to business. In Saudi Arabia, for example, the Committee for Settlement of Commercial Disputes operates in a manner that would not be uncongenial to a Westerner.

The differences in legal systems are important to decision makers in a firm. They must study the legal systems and seek appropriate local legal advice when necessary. The following section merely alerts the manager to some of the variations in legal systems abroad.[21]

FOREIGN LAWS AND STRATEGIC DECISIONS

Anyone who is familiar with regulations in the United States will not be surprised at the range of laws affecting businesses in other nations, although he or she may be surprised at the lack of regulation in some less developed countries.

To Fight the Pirates

Holograms were an early high-tech solution used to prevent piracy and counterfeiting. They appeared on credit cards, CD and DVD packages, and on some currencies (the euro paper money). Now, though, the machines used to produce the prototypes have fallen in price to about $2,500—well within the reach of serious counterfeiters.

New high-tech solutions are being developed to combat piracy, though. An Israeli firm, Bsecure (formerly Pitkit Technologies), offers a variety of products that can tell what is genuine and what is fake. The company manufactures inks that contain signature chemicals, microwires thinner than a human hair, and unique polymers with embedded codes used to coat identification badges and packaging—all of which can be detected with special scanners to make sure the products are genuine. Bsecure also makes tamperproof packaging substances that prevent counterfeiters from opening product packages and substituting imitations. Bsecure's clients include New Balance Athletic Shoe, Inc.; Intel; Seagram's; and the motor vehicle departments in Israel and Belarus.

Wal-Mart and Procter & Gamble have been investigating radio-frequency identification (RFID) tags, currently used by Mobil in their Speedpass program and the E-ZPass toll system. The idea is to track ship-

There are laws about taxes on Internet sales, royalty payments for downloading songs and software, privacy, what managers may or may not do with the information they gather, protection of minors, use of screening or blocking software, and a host of other concerns that were unheard of ten years ago. While the Internet and e-commerce advancements have opened a broad spectrum of opportunities for businesses (and individuals), many new legal and ethical issues must be addressed (and see: Chapter 7). Discussions about these issues highlight the differences in how they are viewed from country to country. For example, privacy laws in the United States and the EU are quite different and clearly show that some subjects are long-standing and culturally related. These differences make it more difficult to come to an international agreement about how to treat the issues.

Instead of a presenting a catalog of foreign laws, the following material deals with how laws influence the selected decision areas—specifically those that relate to product, price, place (distribution), and promotion. The treatment is brief and suggestive of the problem areas. A more extensive study is in order when considering a specific market. For example, Japan has more than 10,000 laws to regulate business.

Global firms will find many regulations affecting a product. The physical and chemical aspects of a product are affected by laws designed to protect national consumers with respect to its purity, safety, and performance. As the thalidomide tragedy showed, nations differ as to strictness of their controls. The Food and Drug Administration (FDA) had not cleared the drug for sale in the United States; but many deformed babies were born in Europe, where it was legal.

In a similar vein, European manufacturers were disturbed by U.S. safety requirements for automobiles, which had to be modified to meet the needs of one market. Because the U.S. marments more closely and ensure arrival of genuine goods by putting small RFID tags in product cases. The problem is cost. The price of the microchips would have to fall to 5 cents or less to make them a cost-effective option.

Mention "Los Alamos" and many people think of the atom bomb, first developed and tested in the United States in this remote part of New Mexico. It was also the home of Isotag, the manufacturer of nanotechnology isotags. These unique and identifiable single molecules can be added to a variety of products (including cosmetics, gasoline, and pharmaceuticals) to help firms distinguish real from counterfeit. (Isotag merged with other firms to form Authentix, a company that specializes in technologies designed to combat counterfeiting and piracy.) Scanned products that do not contain the isotags can be removed from store shelves—and possibly traced to their source so the pirates can be caught. What's the best part? Isotags cost less than 1 cent per unit.

There are other product defense techniques: ink that becomes visible when copied (the word *counterfeit* appears), tamper-evident glue, self-destruct technologies for sound and video recordings, and activation and deactivation codes for software.

Bsecure estimates that the amount of counterfeit products sold annually totals $1 trillion. While the market for products to defend against piracy was only about $24 billion in 2002, it is growing by 16 percent per year.

Sources: "Forgery Fighters," *Jerusalem Report*, October 7, 2002, page 36; "Tech Goes Undercover," *Optimize*, November 1, 2002, page 15; "Beam Me Up Some Ivory Soap," *Fast Forward*, October 2002, Issue 12 (http://www.optimizemag.com/issue/012/fast.htm); accessed December 6, 2002; Authentix site (http://www.authentix.com); accessed February 26, 2005.

ket is large, the adaptation was not as serious as that needed to meet the peculiar requirements of a small market. There are exceptions. The EU ban on hormone-treated beef effectively closed the market of over 375 million people to American cattle ranchers. American farmers rely on hormone treatments to get their cattle to market quicker and cheaper than producers in other countries and, therefore, have been unwilling to change their husbandry practices. This example highlights what frequently appears to be the protectionist use of these laws. Although consumers should be protected, different safety requirements are not necessary for consumers of every country. By maintaining different standards, nations imply that consumers in other countries are not being adequately protected. One reason nations often persist in demanding particular legal requirements is to protect their own producers. For example, Britain kept French milk out of the country by requiring it to be sold in pints rather than metric measures. German noise standards kept British lawn mowers off German lawns.

Fortunately, in the late nineties, the United States and the EU drafted an agreement to accept each other's standards for a wide range of products. This Mutual Recognition Agreement will save millions of dollars on both sides of the Atlantic. Automobiles were not included, and the FDA retained its control over pharmaceuticals.

China now has a product liability law to protect its consumers. Some, unfortunately, have used the law to target foreign companies. Procter & Gamble was sued by a woman who said its shampoo melted her hair. It turned out the shampoo was counterfeit.

Labeling is subject to more legal requirements than packaging. Labeling items that are covered include (1) the name of the product; (2) the name of the producer or distributor; (3) a description of the ingredients or use of the product; (4) the weight, either net or gross; and (5) the country of origin. As to warranty, there is relative freedom to formulate a warranty in all countries, but the rights of consumers and responsibilities of firms differ from nation to nation.

Brand names and trademarks also face different national requirements. Most nations are members of the Paris Union or some other trademark convention, which ensures a measure of international uniformity. However, differences exist between code law countries (ownership by priority in registration of a brand) and common law countries (ownership by priority in use) in their treatment of a brand or trademark.

Cybersquatting—registering domain names and not using them—is a common practice, especially with the release of new extensions such as .biz, .name, and .info. Companies around the world are fighting over Internet addresses and domain names. WIPO arbitrates and provides details of many of these disputes, one of which was the use of the address HardRockCasinos.com. The case was brought by Hard Rock Café International (USA) against WW Processing, "an entity of unknown legal status, with headquarters in Nevis, Saint Kitts and Nevis," which had already registered the domain. There were many issues in the case. One deciding factor was the fact that Hard Rock Café owned the name "Hard Rock Casino" and had been using it in other business activities, while the respondent, WW Processing, had not been using the name or the Internet address. ("Neither Respondent nor its predecessors-in-interest is making or made a legitimate non-commercial or fair use of the disputed domain name.") In April 2002, WIPO ordered that the domain name be transferred to Hard Rock Café International.[22]

Other recent cases have involved well-known names and companies such as Toyota, Intel, Air France, Coca-Cola, Playboy, and Victoria's Secret.

Price controls are another concern for many businesses, and laws related to pricing are pervasive in the world economy. **Resale price maintenance (RPM)** is a common law relating to pricing. Many nations have some legal provisions for RPM, but with numerous variations. Another variable is the fact that some countries allow price agreements among competitors.

Another law in many nations is that of government price control. The price controls may be economy-wide or limited to certain sectors. For example, France has had a number of economy-wide price freezes. At the other extreme, Japan controls the price on only one commodity—rice. Generally, price controls are limited to "essential" goods, such as foodstuffs. The pharmaceutical industry is one of the most frequently controlled, sometimes taking the form of controlled profit margins.

For example, at one time, Ghana set manufacturers' margins at between 25 and 40 percent, depending on the industry. Argentina allowed a standard 11 percent "profit" on pharmaceuticals, whereas Belgium fixed maximum prices and wholesale and retail margins on pharmaceuticals. Germany did not set margins but had an obligatory price register, making prices and margins available for public scrutiny. In 1998, China introduced price controls on pharmaceuticals, cutting prices of imported and joint venture-produced drugs by over 20 percent. The pricing formula restricted profit margins.

Two other pricing issues that firms face are dumping and transfer pricing. **Dumping** occurs when a firm sells products below the cost of manufacture or when it sells products for a lower price abroad than at home. The basis for the latter is that selling internationally costs more because of added risks, additional transportation and distribution costs, and numerous other factors. The nation being subjected to dumping often applies antidumping or countervailing duties to raise the price of imports to more closely match the domestically made products. Typically, the cases are brought by developed nations (such as the United States) against developing nation manufacturers (China, for instance) who have access to cheap labor. But developing nations have also charged developed nation producers with dumping, such as the steel manufacturers in India who claimed that South Africa, the EU, and Australia were dumping steel products in their country.[23]

There is also the issue of **transfer pricing**, the price at which intercompany transfers take place. Governments are vigilant about these transfers and do what they can to curtail tax avoidance strategies that involve transfer pricing. A recent case was that of British Petroleum, which was charged with taking excessive profits from its operations in Russia via transfer pricing.[24]

Distribution is an area in which a firm has fewer constraints. A firm has a high degree of freedom in choosing distribution channels from among those available in the market. Of course, one cannot choose channels that are not available. For example, France had a specific prohibition against door-to-door selling, but the Singer Company received a special exemption from this law. One major question is the legality of exclusive distribution. Fortunately, this option is allowed in most markets. In fact, the strongest legal constraint does not apply to firms managing their own distribution in foreign markets, but rather to exporters who are selling through distributors or agents.

Careful selection of an agent or a distributor is critical for two reasons. First, the quality of the distributor helps determine a firm's success in the market. Second, the contract with the distributor may bind the exporter to a commitment that is difficult and costly to terminate. The challenge for the exporter is to be aware of national laws concerning distributor contracts in order to avoid potential problems. It is much easier to enter an agency agreement than to end one. (See "Global Environment: Distributor Divorce: Including an Escape Clause.")

Advertising is one of the more controversial elements of what a firm does since, as intended, it is so visible. Advertising tends to be subject to a lot of government control. Most nations have some law regulating advertising, and advertising groups in many nations have self-regulatory codes. Advertising regulation takes several forms. One pertains to the message and its truthfulness. In Germany, for example, it is difficult to use comparative advertising and the words *better* or *best*. In Argentina, advertising for pharmaceuticals must have prior approval of the Ministry of Public Health. Even China brought foreign firms to court over their advertising claims under its new law.

Another form of restriction relates to control over the advertising of certain products. For example, Britain allows no cigarette or liquor advertising on television. Finland is more restrictive and allows no newspaper or television advertising of political organizations, religious messages, alcohol, undertakers, diet drugs, immoral literature, or intimate preparations. Another restriction is through the taxation of advertising. For example, Peru once implemented an 8 percent tax on outdoor advertising; Spain taxed cinema advertising.

Some nations institute greater restrictions on sales promotion techniques than what is found in the United States. In the United States, there is often no constraint on contests, deals, premiums, and other sales promotion gimmicks. The situation is quite different in other countries. As a general rule, participation in contests must not be predicated on purchase of the product. Premiums may be restricted with regard to size, value, and nature. A premium may be limited to a certain fraction of the value of the purchase and may be required to relate to the product it promotes; that is, steak knives cannot be used as a premium with soap or a towel with a food product. Free introductory samples may be restricted to one-time use of the product rather than a week's supply. In the infant formula controversy, sampling was completely forbidden. Variations are great; and laws in both home and host countries must be considered, even when the laws conflict with one another.

Distributor Divorce:
Including an Escape Clause

Escape clauses are designed to protect the parties of an agreement in the event a disagreement or circumstance arises that prevents completion to the expectations of those involved. In the case of hiring sales representatives in other countries, the desire to get out of a contract is most commonly due to the salesperson not meeting the company's goals. The U.S. Department of Commerce and an American export compliance firm, Unz & Co., have formulated some advice about sales representative agreements.

In international contracts, escape clauses may be limited by local laws, regardless of what the parties agreed to, whether verbal or written. Therefore, one should learn as much as possible about appropriate commercial laws and seek local legal advice. When talking to a lawyer, one should consider asking the following questions:

• What is the required advance notice for termination? (possibly 180 days or more)

ENFORCEMENT OF THE LAWS

A firm needs to know how foreign laws will affect its operations in a market. It is not sufficient to know only the laws; a firm must also know how the laws are enforced. Most nations have laws that have been forgotten and are not enforced. Other laws may be enforced haphazardly, and still others may be strictly enforced.

An important aspect of enforcement is the degree of impartiality of justice. Does a foreign subsidiary have as good a standing before the law as a national company? Courts have been known to favor national firms over foreign subsidiaries. In such cases, biased enforcement means that a law is interpreted one way for the foreigner and another way for a national. Knowledge of such discrimination is helpful in evaluating the legal climate.

The Firm in the International Legal Environment

Firms that have had little experience with international transactions may not realize that there may be little recourse when another party in a contract does not pay for goods or services received, the product received is defective, or the service is not up to agreed-upon standards. Whatever the resolution of a contracted dispute, the time it takes to reach that point is often much longer and more costly than expected.

WHOSE LAW? WHOSE COURTS?

Domestic laws govern businesses within a country. Questions of the appropriate law and the appropriate courts may arise, however, in cases involving international business. As noted, few international laws apply to international business disputes. Nor is there an international court in which to try them, except for the European Court of Justice for the EU.

When commercial disputes arise between principals of two different nations, each would probably prefer to have the matter judged in its own national courts under its own laws. By the time the dispute has arisen, however, the question of jurisdiction has usually already been settled

- What are justifiable reasons for termination? (Not meeting a sales objective may be insufficient grounds.)
- What compensation is due on termination? (Cost can be substantial, including lost *potential* sales.)
- In what language are contracts to be written? (Careful translation is a necessity.)
- Whose laws apply? (Even with a written contract, some nations do not allow the salesperson [or the firm] to waive the nation's jurisdiction.)
- Is the representative to be referred to as an agent? (In some instance, "agent" implies power of attorney and more authority than desirable.)
- What happens to proprietary property upon termination (including sales records, customer data, patents, trademarks, and similar materials)?
- Are the host country laws in conflict with home country laws? (Sales exclusivity, labeling, and other components may be in violation of antitrust regulations, antiboycott laws, or other home country regulations.)

Source: *A Basic Guide to Exporting*, 1998, prepared by the U.S. Department of Commerce with the assistance of Unz & Co., Inc. (http://www.unzco.com/ basicguide/c4.html#negotiating); a more recent counterpart is the Exporting Guide produced by Team Canada, Inc. (http://exportsource.ca/gol/exportsource/interface.nsf/engdocBasic/0.html) or the *Export Programs Guide*, published by the U.S. Department of Commerce, International Trade Administration.

by one means or another. One way to decide the issue beforehand is by inserting a jurisdictional clause in a contract. Then, when the contract is signed, each party agrees that the laws of a particular nation (or state in the case of the United States) govern the content of the contract.

If the parties do not have a prior agreement as to jurisdiction, the courts in which the appeal is made decide the issue. One alternative is to apply the laws of the nation in which the contract was signed. Another is to use the laws of the country where contract performance occurs. In one of those ways, the issue of which nation's laws shall govern is already out of the company's hands when a dispute arises. Most companies prefer to make that decision themselves. Therefore, they insert a jurisdictional clause into the contract, choosing the more favorable jurisdiction. Of course, the choice of jurisdiction must be acceptable to both parties.

The decision as to which nation's courts will try the case depends on who is suing whom. The issue of which courts have jurisdiction is separate from the issue of which nation's laws are applied. Suits are brought in the courts of the country of the person being sued. For example, a U.S. company might sue a French firm in France. This kind of event often leads to the situation in which a court in one country tries a case according to the laws of another country; that is, a French court may apply the laws of New York State. This would happen if the parties had included a jurisdictional clause stating that the laws of New York State govern; it would also happen if the French court decided that the laws of New York State were applicable for one of the other reasons mentioned.

Some U.S. laws have a particularly long reach. Corporate fraud and embezzlement of millions, sometimes billions, of dollars by executives at Enron, Tyco, WorldCom, Allegheny Health System, and others led to new corporate reporting and personal liability laws in the United States. Those laws apply to all publicly traded firms, even those whose headquarters are in other nations. This means that foreign firms listed on the New York Stock Exchange must also comply. The European governments and companies are asking that they be subject to looser rules; but so far, the U.S. Securities and Exchange Commission (SEC) is standing firm. The Japanese, on the other hand, are less concerned since some of their laws are similar and since they, too, went through recent fraud cases involving giants such as Mitsui and the Tokyo Electric Company.

The Economic Espionage Act of 1996, designed to protect trade secrets, is far-reaching in that it applies to the theft of trade secrets or corporate espionage by U.S., as well as non-U.S. individuals or entities, and that "the district courts of the United States shall have jurisdiction of civil actions." Penalties may include fines of $500,000 and jail sentences of 15 years.[25]

ARBITRATION OR LITIGATION?

An international manager must be knowledgeable about laws and contracts. Contracts identify two things: (1) the responsibilities of each party and (2) the legal recourse to obtain satisfaction. Actually, however, businesses consider litigation a last resort and prefer to settle disputes in some other way. For several reasons, litigation is considered a poor way of settling disputes with foreign parties. Litigation usually involves long delays, during which time inventories may be tied up and trade halted. Further, it is costly—not only in money, but also in customer goodwill and public relations. Firms also frequently fear discrimination in a foreign court. Thus, litigation is seen as an unattractive alternative, to be used only when all else fails.

More peaceful ways to settle international commercial disputes are offered by conciliation, mediation, and arbitration. Conciliation and mediation are informal attempts to bring the parties to an agreement. They are attractive, voluntary approaches to the settlement of disputes. If they fail, however, stronger measures (such as arbitration and litigation) are needed. Because of the drawbacks of litigation, arbitration is used extensively in international commerce.

Litigation costs are high, particularly in the United States, which is a litigious society (suing someone is a common way to resolve disputes). The *American Arbitration Association* (AAA) provides alternatives; it administered over 200,000 cases in 2001 via mediation, arbitration, and less formal *alternate dispute resolution* (ADR) formats. While the AAA claims to be the largest full-service ADR provider, other agencies in the United States, such as the Better Business Bureau (BBB), handle a large number of arbitration cases as well. The savings to the U.S. court system and to the parties involved in the disputes are incalculable.[26]

Arbitration generally overcomes the disadvantages of litigation. Decisions tend to be faster and cheaper. Arbitration is less damaging to goodwill because of the secrecy of the proceedings and its less hostile nature. This means that the climate for conciliation is better so that almost one-third of the cases are settled in direct talks before the judgment stage is reached. Decisions are more equitable and informed because of the expertise of the arbitrators, who are not judges, but people with practical experience. Arbitration allows business to continue while the dispute is being settled. It neutralizes the differences between legal systems because decisions are not based on points of law, but on practical considerations of equity. Each party also has the satisfaction of avoiding the courts of the adversary's country.

In an increasing number of countries, including the United States, arbitration awards have the status and enforceability of court decisions. This practice is supported by the large number of arbitral awards that are upheld in courts around the world. There are even examples of cooperative international arrangements, such as the one recently reached between the AAA and the Malta Arbitration Centre for the use of ADR to resolve commercial disputes between American companies and those located throughout Europe and North Africa.[27]

The arbitration procedure is relatively straightforward. If firms want to settle disputes by arbitration, they include an arbitration clause in the contract. A common form is the one suggested by the AAA:

> Any controversy or claim arising out of or relating to this contract, or the breach thereof, shall be settled by arbitration administered by the American Arbitration Association under its Arbitration Rules, and judgment on the award rendered by the arbitrator(s) may be entered in any Court having jurisdiction thereof.

Because of its advantages, arbitration is increasingly popular for settlement of commercial disputes. A number of examples support this trend. One is from UNCITRAL, which formulated the Model Law on International Commercial Arbitration. Because of its multinational source, this law could be used to combine national arbitration rules into a single global standard.

Another development is the increase in the number of centers for hearing arbitration. The ICC in Paris is one of the leading, more well-established and well-respected centers in the world, receiving more than 500 arbitration cases every year. The ICC also supplies samples of arbitration clauses, but in a variety of languages, and allows users to access an "arbitration cost calculator" to estimate the cost of pursuing a claim. All of those resources are available on the ICC web site at http://www.iccwbo.org. Estimates are that fewer than 10 percent of the ICC decisions are challenged.

In 2001, the International Centre for Dispute Resolution (ICDR), a division of the AAA, handled over 600 cases involving 63 countries and claims in excess of $10 billion. The ICDR has cooperative arrangements with more than 50 arbitral agencies in 40 countries, including the Permanent Court of Arbitral Awards at The Hague. Many resources and agencies for ADR are helpful in reducing the costs and other problems often associated with litigation, but the following offer a starting point.

China created its own arbitration tribunal in 1989, and Beijing is now one of the busiest arbitration centers in the world. Even with this tribunal's problems, foreign firms find it far superior to going into a Chinese court. Although it does not recognize awards of other tribunals, the AAA signed a cooperation agreement with China's International Economic and Trade Arbitration Commission in 2001. With a goal of capturing more of the large arbitration cases, in 2002, the Singapore International Arbitration Centre drastically reduced the fees it charges for its services. The management fees are lower than those charged by the arbitration associations in Stockholm, Kuala Lumpur, China, and the ICC in Paris. For example, the fee for a case involving a $10 million claim was lowered from nearly $24,000 to $14,000. The maximum fee for a case is now $25,000, versus $68,375 the previous year in Singapore.[28]

The International Centre for Settlement of Investment Disputes (ICSID), an autonomous unit of the World Bank, provides facilities for arbitration of disputes between member countries and investors of other member countries. It is especially useful when a government is a party in the dispute.

The advantages of arbitration and other forms of ADR over litigation have been emphasized. Although it is very important, arbitration should not be considered a panacea. Cases can take as long as two years and can cost over $100,000. (Rates vary according to the amount in dispute and the arbitral board.) Nevertheless, if disagreements do arise, arbitration is a preferred alternative to litigation.

There is another way of dealing with disputes among business partners. Rather than relying on "fixing" the problem after it occurs, businesses are taking time before a contract is signed to more carefully evaluate potential partners. This trend is supported by the findings of one study of the English court cases between 1990 and 2001. Despite a significant decline in suits, the researcher did not find a corresponding increase in arbitration, but did find that businesses took more care in establishing partner relationships initially and put more effort into resolving disputes before involving third parties. Reasons cited for more careful prearrangement assessment included the expense of litigation, but also the distraction to the businesses' personnel and the cost in terms of partner and consumer relations.[29]

E-LAW

E-commerce is not new, but it certainly becomes more pervasive every year. New opportunities and challenges face businesses, whether they are considering new methods of distribution for software, videos, and reading material; advertising using a relatively new medium (the Internet); dealing with transparent pricing; developing new products such as Internet security; or developing interactive gaming software, web site consultant services, or the Combined DNA Index System (CODIS) data management system.

E-commerce also introduces new legal issues. Businesses must deal with topics such as privacy. Also difficult to contend with are the differences between countries. For example, the United States wants to reduce privacy in order to combat terrorism (the establishment of the Directorate for Information Analysis and Infrastructure Protection), while the EU, Canada, Singapore, and other nations have enacted rules such as the Consumer Credit Directive to ensure that consumer information is carefully regulated. Fraud, spam (junk e-mail), and IP theft take place on an unprecedented scale—all made easier by the Internet. Examples of e-terrorism include the theft of customer records and subsequent threat of release unless a ransom is paid, spy software capable of snooping competitors' records, and virus attacks that destroy vital records or close web sites—all becoming much too common. Laws establishing punishments for those crimes and the way perpetrators are to be prosecuted must also cross national boundaries if they are to be effective.

Governments are particularly interested in the issue of taxation. With billions of dollars in transactions taking place on the Internet, governments are losing money because of uncollected sales tax and value-added tax (VAT). Attempts to regulate or control sales and taxes have not been successful, but the United States and the EU are at the forefront of designing and implementing new regulations. It may become the responsibility of firms such as eBay to collect the sales taxes and distribute them to the appropriate authorities.

Whether selling products through e-mail, offering promotions on its web site, or making statements about its products, a firm's after-sales responsibilities and liability are issues being debated in the press, in courts, and in international agencies around the world.

The topics mentioned here are only a few of those likely to occupy lawmakers for years to come, but firms must keep abreast of new developments and the regulatory impact those developments can have on them.

The Business Manager Is Not a Lawyer

What are the implications for the international businessperson of all of the legal parameters discussed in this chapter? There are methods to reduce political and legal risks, some of which were shown in Table 4-2. Hiring an expert is usually a good idea. Keep in mind, however, that many lawyers do not have detailed knowledge about all of the domestic, international, and foreign legal aspects involved in global business. While a firm's decision makers cannot know all of the relevant laws, they do need to know what decisions are affected by the laws. A firm can call in legal counsel when special expertise is needed. Expertise includes not only the domestic legal staff, but also legal representatives from the firm's foreign markets.

A firm's need for legal expertise is related to its international involvement. If a firm only exports or licenses, it has fewer legal needs than if it has foreign subsidiaries and joint ventures. Where it operates through licenses or distributors, these parties relieve the firm of some of its legal burden. When a firm has subsidiaries, however, it needs local legal counsel.

With the growth of international business and the proliferation of national and international regulation, the international legal function is becoming more complex. Firms need an international legal staff at headquarters and local lawyers in foreign subsidiaries. In host countries, the task will be largely decentralized because of local practices. However, some coordination and exchange of experience will be necessary to optimize performance of a firm's international legal function.

Summary

A host country's behavior is guided by its national interests, such as security, sovereignty, prestige, and economic welfare. To achieve its goals, a country uses a variety of controls over a firm, such as entry restrictions, price controls, quotas and tariffs, exchange control, and even expropriation. These national interests and controls constitute the political environment of an international firm.

A firm needs to evaluate the host country environment and assess the political risk in every country in which it enters into business transactions. Then the firm needs a plan for managing host country relations, both before and after entering the country.

An international firm often becomes involved in international relations, usually against its will. It needs to know how a given host country relates to its own country and to other nations, as well. Also, a firm's home country may restrict its international activities. The United States, for example, is especially attentive to these issues.

Many U.S. laws affect U.S. firms. These laws relate to the regulation of exports and to antitrust implications of overseas ventures and even help the firms get involved in international business. One example is the U.S. Export Certificates of Review.

Still other U.S. laws concern the behavior of U.S. firms abroad. The FCPA prohibits bribery, and antiboycott provisions are meant to prevent U.S. firms from cooperating with the Arab boycott of Israel.

The FCN Treaty ensures that U.S. firms will not receive discriminatory treatment in a foreign legal system. UNCITRAL's Convention for the International Sale of Goods facilitates the international selling task. IMF and WTO, each in its own way, help to create an environment more favorable to international business. ISO is creating standards for international products that a firm must incorporate into its product planning.

International patent conventions help international firms protect their most valuable IP.

Regional economic groupings, especially the EU, are writing new multicountry laws covering many aspects of business. These laws facilitate global business in a region.

Each foreign country has its own legal system, which is shaped by the common law, by code law, or by Muslim law tradition. These foreign laws affect all aspects of product policy, including the physical product, the package and label, the brand name, and the use of warranty.

Pricing and promotion programs are generally more strictly regulated in foreign markets than in the United States.

In cases of legal disagreements, each party usually prefers its own country's courts. A jurisdictional clause should be included in all international contracts in case a problem arises. However, rather than litigate in a foreign court, many international firms prefer to settle differences by arbitration. Arbitration is often more efficient, more equitable, and less damaging to continuing relations.

E-commerce is causing lawmakers to review current laws about privacy, liability, and taxation in a new light. These regulations will have an impact on how businesses collect and use information about their consumers, what warranties they include with their products, and how they promote their products over the Internet.

Questions and Research

4.1 Explain the threefold political environment of international business.

4.2 Discuss the various kinds of host country controls over an international firm.

4.3 How might a firm analyze its own political vulnerability in a particular host country?

4.4 What can a firm do to help manage its host country relations?

4.5 Identify the elements of the international political environment.

4.6 Explain the foreign policy concerns with regard to U.S. export controls.

4.7 Discuss the various aspects of international business that can be affected by U.S. laws.

4.8 Discuss the ambivalent attitude of the U.S. government toward antitrust in international business.

4.9 Give examples of the kinds of international laws that can influence a firm's international business.

4.10 Explain a firm's concerns relating to international patent and trademark law.

4.11 Discuss the influence of regional groupings—especially the EU—on the development of international law.

4.12 Why is arbitration preferred to litigation?

4.13 Discuss how the Internet will shape business regulations in the future.

Endnotes

1 "Bank Lending Rates for Exporters Drop to 15%" *Financial Gazette*, August 1, 2002.

2 "Mexican Bill Could Affect U.S. DMers," *Marketing News*, October 14, 2002, page 5.

3 Oetzel, Jennifer M., Richard A. Bettis, and Mark Zenner. "Country Risk Measures: How Risky Are They?" *Journal of World Business*, Summer 2001, Volume 36, Number 2, pages 128–145.

4 Guiding Principles of the Bureau of Industry and Security (http://www.bxa.doc.gov/ManagementTeam/BISGuidingPrinciples.html); accessed November 8, 2002.

5 Commerce Department Renames Agency "Bureau of Industry and Security," Bureau of Industry and Security News Release, April 18, 2002 (http://www.bxa.doc.gov/press/2002/CommerceRenamesAgencyBIS.html).

United States Department of Treasury, Export License Requirements (http://www.itds.treas.gov/licenseinfo.html); accessed November 12, 2002.

6 "Commerce Department Imposes Civil Penalty on Minnesota Firm in Settlement of Export Violations," BIS Press Page (http://www.bxa.doc.gov/press/Archive2001/MinnFirmFined.html); accessed November 12, 2002.
"Commerce Department Imposes $2.12 Million Civil Penalty on McDonnell Douglas for Alleged Export Control Violations," BIS Press Page (http://www.bxa.doc.gov/press/Archive2001/McDonnellDouglasFined.html); accessed November 12, 2002.
"German Company Fined for Illegal Shotgun Sales," BIS Press Page (http://www.bxa.doc.gov/press/2002/GermanFirmFined.html); accessed November 12, 2002.
"New Jersey Company Pays $30,000 to Settle Charge of Illegal Exports to Iran," BIS Press Page (http://www.bxa.doc.gov/press/2002/MercatorExports2Iran.html); accessed November 12, 2002.

7 "Carnival Bid for P&O Falls Beneath Royal Caribbean," *Financial Times*, Global News Wire, July 28, 2002.
"Infineon Contacted About U.S. Probe Into Chip Makers," *Financial Times*, Global News Wire, June 20, 2000.
"European Executive Agrees to Plead Guilty for Participating in an International Antitrust Conspiracy," U.S. Department of Justice News Release, Wednesday, August 7, 2002.
"Monti Defends EU After Blocking General Electric-Honeywell Merger," *Financial Times*, July 10, 2001, page 8.
"EU Told to Reconsider Microsoft Case," *Financial Times,* Global News Wire, May 16, 2002.
"A Welfare State for Aggrieved Market Losers," *Financial Times*, Wednesday, March 24, 2004, page 17.

8 "U.S. Dam Says Bush Administration to Work on International Corporation Tax Overhaul," *AFX European Focus*, Economic News, November 14, 2002.

9 Rasmussen, C. (Economist, Office of Export Trading Company Affairs, personal communication; November 19, 2002); The Office of Export Trading Company Affairs (OETCA) web site (http://www.ita.doc.gov/td/oetca); accessed November 19, 2002.

10 Ensminger, John J. "September 11 Brings New Anti-Terrorism and Anti-Money Laundering Responsibilities to Financial Institutions," *Review of Business*, Volume 23, Number 3, Fall 2002, pages 29–34. In the United States, the agency responsible for coordinating activities among the 25 or so other federal bodies and enforcing the regulations is the Financial Crimes Enforcement Network (FinCEN).

11 United Nations Commission on International Trade Law (UNCITRAL) (http://www.uncitral.org/en-index.htm); accessed November 22, 2002.

12 Corporate Governance Forum (http://www.gcgf.org); accessed November 22, 2002.

13 Ensminger, John J. "September 11 Brings New Anti-Terrorism and Anti-Money Laundering Responsibilities to Financial Institutions," *Review of Business*, Volume 23, Number 3, Fall 2002, pages 29–34.

14 The United Nations, *Universal Declaration of Human Rights* (http://www.un.org/Overview/rights.html); accessed February 9, 2005.

15 The World Intellectual Property Organization (WIPO) (http://www.wipo.int/about-ip/en/patents.html); accessed November 26, 2002.

16 "Description of the IIPA," International Intellectual Property Alliance (IIPA) (http://www.iipa.com/aboutiipa.html); accessed November 26, 2002.

17 "High Prices Encourage Software Piracy," *Australian Financial Review,* September 4, 2002, page 52; "China Faulted for Rampant Product Piracy," *Philadelphia Inquirer,* September 17, 2004, section B, page D3.

18 United States Patent and Trademark Office (USPTO), Performance and Accountability Report: FY 2003 (http://www.uspto.gov/web/offices/com/annual/2003/index.html).

19 Calculated based on World Intellectual Property Organization (WIPO) patent application statistics for 2000—"25 Years of Industrial Property Statistics (1975–2000)" (downloaded in MS Excel format from http://www.wipo.int/ipstats/en/index.html on November 27, 2002).

20 *Yearly Review of the PCT: 2003*, World International Property Organization, 2004, pages 3–4; memorandum of the Director General, World Intellectual Property Organization (http://www.wipo.int/about-wipo/en); accessed December 1, 2002.

21 There are different classification schemes and criteria used in classifying countries' legal systems. Most sources include a number of types; but one of the more trustworthy and clear is that developed by the law faculty at the University of Ottawa (http://www.uottawa.ca/world-legal-systems), which is used here.

22 WIPO Arbitration and Mediation Center; ADMINISTRATIVE PANEL DECISION; Hard Rock Café International (USA), Inc. v. WW Processing; Case No. D2002-0021 (http://arbiter.wipo.int/domains/decisions/html/2002/d2002-0021.html); accessed December 16, 2002.

23 "Essar Steel, SAIL Move Court Against Dumping," *Financial Times,* Global News Wire, March 27, 2004; accessed September 17, 2004.

24 "Russian Arm of BP to Meet Minority Shareholders' Demands," *Sunday Business* (London), August 22, 2004.

25 United States Code, Title 18; see, in particular, sections 1831–1832 and section 1837; for an explanation of the Federal Protection of Trade Secrets and the Economic Espionage Act of 1996, see http://www.cybercrime.gov/EEAleghist.htm and the *Washington State Bar News* (http://www.wsba.org/media/publications/barnews/archives/sep-97-federal.htm).

26 American Arbitration Association 2001 annual report.

27 "American Arbitration Association Announces Cooperative Agreement With Malta Arbitration Centre" (http://www.adr.org/index2.1.jsp?JSPssid=15780&JSPsrc=upload\LIVESITE\About\..\NewsAndEvents\Press\Malta%20Coop%20Release.htm); accessed December 18, 2002.

28 "Fees Slashed to Attract 'Big-Ticket' Arbitration Cases," *Business Times Singapore*, September 21, 2002.

29 Ede, Justin. "It's Good to Talk—Rather Than Sue," *The Times* (London), November 26, 2002, page 7.

Further Readings

Anspacher, Jeff. "Export Trade Certificates of Review," *Export America*, August 2002, Volume 3, Number 8, pages 14–15.

"Brussels Extends Powers to Crack Down on Cartels," *Financial Times*, November 27, 2002, page 8.

"Clear Sailing for Pirates," *Business Week*, July 15, 2002, page 53.

Comeaux, Paul E. and N. Stephen Kinsella, *Protecting Foreign Investment Under International Law: Legal Aspects of Political Risk*, 1997, Dobbs Ferry, NY: Oceana Publications.

"Customs Solution," *Forbes*, May 24, 2004, page 172.

Finkel, David. "Crime and Holy Punishment," *Washington Post*, Sunday, November 24, 2002, page A01.

"Fixing a Lock and Key to Your Identity," *Financial Times*, December 5, 2002, page 24.

Hadjikhani, Amjad and Pervez N. Ghauri, "The Behaviour of International Firms in Socio-Political Environments in the European Union," *Journal of Business Research*, 2001, Volume 52, Number 3, pages 263–275.

"India Court Rejects Union Carbide," *Washington Post*, August 28, 2002.

Keillor, Bruce D., Gregory W. Boller, and Robert H. Luke. "Firm-Level Political Behavior and Level of Foreign Market Involvement: Implications for International Marketing Strategy," *Journal of Marketing Management,* 1998, Volume 8, Number 1, pages 1–11.

Kobrin, Stephen. "Territoriality and the Governance of Cyberspace," *Journal of International Business Studies,* 2001, Volume 32, Number 4, pages 687–704.

"Making Sense of Transfer Pricing," *Financial Express,* Global News Wire, August 14, 2004.

Mewhirter, Erin and Michael Fullerton. "The Trade Act of 2002," *Export America,* November 2002, pages 20–21.

"Russia May Restrict Beer Advertising," *Philadelphia Inquirer,* August 8, 2004, page E2.

"Taxing Multinationals: The Donnybrook Ahead," *Business Week,* September 9, 2002, pages 86–89.

"Washington Alters Line on U.S. Investor Protection," *Financial Times,* October 2, 2002, page 13.

Recommended Web Sites

Antiboycott laws (http://www.bxa.doc.gov/AntiboycottCompliance/Default.htm) for U.S. firms. The U.S. Bureau of Industry and Security maintains information about antiboycott rules.

Bribe Payers Index 2002 (http://www.transparency.org/cpi/2002/bpi2002.en.html). Transparency International (TI) is an international nongovernmental organization "devoted to combating corruption by bringing civil society, business, and governments together in a powerful global coalition." Its founder and chair is a former World Bank official, and members include journalists and academics. Among other activities, TI publishes the *Corruption Perceptions Index* for 91 countries and the widely referenced *Bribery Index* that is the result of surveys of business executives in 21 nations.

International Standards Organization (http://www.iso.ch/iso/en/ISOOnline.frontpage)—information about the organization, ISO 9000, and 14000 certification; "In the beginning" is especially descriptive (http://www.iso.ch/iso/en/iso9000-14000/basics/general/basics_2.html).

Laws for nations of the world (http://www.loc.gov/law/guide/nations.html). The U.S. Library of Congress provides many resources for country-specific legal information.

The International Chamber of Commerce (ICC) (http://www.iccwbo.org/); organization information, dispute resolution services, documentation, information, and standard arbitration clause—MS Word documents in Arabic, Bulgarian, Dutch, English, French, German, Greek, Italian, Spanish, Vietnamese, and other languages.

Organization for Economic and Cooperation and Development (OECD)—the Convention on Combating Bribery of Foreign Public Officials in International Business Transactions (http://www.oecd.org/EN/home/0,,EN-home-86-3-no-no-no,00.html).

United States Government sites:

- United States Department of Commerce:
  - Bureau of Industry and Security (BIS) provides information about export controls (http://www.bxa.doc.gov/licensing/exportingbasics.htm). The BIS is a department within the Department of Commerce that is the primary licensing agency for "dual use" exports—items that can be used for private or legitimate business applications as well as for military purposes. This site provides information on the type of export controls U.S. businesses are subject to as well as the best ways to comply with the regulations.

  - United States Department of Commerce, Office of Export Trading Company Affairs (OETCA), Export Trade Certificate of Review (COR) information (http://www.ita.doc.gov/td/oetca/etc.html).

- United States Customs Service (http://www.customs.ustreas.gov) is the agency responsible for ensuring that U.S. imports and exports enter and exit the country in accordance with all U.S. laws and regulations.

- United States Export Administration Regulations (EAR) web site (http://w3.access.gpo.gov/bis/ear/ear_data.html) provides information about current changes to export regulations, general export prohibitions, special reporting requirements, applications (classification, advisory, and license), and documentation.

- United States Federal Trade Commission (FTC) (http://www.ftc.gov).

- United States Copyright Office at the Library of Congress (http://lcweb.loc.gov/copyright) provides copyright information, including "copyright basics," fees, and more.

- United States Department of Justice (DOJ), Antitrust Division (http://www.usdoj.gov/atr/index.html). It also maintains a portal of Internet links to antitrust agencies in other nations (http://www.usdoj.gov/atr/contact/otheratr.htm).

- United States Patent Office (USPTO) provides patent information, including "patent basics," fees, statistics, and more (http://www.uspto.gov).

- United States Department of State's annual Patterns of Global Terrorism report (http://www.state.gov/s/ct/rls/pgtrpt) provides statistics and information on worldwide terrorism.

- United States Department of the Treasury, Office of Foreign Assets Control (OFAC) (http://www.treas.gov/offices/enforcement/ofac) administers and enforces economic and trade sanctions based on U.S. foreign policy and national security goals against targeted foreign countries, terrorists, international narcotics traffickers, and those engaged in activities related to the proliferation of weapons of mass destruction. Application instructions for export licenses and a description of the Export Control Commodity Number (ECCN) and Commodity Control List is available on a Department of Treasury web page (http://www.itds.treas.gov/licenseinfo.html).

The World Intellectual Property Organization (WIPO) is an international organization dedicated to promoting the use and protection of intellectual property. Headquartered in Geneva, Switzerland, WIPO is one of the 16 specialized agencies of the United Nations system of organizations. It administers 23 international treaties dealing with different aspects of intellectual property protection. The Organization counts 179 nations as member states (http://www.wipo.int). WIPO also supplies detailed information on the IPP treaties (http://www.wipo.int/treaties/en/index.jsp) it administers, which include, among others, the Paris Union, Berne Convention, Brussels Convention, Madrid Agreement, and Rome Convention. See also "Global Protection Treaty Systems" (http://www.wipo.int/treaties/registration/index.html) for information on the Madrid Agreement Concerning the International Registration of Marks as well as the Patent Cooperation Treaty (PCT).

Check the website & the Invisible website on the Meta page

Case 4.1

The Legal and Political Environment of Cigarette Manufacturers

Tobacco has been used in one form or another—seemingly for as long as humans and the plant coexisted but certainly as long as recorded history. Humans have had a love-hate relationship with tobacco—the product sometimes being extolled as a cure-all and other times being labeled a wicked, insidious killer. To curb its use, or sometimes as a means of financing wars, governments have banned, taxed, and regulated tobacco. Typically, banning tobacco products affects demand and, ultimately, sales, while taxes or tariffs are passed along to consumers as higher prices. Other regulations have been aimed at the distribution or promotional aspects of selling tobacco products.

NORTH AND SOUTH AMERICA

Americans smoke over 450 billion cigarettes every year (more than 2,255 per capita), making it the largest market in the world. In Canada, the per capita consumption is also high, nearly 2,000; but with a population of 31 million, total annual consumption is only one-tenth that of the United States. Most countries in Latin and South America are currently experiencing annual per capita consumption rates of between 500 and 1,500 cigarettes.[1]

New York City has recently adopted a ban on smoking in public places that is perhaps the toughest in the nation. Other than in a handful of places (such as private clubs), smoking is prohibited. It will even affect inmates, since the no-smoking policy also applies to New York jails.[2]

We Card, the placard that is (or should be) present in stores selling tobacco, tells people that if they want to buy cigarettes or other tobacco products and they look to be under the legal age to buy them, the sales agent is supposed to ask for identification that includes a birth date. This is simple compared to the requirements under the Tobacco Free Internet for Kids Act. Under this law, anyone selling tobacco on the Internet and shipping to a consumer in the United States must verify the age of the purchaser. One idea being tested includes requiring customers to provide their name, age, and driver's license number (subject to verification). Internet tobacco vendors must be able to supply hard evidence that they are not selling to underage smokers. Anyone selling to minors would be subject to a fine of up to $5,000, but only if the sale was made unintentionally. If vendors intentionally sell tobacco to minors, they could get even stiffer fines and face prison terms of up to five years![3]

A study conducted in the United States by the National Cancer Institute concluded that ultra light, light, mild, and similarly labeled cigarettes are no less harmful than regular cigarettes because smokers inhale harder and longer and they smoke more cigarettes to make up for lower nicotine levels. Philip Morris is taking a proactive stance by including literature with their cigarettes that explains this fact to smokers, although doing so is not a law in the Unites States. Other firms in the industry are likely to follow suit.[4]

The DOJ wants new regulations to limit tobacco promotions to black and white, with no "alluring" and "lifestyle" images (no woman reclining on a couch or no bare-chested man). The law would also require that warning messages cover at least 50 percent of the package and would include a ban on all point-of-purchase promotion (no racks or display signs). All of the following are examples of how promotion of tobacco products is being regulated in the United States: prohibition of the use of cigarette brand names or trademarks on clothing and other nontobacco products, cease-and-desist orders for advertising on newspaper home-delivery bags, fines for giving too much TV exposure to billboards at baseball games and car races, and penalties for ads placed in magazines that have teenage audiences.[5]

Huge awards, such as the Master Settlement Agreement of 1998 that awarded over $200 billion to 46 states (and the earlier four-state award of $40 billion), as well as individual awards, such as the one for Ms. Betty Bullock of California (the $28 billion award against Philip Morris was later reduced to *only* $28 million), have an impact on firms' profits; and as with taxes, these expenses are generally passed along to consumers in the form of higher prices. Even though tobacco products are addictive and therefore relatively *demand-insensitive* to price increases, multimillion and multi-billion dollar awards and steep tax increases have more than tripled cigarette prices to consumers in many areas. Demand is declining, especially among younger smokers (the prime target of anti-smoking campaigns and, some would argue, the tobacco firms); and high prices seem to be an effective deterrent for young smokers. Since smoking in this age group causes the most concern, lawmakers will likely keep using tax hikes as one tool in the arsenal to reduce smoking.[6]

Aside from the regulations, special interest groups are pressuring governments, lawyers, and even intermediaries for change. One example is the recent call from religious groups for Wal-Mart to explain its inconsistent selling practices of cigarettes in the United States, where Wal-Mart has minimal point-of-purchase display material, and in Mexico and South Korea, where banners, large cardboard displays, and other promotional items are aggressively exhibited.[7]

On every pack of cigarettes, Canada requires graphic pictures that depict diseased lungs, yellow teeth, a hospital patient on a respirator, or one of another dozen or so explicit photographs to remind people of the dangers of smoking. The concept is designed to reinforce the text messages that warn of lung disease, cancer, and death. Legislators in the United States (as well as in Brazil and other nations) are contemplating similar laws.[8] A ban on cigarette manufacturers' sponsoring sport and cultural events took effect in October 2003.[9]

Nova Scotia's Act to Protect Young Persons and Other Persons from Tobacco Smoke, which became effective on January 1, 2003, makes it illegal for anyone under the age of 19 to possess a cigarette.[10]

In Mexico, despite an increase in population between 1985 and 2002, from 60 million to 100 million people, cigarette consumption declined from 54 billion to 49 billion per year. Cigarette consumption is expected to decline further as new regulations take effect, especially the ban on television and radio advertisements and the 100 percent increase in cigarette tax.[11]

MIDDLE EAST AND AFRICA

In the Middle East, average cigarette consumption is between 500 and 1,500 cigarettes per year per person. In Bahrain, Israel, and Jordan, cigarette smoking is higher (2,000); but in Kuwait, smoking is higher than in the United States, Japan, and nearly anywhere else in the world—over 3,000 cigarettes annually for every person! Statistics from the last half of the 1990s indicate that except for South Africa, where cigarette consumption is slightly over 1,500 per person per year, most African nations have per capita consumption rates below 500. Trends indicate that these numbers are rising rather quickly. Within this region, people in Morocco, Libya, Algeria, Egypt, and other Northern African nations smoke an average of three times more, 1,500 per capita annually, than people in other nations. Somewhat surprising is the fact that it was the officials of African nations, not those in rich, developed countries, who provided the leadership behind the WHO's Framework Convention on Tobacco Control in 2002.[12]

Relatively few restrictions exist on cigarette consumption in Africa and the Middle East. Algeria, Iraq, Israel, and the Sudan have comprehensive advertising bans; and smoking is prohibited in some public areas in Benin, Botswana, Israel, Mali, Morocco, Nigeria, Sudan, South Africa, Syria, and Zambia. Voluntary employer restrictions are in place in a handful of other nations (including Kuwait, Lebanon, and Tunisia). In 2002, there were calls for bans on public smoking in Ghana, Kenya, and Uganda. That same year, Nigeria enacted advertising bans on billboards, print, and electronic media for tobacco products and banned public smoking in movie theaters, on public transportation, in offices, in schools, and in a host of other areas.[13]

EUROPE

Consumption trends across Europe are in some respects regional. Those people who smoke the least are found in the northern European nations of Norway (725 per capita), Sweden (1,200 per capita), and Finland (1,350 per capita). Most other nations in both eastern and western Europe (including France) have consumption rates of between 1,500 and 2,500 cigarettes annually. There are some exceptions. Heavy smokers exist in Spain (2,800 per capita) and Switzerland (2,700 per capita), as well as in Bulgaria, Belarus, Slovenia, Hungary, and Modova. Worst, though, is Greece, where consumption is over 4,300 cigarettes for every man, woman, and child, which is the highest rate in the world according to the WHO.[14]

The United Kingdom, Germany, and Romania have the laxest rules about smoking in public areas; while the rest of the European nations have varying degrees of regulations about smoking in public spaces. Advertising bans exist in Finland, Iceland, Italy, Norway, and Portugal.[15]

An attempt to impose a near complete ban on all tobacco advertising across the EU in 2000 was halted by Germany, which saw the restrictions as too harsh. In 2002, though, a revised ban was approved by the EU Parliament that prohibited sponsorship of sporting events and limited advertising to tobaccophile journals (such as *Cigar Today*) and magazines for executives in the tobacco industry.[16]

Effective January 2003, smokers in France began paying an additional 17 percent for a pack of Marlboro cigarettes. The money raised from the new tax on tobacco, the largest increase ever in that country, is to be used to help fund the country's health-care system.[17]

Sweden has had strict restrictions on cigarette advertising for over 25 years, including prohibition on print and electronic media ads, as well as point-of-purchase requirements that allow promotion in "moderation." Now, however, the Swedish government is working on laws that would require harsher messages on tobacco product packaging (such as "smoking kills" and "smokers die younger"), a ban on tobacco-branded merchandise (clothing, for example), and further limits on point-of-purchase displays. If passed, virtually all tobacco advertising would be outlawed. Besides packaging and promotion, Swedish laws include limits on product content, specifying the number of milligrams of nicotine allowed in cigarettes.[18]

ASIA-PACIFIC

Three of the top five cigarette markets in the world are in Asia. The Chinese smoke 1.6 trillion cigarettes each year. Add to this the Japanese (325 billion) and Indonesian (215 billion) markets, and these three nations account for over 2 trillion (or 40 percent) of the total 5.5 trillion cigarettes sold in the world each year. In Asia, consumption rates for cigarettes vary from relatively low rates of fewer than 150 per person in India to rates over 3,000 per person in Japan. More alarming are the statistics about China, where per capita consumption is 1,800 annually. According to the WHO study, consumption has increased by over 50 percent between 1990 and 2000 and the Chinese now smoke more that one-third of all of the world's cigarettes![19]

While tobacco advertising has been banned in Malaysia for about ten years, a new law also forbids cigarette manufacturers from sponsoring sporting and entertainment events. New laws would also prohibit the showing of movie scenes that depict smokers.[20]

Tougher new laws in Australia include banning public smoking in restaurants and bars while food is being served. Establishments must provide smoke-free areas for nonsmokers when food is not being served, and designated no-smoking areas must be made available around counters and bars (admittedly difficult to enforce). Tobacco companies that violate advertising regulations will also face million-dollar fines, rather than the $9,000 "slap on the wrist" that Philip Morris received for hosting a rave at Fox Studios.[21]

The Smoke-Free Environments Act in New Zealand prohibits tobacco promotion in most forms. This includes print/electronic advertising, sponsorship (cultural or sporting events as well as scholarships), and the use of trademarks or other identification on nontobacco products and items (clothing, for example).[22]

India is also concerned with the number of smokers in the country. Its sentiments are conveyed in a recent award-winning promotion. Ogilvy & Mather won the 2002 Gold Outdoor Award at the International Advertising Festival in Cannes for its antismoking ad that shows a cowboy standing over a dead horse with the copy "secondhand smoke kills."[23]

GLOBAL

The WHO is calling on the nations of the world to make a concerted effort to reduce smoking and to take a unified stance against promotion of tobacco products. In its Framework Convention on Tobacco Control, the WHO suggests that (much) higher prices and less promotion would reduce tobacco consumption and it asks that nations enact stricter rules about promotion (bans preferably), raise prices by instituting higher taxes, and help fund training and other costs associated with getting tobacco farmers to grow other crops.[24]

How will tobacco be sold in the future? Some new cigarette slogans are hinted at in pamphlets and from tobacco executives. Witness advertising copy for Advance cigarettes: "All of the taste, less of the toxins!" A possibility for Omni cigarettes: "Will not kill you as quick, or as much!" The former statement is an excerpt from the pamphlet included with Advance cigarette packages; the latter is a statement made by Bennett LeBow, CEO of the Vector Tobacco Company, about the advantages of the firm's new Omni cigarettes.[25]

According to the WHO, the future holds some interesting possibilities. Its predictions: by 2020, more cigarettes will be sold illegally (smuggled) than legally and tobacco advertising will be illegal. A decade later cigarettes will be sold only by prescription in developed nations and 75 percent of the price of cigarettes will be its tax. Tobacco-related costs in health care, insurance, and other expenses will reach $1 trillion annually by 2040.[26]

Questions and Research

1   Enter *buy cheap cigarette* in any search engine and see how many hits you get. What kind of proof of age is required? Are you able to identify the seller's location? Explain.

2   Identify in some detail the legal, political, and other challenges facing cigarette manufacturers in the United States and abroad.

3   Identify the various interest groups, organizations, and institutions that companies must consider if they plan to continue selling cigarettes.

4   Identify in detail strategies and tactics that cigarette companies are using to meet the challenges facing them. Suggest some other approaches.

5   Apart from the legal and political dimensions, do you see any ethical dimensions to these issues? If so, what questions would you raise and how would you respond to them?

Case Endnotes

1 Mackay, Judith and Michael Eriksen. *Tobacco Atlas,* 2002, Geneva, Switzerland: World Health Organization (available free of charge in PDF format: http://www5.who.int/tobacco/page.cfm?sid=84), Table A, pages 94–101.

2 "Smoking Bill Is Adopted as Council Ends Year," *New York Times,* December 19, 2002, page 3B; "A Smoking Ban in City's Jails Worries Correction Officers," *New York Times*, January 5, 2003, page 27.

3 "New Bill Aims to Separate Kids, Cigs Online," *Marketing News*, February 4, 2002, pages 6–7; Tobacco Free Internet for Kids Act (HR 2914 IH); *Tech Law Journal* (http://www.techlawjournal.com/cong106/tobacco/hr2914ih.htm); accessed December 6, 2003.

4 "Philip Morris Tells Smokers 'Light' Cigarettes Aren't Safer," *Wall Street Journal*, November 20, 2002, page B3.

5 "U.S. Seeks Tough Tobacco Restrictions," *Wall Street Journal*, March 11, 2002, page A1; "Bold Promotions Land R.J. Reynolds in Controversies," *Wall Street Journal*, September 6, 2002, pages A1, A6.

6 "Accepting $28 Million In Tobacco Suit," *New York Times,* December 25, 2002, page A21; "RL30058: Tobacco Master Settlement Agreement (1998): Overview, Implementation by States, and Congressional Issues," National Council for Science and the Environment, November 5, 1999 (http://www.ncseonline.org/NLE/CRSreports/Agriculture/ag-55.cfm); accessed January 6, 2003.

7 "Wal-Mart Rejects Shareholder Call to Explain Policies on Tobacco Ads," *Wall Street Journal*, March 1, 2002, page B2.

8 "Canada Hopes Photos Will Coax Smokers to Kick the Habit," *Washington Post,* October 6, 2002, page A30.

9 "Tobacco Companies Appeal Quebec Court Ruling On Law Banning Advertising," cnews (http://www.canoe.ca/NationalTicker/CANOE-wire.Tobacco-Ruling.html); accessed January 12, 2003.

10 "Cigarette possession becomes illegal for Novia Scotia's under 19," *British Medical Journal*, January 11, 2003.

11 "Mexico Strives to Snuff Out Tobacco Use Among Youths," *San Diego Union-Tribune*, June 2, 2002, page A24; "Tobacco Ads to Be Banned on Mexican TV and Radio," *Bloomberg News*, May 31, 2002 (http://quote.bloomberg.com/fgcgi.cgi?T=marketsquote99_news.ht&s=APPftXxM4VG9iYWNj); accessed January 6, 2003.

12 Mackay, Judith and Michael Eriksen. *Tobacco Atlas*, 2002, Geneva, Switzerland: World Health Organization (available free of charge in PDF format: http://www5.who.int/tobacco/page.cfm?sid=84); Table A, pages 94–101.

13 Mackay, Judith and Michael Eriksen. *Tobacco Atlas*, 2002, Geneva, Switzerland: World Health Organization (available free of charge in PDF format: http://www5.who.int/tobacco/page.cfm?sid=84; pages 74, 75.

Ban Smoking in Public, KNH Boss Urges Government," *Africa News,* October 14, 2002.
"Muhwezi Wants Ban on Smoking in Public," *Africa News,* August 22, 2002.
"Ban Smoking in Public Places," *Africa News,* June 17, 2002.
"House of Representatives Bans Tobacco Advertisement," *Africa News,* March 22, 2002.

14 Mackay, Judith and Michael Eriksen. *Tobacco Atlas*, 2002, Geneva, Switzerland: World Health Organization (available free of charge in PDF format: http://www5.who.int/tobacco/page.cfm?sid=84; pages 74–77.

15 "Europe Curbs Cigarette Promotion," *Wall Street Journal,* November 21, 2002, page B10.

16 "Europe Curbs Cigarette Promotion," *Wall Street Journal,* November 21, 2002, page B10.

17 "France Passes Largest Tobacco Tax Increase in Its History," *Tobacco Reporter* (http://www.tobaccoreporter. com/news/LateBreak.asp#france); accessed January 12, 2003.

18 "Match Game: Globally Speaking, U.S. Tobacco Laws Relatively Lax," *Marketing News*, November 11, 2002, pages 1, 11–12.

19 Mackay, Judith and Michael Eriksen. *Tobacco Atlas*, 2002, Geneva, Switzerland: World Health Organization (available free of charge in PDF format: http://www5.who.int/tobacco/page.cfm?sid=84), pages 74–77. Note that the Chinese market is tightly controlled and largely closed to foreign-made cigarettes. One concern is that if the market is opened to sophisticated foreign manufacturers, the allure of foreign-made tobacco products may increase overall consumption.

20 "Malaysia Bans 'Sly' Tobacco Ads," *Marketing News,* September 16, 2002, page 7.

21 "Tough New Law Stays on Pub, Club Cig Bans," *Sunday Mail,* March 17, 2002, page 3.
"Huff Away, Just Don't Puff," *Sydney Morning Herald,* December 18, 2002, page 13.
Million Dollar Fines for Tobacco Ads," *Sydney Morning Herald,* November 21, 2002, page 6.

22 Hoek, Janet and Robert Sparks. "Tobacco Promotion Restrictions—An International Impasse?" *International Marketing Review*, 2000, Volume 17, Number 3, pages 216–230.

23 "Applause for Commercial Breaks," *Philadelphia Inquirer*, November 16, 2002.

24 World Health Organization, "Intergovernmental Negotiating Body on the WHO Framework Convention on Tobacco Control, Fifth Session; New Chair's Text of a Framework Convention on Tobacco Control," June 25, 2002.

25 "Tobacco Industry Unleashes New Generation of Deceit," *USA Today,* November 11, 2002, page 1A.

26 Mackay, Judith and Michael Eriksen. *Tobacco Atlas,* 2002, Geneva, Switzerland: World Health Organization (available free of charge in PDF format: http://www5.who.int/tobacco/page.cfm?sid=84, pages 90–91.

Web Sites

Advertisements (http://tobaccofreekids.org/adgallery); examples of tobacco ads around the world.

American Medical Student Association Comprehensive List of Tobacco Texts (http://www.amsa.org/hp/tobtexts.cfm).

Smithsonian Institute, Marlboro Advertising Oral History and Documentation Project, ca. 1926–1986 (updated in 2000) (http://americanhistory.si.edu/archives/d7198.htm).

Parker-Pope, Tara. "Safer" Cigarettes: A History—PBS, NOVA presentation (http://www.pbs.org/wgbh/nova/cigarette/history.html).

Tobacco.org (http://www.tobacco.org) for the latest tobacco news and resources; World Health Organization (WHO) (http://www.who.int/health_topics/tobacco/en); and the WHO Tobacco Control Country Profiles (http://www5.who.int/tobacco/page.cfm?sid=57) — see especially Appendix B (PDF file) on legislation by nation.

World Bank (http://www1.worldbank.org/tobacco); tobacco control, including PowerPoint presentation on smuggling, tobacco controls in developing countries, health-related issues, and economic concerns.

Case 4.2

U.S. Pharmaceuticals, Inc. (B)

U.S. Pharmaceuticals (USP) is a U.S. firm with about 30 percent of its sales outside the United States. USP concentrates on the ethical drug business; but it has diversified into animal health products, cosmetics, and some patent medicines. Those other lines account for about one-fourth of USP's $800 million sales.

USP's international business is conducted in some 70 countries, mostly through distributors in those markets. In six countries, however, USP has manufacturing or compounding operations. (Compounding refers to the local mixing, assembling, and packaging of critical ingredients shipped from the United States.) USP's only Latin American manufacturing/compounding operations are in Latinia, a country with a population of about 30 million. Some products are shipped from Latinia to other Latin American markets.

Recently, USP has run into a problem in Latinia with its newest drug, Corolane 2. This drug is effective in treating certain intestinal diseases and infections. The drug has been under development for several years. Three years ago, when it showed considerable promise in the extensive testing process, USP registered the name *Corolane 2* in the United States and several other major world markets. Last year USP introduced Corolane 2 in the United States and several large foreign markets. Its early promise was confirmed by its quick acceptance by the medical profession in those countries.

Because of Corolane 2's initial success, USP plans to introduce the drug in all of its foreign markets. It planned to both manufacture and sell the drug in Latinia. A problem arose, however, because Jorge Rodriguez, a Latinian citizen, had already registered local rights to the name *Corolane 2*. Though a questionable procedure, this is perfectly legal, for Latinia is a code law country that gives exclusive rights to trade names according to priority in registration rather than to priority in use, which is the basis for exclusive rights in the United States. Furthermore, Latinia is one of several countries around the world that is not a member of the international patent and trademark agreements.

The problem for USP was that it could not sell Corolane 2 under that name in Latinia because Rodriguez owned the rights. Of course, Rodriguez was quite willing to sell his rights to the Corolane 2 name for $20,000.

Registering foreign brand names was Rodriguez's way of supporting himself. He made a good living by subscribing to foreign trade and technical publications (especially in the medical field) and registering all of the new names he found. Not all of the names would be exploited in Latinia, but enough of them were to make it profitable for him. Corolane 2 was an atypical case. Early in the drug's development process, journal articles told of successful tests and applications. As soon as the name *Corolane 2* was mentioned in one of the articles, Rodriguez registered it in Latinia, beating USP lawyers by just two weeks.

USP had encountered problems like this before in Latinia and other countries. It conducted R&D on many projects, most of which never reached the market. Some company officials believed it was not profitable to register every new product name in every market.

Questions and Research

1   Identify and evaluate the alternatives open to USP in Latinia.
2   What variables are important in this decision?
3   How could this kind of problem be avoided?

Case 4.3

What Is International Law?

If you were to ask someone for a straightforward definition of *international business*, the person might say something like "it is business conducted across national boundaries." So international law must be "law that is conducted across national boundaries." That might be possible were it not for **national sovereignty**, which, in simplest terms, can be described as a nation's inalienable right to govern itself without outside interference.

National sovereignty was at the heart of the Gulf War in the 1990s and the dispute between Iraq and the UN about weapons inspection. The allied coalition (the United States, France, the United Kingdom, Saudi Arabia, and other countries) defended Kuwait because Iraq sent in troops, which was a violation of Kuwait's sovereignty. The rationale for the Iraqi invasion, to some extent, was that Kuwait had been taking oil from Iraq's Rumaila field (theft of Iranian property and a violation of Iraqi national sovereignty). Iraq stated that the subsequent weapons inspections were a violation of its national sovereignty—that it has the right to do whatever it wants within its own borders.

China, France, and Mexico enact laws to which they hold their corporate and individual citizens responsible. Perhaps the best or truest form of international law takes place in the EU. The EU is a group of nations, each with its own national sovereignty; but the nations have agreed to policy making and legal restrictions that supersede national laws in certain circumstances and areas. No other international entity had the right to govern the activities of citizens from different nations.

Controversy over the use of child labor, poor working conditions, and exploitation in manufacturing products around the globe are issues raised by nations and consumers alike. Response may take the form of product boycotts, demonstrations, or government-imposed sanctions. The response from the offending nation is that these actions violate national sovereignty. It is an important issue that has consequences for everyone—consumers, CEOs, wage earners, policy makers, and responsible global citizens.

Recently, however, much to the dismay of American firms, lawyers representing foreign claimants have been using an arcane 1789 U.S. statute to sue American companies. The Alien Tort Claims Act was originally intended to reassure Europeans that the new United States of America would not provide protection to pirates and assassins. Recently, however, the law was used in a suit brought by Burmese citizens against Unocal, a southern California energy giant. In essence, the complaint was that Unocal was "vicariously responsible" for the Burmese government's use of peasants (forced at gunpoint, some of whom were tortured and killed) to build a pipeline to be used by Unocal to transport natural gas. Even though Unocal did not participate in building the pipeline, it was being held accountable for "providing practical assistance or encouragement" to the Burmese government. The terms were not disclosed, but the case was settled out of court in April 2005. Had the case gone to trial and Unocal lost, the amount of the monetary award would have been enormous and, more importantly, would have laid the foundation for similar claims against multinationals. More disturbing to American firms is that U.S. law is based on precedence; therefore, if this law had been successfully applied in the Unocal case, it would have been used in other cases as well. Coca-Cola and Citigroup are also facing suits under this law. It is estimated that over 1,000 American and foreign firms could be facing similar suits. The awards would be in the trillions of dollars, likely forcing some firms into bankruptcy.

What does this mean for international businesses? If someone breaks a contract with them in their home market, businesses can often sue for restitution. Between parties of different nationalities, though, this may be difficult or impossible because of national sovereignty and the refusal of one nation to allow its citizens to be subjected to the laws of another nation. In essence, it means that *any* contract that involves parties from different nations requires careful scrutiny and that all methods of reducing commercial and political risk should be considered—from using forward exchange contracts, arbitration clauses, and political risk insurance to withholding proprietary information and being a good corporate citizen.

Source: "Making a Federal Case of Overseas Abuses," *Business Week*, November 25, 2002, page 78.

Questions and Research

1   Identify an EU law that has an impact on business. Discuss how it might best be addressed.

2   Review ways in which contract disputes can be managed.

Case 4.4

SWOT Analysis

New laws need not mean new threats to businesses; rather, the laws should be evaluated as potential opportunities. For example, newly required security measures and regulations have been a boon to some companies. Consider Iridian Technologies, a company that has developed a relatively low-cost biometric iris recognition system that can be used at airports, sensitive installations, and other areas where security is a concern and access must be limited. This unobtrusive, fast, and accurate identification process is currently in use at Schiphol, JFK, and Heathrow airports, as well as at the Pentagon. The UN uses the Iridian system to allow fairer distribution of supplies by identifying double-dippers at food aid stations in Pakistan.

Environmental concerns spurred by conservationists, multilateral agreements such as the Kyoto Accord, and host government regulations have increased incentives to develop green products. Examples include hybrid vehicles, such as the Toyota Prisus, Honda Insight, and Civic Hybrid, and concepts that will likely arrive to market shortly, including Honda's RDX (a sport utility electric and gasoline hybrid) and the Acura DN-X (a 400-horsepower muscle car that gets a reported 42 miles per gallon versus the more traditional 10 to 15 miles per gallon for similar cars).

To help power the natural gas hybrid vehicles, the FuelMaker Corporation of Toronto, Canada, has developed a home fueling system that connects a car to a natural gas line in an owner's home. Initially priced at $2,000, "Phill" allows consumers to "gas up" the Honda GX or a similar vehicle at home rather than hunt for a station with the equipment needed to fuel hybrid gas cars.

Sources: "Eyes Have It for Identification," *Philadelphia Inquirer*, Wednesday, October 24, 2002, pages C1, C4; "Green Garage," *Los Angeles Times*, Wednesday, October 16, 2002, page 1.

Questions and Research

1 Research, identify, and discuss new products being developed to reduce piracy.

2 What are some potential threats facing firms as new, stricter environmental laws are enacted? What if the laws are relaxed or adherence is postponed (for example, car emissions)?

CHAPTER 5

Information Technology and the Global Business

Learning Objectives

Information technology (IT) has changed the way business is conducted, and information has become a strategic weapon.

The main goals of this chapter are to

1 Describe recent IT innovations, focusing on global linkages with customers and suppliers.

2 Provide examples of how the Internet and electronic data interchange (EDI) are used effectively to communicate with customers and coordinate transactions between customers and suppliers.

3 Develop information about customers around the world, using Internet-based interaction and point-of-sale information-gathering techniques.

4 Demonstrate how firms involve customers in new product design and interact with them after the sale, enhance customer loyalty, and stimulate repeat business.

5 Present new international market research techniques, such as using virtual shopping environments to collect data and tracking customer behavior on the Internet.

Global Linkages: An Overview

IT has dramatically changed the way companies conduct international business. Global IT linkages can connect a firm, its partners, and its customers in a way that strengthens relationships not possible in the past.[1] Significant linkages, which are summarized in Figure 5-1, include the following:

1. The company can *monitor the POS* to obtain detailed information on consumer purchase behavior. POS information systems include data on sales sorted by brands, quantities, prices, package size, time of day and day of week, and month. Data may also be collected on whether coupons were used and competing products were purchased, providing instant feedback about customer decisions, letting a firm know exactly what was sold, at what prices, in what quantities, and at which location. The company can use that information to update inventory records, make decisions about additional production runs, adjust prices and launch sales, and design new products.

   The information collected feeds into **database marketing**, where vast stores of knowledge about customers and potential customers are analyzed and utilized to develop products and business strategies. Information, aggregated by individual store and then by larger groupings such as city, region, and sales territory, allows managers to relate actual sales to historical data, competitive market share, advertising, promotion, and pricing. In turn, this leads to better information about the effectiveness of business strategies.

   For example, a company can collect general information about visitors who access its web site—frequency of visits, number of unique visitors, length of time spent at the site, frequency of downloads, etc. Firms can use the web statistics they collect through tracking software to redesign the site (suggesting the addition or deletion of content) or to change site navigation. Since a company can identify the locations of users, it may offer different products (more beach wear in coastal areas, for example) or change the language of its site. If a company finds that it receives repeated requests for information, it may decide to add a link or a section of frequently asked questions. The data from the tracking software may also indicate that the firm should emphasize after-sales service.

   Data mining (analysis of data to identify patterns for predictive purposes) is not an easy task, in part because of the vast amounts of data involved. Data mining is akin to getting 10,000 hits, using a web search engine—no one has time to look at all of the results. Data, if not used in a timely fashion, becomes useless; and the money spent on collecting it is wasted. Software manufacturers are addressing this issue by making it quicker and easier to analyze data. Enterprise Miner software, developed by SAS, used in conjunction with a new version of Predictive Model Markup Language (PMML), allows users to integrate predictive and descriptive models more easily. IBM's DB2 Information Integrator provides an efficient means of caching data from a variety of sources that permits users to maintain data in a way that is more easily and quickly accessible. Microsoft is competing with its Analysis Services, which is being purchased by smaller firms because of the database's ease of use and compatibility with other components of the data mining functions.

2. The company can *interact with the customer*, both pre- and postsale: at presale by allowing customers to communicate wants and desires and to be involved in designing and testing the product; at postsale by collecting and using information about customer satisfaction and about events and problems surrounding pre- and postsale service. The goal is to enhance customer loyalty and encourage repeat purchase behavior.

3. The company can use IT to *develop new international research techniques* like those based on simulated, or virtual, shopping environments. The company can monitor consumer behavior in the virtual shop to trace the effects of a variety of decisions about product features, price, packaging, and promotions in a simulated environment.

4. The company can *use information networks, principally the Internet, to sell and develop a new direct channel of distribution* to the customer, allowing customized shopping at the convenience of the customer. The Internet allows even small firms to interact directly with customers around the world who have access to the Internet.

5. The company can *use the Internet and EDI to deal directly with business partners, customers, and suppliers*. The Internet is the central medium for that purpose—ubiquitous, inexpensive, and available nearly all over the world to small as well as large companies. Combining the Internet with the intranet (internal corporate networks) allows firms to communicate both internally and externally. Companies can use those networks to send orders, negotiate prices, set up auctions at which prequalified suppliers submit bids, exchange product specifications, track production status, track shipments, and handle billing and payments.

   Advanced use of the Internet would include interaction at the product design phase where suppliers and customers interact with a firm in developing new products, with a view to reducing time to market and reducing cost to manufacture. EDI is the principal technical communication vehicle for such information exchange between a company and its business partners in the world today, displacing the telephones, faxes, and memorandums of yesteryear! Corporate data networks and EDI facilitate accurate interaction, simplifying the use of techniques such as quick response production planning based on up-to-date sales figures. Another major innovation has been just-in-time supply chains, with EDI allowing communication of quick-response production schedules and required delivery quantities.

Figure 5-1 Information Technology and Global Business

Information Technology as a Strategic Business Tool

Global Customer Linkages:	Global Supplier Linkages:
Point-of-Sale Data Collection	Development of Direct Distribution
Presale and Postsale Interaction with Customers	to the Customer, Primarily Internet-Based
Research Using Virtual Shopping Techniques	EDI to Deal Directly with Business Partners

Changes in the information environment, technological infrastructure, and communication culture and related factors have had dramatic implications for strategy development. Those changes have affected a firm's evaluation of market attractiveness, its competitive position, and all other aspects of planning and implementation. Information systems development also influences a firm's organizational structure, dissolving boundaries between the firm and its environment, its suppliers, and its competitors and customers, as well as boundaries within the firm (reducing barriers among finance, marketing, and manufacturing, for example). Information content also becomes a feature of the product and even becomes a product in its own right. Applied systematically, information systems can affect the performance and delivery of a product or service.

Democratization of Technology

This information transformation is comparable to the industrial revolution in the nineteenth and twentieth centuries in that it impacts nearly everything people do. How they live and interact with one another is changing dramatically. But technological advances and new ways of using technology are taking place at a more rapid pace than what occurred during the industrial revolution. Not only is the cost of connecting to others decreasing rapidly, but wireless technologies are allowing people in even the most remote regions (those without the traditional infrastructure) to tie in to the information systems if they so choose. Thomas Friedman, in *The Lexus and the Olive Tree,* refers to this as the democratization of technology and information.[2] The advances in information availability afford greater interactivity and transparency for anyone participating in the global business environment. Furthermore, the relationships between a company and its customers are changing dramatically, with the balance of power shifting toward well-informed consumers who are seeking long-term integrated solutions rather than a one-time product purchase.[3] Companies that recognize the shift will thrive, while those stuck in the perceptions of the last quarter-century will be replaced by savvy competitors. Relationship marketing will become increasingly important, which may, at times, go counter to outsourcing of customer service.[4, 5]

At the core of many of the advances in IT is the Internet, allowing people to exchange information at a rate and volume not possible only a short while ago. While speed of transmitting data has increased, more importantly, perhaps, is the rapid penetration of devices and software that allow people access to the technology. More people are using the Internet every day, whether they are sending pictures to relatives around the globe or downloading maps to the car for directions to the nearest electronics store. The Internet has changed how people communicate with one another and has altered the nature and process of making strategic and tactical decisions. The Internet impacts everything that businesses do—whether dealing with price, promotion, or the physical distribution of goods and services or communicating with employees, providing training for partners via e-learning, or sharing company data. Businesses also shape the Internet, acting as **change agents** when they allow customers to print out cents-off coupons for groceries rather than clip coupons or to download a movie rather than go to a theater or video rental store.

Consumers are also becoming more powerful. The Internet is more interactive than other avenues of communication with consumers and others, providing them with the power and control to select what they see; to compare product, price, and delivery offerings among competitors; and to access broader sets of alternatives in nearly every product category. (Firms must put a lot of information on the Web, making it easily accessible and allowing consumers to pick and choose.) Consumers rely on the Internet as a search tool in large part because it is cheaper, is less time-consuming, and offers a broader assortment than conducting a search by calling companies or writing to providers with questions. Consumers are able to become better informed (or ill-informed depending on the source) quicker. Consumer power comes from the ability to direct the message received.

IT also raises new issues, perhaps the most controversial of which is personal privacy. Security against theft and destruction of data, accuracy of information, morality, taxes, and cultural invasion are also concerns that accompany enhanced IT capabilities. Table 5-1 provides some of the issues surrounding web-based communication, which is inherently global in nature.

Table 5-1 Web-Based Global Communication	
Foci of Web-Based Communication:	**Web Communication Strategy Issues:**
• Development of a presence	• Web site design and positioning
• Potential sales outlet and distribution	• Infrastructure for web-centric communication
• Product and services information	• Coexistence with other distribution channels
• Collection of customer/visitor information	• Product range for Internet site sales
• Communication and interaction with customers	• B2B communication
• After-sales service, user support	• B2C communication
	• Data use and protection

A Global Network Illustrated

Figure 5-2 shows global linkages at Mattel, providing an example of global networks. This U.S.-based toy designer depends on feedback from customers around the world for new product ideas. Mattel takes new toy ideas and selects independent Far East-based companies as manufacturing subcontractors. Inventory statistics from a network of global warehouses are analyzed at the U.S. headquarters to arrive at follow-on orders that are given to the manufacturing subcontractors. Finished products ship directly from the Far East subcontractors to the various global warehouses, with allocations based on sales figures attained from global customers, which are analyzed at headquarters and at regional offices. Sales figures and inventory levels are also relayed to and analyzed by management for monitoring and changing prices, when indicated, to achieve increased sales in an industry where the bulk of demand is concentrated in a short selling season. Management's twin imperatives are (1) to ensure that popular toys are available in sufficient quantities around the world to satisfy demand (hence, the need to transmit rush follow-on orders to distant manufacturing subcontractors) and (2) to price efficiently enough to clear toy inventories to prevent losses from obsolescence of outdated toy inventories. Without the global information network in use at Mattel, such market responsiveness would be difficult.

Figure 5-2   Global Linkages at Mattel

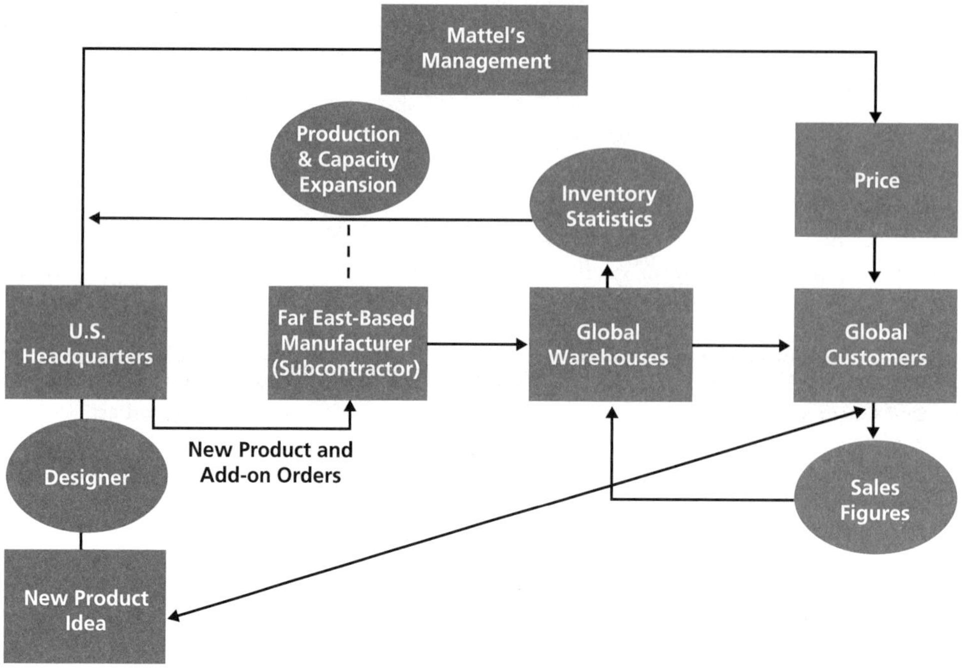

Developing global networks is complicated by the very nature of the international environment. Difficulties arise from:

- Differences in the level of infrastructure across countries, including (1) the depth and sophistication of computer networks; (2) the availability, reliability, and cost of telephone systems; and (3) the penetration of computer hardware and software usage across companies. Arguably, those three areas are fundamental to the development of IT-based business.
- Traditional barriers, such as tariffs, quotas, and NTBs (for example, customs formalities and local content laws).
- Cultural differences such as those created by language and business practices.
- Legal differences that complicate the establishment of commercial relationships with overseas partners and require close attention to questions of data security and network access.
- Geographical distance and different time zones, which make communication difficult.
- Barriers created by government regulation, such as limits on transborder data flows and use of value-added networks (VANs).
- Differences in the level of technological sophistication of overseas partners, such as in the use of information systems, computer hardware and software, incompatible standards, and differences in managerial expertise brought to bear on subjects such as quality control, inventory management, customer service and support, and global market research. Those differences complicate efforts to tie partners into the global network.

Global Networks: A Conceptual Framework

Figure 5-3 outlines an idealized framework for global networks that would include the following major elements:

1. Linkages between a firm and its customers and suppliers around the globe.

2. Integrated global communications aimed at global markets and global service needs that connect a multinational sales force with distributors and suppliers as well as customers.

3. A set of major environmental linkages with outsiders, including host governments, multinational competitors, and the global logistics infrastructure, with both in-house entities and independent third parties.

4. Linkages to the implementation aspects of such global networks. This is principally comprised of control, organizational structure, and personnel. Equally important are technical issues crucial to the smooth functioning of such global networks.

The remainder of this chapter will examine in greater detail the various elements of such a global network.

Figure 5-3 A Conceptual Framework for Global Networks

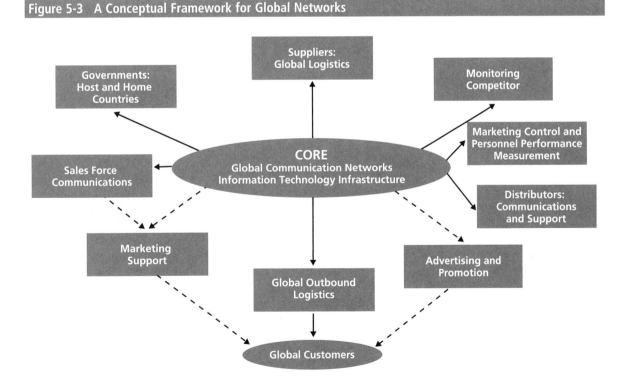

Linkages With Customers

As IT becomes more closely intertwined with the very fabric of doing business, information becomes both a critical resource enabling a company to compete in the marketplace and a service in its own right that the company can offer and sell to its customers. A company competes in two arenas: the physical *marketplace* and the virtual *marketspace*. Information changes the way a company creates value and competes within the virtual value chain. A well-known example is Federal Express's system, which allows its customers to access the FedEx database and verify where a letter or parcel is in the system: whether it is en route, whether it has been delivered, who received it, and when it was delivered. Providing that information allows FedEx to provide an additional service of value to the customer, differentiating itself from the competition, building customer loyalty, and increasing repeat business. Value chain activities in the virtual world include *gathering, organizing, selecting, synthesizing, and distributing information.* Often those steps result in a company entering a new business. Table 5-2 summarizes the information needed for specific strategic decisions.

Consider the opportunities offered by a central database of books, music, videos, and other forms of digital material:

- Customers can preview or try out the product before deciding whether to buy it. As part of the interactive experience, customers can also contribute reviews and suggestions for other potential buyers.
- A distributor can construct customer profiles based on customers' previous choices or searches and suggest additional items that are likely to be of interest. Thus, the distributor can customize the message for each customer. Coupled with customer reviews and suggestions, a firm can direct its product development and acquisition to meet changing buyer patterns.
- A company can offer to act as a reseller for other providers for materials they do not carry (for example, used books and DVDs).
- A company can store all of its recorded movies, music, and books in digital archives, particularly when the files are compressed. The material, now a new product, requires little in terms of inventory carrying costs and affords customers a broader array of products from which to choose.
- With direct links between store and customer, traditional intermediaries become less important, reducing distribution costs.

Amazon is one firm that uses this technology effectively. The virtual marketspace opportunities described previously are available to consumers anywhere in the world who have access to the Internet and who can access a company's databases and home page. Suddenly, a company is close to customers in distant lands—to teenagers in Tokyo as well as in Tucson. Imagination and creativity are a firm's only limits in using the virtual marketspace to attract and serve international customers. As illustrated, companies can:

- Develop new products and services tailored to the needs of small customer segments—even individual customers.
- Interact directly with customers to capture and store information about them and to use that

Table 5-2	Global Networks and Information Needs
Strategy Area	**Information Needs**
Global Sourcing	Manufacturing lot sizes of parts and subassemblies by location; monitoring inventory, costs, and quality; allocating production; exchanging design information; and changing product specifications
Global Logistics	Servicing overseas subsidiaries: up-to-date information on inventory, manufacturing output, demand in various markets, shipping details, and delivery dates, all categorized by finished goods and parts numbers
Global Servicing	Achieving service quality levels; offering warranty and after-sale services; providing worldwide personnel and parts; and providing training and documentation, including service updates
Global Competitors	Monitoring competitive new product offerings and analyzing competitor market share, cash flow, and profits
Strategic Partners	Exchanging R&D results; communicating strategic goals and tactics; and coordinating transfer of technology, manufacturing, and marketing
National Governments	Providing local output and value-added statistics, company-specific export and import flows, local pricing, promotion, and service and complying with national interests
Global Customers	Coordinating multinational strategies (adapting products, offering discounts, coordinating pricing and credit, and allocating product to markets), developing and maintaining customer and sales leads databases, and utilizing a global sales force and distributor management

information to better serve them. A major gain is that such information allows a firm to more precisely forecast demand and shifts in preferences, avoiding both stockouts and excess inventory that could become obsolete and have to be discounted.

- Move a product's utility (the reason for purchasing a product) from the physical to the virtual world, affecting scale and scope economies. In general, such a move makes it easier for small companies to sell around the globe. Information-based products and services have low or no variable costs of production while the fixed costs of production are high, resulting in a disproportionate investment in infrastructure. Such products are often patentable, and a patent can serve as a barrier to entry.

- Provide access when and where customers want it. As long as a server is running and connected to the Internet, anyone can view the material on a web page, regardless of location. Promotion via the Internet can act as mass personal selling, where communication is tailored to the individual. No longer is promotional timing a problem (the policy of advertising windshield wipers only when it rains); the Internet is "on" 24/7/365. No longer is geography a problem (a billboard on Route 76 is not seen by people on Route 23, for example); the information is available for individuals in Toledo, Ohio (in English), and Toledo, Spain (in Spanish).

Virtual Shopping Environments and Experiments

Virtual shopping environments allow researchers to observe consumers under near-real circumstances. Those experiments provide firms with an opportunity to gather valuable information, incurring fewer competitive risks and lower costs than traditional field research, which uses controlled field experiments and focus groups.

In a virtual shopping environment, a customer interacts with a grocery store or any other retail outlet as simulated on a computer. The customer can survey the layout of the store, pick directions to walk, stroll down an aisle, and watch the display of goods on shelves unfold. The customer can stop and examine a product more closely, read the label, and peruse product literature. The customer can see the price, conduct comparison shopping, look for promotions, and perhaps buy the product. The computer records many aspects of customer behavior, including the time spent shopping, alternatives compared, the order in which products and categories were examined, the decision to purchase, as well as the quantity purchased and the price paid.

The simulation can be quite realistic, offering 3D representations of products. Such tests may be costly to set up; but once the store layout and product assortment have been digitized and stored in a simulation database, companies can conduct experiments that monitor customer response to variables such as changes in price, packaging, and promotions; new display techniques; and new products. Companies can explore questions such as the drawing power of a brand under different competitive conditions, the impact of price cuts, and expanded offerings. Researchers can study whether a firm's product line meets customer needs and understand which display mode (arraying a firm's products all together next to the competition's or according to size of package, for example) best elicits a desired customer purchase behavior.

Virtual shopping experiments have many advantages: They are easy to set up and can be modified easily. They can be kept secret from the competition. Experimental design methodology can be used to study the effects of key variables such as price cuts and package size. Such experiments can also help managers understand the shopping process; that is, how customers buy products. Virtual shopping makes international research relatively easy because the virtual shop can be presented to customers in different countries via a computer network. In addition, the shop can be modified to offer local products priced in local currencies and in the local language. Comparing standardization versus adaptation strategies is more easily accomplished using this approach.

Of course, not all products can be tested or sold in virtual shopping environments; products that customers want to touch or smell or taste are harder to simulate. It has been shown that sensory input has an impact on the purchase decision.[6,7] The capability of equipment and software is improving, though; and the improvements will allow the senses to play a part in these virtual spaces in the near future. Work is being conducted to improve a virtual haptic display device—a glove that connects to the computer—that will allow consumers to "feel" soft objects such as fabric. Adding smell to visual displays, such as movies, has been attempted for decades; and progress is being made in this area as well. VirTra Systems (http://www.virtrasystems.com) offers virtual reality market testing and promotion that promises total "immersive virtual realty," including a 360 degree visual experience and simulations that include tactile sensations and real-life smells. In summary, virtual shopping illustrates the gains to be realized from using IT in conducting research.

Online and Internet-Based Shopping

With the creation of virtual shops, it is a short step to allowing customers to do their shopping in these online stores. The difference is that in virtual shops, customer shopping is simulated; in online shopping, actual transactions take place, with money being exchanged for goods and services. As issues such as confidentiality and security of payment are addressed to customers' satisfaction, more people will shop online. According to the Association of National Advertisers, 80 percent of U.S. companies are selling products online—providing a wide array of services and goods.[8] Recent trends in Internet shopping include the following:

- Large retailers such as Wal-Mart are influential in determining which products are made available to consumers, and they can squeeze suppliers to get better margins for themselves. Online shopping allows suppliers to bypass the retailer, go directly to the customer, and offer consumers a wider array of choices.
- The Internet allows businesses to expand consignment-like models, which means e-businesses can offer a broader product line to consumers. For example, Amazon.com sells books and DVDs that it carries in its own inventory, but it also allows other firms to advertise and sell books and DVDs through its web site. (Amazon collects and forwards the charges for the merchandise, shipping, and handling and provides an assurance about the sellers' products.) While the Internet allows consumers to shop the world, the Internet also allows businesses from different geographic areas to combine resources in a synergistic manner. Amazon.com quickly expanded from being a seller of books to a company in the entertainment business to a firm that fulfills a variety of shopping needs.
- Firms must be aware, though, that the nationality of users is expanding and changing. While the majority of people with Internet access currently reside in the United States (30 percent), 23 percent are now Europeans and nearly 15 percent reside in Asia. In 2003, Spain posted a 23 percent increase in the number of its population that used the World Wide Web, versus 3 percent in the United States. Increasingly, this will force companies to "go global" if they are to remain competitive.
- Online shopping offers convenience, allowing customers to shop 24/7/365, and affords more choices in products and suppliers. Time and place become less relevant. Online shopping also increases value because part of the savings from not incurring retailers' margins can be passed on to shoppers. Online shopping also allows customizing based on customers' needs in product areas as diverse as computer systems, clothing, and home furnishings—referred to as "customerization."[9]

The Internet's Impact On Global Business[10]

Firms find that as customers gain increased access to the Internet, it becomes a more viable approach to interacting with customers and their households. Through the Internet, a company can:

- Develop a presence on the Internet, enhancing its image and using the Internet as a vehicle for advertising—both broad corporate image advertising as well as product- and service-specific advertising. A company's image is a precious asset, difficult to replicate but easy to lose.[11] However, customers on the Internet typically approach sites because they are looking for information, interaction and communication, or entertainment or because they want to close a transaction. Customers are likely to bypass advertising unless the message is informative and helps them in the decision-making process. A danger is that online shoppers may have difficulty separating advertising from objective content, leading consumers to question the validity of information provided at a company's web site.[12] More on the topic of web site design will be discussed in a later section.
- Provide information about products and services, prices, product availability, order status, access to its databases, and links to other useful sites on the Web. The more useful such infor-

mation is to customers, the more customers will visit the site and the longer they will stay, making the site "sticky" and allowing the company more time to capture their business.

- Communicate and interact with customers by handling queries from them, responding to complaints and feedback about products, and conducting research by persuading customers to respond to queries and forms on the Web (giving the firm the ability to conduct research in real time and continuously update its information).

- Provide after-sales service, product upgrades, and access to online experts and facilitate the formation of user groups. Firms can offer a chat room in which users communicate with one another about product use and new features desired, make complaints, and ask questions. This value-added service enhances customer loyalty and encourages repeat business even as it builds confidence in the company. Adding free e-mail service is an example of providing clients with a reason to keep coming back to a company's web site.

- Sell to the customer. The most enticing aspect of the Internet is a firm's ability to close commercial transactions with clients and obtain payment. The news and music industries are leading the way with micropayments (sales involving prices below $1 per unit). Other payment technologies—such as use of cell phones to make purchases from vending machines (payments are collected by the cell phone service provider or are prepaid and stored on cell phone microchips), advances in biometrics (allowing account access via fingerprint or retinal scan), and acceptance of digital checks to speed transaction processing—are changing business practices. Technologies that provide convenience to consumers; cost-effective transaction processing for firms; and, perhaps more importantly, security for all participants will make buying and selling via electronic means increasingly attractive and profitable.

Pricing on the Internet

The Internet allows customers to be fully informed. They can use search agents to learn about competing products' features, warranties, return policies, prices, shipping and handling costs, and taxes. This means that in many instances, companies will find themselves competing more on price than on features. How does this help firms selling products that are differentiated by superior quality and service? Those companies must be able to communicate to customers that the lowest price may not provide the desired bundle of attributes. Firms that compete on attributes other than price must also realize, though, that price competition will only intensify. This means they must develop business models that allow profitable operations at lower prices by seeking lower manufacturing costs, reducing distribution costs (bypassing channel intermediaries), and cutting costs by carrying smaller inventories. Closer and faster communication between company and consumer allows firms to practice just-in-time manufacturing and better customization of product. As mentioned previously, new payment technologies are allowing firms to profitably unbundle products such as music and news and deliver specific songs and stories to individual users.

In the United States, another issue is sales tax. Most U.S. Internet sales do not require payment of sales tax. However, Wal-Mart and other large retailers with physical locations in many states are lobbying that sales tax be applied to all online sales so they can compete in price with retailers that have no brick-and-mortar outlets.

Can the Internet Coexist with Other Channels?

Many large firms that dominate their industry have assiduously developed close channel relationships with distributors, wholesalers, and retailers. The major U.S. car companies are an example, relying on a nationwide network of car dealers who sell in a time-honored ritual of haggling over car price, an options package, and financing. The dilemma faced by automobile manufacturers is that, by developing Internet-based purchase alternatives for their consumers, they cannibalize sales from existing channels, taking sales from existing outlets (such as the car dealer up the street). They are not generating additional sales. (This would anger the bricks-and-mortar dealers and the salespeople who work there, having no impact on total sales.)

Using the Internet as a channel of distribution can also upset corporate culture, which has been built up over a long period of time. Yet firms have no alternative. Companies that delay or make a desultory attempt because they are afraid of the impact on current channel relationships simply allow newcomers to obtain first-mover advantages with the new channel (the Internet). For example, in book retailing, Barnes & Noble was a "late mover," slow to recognize the Internet as a new channel; a newer firm, Amazon, became an industry leader very quickly. The Internet will become a dominant new channel. Therefore, firms must establish their position while working with existing channels and salespeople, perhaps by giving them a portion of sales commissions during a transition period. Otherwise, firms are likely to disappear.

Firms are also learning to use both traditional and online outlets by offering the convenience of online shopping with instant delivery for products that cannot be downloaded. Best Buy, for instance, encourages consumers to shop online, order and pay for the merchandise, and pick up the purchase at the bricks-and-mortar store (convenient because the stores are nearly ubiquitous).

Can Everything Be Sold on the Internet?

Products such as books, airline tickets, hotel rooms, vacations, computer hardware and software, and stocks and bonds are some of the products that first made a splash using the Internet as a channel of distribution. Those products still dominate Internet sales. But as customers become more comfortable with shopping on the Internet, other products are being sold online: homes, flowers, mortgages, insurance, office products, home furnishings, and apparel, to name a few. Certain products are better suited to Internet sales—products whose features can be assessed online; products for which competing offerings can be ranked; products that are nonperishable, light in weight, and easy to ship; and products that are familiar to customers. But if you include what is available on auction web sites, *anything* can be purchased on the Internet (including, purportedly, a human liver). Consumers must also be willing to postpone consumption gratification until the product arrives; for example, buying a bottle of wine to take to a dinner that evening would still be purchased at the corner store. But the expanding range of products sold online suggests that merchants are using their ingenuity to adapt their products for sale on the Web.

B2B Communication and Transactions on the Web

Even while firms grapple with consumer marketing on the Web, over half of all Internet transactions are between businesses (i.e., B2B transactions). Businesses find that they can more easily procure product inputs, supplies, and components on the Web. Firms can clearly lay out specifications, prequalify suppliers, and post projects for bids. Such procurement saves immensely on product purchasing costs and can be speedy. EDI allows for rapid interchange of information and payment.[13] Integrated web-based sourcing, production, and tracking systems allow manufacturers to manage production, movement, and storage of products in ways not possible previously. Smaller inventories, fewer stockouts, and less obsolete merchandise mean higher profits.

Infrastructure for Web-Centric Business

Secure networks are a must for preserving company confidentiality and for providing peace of mind to customers as they arrange to pay for their purchases. Speed of Web response is also important because customers are likely to become impatient when secure transaction processing networks are slow. Consumers also worry about the integrity of the companies they buy from; arrangements that guarantee customer rights, the ability to effect product returns and exchanges, and the ability to settle disputes will help alleviate such worries and win the customers' trust. To better understand consumer behavior and trends, firms use measurement tools to gather data on visitor traffic and interest. Services such as Media Metrix, tracking software such as DeepMetrix, feedback on customer satisfaction surveys, and cookies (small bits of information stored on visitors' computers) are ways in which companies learn more about their consumers, both actual and potential.

Web Site Design and Positioning

Attractive, well-designed web sites are important if a firm expects to get and maintain customers' attention, ultimately resulting in purchases. Sites that load quickly are essential, as are sites that are structured so that clients can quickly and easily find the information they are seeking. A web site is an advertisement as much as it is a source of information about the company and its products. Thus, the same level of attention and graphic design expertise that is devoted to print and other media ads should also be given to web site design. (See Table 5-3.)[14] Major firms attempt to make their sites comprehensive so that visitors stay as long as possible; for example, Microsoft provides one-stop access from its msn.com site to e-mail; chat facilities; and travel, brokerage, news, and entertainment links—all under its aegis. Smaller companies often form consortia, linking each other's sites, such as those between purveyors of books and CDs, software, movies, travel services, toys, and brokerage services.

Portals that contain narrow but deep coverage of a particular topic (such as the EU) are expensive to construct and maintain, whether updating statistics, stories, and other content or linking to other resources (since web addresses, or URLs, change constantly, which leads to user frustration because the hyperlinks no longer work). The other extreme is represented by firms such as Amazon, which tries to be a one-stop shop on the Internet, having expanded from books into movies, music, and games, then beyond entertainment into jewelry, electronics, and more. The chief competitive advantage is not so much the range of product offerings as it is a base of shoppers who like to shop online, were early adopters of this technology, and are repeat buyers, likely to exhibit loyalty as long as their shopping experience is satisfying.

Table 5-3 Developing a Global Web Presence	
1. Use simple language.	5. Use graphics to help communicate written concepts.
2. Avoid complicated sentence structures.	6. Avoid complicated and unnecessary graphics.
3. Use the active voice.	7. Translate the web site into selected target languages.
4. Avoid humor.	

Companies must incorporate their domain name, which is part of the URL, into their branding strategy. No one wants to key in an address such as http://www.getabettermousetrap forlessmoney.com. A firm's web site must also be easily found using search engines, which is partly a function of how a web site is designed (meta tags and the like) as well as how useful people find the site (the more a site is referenced, the more likely it is to be near the top of search engine results). And as multinationals have learned, language is important when branding. For example, in a Hispanic market, General Motors used the brand name Nova, meant to illicit an image of a bright star. Unfortunately, in Spanish, the brand name means "'doesn't go"—not a good name for a car.

Despite the claim that promotion via the Internet is relatively cheap compared with other methods, it is costly to design, upgrade, and maintain a web presence. Even though their resources may be somewhat limited, small companies can compete more directly with larger firms. Small companies must spend the time, energy, and money needed to design an effective web site that is easy to navigate, is stimulating, and provides the content consumers are seeking. Sending bulk e-mail may be a less expensive option than sending bulk land-based mail, but designing the message and harvesting (or purchasing) e-mail addresses is not cost free.

Customization

One of the most exciting aspects of using IT in business is the ability to find out exactly what customers want, then customizing to meet individual customers' needs. What can be digitized can be customized! The new hybrid consumers expect to be able to customize the products they buy and the information they seek at a price they are willing to pay.[15]

Customization requires continuous learning by both a company and its customers. Firms that listen to their customers create a sense of caring, which leads to customer loyalty. Of course, this built-in loyalty advantage must be supplemented with competitive, quality products; in addition, products must evolve to accompany technological improvements.

An example of such customization is Peapod, a company that allows customers to buy groceries online. Peapod works with grocery chains to present the available assortment of goods and services online. The products are displayed in whichever format the customer requests: displayed by produce category, by items on sale at that time, by brand name, by package size, etc. Then the customer indicates what items he or she wants to buy. Peapod's buyers purchase and deliver the groceries for an additional charge. Despite the higher price, customers find that they save time and money by taking advantage of sales, doing comparison shopping, and avoiding impulse purchases. Peapod has a high rate of repeat business; and by asking customers to rate their shopping experience, it learns from its customers. This allows Peapod to modify and improve its service, particularly in critical areas such as handling customer complaints and correcting erroneously filled orders.

Who controls and learns from interaction with customers—the retailer or the manufacturer? Whichever party controls the information gains power. One solution is an alliance, as in the auto industry, where car manufacturers work with dealers to deliver mass customization. In such instances, dealers receive special training that allows them to deal effectively with customers who are armed with information about buying cars and to respond quickly to customers' e-mail queries.

What are some key steps in developing an information-based mass customization approach? In adapting to today's consumer, firms must address four key areas:

1. Companies must gather information to learn about their customers, recognizing, however, that not all customers are equally important. Initially, companies need to concentrate on large-volume customers and customers who are at the user frontier, enabling the company to learn from them (for example, customers who are willing to test prerelease software). Companies can benefit from collaborating with such customers in creating new products. Involving customers in the design process can result in a better product and win their loyalty and their willingness to buy the new product, reducing the time it takes for product acceptance. Beyond individual product design, companies can maintain a continuous dialogue. This implies accepting and encouraging interaction instead of employing a one-way broadcast.

    Therefore, it is important to train the frontline sales force and others who interact with customers to gather and transmit information. Not unsurprisingly, customers are resistant to providing personal information because of their all-too-realistic fears of being deluged with junk mail. Customization of messages for small groups of people can lose their effectiveness when many companies, armed with the same databases, bombard customers with multiple direct mail pieces. Companies need to make a special effort to respect customers' privacy if they are to gain the customers as allies. The information gathering needs to focus on two areas:

    - How hard is it for a customer to do business with the company (customer sacrifice)?
    - How much of a customer's total business does the company get (customer share)?

2. IT can be used to facilitate the purchase and delivery of goods and services. This suggests that there are two distinct skill sets that are relevant to satisfying customers. One set focuses on what new products and services should be offered and customized; while the other skill focuses on how to deliver the goods, whether delivery is possible, and whether the newly customized offerings should be produced in-house or subcontracted.

3. Companies can offer IT-based follow-up services, including handling of complaints and customer retention campaigns. Customer problems can form the basis of product modifications and better service. But increased customer access raises customers' expectations, resulting in customers becoming frustrated when a response is not immediately forthcoming.

4. Using database management, companies can organize and store information for ease of retrieval and for use in distinct phases of the consumer business transaction (such as new product development, information gathering prior to purchases being made, current product purchases, and postpurchase follow-up). The latter can be categorized into after-sales training and service, the generation of repeat business, and enhancement of retention. Successful use of a database requires that the database design be linked to decisions that use such information. As mentioned, one well-known example of that approach is FedEx, which offers Internet-based tracking of packages so customers and suppliers know exactly where a critical shipment is and when it is scheduled to arrive at a customer's site.

The Internet's Impact on Business

The studies and concepts reviewed previously suggest that customer linkages can be divided into two broad categories: customer interaction variables and customer information variables. *Customer interaction* variables affect the nature of the relationship established with a customer and shape the parameters of the network to be developed. *Customer information* variables are concerned with the information content of the network; that is, what kinds of information will flow from the firm to the customer and vice versa. The information content aspect is concerned mainly with understanding the buyer and the role the firm's product plays in helping the buyer improve his or her business performance. Strong customer-business relationships are based on the purposeful development of systems and processes that allow for close contact between a firm and its customers—from product design through sales, warranty, and repurchase. Table 5-4 summarizes how those two categories of variables shape global linkages with customers.

Table 5-4   Variables Affecting Global Linkages with Customers

Customer Interaction	Customer Information
Relationship: one-time; ongoing	Customer database and buying history; market demographics
Product complexity: straight sales versus after-sales support and complex service	Customer segment positioning; vertical industry segments
Length of selling cycle: necessary for repeated interaction to close the sale? team selling effort?	Key decision makers; team buying?
Intensity of competition for order; first-time or repeat sale?	Client importance: size and frequency of order; lead user
	Competitive presence among the following: • Existing customers • New prospects/sales leads
Price: fixed or negotiated; volume and use-based pricing	Differences across country markets
Upstream involvement: customer participation in product design, modification, and customization	Customer input and feedback during product design; role in prototype (beta site) testing; feedback on product performance
Distribution channel in reaching customer: independent distributors, personal selling, direct mail, telemarketing, or an original equipment manufacturer (OEM) arrangement?	Channels used to reach customer: alternative distribution approaches; volume and efficiency
Downstream involvement: customer participation in joint selling; promotion	Customer capabilities; convergence of interests; perceived strategy development
Service relationship: extent of service interaction, quality of service, and parts shortages; debriefing service personnel	Customer service: monitoring of service quality
Other: exchange rate risk and risk sharing	Monitoring exchange rate changes and effects on customers; development of risk-sharing formulas based on exchange rate bands

Examples of Global Customer Linkages

Liz Claiborne has been developing links with retailers that allow buyers to view new fashion lines and specific styles on a high-resolution graphics computer. The high-definition image is digitized and transmitted to a retailer, saving the person time and providing for feedback as the design process is occurring. The retailer does not have to wait for visits from a factory representative, but can view the line whenever he or she chooses. The system also allows the retailer to zoom in on details of a product, such as the detailing over pockets or the weave of the fabric, and then transmit an order. Similar CAD/CAM-based linkages transmit design information to Liz Claiborne's overseas suppliers, which allows retail buyers, executives, and representatives of manufacturing subcontractors to interact in shaping the final product.

Gould Pumps has been manufacturing pumps for more than 150 years. Today it produces many varieties of industrial pumps; and because pumps wear out, replacement demand is a major component of sales. Gould had five geographically separated product divisions, which meant that salespeople might have to place five separate orders (with each manufacturing division) for one customer order. The 34 sales offices, including seven international offices, were widely dispersed, which further delayed order processing and sometimes resulted in nonstandardized price quotes. Gould wanted to create a system to retain customers, increase sales, and speed up shipping and delivery. It wanted to provide customers with immediate information on pricing, order status, inventory availability, and shipping schedules. Further, Gould wanted to allow customers to dial into the company's computers and look up the information themselves. The goal was a centralized system that would bypass and reduce the load on local sales offices, agents, and distributors. Lastly, Gould wanted an international order-entry system that would eventually be integrated with inventory, plant scheduling, and shipping systems.

The global network would link markets in the United States, Canada, Italy, West Germany, and Hong Kong. A planned next stage would link the customer order to the factories producing the pumps, thus automating purchasing and providing links with preferred suppliers for components and subassemblies. In turn, this could lead to integrating all of the manufacturing plants to provide just-in-time deliveries to customers. In short, an attempt to provide better customer service could lead to integration of several parts of the company, including purchasing, material requirements planning, outside sourcing, production control, and costing.

In summary, an understanding of the buyer, together with interaction variables as depicted in Table 5-3, helps shape a global network that can aid a firm in improving the quality of its relationship with industrial customers worldwide. A supplementary benefit is that aggregating information gathered from customers scattered around the world will result in data about individual country markets, as well as about individual products in a product line.

Linkages with Suppliers

After customer influence, the second major focus of global networks is linkages with suppliers. Several factors mediate this relationship. Foremost is the intent behind the business purchase transaction. Is the relationship intended to be long-term; that is, a strategic partnership? Why does the client firm seek a supplier? A strategic orientation arises out of a mandate by the client firm to reduce fixed costs and investments while seeking quality and lowered outsourcing costs.

In turn, this often leads to favoring a few suppliers in an effort to gain improved quality and closer coordination in design and manufacturing, as well as the traditional economies of scale. Table 5-5 outlines the variables affecting global linkages with suppliers.

Arising out of such a strategic orientation in seeking suppliers, the next question is this: "When does the supplier become involved?" A critical concern is whether the supplier should be involved at the design stage of a product's development—affecting a final product, manufacturing costs, quality, ease of service, etc. Other kinds of involvement may include supplying a long-term open order, guaranteeing incremental product performance improvements over the life of the order, providing customer support and warranty services, and engaging in joint promotion.

Table 5-5   Variables Affecting Global Linkages with Suppliers

Strategic Orientation	Subcontractor or Partner
Stage of Involvement	At design? (designs for ease of manufacture)
Pricing Relationships	Sharing of cost reductions achieved by supplier (volume-based discounts)
Delivery Terms	Just-in-time
Quality Standards	Contracted for targeted improvement
Compatibility of Capital Equipment and Communications Network	CAD/CAM standards; EDI; transparent document interchange
Service Responsibilities	Subassemblies replaced by suppliers; joint service teams; spare part provisions; service data interchange
Technology Transfer	Safeguarding technology; technical assistance in implementing technology; second sourcing

Most shirt buyers have never heard of TAL Apparel Limited, but this company supplies all of the shirts sold by JCPenney. TAL, a company based in Hong Kong, collects point-of-sale information from all JCPenney retail outlets around the world; analyzes the data using a software model designed by TAL; and manufactures the sizes, colors, and designs specified. TAL has the shirts shipped directly to each store, bypassing the JCPenney buyers, shippers, and warehouses. JCPenney was able to cut inventories from thousands of shirts that they would hold for as long as six months to zero.[16]

Favoring more efficient inventory management, JCPenney leaves many decisions to the supplier. This practice is in contrast to a typical North American pattern, where suppliers perform mainly as subcontracting manufacturers, with all product design and test phases carried out by the client (OEM) firm itself. Outsourcing is a strategic decision that requires supplier involvement; it is the first and most important question that firms need to ask. Several other consequences follow from that strategic decision.

Li & Fung, which began as a Chinese import-export business in 1906, is a supply chain management firm that orchestrates the manufacture and delivery of a vast array of consumer goods, including garments, fashion accessories, toys, sporting goods, promotional merchandise, handicrafts, shoes, travel goods, and household items. The firm's network of suppliers spans 40 nations; while Li & Fung customers are located throughout North America, Europe, Africa, and Asia. While the company still focuses on trade as a core competency, it has continuously updated its supply chain technology and today uses BizTalk and the Supplier SCMTalk Solution to manage the huge amount of data that pass through its network every day.[17]

Examples of Global Supplier Linkages

To provide evidence of the previous concepts, the following examples highlight recent corporate efforts in developing global networks with overseas suppliers.

Mast Industries

Mast is the manufacturing and sourcing arm of The Limited, responsible for supplying Limited subsidiaries such as The Limited, Lerner, Abercrombie & Fitch, Victoria's Secret, and various catalog businesses. Mast does not generate clothing ideas itself. Instead, buyers for the various Limited retail subsidiaries come to Mast with garment ideas for their stores. Mast's job is to get the clothing produced and make it available on time for the various Limited subsidiaries. Mast works with independent factories in Hong Kong, Taiwan, Singapore, Korea, and Europe. One of its objectives is to reduce the turnaround time necessary to get the items into the stores (that is, reduce the offshore production and sourcing time). The MAST Connection is the network of suppliers, transport companies, and retailers that allows apparel orders to be filled within 30 to 60 days—compared to 3 to 10 months taken by competing specialty and department stores. The reduced turnaround time allows buying decisions to be delayed until consumers' needs can be more clearly assessed. The short production time also means that smaller repeat orders can be placed, instead of one large order early in the buying season. In turn, this process reduces the risk of having excess unsold inventory at the retail stores, which obviates the need for end-of-season sales at discount prices. Thus, initial prices need not be set at high levels in order to cover losses on unsold end-of-season merchandise. The lower initial prices can translate into increased market share. Figure 5-4 details the workings of Mast's global supply network.

Mast's system uses EDI bar coding, product data management, and event management to facilitate global coordination of orders. Mast uses videoconferencing and high-definition TV (HDTV) to facilitate global discussions on fabric colors and textures. The 35mm photograph quality of HDTV allows fabric comparisons to take place between the Far East and the United States. The technology allows buyers and suppliers to zoom in on a complex print, seeing enough detail to count the stitches in the cloth. Using this technology cuts down on travel time and, more importantly, allows for quick decisions; a decision about fabric can be made in a few hours instead of five days. Quick results also come about through use of an e-mail system that links Mast to its suppliers. An employee can request a quote from the company's overseas production network and receive a cost sheet overnight. Communicating via e-mail increases overall responsiveness while it deals with the major time difference between Mast's East Coast U.S. offices and the company's Far East suppliers.

Developing such global networks means overcoming several problems—one being the building or leasing of high-speed communication facilities, which are not available worldwide. Countries that do not develop the communication infrastructure needed to conduct business place their firms in the position of being unable to compete in global trade.[18] There are also regulatory problems, ranging from government controls over the kind and type of equipment to be used on a network to controls over the transmission of data across borders (transborder data flows). Customs clearances can also hold up shipments. In response to this, Mast has developed artificial intelligence systems to automatically determine the tariff classification of a garment and its duty rate. Those systems expedite the import and export of garments between Hong Kong and the United States (since trade barriers are commonly found in the apparel and textile industries).[19]

Figure 5-4   Global Supply Network at Mast Industries

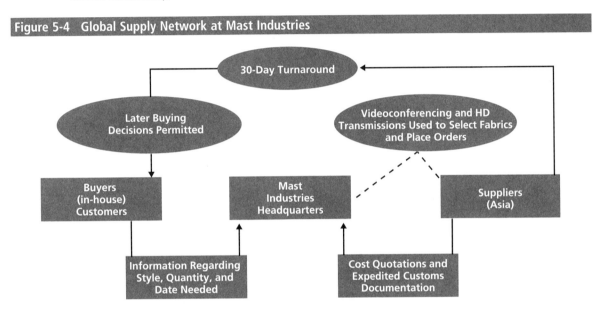

Benetton

Figure 5-5 shows one of the more advanced systems linking a firm with suppliers and customers. The system is found at Benetton, another apparel retailer. Benetton's network includes company-owned retail outlets and franchisees, and the firm uses both in-house and subcontract manufacturing. Benetton analyzes sales from its owned outlets to forecast sales by product lines. That information is relayed to independent agents who use the information to increase orders from franchisees. Such orders are grouped and transmitted to Benetton factories and to subcontractors. Up-to-date information allows orders to be closed closer to the selling season, cutting down on unsold goods; and the speed of the system allows smaller orders to be placed later in the season. Close ties to manufacturing allows headquarters to respond to order status inquiries; and a subsystem allows Benetton to automate preparation of shipping and customs documents for a large number of countries, each with its own import, tariff, and shipping rules.

Benetton uses RFID—technology-embedded shipping labels—to help its retailers keep track of shipments, manage inventory, and cut costs. The system includes an antenna and semiconductor that are less than a millimeter in size and, therefore, can be sewn directly into clothing tags. While discreet, they are more durable than the paper bar codes that consumers often see hanging from the sleeves of new garments.[20]

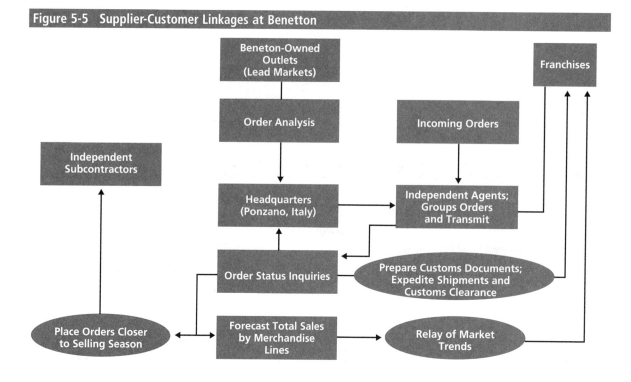

Figure 5-5   Supplier-Customer Linkages at Benetton

IT and the Obsolete Inventory Problem

IT can help alleviate a serious problem that consumer goods manufacturers face: goods with short product life cycles that become obsolete, resulting in large losses to firms because they must write off excess inventories that cannot be sold through regular channels at normal retail prices. Firms have typically responded to that problem by reducing production quantities, in which case they run the risk of lost sales on popular products whose demand exceeds the supply.

Quick response production planning techniques, in which early sales figures are used to adjust subsequent production schedules, rely on IT. For example, in the case of apparel, losses from obsolescence for a company selling fashion-conscious clothing were traditionally very high. Lead times in the garment industry were generally long—ordering fabric, zippers, buttons, and other notions; contracting with manufacturers in Asia or Eastern Europe; and shipping finished goods well in advance of the season. Exacerbating the problem was the fact that potential sales were often misjudged, blamed in part on the length of time between demand estimate and receipt of the merchandise (often separated by as much as 8 to 12 months). Markdowns and lower profit from end-of-season merchandise was the result.

Increasingly, sophisticated application of IT is leading to shorter time periods between the design and delivery of apparel. One solution is a **risk-based multistage production sequencing**, which allows for development of production plans for the manufacturing process based on predictability or stability of demand. It is graphically displayed in Table 5-6. The process, which is described in the following steps, shows how an apparel firm can shorten the time between concept design and sales to consumers.

1. Divide the product line into two major categories, with one category containing items with more predictable demand and the other category including products with more volatile demand.

2. Develop a team of seasoned sales professionals, each one asked to develop a forecast by color and style for the more volatile products.

3. Statistically analyze the forecasts to develop a group mean or average forecast and identify the variance among the forecasts. Forecasts that are substantially different (variance is high) indicates a product with highly volatile demand.

4. Use the initial forecasts to develop a production schedule. The firm then contracts to buy a certain amount of production capacity to be used over a period of months. Some of that reserved production capacity is used during the initial months to produce products with less volatile demand as well as a portion of the total forecasted demand for the more fashionable items; that is, not all of the forecasted demand is scheduled for production.

5. Obtain advance orders from a select group of influential retailers who together account for a significant portion of annual sales. Use the early orders as additional information to help team members develop revised forecasts. Based on those revised demand forecasts, allocate the remaining production capacity among the various fashion products in accordance with the revised demand figures.

The net result of the above system is fewer losses due to the write-off of obsolete goods in inventory. At the same time, point-of-sale information and order-taking systems allow a firm to keep track of stockouts (unmet demand) so the forecasting system can be continually revised. This ensures that foregone profits, because of stockouts, are balanced against losses caused by excess inventory. The heart of the system is developing timely information and letting production schedules react to that timely market information.

Table 5-6   Multistage Production Sequencing

Predictive Demand Criteria
1. Manufacture goods in advance of season based on internal forecasts.

September–March	March	March–April	September–October	September–December
Design	Show samples to retailers	Place orders	Receive goods at	Ship to retailers
	Receive orders	with suppliers	distribution center	

Volatile Demand Criteria
2. Use averages and variances of team member forecasts to order items with predictable demand in November. Obtain advance orders from select retailers in February to fine-tune forecasts and place orders for items with less predictable demand.

September–December	November	February	March	March–April
Design	Place advance orders	Receive advance	Receive orders	Place remainder of
Develop internal	with suppliers based on	orders from retailers		orders with suppliers
team forecasts	team forecasts			

August–October	August–December
Receive goods at distribution center	Ship to retailers

Using models and techniques such as those described above, industrial buyers throughout the world are seeking to reduce the number of suppliers they buy from, while negotiating longer-term agreements. They seek to link manufacturing with product design, inventory and shipping, and customer information. In some industries, designers seek closer links to suppliers to reduce excess inventory that may become obsolete. A firm not only has to communicate with outsiders, but also must break down functional barriers within the organization. Given the hybrid consumer and demands for customization, marketing and manufacturing must work together to design products that can be manufactured at a low cost and to choose and coordinate outside suppliers. Such networks are complex and costly, but they are necessary to doing business as a multinational firm.

Subsidiary Linkages: Sales Force, Distribution, and Service

While buyers and suppliers represent two principal nodes of the global network, other interests must also be integrated. They include sales force interests, distribution and other aspects of the system (promotion, for example), and service.

Sales force interests concentrate on sales leads, up-to-date customer profiles and sales histories, a sales call scheduling and monitoring system, inventory availability and shipping dates, prices and discounts or deals allowable, and competitive pressures pertinent to each sales lead. In global industrial markets, a special issue is the use of multinational and multifunctional leads, with a drawn-out selling cycle. Necessary elements of the network are a reporting subsystem used to monitor and summarize progress made through a sales lead at each visit as well as communication capabilities between members of the sales team.

Service has emerged as a major element of successful industrial selling. Hence, global networks must include service subsystems. Basically, there are two central service issues: providing field service to enhance customer satisfaction at a reasonable cost and using service feedback to enhance product design and quality of next-generation products. Related issues include maintaining failure and service records, forecasting future failures from the service history of a product or parts family, keeping track of the cost of service, facilitating feedback about product design in order to facilitate incremental product improvements, and facilitating similar feedback about parts and subsystem suppliers for similar corrective action. Also important is record keeping with regard to the cost of providing service; customer satisfaction with service; an adequate parts inventory in the field, used for service calls; and comparative competitor performance in the service area, including comparative warranty information and comparative "mean time between failure" statistics. Providing service in the international arena is complicated by distance, the number of locations from which service is provided, the location and availability of warehouses and parts, training and the dispatching of technical personnel, and technical information available to enhance the quality of service performed.

When reconsidering outsourcing, firms are learning that outsourcing to reduce costs sometimes leads to other kinds of costs—frustrated customers. Both Web.com and Dell moved their call centers for after-sales support back to the United States after months of customer complaints.[21]

Global Networks and Management Control Issues

The shape of global networks is also affected by organizational structure and management control needs.[22] The management control and organizational issues that surround the implementation of global communication systems are summarized in Table 5-7. Critical points outlined in the table include the following:

- **Enhancing management efficiency** through applications in areas such as order entry, sales calls, expense reporting, analysis of product profitability by region and customer, and databases of technical product specifications.
- **Managing the selling process** through information that permits client and product profitability analysis, comparing actual sales with targets or quotas, and sales trend forecasting.
- **Managing the manufacturing subcontracting process** with data on costs, quality, and delivery performance; spending on joint design and research; and comparative information on product and process improvement.
- **Managing the customer relationship** through databases of customer purchases, customer complaints, and other feedback and through direct links with customers, using approaches such as EDI (covered in detail in a subsequent section).
- **Facilitating management control** with immediately accessible, up-to-date information that allows managers to perform the computer equivalent of "management by walking around." "Strolling" through successive levels of a customer database can help trace causes of sales declines. For example, a shortfall in a regional quota may be traced to a particular customer, where a change in a manufacturing process led to a switch in the raw material specifications, resulting in the customer's preference for a competitor's product. While the salesperson may know this information, placing the information in a central database can ensure a faster reaction and a more appropriate response at a higher level of the organization.
- **Environmental monitoring** that is particularly important when a firm is dealing with diverse country markets and national differences in regulations and standards.
- **Statistical analysis capabilities** in areas such as market share shifts; isolation of market segments across countries; and customer reactions to management actions such as promotions, new product improvements, changes in service levels, enhanced delivery, and the like. For example, Frito-Lay, the snack foods company, used such capabilities to trace reduced market share in a region to the introduction of a generic store brand. Possessing such data allowed a quick counterresponse and eliminated the problem.

Management control draws on a set of databases and statistics that is also relevant to linkages with customers and suppliers. The difference is in the level of aggregation and analysis to which such data are subject; timeliness and speed of response are what interests management. Hence, from a management control perspective, greater emphasis will be placed on the communication network itself and on cost/benefit trade-offs in articulating the database and communications network configuration. Implementation is always a management preoccupation, and it is clear that a full-blown global network is a major corporate undertaking, requiring considerable analysis and commitments of time and money. Hence, management is more likely to opt for implementation in phases—building a full-scale global network for one product line, then using the learning from that effort to extend the concept to other product lines. Such an approach more clearly identifies the difficulties involved in extending global networks to various countries and in coordinating the tie-in of suppliers and customers to such a network.

Table 5-7	Implementing Global Communication Systems
Managerial Issues	Managing customers and suppliers Marketing efficiency: sales force control; forecasting, analysis, and planning; statistical capabilities; competitive assessment Environmental monitoring: governments, consumers, competition, technology, and legal aspects Database commonality
Organizational Issues	Opening up the firm: • Externally, with customers/suppliers • Internally, with manufacturing and others Sharing data: value of information; availability of information, access levels, and frequency of access
Technological Issues	Use of EDI; data transfer problems; transmission protocols Data networks: use of third-party VANs and VSAT private data (satellite-based) networks Data security: controlling access—hackers and viruses Government regulation on transborder data flows; data privacy issues Compatibility of equipment: computers and data transmission Legal responsibilities in using computer linkages with suppliers and customers

Note: VANs = Value-Added Networks; VSAT = Very Small Aperture Terminal

The Valuation of Information

An important question is the value of information. Firms must decide how much information to make available to outside partners such as customers and suppliers (while the technology needed to create and maintain a large, complex database that contains sensitive information about the partner firms and clients has existed for many years). Equally important is software that restricts access to specific areas within a complex database, allowing database managers to control what each user can view, change, add, or delete. The access control provides firms with the ability to maintain one database for all users, rather than have separate databases that may contain the same data. Entering and updating data in multiple locations is expensive and increases the likelihood that mistakes will be made. Therefore, the software that controls access adds considerable value to the data and the database.

Firms must also be concerned about the cost and time required to implement such networks, including finding or designing appropriate software and getting partner collaboration in implementing such efforts. In addition, technologies and management styles inherent in using a global network are being adopted at different rates in various overseas markets. As a consequence, overseas suppliers may be unable to successfully implement their end of a network. Their unfamiliarity or resistance to change may also lead them to oppose such networking attempts. Such reluctance slows down the pace of implementing a global network. Technology and access to technology is uneven worldwide. Thus, firms must spend time and effort on training their partners to make full and effective use of global networks. One such example is Pier 1 Import's approach to supply and distribution networks, which is illustrated in Figure 5-6.

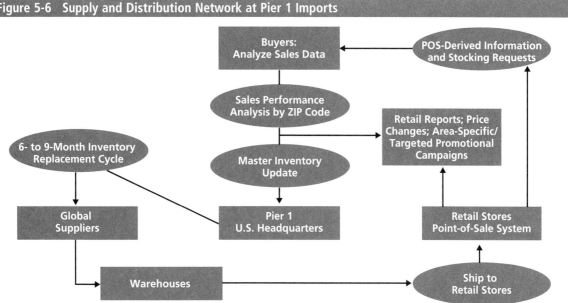

Figure 5-6   Supply and Distribution Network at Pier 1 Imports

Technological Issues in Developing Global Networks

Developing global networks is partly an exercise in developing a global information and communications network. Several computer-related technical issues affect such network development. Foremost is the growing global use of EDI and of third-party VANs. Figure 5-7 summarizes the basic characteristics of using EDI.

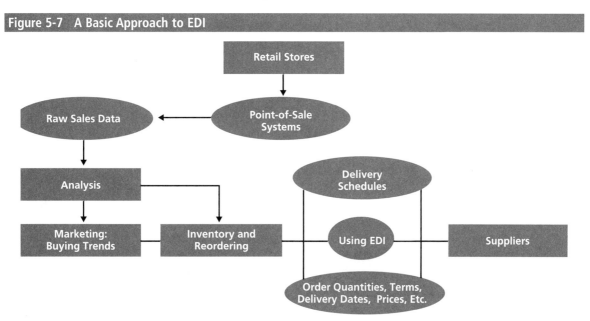

Figure 5-7   A Basic Approach to EDI

EDI DEFINED

EDI can be described as business being conducted between computers or, more accurately, the direct transfer of business transactions between computers. EDI is a process used to automate standardized data exchange between business partners. Thus, a buyer could set up EDI with vendors to buy on a just-in-time basis, with all orders being electronically transmitted directly to the vendor's computer systems. In turn, the buyer could query the vendor's manufacturing database to ascertain what the status of the order is, how far along it is, and when delivery is likely to be scheduled. Then upon shipment, the buyer could use EDI to instruct the bank to electronically transfer funds in payment.

A major advantage of EDI is the decrease in duplication of data entry, which decreases the possibility of errors and raises productivity. EDI can reduce pipeline inventory and the length of time goods wait at loading docks and in warehouses. The problem in implementing EDI globally is that foreign suppliers, who may be small in relation to the client firm, often do not have EDI capability and must make an effort to learn how to do business using EDI. EDI, of course, requires a telecommunications network that can connect users on disparate computer systems. Such networks are available to a far greater extent in the United States than in Japan or Europe, with the smaller emerging markets lagging.

Implementing an EDI system has its difficulties, including the following:
- User access to hardware and software must be compatible with others using the system.
- There is a high cost of telecommunications infrastructure development and maintenance (hardware and software and upgrades of both).
- Adoption of a new system is easier and quicker when it is compatible with the existing order-entry and inventory systems.
- Data must be secure (outsider access to a host computer via a network).

Table 5-8 outlines some of the managerial and technical network issues relevant to EDI implementation. However, the biggest factor hindering EDI's widespread adoption is a lack of confidence in a system that does away with paper forms in triplicate and with tried and trusted accounting systems. In conducting such data interchanges, a common data format is essential.

When Greenwood Mills, a fabric producer, used EDI to link up with customers, an impediment was fabric bolt sizes. Greenwood used standard measurements, such as 36-inch and 48-inch fabric sizes (minimum measurements). But customers who used numerical control machines needed to communicate exact sizes to their fabric-cutting machines, whether the bolt was actually 37 or 37.5 inches wide. Hence, they had to remeasure the shipments. Fabric color required similar standardization. (Greenwood used names for different colors, while customers measured fabric color by its variance from a standard color, such as red.) In order to use EDI with customers, Greenwood had to reconfigure the product database for exact bolt sizes and color variances. A Textile Apparel Linkage Council (TALC) has been formed to standardize terminology among the various companies, suppliers, and customers in the U.S. textile industry. Similar vertical industry groups have formed across industries in the United States, Europe, and the Far East. Thus, a major implementation problem is that standards are incompatible within and across industries.

Table 5-8   EDI: A Checklist

Managerial Issues

- Correct orders (timely receipt of and acknowledgement of orders).
- Accurate remittance notices, advising that a payment has been made.
- 100 percent accuracy of payments made with EDI to suppliers (correct amount credited to the correct account on time).
- Separation of payment details from remittance data (information on what is being paid for, which account should be credited, etc.). Separation creates a reconciliation problem: payments to client accounts.
- Ample time for implementation, permitting a careful evaluation before move from pilot use to full-scale volume and time for installation and training.
- Expandability, to be able to add new trading partners (necessity of low cost of adding partners facilitated by VAN support programs to educate new trading partners and get them up and running).
- Confidentiality and data ownership issues (preserving confidentiality since sensitive firm and client data are being sent over the network).
- Security, prevention of unauthorized access, error correction, and audit trails.
- Legal responsibility: When errors are made, who is responsible for consequences? the firm? the client? the provider of the physical VAN?
- Government regulations governing access to and the cost of using data networks and satellite communications; also, national data privacy laws affecting the database design of such networks.
- Build your own or use a third-party network (VAN)? As the volume of EDI transactions increases, larger EDI users find it more economical to develop their own EDI transmission networks, though this means investing in special fault-tolerant hardware and software combinations.

Technical Network Issues

- Volume of data transmitted: network must be able to handle peak data traffic.
- 24-hour access to the network, 24-hour uptime (that is, using alternative routes to avoid parts of the network that are defective, guarding against disasters such as power outages, electrical storms, hurricanes, etc.).
- Storage and forwarding capabilities (users must be able to access data and documents at their convenience), which requires developing fast search and query capabilities when dealing with diverse databases and database software.
- Ability to handle different physical data characteristics, such as SNA and asynchronous.
- Ability to handle different rates of data transmission speeds.
- Data standards and security of payment because of competing and sometimes incompatible standards between the United States and Europe.
- Cost: Generally, a fixed fee plus charges based on volume of data traffic and software to handle EDI, covering the technical issues outlined above.
- EDI software supporting multiple software platforms, such as workstations, mainframes, Windows, and Unix, and integration with in-house financial software so that one company's purchase order system can communicate with another company's order receipt and processing system.
- Internetworking capability (a trading partner working through a different third-party EDI network), which is crucial for global EDI since local VANs often provide EDI services in their countries and may have incompatible equipment and standards.

Summary

Multinational corporations face an increasingly complex task of communicating and coordinating with their global customers and suppliers. The main components of such a network include linkages with customers; suppliers; the sales force; and other elements of the system, including distribution, promotion, and after-sales service. Factors such as customer profiles, the complexity of the product and the selling cycle, the strategic nature of the partnership, and the level of interdependence all influence the design and detail built into the network. Another set of influences on the network are managerial issues such as efficiency, market research needs, forecasting, analysis and planning, environmental monitoring and competitive assessment, and sales force control. Just as important are organizational issues, since creating such a network forces greater openness with customers and with other functional areas within a corporation. Also important are technical issues such as the value of information made available to outsiders, the use of technologies such as EDI, third-party VANs, data security problems and controlled access, and government regulations limiting freedom of transborder data flows.

Questions and Research

5.1 How can IT change international business communications?

5.2 What are some principal features of a global communications network? What obstacles make it difficult to create such a network?

5.3 What are the different kinds of information needed by global communication networks?

5.4 How can a company be said to compete in both the marketplace and the marketspace?

5.5 What is a virtual shopping environment? How can it be used?

5.6 How does IT help implement the concept of mass customization?

5.7 Distinguish between customer information and customer interaction variables.

5.8 What variables should a company keep in mind when designing global supplier linkages?

5.9 How can IT help firms reduce losses from obsolete goods?

5.10 What are some management control and organizational issues underlying the implementation of global communication networks?

5.11 What is EDI? How can it help a firm's international business efforts?

Endnotes

1 Speier, Cheri, Michael G. Harvey, and Jonathan Palmer. "Virtual Management of Global Marketing Relationships," *Journal of World Business*; Volume 33, Issue 3, September 22, 199, page 263.

2 Friedman, Thomas L. *The Lexus and the Olive Tree,* 2000, New York: Farrar, Straus, Giroux, pages 41–88.

3 Wind, Yoram, Vijay Mahajan, and Robert E. Gunther. *Convergence Marketing: Running With the Centaurs,* Upper Saddle River, NJ: Prentice Hall, 2002, pages 205–214.

4 "Philippines, India, China to See Sharp Rise in Call Centers," *Company News*, Thursday, September 25, 2003.

5 "Hang-ups in India: Call Center Backlash! India Isn't the Answer, Say Some Firms," *Fortune*, December 2, 2003, page 44.

6 Citrin, Alka Varma, Donald E. Stem, Eric R. Spangenberg, and Michael J. Clark. "Consumer Need for Tactile Input: An Internet Retailing Challenge," *Journal of Business Research*, Volume 56, Issue 11, November 2003, page 915.

7 "New Luxury-Car Specifications: Styling. Performance. Aroma," *New York Times,* Saturday, October 25, 2003, section A, page 1, column 5, Business/Financial Desk.

8 "The Internet and Business," *Internet Indicators* (http://www.internetindicators.com/facts.html); accessed December 29, 2003.

9 Wind, Yoram, Vijay Mahajan, and Robert E. Gunther. *Convergence Marketing: Running With the Centaurs,* 2002, Upper Saddle River, NJ: Prentice Hall, pages 205–206.

10 "The Internet: Selling Points," *Wall Street Journal*, Special Report, December 7, 1998; Hamel, Gary and Jeff Sampler, "The E-Corporation," *Fortune*, December 7, 1998.

11 Kanner, Bernice. "The Bad Man Cometh: Interview with Saatchi and Saatchi Worldwide CEO Kevin Roberts," *Chief Executive*, December 1998.

12 Fellman, Michelle Wirth. "Globalization: Worldwide Economic Woes Force Global Marketers to Seek New Opportunities—or Ways to Ride Out the Storm," *Marketing News*, December 7, 1998.

13 Smith, Gwendolyn. "Mastering the Art of Global Marketplace Exposure," *Marketing*, July 20, 1998.

14 Terpstra, Vern and Lloyd Russow. *International Dimensions of Marketing*, 4th Edition, 2002, Cincinnati, OH: South-Western Publishing, page 140.

15 Wind, Yoram, Vijay Mahajan, and Robert E. Gunther. *Convergence Marketing: Running With the Centaurs*, 2002, Upper Saddle River, NJ: Prentice Hall, pages 205–206.

16 "Made to Measure: Invisible Supplier Has Penny's Shirts All Buttoned Up," *Wall Street Journal*, September 11, 2003, A1.

17 Li & Fung Limited web site (http://www.lifung.com); accessed September 25, 2004.

18 Friedman, Thomas L. *The Lexus and the Olive Tree*, 2002, New York: Farrar, Straus, Giroux.

19 Mast Industries web site (http://www.mast.com/about/mastconn.htm); accessed December 30, 2003.

20 "Benetton to Add Electronic 'Smart Tags' to Clothing Line," *ComputerWorld* (http://www.computerworld.com/printthis/2003/0,4814,79286,00.html); accessed September 25, 2004.

21 "Hang-ups in India," *Fortune*, December 22, 2003, Volume 148, Issue 13, page 44.

22 Schultz, Don E. "Structural Straitjackets Stifle Integrated Success," *Marketing News,* March 1, 1999.

Further Readings

Anderson, Alex. "The language of e-Business: Microsoft partnership blends XML and EDI," *MSI* (Manufacturingsystems.com), September 2003, Volume 21, Issue 9, page 14.

Bishop, Bill. *Global Marketing for the Digital Age*, 1999, Lincolnwood, IL: NTC Business Books.

Dann, Susan and Stephen Dann. *Strategic Internet Marketing*, 2002, Hoboken, NJ: John Wiley & Sons.

Darrow, Barbara. "IBM Speeds Up Information Integration," *Financial Times*, June 21, 2004 (Global News Wire).

Farhoomand, Ali and Peter Lovelock. *Global e-Commerce: Text and Cases*, 2001, Upper Saddle River, NJ: Prentice Hall.

Forrest, Edward. *Internet Marketing Intelligence: Research Tools, Techniques, and Resources*, 2003, Boston: McGraw-Hill/Irwin.

Hayes, Frank. "Wal-Mart says so," *Computerworld*, November 17, 2003, Volume 37, Issue 46, page 70.

Jesdanum, Anick. "Erecting Borders on the Web" *Philadelphia Inquirer*, July 11, 2004, Business, E03.

Lee, Sangjae and Gyoo Gun Lim. "The impact of partnership attributes on EDI implementation success," *Information & Management*, Amsterdam, December 2003, Volume 41, Issue 2, page 135.

Miller, Thomas W. *Data and Text Mining: A Business Applications Approach*, 2005, Upper Saddle River, NJ: Prentice Hall.

"Plugging in with Gary Thompson, Highlights from Talks with IT Strategists," *Intelligence Enterprise*, August 7, 2004, page 48.

Roberts, Mary Lou. *Internet Marketing: Integrating Online and Offline Strategies*, 2003, Boston: McGraw-Hill/Irwin.

Senn, James A. *Information Technology: Principles, Practices, and Opportunities*, 3rd Edition, 2004, Upper Saddle River, NJ: Prentice Hall.

Taylor, David A. "Supply chain vs. supply chain," *Computerworld*, November 10, 2003, Volume 37, Issue 45, page 44.

Thomas, Jerry W. "Brave New World: Strategic Impact of the Internet," *Communication World*, Issue 4, March 1998, pages 15, 38.

Turban, Efraim. *Electronic Commerce 2004: A Managerial Perspective,* 2004, Upper Saddle River, NJ: Pearson/Prentice Hall.

Wind, Yoram, Vijay Mahajan, and Robert E. Gunther. *Convergence Marketing: Running With the Centaurs*, 2002, Upper Saddle River, NJ: Prentice Hall, pages 205–206.

Zimmerman, Ann. "B-2-B—Internet 2.0: To Sell Goods To Wal-Mart, Get on the Net," *Wall Street Journal*, November 21, 2003, B.1

Recommended Web Sites

European Society for Opinion and Marketing Research (ESOMAR) (http://www.esomar.org).

StatSoft (http://www.statsoft.com), particularly the description of data mining, data mining techniques, and terminology (http://www.statsoft.com/textbook/stdatmin.html).

Thearling.com (http://www.thearling.com) for information about data mining, data mining defined, recommended readings, ethical issues, and uses.

CHAPTER 6

Planning, Organization, and Control: The Global Enterprise

Learning Objectives

The focus of previous chapters was how the world environment shapes international business. The focus of this chapter is on how the separate functional tasks of planning, organization, and control are blended together into an effective international business operation.

The main goals of this chapter are to

1 Identify the elements of the planning process.

2 Describe how firms develop and coordinate plans for national markets.

3 Describe the nature and role of long-range planning.

4 Identify the variables that affect organizational design for global business.

5 Describe the alternative designs available for international business organization.

6 Study examples of how companies organize internationally and what roles headquarters can play.

7 Discuss how companies control international business.

8 Explain the role of the information system in international control.

Planning for Global Business

Planning consists of identifying systematic steps that will help a company formulate detailed actions to implement broad strategies. Planning can be for the short- or long-term. Typically, firms plan for three to five years, revising the long-term plan annually. The year immediately ahead then becomes the short-term plan, with more detailed strategies.

There is an advantage to having the annual plan be part of a longer planning horizon. It keeps planners from becoming shortsighted by forcing them to consider the future impact of each year's operating plan. The short-range plan for international business can be composed of several elements, including, for example, a business plan for each foreign market, plans for individual product lines, and a plan for international product development.

There are several elements of the business plan:
- *Situation analysis:* Where are we now? The company must analyze its current environment in each of its markets: What are the important characteristics of demand, competition, distribution, law, and government? What problems and opportunities are evident in the current situation?
- *Objectives:* Where do we want to be? Given an understanding of the firm's current situation in markets around the world, management can propose objectives that are appropriate for each country, market, and region. While those objectives should be challenging, they should also be reachable. And they must be specific if they are to be operational.
- *Strategy and tactics:* How can we best reach our goals? Once the firm has identified concrete objectives for foreign markets, it must prepare a plan of action to meet the goals. The approach includes assigning specific responsibilities to business personnel and to the business functions.

These three basic elements—situation analysis, objectives, and strategy and tactics—provide a framework for the planning needs of the international business manager. In turn, the short-range planning task has two basic parts: (1) developing the plan for each foreign market and (2) integrating the national plans into a coherent international plan, both regional and global.

Developing Plans for Individual Markets
The mode of entry affects the extent to which a firm takes responsibility for and control of planning. Exporting may rely more heavily on export intermediaries for planning; similarly, licensing cedes principal control and responsibility to the licensee. In a joint venture, a partner may share or take a controlling role in planning, depending on how the joint venture has been structured. It is in wholly owned subsidiaries that a firm's planning role takes center stage.

Setting Objectives for a Subsidiary
A firm must first evaluate the environment and industry context, which can be unique for each subsidiary. It must also clarify the governmental actions and role that may affect the subsidiary and determine what competitors are up to—their strengths and weaknesses, the threats they pose, and their strategic actions and tactics. The firm can then set detailed subsidiary objectives, including:

- Target sales, in units, in local currency and in the parent company's home currency, possibly at a predetermined exchange rate.
- Target market share by product and line of business.
- Goals for distribution channel penetration, coverage, and extension to new distributors and channels.
- Goals for brand image creation and awareness.
- New product introduction plans, as appropriate, with detailed plans for product launch, covering issues such as pricing, positioning, channels, media plans and spending, target sales, logistics, and service and support.
- Export and international business plans. These plans require the development of sourcing and supply proposals with the identification of countries and regions to be evaluated as possible new markets or as sources of components and finished products.
- Market research goals and specific programs.
- Business personnel training, hiring, and motivation, including sales force plans.

FROM STRATEGY TO TACTICS AND BUDGETS

Each planning goal can be subdivided into more detailed targets, with operational plans providing the details of implementation, budgets, and managerial responsibilities. At this stage, individuals within the business department can receive specific assignments, including details for working with third parties such as advertising agencies, market research firms, value-added distributors, and product servicing companies.

Stages in the Planning Calendar

Thus, a series of typical planning steps can be constructed:

1. Market environment analysis of the macroeconomic environment and the industry to identify opportunities and threats and ways they will affect company objectives
2. Communication of company-wide goals, subsequently divided into global, regional, and country-specific goals and goals for each product line
3. Detailed country and product-manager plans showing how goals such as market share, competition containment, and return on investment will be achieved
4. Aggregation of detailed country and product-line plans to determine whether the overall result is compatible with corporate headquarters' goals
5. Translation of plans into budgets, setting out quantitative and qualitative targets in terms of market share, unit volume growth, prices, target-market segments, distribution channels, advertising budgets, new product introductions, and personnel and training needs
6. Actions by product-line managers and country managers (CMs) based on plans and budgets, which also form the criteria used to judge performance

Adapting Plans to Individual Countries

A centralized coordination of programs is necessary so, for example, global products can be introduced into different markets on a staggered basis. The experience of lead markets may be used to tailor product-introduction programs for other markets. In addition to country and product-manager initiatives, some programs may be initiated at headquarters and communicated to subsidiaries.

An example is Avon's planning process for Latin America. Local executives gather information and develop preliminary country business strategies. Scrutiny of the operating environment is given precedence, focusing on the political, economic, and regulatory environment in each market, as well as making forecasts for the next five years. Next, competitors are identified and their products, market share, strengths, and weaknesses assessed. Avon seeks to learn the sources of its competitors' competitive advantages and compare them with Avon's own competitive advantages. Out of such analysis emerges a plan designed to capitalize on opportunities and competitive weaknesses. Contingency planning is emphasized, the question being what actions are necessary to achieve planned results in the face of unforeseen events?

The Avon planning process is initiated by top management, which visits each firm's key country subsidiaries over a period of two months. While the general manager of each country's subsidiary prepares the plan, a planning staff at headquarters, including a planning director, help key markets with their plans. Once all of the plans are completed, they are forwarded to headquarters for review and integration. Country proposals are reviewed and prioritized; and through comparison, headquarters can detect unexploited opportunities and suggest imitation or adaptation of plans currently scheduled for implementation in one country.

FACTORS THAT DETERMINE WHETHER FORMAL GLOBAL BUSINESS PLANS WILL BE DEVELOPED

What factors influence whether a firm formally develops strategic business plans? As depicted in Figure 6-1, Chae and Hill found:
- A corporate culture that believes in and is supportive of planning.
- Supply chain complexity.
- Complex and uncertain foreign environments.
- Higher levels of governmental involvement with and impact on the business environment.
- Higher levels of competition.

All of those factors influenced the degree of planning formality. Involvement by chief executive officers (CEOs) and firm size were not as important; furthermore, such formal planning generated competitive and organizational benefits.[1]

Division of Labor in International Planning

Avon's approach, discussed earlier, highlights the importance of organizational arrangements in international business planning. How a company is organized will affect the quality of the plan and the likelihood of its implementation. Who contributes what to national operating plans? What are the respective roles of corporate headquarters and the national subsidiaries? Usually corporate headquarters can contribute planning know-how based on its domestic and international experience. That expertise would include planning guidelines, a planning schedule, and training of subsidiary personnel.

The national subsidiary should do most of the actual planning. Whereas the international parent has planning expertise, only the subsidiary has the intimate local knowledge needed. Most of the data for the plan, therefore, must be supplied locally. The resulting plan is more effective because of the complementary contributions of the two parties.

Nestlé provides an example of interactive planning, but with a bias toward decentralization. Some guidance comes from headquarters, but each national company prepares the annu-

Figure 6-1   A Model of Global Strategic Planning

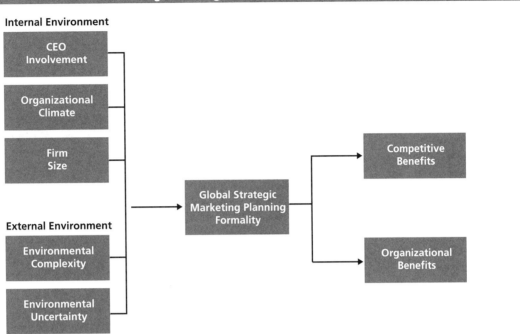

Source: Adapted from Myung-su Chae and John S. Hill, "Determinants and benefits of global strategic marketing planning formality," *International Marketing Review*, Volume 17, Issue 6, pages 538–562.

al plan and budget. Once a year each affiliate meets at headquarters in Switzerland to review the plan with specialists. Compromises and adjustments are made at that time.

International Coordination of National Plans

The final role of the international planner is to form the national plans into an international plan. This coordination is not done after the national plans have been completed; rather, it starts at the beginning of the planning process. Otherwise, national plans will make conflicting claims on company resources and require time-consuming revision. Therefore, coordination begins with guidelines sent to each national operation at the beginning of the planning period. National plans may be modified during the planning process, but good communications ensure that those changes can be coordinated with the overall international plan.

For example, imagine that a company begins its planning cycle in August. Each country prepares its plan, which goes to regional headquarters and then to international headquarters in the United States. Between September and November, continuing exchange of information may occur among the three levels. The final coordination takes place at area-wide meetings in December, where CMs, regional managers, and headquarters staff meet for one or two weeks. Those meetings are held in the area—Europe, Latin America, Asia, Africa, and sometimes the United States.

Incorporating Government Policies in Global Business Planning

How should government policy be included in conducting business planning? Leclair uses the EU as an example to set out a model, including dimensions such as:

- Policy-making process.
- Broad policy climate.
- Categories of relevant legislation.

Those dimensions should then be assessed for their effect on business objectives and strategy in areas such as market research, the communication strategy, product development, product liability, labeling, distance selling, data collection and privacy, and electronic commerce. Also broadly relevant are competition policy and the move toward monetary union (the Eurozone) that affect choice of partners, channels, control over the entities, pricing, etc.[2]

Comparative Analysis for International Planning

As firms increase their multinational presence and the number of subsidiaries increases, regional and headquarters managers begin comparing subsidiaries against one another by region, by product line, and by stage of evolution of their respective markets. Such comparisons can help determine if targets set for individual subsidiaries represent challenging but achievable goals. Comparisons can be helpful if the subsidiaries being compared are similar in their markets and competitive environments and when they face roughly the same degree of governmental controls. Thus, it may make sense to compare business plans for selling razor blades in Brazil, Argentina, and Mexico, perhaps extending to Turkey and the Philippines. However, including significantly poorer countries such as China and India, with their larger populations and lesser degree of infrastructure development, may blur the comparisons. Hence, care is necessary in choosing subsidiaries for comparison.

A-M International provides an example of how to plan for international markets by using an analytical approach. The company is a leader in the global graphics industry, with divisions selling offset presses and printing equipment and engineering and architectural graphics equipment. International sales are about 40 percent of total sales. A-M's strength is its worldwide sales and service infrastructure, having sales branches in countries on six continents and a worldwide base of installed equipment that is a continuing market for supplies and service. To manage this global business, the company operates warehouses, has a worldwide logistics system, and offers worldwide service capabilities (including training). A large portion of the costs of this infrastructure is fixed; hence, A-M's primary goal is to maximize sales from the worldwide infrastructure already in place. In practical terms, this means selling more products through the sales and service organization. To accomplish this, A-M analyzes the outlook for international markets for each of its product segments. Using this approach, A-M developed a new international presence in copiers, an area in which it had not been active previously. The A-M international division agreed to sell the entire line of Konica copiers in Europe under the A-M label. This was part of the company's plan to leverage the existing distribution channel by taking on worldwide distribution rights to sell "contiguous" products under the A-M brand name; A-M expected considerable overlap with its current customer base.

A-M further analyzed markets by geographic area, recognizing that growth rates of over 30 percent per year registered in the Asia/Pacific region would continue and should be exploited aggressively. At the same time, the above analysis, extended to include current market share and future potential, disclosed areas for further attention. Such comparative information gathering is the cornerstone of successful global planning.

Long-Range Planning

Long-range planning deals with the future of a company over a period of five to ten years. Uncertainty is high, and the level of detail that can be forecast is low. The major concern is determining the shape of future markets and competition. How will the environment change, how will competition change, how will the customer base change, and what will future needs be? A firm seeks to learn enough about the future to prevent unpleasant surprises that can reduce its competitive advantage.

The flavor of long-range planning can be seen in TRW's approach. It addresses questions such as the following: What markets should we be in at that time? What products should we be making then? What business and operations methods will be valid then?

Such plans can be prepared at group headquarters by a planning and development department. It can draw on data assembled by the group's product divisions and foreign subsidiaries.

The plan can cover several variables:
- Historical trends in the industry
- Forecasts of demand from end-user segments such as cars, trucks, and off-road vehicles
- Forecasts of the economies of the countries where the group has operations
- The competitive situation in those countries
- Possible future modes of transportation
- Possible future energy problems

Such short-range and long-range plans will reflect a company's dependence on the plans of its key customer segments. Planners will rely heavily on contacts within customer companies for input to the plan.

Strategic Alliances

A central aspect of planning is responding to competition. In a global context, this may involve activities in more than one market, making integration of activities across markets essential. Response may be defensive or aggressive and may involve waiting for a competitor to act; or it may be preemptive, seeking to ward off competitors or warn them of rival actions such as price cuts, competitive product introductions, and expansion of dealer networks.

Being ready to respond to competition is partly a matter of contingency planning. Although a firm does not know what a competitor will do, it can make reasonable guesses about a competitor's options over the planning horizon. Planning should, therefore, include appropriate responses to those options.

Strategic response sometimes entails cooperating with the competition by forming a **strategic alliance**. This action is becoming increasingly popular as companies realize the importance of having a global strategy. The problem for many companies is that their global ambitions exceed their resources; and if they move too slowly in developing global markets, they may be swallowed up by stronger, already established global competition. Strategic alliances sometimes solve that problem. A review of a variety of strategic alliances follows, with examples from the pharmaceutical and tire industries.

COMPETITIVE RESPONSE IN THE PHARMACEUTICAL INDUSTRY

The pharmaceutical industry presents an interesting arena for competitive response. It is stable, with an aging population in rich countries, boding well for growing demand. Major markets include the economies of Japan, Europe, and the United States. Fast-growing developing countries such as India, China, and Brazil represent major markets of the future. International health-care crises such as the devastation rendered by the HIV/AIDS crisis in Africa create ethical dilemmas for the industry, leading companies to consider the importance of balancing drug affordability criteria with shareholder wealth.

Developing a new drug is costly and time-consuming, exceeding $500 million and taking 10 to 15 years. Drug companies must be able to sell the drug quickly in all three major economic regions before their drug patents expire. Therefore, they may need partners to help sell a drug or defray the cost of developing a new one. In addition, they may want partners who have something of their own to offer: ideally, a new drug, exchanging distribution rights for the firm's own new drugs.

Drug companies also feel pressure to reduce costs because governments pay for many health-care costs and want to keep drug prices low. Hence, drug companies have to increase their sales volume to make up for lower margins. Generic drug companies also pose a threat, making drugs that are no longer protected by patents. Because generic drug companies do not have to invest in R&D, they can charge lower prices.

The global pharmaceutical industry has seen a changing environment in which customers are gaining power, forcing down prices and profit margins. The growth of large buyers such as health maintenance organizations (HMOs) has increased their power. Patents on many major drugs are expiring; and the industry is fragmented, with the largest company, Pfizer, controlling a little over 10 percent of the global market. The drug companies need to become larger in order to reap economies of scale, and they may need to diversify so they are not dependent solely on research success within pharmaceuticals.

Pfizer became the industry's largest company by acquiring the European company Pharmacia in an acquisition valued at nearly $60 billion. Other pharmaceutical companies have followed similar strategies of acquisition, as shown in Table 6-1.

The 1996 merger between Ciba-Geigy and Sandoz, which together became Novartis, illustrates why mergers have become the central strategic response to pharmaceutical industry change and globalization. It is instructive to consider the strengths and motivations that each company brought to the merger. Both companies were facing threats from generic drugs to their own lines, whose patents were expiring. They did not have blockbuster drugs in their research pipeline, and Ciba had experienced negative clinical results in two major research efforts on acute heart disease and therapies to limit damage from head injuries and strokes. A merger would allow for elimination of redundancies and lead to cost reduction. Moreover, neither company would have to take on debt or spend large sums of money, as the merger was a friendly one.

Corporate culture clashes, while inevitable, might be reduced because of a shared Swiss culture, with companies headquartered in Basel, Switzerland. The merged company would be diversified, with 40 percent of total revenues coming from agricultural chemicals and human nutrition. Lastly, power would be shared, with each company contributing eight members to a

Table 6-1 Pharmaceutical Company Acquisitions

Company	Strategic Moves
Sanofi	Acquired Aventis, another French pharmaceutical firm, to stay all-French and to become the third largest drug firm in the world in 2004
Pfizer	Acquired Pharmacia for $60 billion, with resulting combined sales of $48 billion
Pharmacia	Acquired Monsanto in 2000 Monsanto Acquired American Home Products (AHP), which was somewhat controversial; AHP is now Wyeth
Pfizer	Acquired Warner Lambert; the principal attraction was Lipitor, a statin to treat high cholesterol
Glaxo	Merged with Smith Kline, the second largest pharmaceutical firm in the world
Merck	Acquired Medco Containment Systems to control the selling of drugs in the United States and to build a detailed database of drugs
Novartis	Merger of Sandoz and Ciba-Geigy; holds one-third of Roche
Hoechst	Became a major drug company with the acquisition of Marion Merrell Dow
Roche Holding	Acquired U.S.-based Synte and Japan's Chugai Pharma in 2001
Bristol-Myers Squibb	Merger of Bristol-Myers and Squibb
SmithKline Beecham	Merger of SmithKline and UK's Beecham; later merged with Glaxo
Pharmacia and Upjohn	Merger between Swedish and U.S. firms to gain size and to ward off hostile takeovers; later merged with Pfizer
American Home Products (AHP)	Acquired American Cyanamid, including Lederle drug division

joint executive board. Aside from those merger synergies, each company had certain strengths, as shown below:

Ciba-Geigy	**Sandoz**
Two strong divisions: over-the-counter medication and eye care	Strong gene therapy research
49% ownership of U.S. biotech leader Chiron	80% global market share in drugs to prevent rejection in organ transplants
Respected worldwide distribution capability	$1 billion research on animal organ transplants in humans

The Sandoz/Ciba-Geigy merger illustrates one effect of globalization on strategy: Fragmented industries begin to consolidate in order to approach the requisite size and to obtain scale economies necessary to be competitive in the global arena.[3]

REASONS FOR FORMING STRATEGIC ALLIANCES

In a strategic alliance, firms join together in some area of their business to reduce risk, obtain economies of scale, and obtain complementary assets—often intangible ones such as access to lucrative markets, brand names, and access to government procurement. The allure of acquiring technology and the pressures of government are also reasons for such alliances. They are typically formed in one of three broad areas: technology, manufacturing, and marketing.

Table 6-2 Motivations to Form Joint Ventures and Strategic Alliances

Motivations	Results
Complement weaknesses in the value chain	Obtain complementary competences in R&D (basic research and/or applications development) and manufacturing (scale/scope economies, new processes, and cost reduction)
Take defensive position to protect market	See examples from the pharmaceutical industry, such as the Sandoz Ciba-Geigy merger
Be proactive by developing new businesses	Keep pace with new technologies and new customer segments
Focus on product line or geographic area	Enhance market access to specific countries, brands, distribution channels, and service capabilities; enhance product line with partners possessing complementary products and services
Think strategically of core and peripheral operations	Reduce dependency on alliance partner and possible cannibalization of the corporation
React to government-imposed regulations	Offer legally necessary ownership stakes in return for political ties and local influence, as in several Asian private energy infrastructure projects
Reduce/share risk	Reduce ownership with attendant reduction in share of profits and losses
Overcome resource scarcity with partner contributions	Obtain resources (materials, components, capital, management, and information technology, such as Computer Reservation Systems in airline and hotel businesses)
Learn from partner	Seek partners from related or unrelated industries, from supplier and customer segments, or from possible multiple partners and coalitions (for example, telecommunications firms bidding for licenses in the U.S. wireless industry)
Obtain fit with global strategy alternatives through licensing, foreign direct investment, and acquisitions	Act cautiously, for alliances are not the universal panacea (over half of all joint ventures and alliances are dissolved within a few years)

Another reason for alliances is that consumers are becoming alike in the developed nations. Consumers tend to receive the same information, and their discretionary incomes are roughly equal. As a result, tastes are becoming homogenized. As Kenichi Ohmae put it, "Everyone in a sense wants to live and shop in California."[4] But no one company can expect to dominate all technologies and create entire product lines for the developing global market. A likely solution, therefore, is to swap products.

An additional factor concerning alliances is that fixed costs account for a larger proportion of total costs. Global sales help a firm recover higher fixed costs even when lower prices are charged. (Volume compensates for a smaller contribution per unit.) The reason firms should consider lowering prices and selling globally is that product life cycles are becoming short and fixed costs are more likely to be covered by resorting to global markets. It is difficult to exploit worldwide markets without global alliances, however. Short product life cycles mean that firms must move quickly to exploit their technological lead. Such a technology lead is actually a disappearing asset, diminishing in value with the passage of time. Strategic alliances allow a firm to penetrate several key markets simultaneously. Table 6-2 summarizes these motivations.

Alliances, however, require that each party has something to swap. In the tire industry, General Tire supplies Japanese auto companies in the United States on behalf of Japanese companies, which in turn supply companies in Japan on behalf of General Tire and Continental. Several alliances can be formed within the same country. IBM, for example, works in Japan with Ricoh to distribute its low-end copiers, with Nippon Steel to sell systems integration services, with Fuji Bank to sell financial systems, with OMRON to penetrate the computer-integrated manufacturing market, and with NTT to sell VANs.

Technology sharing, joint distribution and sales, and supply arrangements are the main foci of such alliances. What is interesting is that these alliances often occur between companies

Table 6-3 Virtual Organizational Models for Alliances

	Location	Work Cycle	Culture	Organizational Relationships	Virtual Management Issues
Shared Partnership (Model 1)	Often share locations, a spin-off approach	Often highly synchronized activities	Typically homogeneous cultures, though distinctive	Typically strong preexisting relationships	Challenges of adapting existing relationships into virtual management
Core/Satellite (Model 2)	Locations shared when performing physical job functions	Often highly synchronized activities	Less emphasis on culture, more contractual relationships	Existing relationships established	Ongoing assessment of partners in constellation Virtual Value Chain
Virtual Value Chain (Model 3)	Typically do not share locations	Highly synchronized across adjoining value chain members	Some emphasis on culture across adjoining members, but more contractual	Often existing relationships limited to adjoining members	Identifying alternative partners for expanding global value chain
Integrated Firm (Model 4)	Often share locations or located in close proximity	Often highly synchronized, coordinated scheduling	Higher emphasis on culture as a competitive advantage	Strong existing relationships among some members	Initiating existing, offensive, and defensive strategies
Electronic Market (Model 5)	Rarely share locations	Highly responsive, not necessarily coordinated	Similar service-oriented cultures, but not necessary	Few existing relationships in many cases	Auditing and exit strategies; competitive response

Source: Adapted from Cheri Speier, Michael G. Harvey, Jonathan Palmer, "Virtual Management of Global Marketing Relationships," *Journal of World Business*, Volume 33, Issue 3, 1998, pages 263–276.

that also compete with each other in other markets. In choosing such partners, several criteria are useful:[5]

- The competitor should have a competitive advantage—economies of scale, technology, or market access—and those areas should be critical in the value-added chain.
- The contributions of each partner should be complementary or balanced.
- The two partners should agree on a global strategy to follow.
- There should be a low risk that the partner will become a future competitor.
- There should be a preemptive value in having the firm as a partner rather than a rival.
- There should be compatibility of organizations as well as top management of the two firms.

How should alliances in different market and cultural settings and with different management and organizational philosophies be managed? Speier, Harvey, and Palmer suggest that alliances be treated as virtual relationships, a web of companies across the value chain.[6] They propose five different approaches to managing such virtual global business organizations, as follows.

- A shared partnership, with nearly equal amounts of commitment
- A core/satellite organization, with a core firm providing the impetus to form the global network
- A virtual value chain to service the end customer
- An integrated firm model where the different companies agree to function as a single vertically integrated firm throughout the world
- An electronic outlet, with firms using technology as the means of interacting with end customers

Such virtual organizations can be difficult to coordinate. Table 6-3 shows some areas for coordination that are essential to continuing success.

Organizing For Global Business

Whatever planning is done will be in vain unless the company is organized to implement the plans. Organizational structure determines who does what, including which employees exercise gatekeeping power in supporting or undermining decisions made by others. Furthermore, organizational structure determines how business activities will be implemented. Implementation should flow from strategy; that is, activities are carried out to implement strategy. Thus, a critical element of designing global business organization is to ensure that it is consistent with strategy, that it leads to activities that help implement strategy.[7] Organizational structure also sets up the rewards that motivate performance and determines the degree to which activities can be integrated. This is particularly important in global strategy since implementation must be carried out by subsidiaries in different countries, without many opportunities for face-to-face communication. Indeed, some of the worst problems facing international managers result from friction between headquarters and foreign subsidiaries.

The basic issue for all organizational structure in global corporations revolves around centralization versus decentralization. Global corporations need strong coordination at headquarters to provide and supervise implementation of global strategy. If local subsidiary managers have different opinions, however, they may pull away from that strategy. Or, pressures by the local government may require greater local responsiveness, even if it means diverging from global strategy. Thus, the major task for organizational structure is to mediate between the opposing needs for centralization and local responsiveness.[8]

Research has suggested that in some industries where consumers around the world buy essentially the same product, as in consumer electronics, centralization and large-scale manufacturing are the keys to success. In industries in which national consumers have distinct product preferences and much product adaptation is necessary, as in branded packaged goods (detergents, for example), a large degree of national subsidiary autonomy is needed. Then there are industries in which scale economies demand centralized, large-scale manufacturing; and yet monopolistic consumers have distinct product preferences, as in the telecommunications industry. Here, both centralization and local responsiveness are needed.[9]

Approaches to Organizing International Operations

A company can organize its international operations as a separate international division, with further subunits within the international division consisting of regional and local entities. It may also prefer to create organizational units structured along products and lines of business. A third approach is to create functional units, with distinct global responsibilities for research, manufacturing, logistics, and other functions. Finally, a company may decide that proper planning and execution of tasks require cooperation between managers, thereby fostering such cooperation by resorting to a *matrix organization*, where responsibilities for achieving goals is jointly allocated to managers with country, functional, and product-line responsibilities.

The International Division

Creating a separate organizational unit to focus on international business and operations allows international expertise, personnel, and vision to be concentrated in one part of the company. It creates a unit whose sole focus is on international business, one that stands up for internation-

Figure 6-2 The International Division Organizational Structure

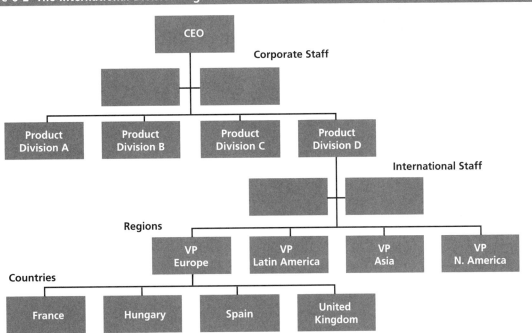

al operations and seeks human and capital resources for that activity. Such an approach is more common in companies with relatively limited international operations, where domestic concerns predominate, and where product-line complexity is limited. Figure 6-2 illustrates the international division structure.

However, a separate international division faces several problems. It may receive a lesser share of resources than its markets warrant, it may be perceived as a backwater that is less relevant to the future of the company, and it may have less political clout in the fight for attention and budget allocations from top management. Resolving international business issues without regard to their integration into the company's overall strategy may result in suboptimization.

STRUCTURING BY AREA

Rather than have a separate international division, a company may develop an organizational structure with distinct responsibilities for each major geographic area. What is "international" is not relegated to second-division status. Instead, world markets are broken up into a series of geographic divisions, one of which happens to include the company's home, or domestic, market.

When a company is structured by area, the primary basis for organization is by divisions for major regions of the world. For example, when CPC International reorganized from an international division to a world company approach, it set up five operating companies—one for Europe, one for Latin America, one for the Far East, and two for North America (consumer products and industrial products). Although the structure is primarily a regional form of organization, the North American area is divided on the basis of product. The regional organizational form is

Internationalizing the Company: Staffing Issues

Organizing the international business function is partly a matter of hierarchies, power, and control. But it is also about finding and putting the best people in key positions. Staffing international positions raises tricky issues not found in the domestic arena. Foremost is the danger that the executive assigned overseas will get "lost," forgotten by colleagues and bosses. In turn, this makes reentry into domestic operations difficult. Very often the returning expatriate finds no job available that makes use of the incremental international business skills gained during the overseas assignment. Overseas executives also supervise large staffs, enjoy high pay and fringe benefits, and have considerable autonomy. Returning to headquarters may mean lower pay and less prestige. Unless they have a mentor or champion at home who smooths reentry and finds them a position commensurate with their new skills, returning managers often believe that their careers are at a dead end and that the firm does not appreciate or want them. Former overseas executives often resign, which is a loss to the firm because the international skills are hard-earned and necessary for the corporation to compete successfully in the global arena. Hence, firms need to set up programs that ensure that the best young managers are selected for overseas assignments and that a clear career path is established, including identifying jobs that will be open and available for returning managers.

As the global economy continues to become more important, one prerequisite to attaining top management positions at large U.S. multinationals is substantial international experience. For example, all eight members of Tupperware's executive committee speak two to four languages and have worked overseas. Samir Gibara, CEO of Goodyear Tire & Rubber, spent 27 years in management positions outside the United States. The chief operating officer (COO) at the Gillette Company and the CEOs at Outboard Marine Corporation, Case Corporation, and ExxonMobil have all spent over half of their management careers outside the United States. Twenty-eight percent of all senior management searches now require international experience. Companies seem to be looking for executives with substantial international experience who have

used primarily by marketing-oriented companies that have relatively stable technology, such as those in consumer nondurables, pharmaceuticals, and automotive and farm equipment.

Several factors favor a regional approach to organization. The growth of regional groupings is one. As nations within a region integrate economically, it makes more sense to treat them as a unit. The proximity of countries provides one logical basis for organization. Certain types of expertise can be grouped within the region to enhance operations in the individual countries. Communication is easy, and coordination of product and functional know-how can take place in the region. A narrow product line and similarity in technology and methods of operation also favor regional organization. The greater the international similarity of the firm's products, the greater the importance of knowledge of an area.

spent several years overseas, immersing themselves in the culture while running operations. U.S. companies in particular seem to value experience in emerging markets such as China, India, and Brazil. The difficulty, of course, is how an executive who spends all of his or her time overseas becomes visible to headquarters' top management in the United States. The answer, presumably, is also to spend time at home in a job with significant managerial responsibilities.

Companies have also begun to assign executives from headquarters units to overseas locations based on the executives' origin and their cultural knowledge of those markets. Payless Shoe Source is one such company. It had set its strategy around expansion into Latin America. Payless, with its many U.S. stores in inner-city locations, appealed to Latin American immigrants to the United States who could afford the prices and liked the range of styles. Those people often gave Payless shoes as presents when they returned home to visit relatives. This practice created strong brand awareness and brand loyalty in the local population in these foreign markets.

In 2000, Payless began to expand by opening 5 stores in Costa Rica, increasing to almost 200 stores scattered throughout Central America, Trinidad, the Dominican Republic, Chile, Peru, and Ecuador. The company informed its U.S. employees of Latin American origin that it was willing to let some of them manage overseas stores in Central and Latin America. Many homesick expatriates were willing to accept such a job offer. One of those employees was Roxana Orellana, who had come to the United States when she was a child, smuggled into the country as a refugee from El Salvador during its civil war. Many years later she had joined Payless, working her way up to manager of an outlet in Los Angeles. When the opportunity arose to go back home, she took it, despite a pay cut from $33,000 to $15,000. She was given charge of a new store in Sonsonate, a regional capital. Customers flocked to the store, which was air-conditioned, carried a full line of popular styles, attractively displayed a full range of sizes, and was decorated with mirrored panels with which to judge potential new shoe purchases in a retail environment where such modern, customer friendly stores were uncommon. Those stores became successful, partly because of local managers who brought with them knowledge of both the U.S. corporate culture and the local culture.

Sources: "Grappling with the Expatriate Issue: Little Benefit to Careers Seen in Foreign Stints," *Wall Street Journal*, December 11, 1989; "An Overseas Stint Can Be a Ticket to the Top," *Wall Street Journal*, January 29, 1996; " 'Repats' help Payless shoes branch out into Latin America," *Wall Street Journal*, December 24, 2003.

In spite of its popularity, the regional organization has drawbacks. It ensures the best use of a firm's regional expertise, but it means less than optimal allocation of product and functional expertise. If each region needs its own staff of product and functional specialists, duplication—and inefficiency—may result if the best staff is not available for each region. Inefficiency is most likely when regional management is located away from corporate headquarters. When regional management is housed at corporate headquarters, a centralized staff can serve all regional units, providing some economies of scale. A regional organization may optimize performance within the region, but there is danger of global suboptimization when no coordination takes place among the regions. Each region must blend into a global operation. Figure 6-3 illustrates a regional organizational structure.

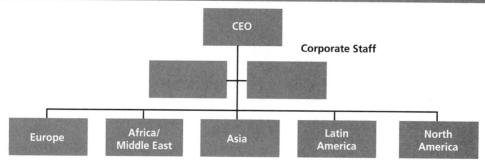

Figure 6-3   The Worldwide Regional Organizational Structure

STRUCTURING BY PRODUCT

Organizing by product line means that product groups have global responsibilities; thus, it is a global company approach by product division. An international division can be organized along product lines, too; but by its very nature, this type of organizational structure also includes area expertise. Structuring by product line is most common for companies with several unrelated product lines because their responsibilities vary more by product line than by region. As Figure 6-4 shows, the global product structure gives each product group what amounts to its own international division.

Figure 6-4   The Worldwide Product Organizational Structure

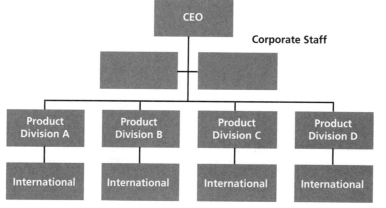

Structuring an organization along product lines has the merit of flexibility; a firm can add a new product division if it enters another business unrelated to its current lines. However, the product division approach has several potential limitations. When the domestic market is more important to a product division, international opportunities are likely to be missed. Limited area knowledge is a common weakness of product-structured organizations. Each product division cannot afford to maintain a complete international staff.

Another problem in a product-structured approach is the difficulty of achieving company-wide coordination. If each product division in a company goes its own way, the firm's international development will encounter conflicts and inefficiencies. The organization must provide global coordination to offset the sometimes contradictory international plans of individual product divisions. For example, it is probably unnecessary for each producing division to have its own advertising agency, service organization, and government relations staff in every market. When foreign plants manufacture products of different divisions, coordination among the divisions also is often a problem for a product organization.

Eaton provides an illustration of how companies with global product organization try to overcome some of its weaknesses. Eaton is highly diversified in the capital goods and automotive industries. It has five worldwide product groups, and each group has a managing director for European operations. To get a better overall corporate understanding and response to European problems in areas such as legislation, labor, and taxes, Eaton formed a European Coordinating Committee (ECC) composed of the five product division managing directors, several European staff, and one executive from world headquarters.

The responsibilities of the ECC's chair rotate among the managing directors, and meetings are at different European facilities. Eaton established country coordinating committees to manage the product groups within each European country. It also formed a Latin American coordinating committee to achieve the same integration in Latin America.

STRUCTURING BY FUNCTION

A functional structure (whereby top executives in marketing, finance, production, etc., all have global responsibilities) is most suitable for firms with narrow, homogeneous product lines, when product expertise is not a variable. Also of benefit is when regional variations in operations are not great, thus lessening the need for regional expertise. Because those conditions are not usually met, the functional form of organization for international operations is not common among U.S. firms except in extractive industries, such as the oil and gas industry. The functional structure is more common in European companies. Although functional executives in U.S. firms do have international responsibilities, those responsibilities are usually in conjunction with a product or regional form of organization.

One of the more interesting organizational developments in recent decades has been the matrix form of organization. Companies became frustrated with the shortcomings of unidimensional organizational structures (product, area, function) that were noted previously. Therefore, they moved to a more complex organizational form that allowed two dimensions to have more or less equal weight in the organizational structure and decision making. A **matrix organization** has a dual rather than single chain of command, meaning that many managers have two bosses. Matrix also involves lateral (dual) decision making and a chain of command that fosters conflict management and a balance of power. Product and market (geography) are the two dimensions receiving equal emphasis in matrix organizations in international business. For example, AGCO Corporation's 2004 matrix restructuring created operational control of sales and engineering by geographic brand, with functional supervisory responsibility on a global basis.[10] Matrix can solve some problems of the simple product or area structure, but matrix organizations have many problems of their own that arise from inherent conflicts and complexity.

Evolving to a Transnational Organization

To summarize, multinationals evolve from a structure consisting mainly of domestic operations — with some overseas business—to the multinational stage in which international business becomes more important. This typically results in independent, locally responsive subsidiaries that display greater sensitivity to local customers, governments, and culture and that are headed by local CMs with an entrepreneurial bent. At some point, competitive forces and environmental pressures from globalization of the industry lead headquarters to want greater global integration of relatively autonomous local subsidiaries. One solution is to implement a matrix approach. The problem, however, is that a global matrix organization is both complex and bureaucratic, with its two-boss structure. The possible consequence is conflict and confusion with overlapping responsibilities. Negotiation is necessary; and the organization may become bogged down with information, while multiple time zones and distances render the resolution of face-to-face conflict difficult. Hence, top management attempts to rein in national subsidiaries and begins to eliminate redundancies that may have developed in products, manufacturing sites, and staff functions.

Greater centralization focuses on developing global products and rationalized global manufacturing. Such steps require more central coordination and control. At this point, local managers begin to chafe against the dictates of central headquarters and market forces lead top management to realize that some local responsiveness and autonomy are necessary. *This leads to the emergence of the transnational form of organization,* with the goal of mediating between the conflicting drives of global integration and local responsiveness. Such an organizational form brings the added benefit of stimulating worldwide innovation because it also facilitates knowledge sharing and transnational cooperation.

The importance of local responsiveness is growing as multinationals increase their presence in environments that are quite distinct from their home markets and from markets in other developed nations. Quelch points out that U.S. multinationals, in particular, have limited presence in Islamic countries and have few Muslims in upper levels of management. That limits the firms' ability to engage Islamic markets, take into account the sensibilities and culture of those markets, adapt products, and learn from the markets. He notes that Saudi Arabia is a lead market for film finishing. Saudi culture does not accept that women in the family be viewed by strangers. Therefore, there is a need for rapid film processing so that when men pick up their processed film, they can rest assured that strangers have not seen photographs of any female family members. Thus, companies such as Fuji and Kodak are often first to introduce innovations in high-speed film processing in such markets. Quelch observes that more of this localization will be needed as such markets increase in importance.[11]

Why become transnational? The multinational can achieve scale and scope economies and obtain lower factor costs for raw materials, labor, and capital. At the same time, growing convergence of tastes allows the multinational to concentrate on developing global products and standards, with some local variation. The multinational is better able to confront global competitors by supporting weaker or embattled subsidiaries, using cash flow from stronger subsidiaries that have operations in healthy markets. Such a structure also allows the multinational to respond to environmental volatility, including discriminatory industrial policies by local governments, currency volatility, short product life cycles, economic cyclicality, and cultural differences. Because the environment is constantly changing, the challenge facing the transnational organization is to continue to stimulate worldwide innovation and organizational learning while still maintaining organizational flexibility.[12]

Transnational corporations are the conceptual translation of the rule to "think local, act global." Transnationals often have products that require adaptation to the needs of local markets. At the same time, the size of transnationals results in benefits from the centralization or regionalization of functions such as finance and product development. And as ideas can develop anywhere in the world in a large, far-flung corporation, the transnational form of organization creates communication links that encourage the sharing of information and ideas across entities, whether demarcated by function or geography or product line. Transnational organization is an evolution of the matrix form of organization; however, responsibility and authority are clarified.

Examples of Global Organization

It is difficult to appreciate arguments about organizational structure in the abstract. The subtleties of structure are more easily grasped in the context of a product and a market. Hence, this section presents specific examples of the evolution of organizational structure to show how market realities are incorporated in the process of organizational change.

REYNOLDS: EUROPEAN REGIONAL AUTONOMY

The EU has led many global corporations to reexamine how they structure their European operations. Reynolds Metals Company used to have 25 European subsidiaries report to the international division located at headquarters in Richmond, Virginia. This meant that each European CM dealt directly with the United States and rarely attempted to coordinate operations with the other European countries. Thus, salespeople from different national units would compete against one another for the same multinational client. There was duplication of manufacturing operations and differences in cost and quality. The changes in Europe meant that Reynolds had to integrate European operations because it would be facing intense competition from pan-European companies such as Pechiney and Alusuisse.

Consequently, Reynolds created a European headquarters in Lausanne, Switzerland, to oversee all European operations so they would have a "single voice." Lausanne was headed by a top management team consisting of a president, a chief financial officer (CFO), an executive vice president in charge of manufacturing, and several vice presidents with responsibilities in areas such as finance. The Lausanne location was chosen over others because Switzerland was viewed as being politically neutral, which may not have been the case for operations located in France or Germany, for example. Reynolds (Europe) Ltd. had direct responsibility for manufacturing facilities.

Reynolds planned to focus on downstream, household-oriented products as well as the aluminum can market since European consumption of cans lagged far behind the 74 billion sold in the United States. Reynolds expected several benefits to flow from the organizational change:
- Rationalized manufacturing, resulting in lowering costs
- Faster decision making
- A pan-European thrust in production and marketing strategies
- Greater influence in Brussels, a city fast becoming the seat of European government

UNILEVER: A TRANSNATIONAL ORGANIZATION

In Unilever's transnational organization, product groups are responsible for profits in Europe and North America, while geographically based regional organizations have profit responsibilities elsewhere in the world. Unilever's transnational organization is the result of a long evolu-

Bringing Global Vision into the Company

Global companies face a problem in that their top management is predominantly a national one; that is, most top managers at U.S. companies are Americans. In Japanese companies, top managers are predominantly Japanese. How can such companies not allow a purely nationalistic perspective to bias their attempts to develop a global vision in their planning? The answer may lie partly in adding nondomestic members to their board of director. Few American firms have non-U.S. citizen directors. Because they have operated in international markets longer, European companies have a larger proportion of foreign directors. The difficulty lies in getting the closed-club world of top executives in one country to accept outsiders from another country. Then there is the matter of finding the appropriate people who are willing to serve. Firms

tion lasting several decades. Initially, Unilever was organized as a series of relatively independent country subsidiaries with strong local management. Later, product groups took over worldwide profit responsibility, which was divided into three major groups: edible fats, frozen food and ice cream, and food and drinks such as tea and soup. Raw materials and distribution systems determined the makeup of those three groups. This change took many years of "patience, persuasion and even some early retirements."[13]

As markets changed, consumer-driven products such as low-calorie, health, and convenience foods and the use of natural ingredients became important. Unilever's response was to form an executive triad of three board directors responsible for all of Unilever's food businesses. Each director received profit responsibility for a group of countries in a region. Five strategic groups centered around edible fats, ice cream, beverages, meals, and professional markets. Today those groups advise the "food executive," providing product expertise; but they don't have profit center responsibilities. Unilever's newest transnational organizational structure seeks to preserve unity within diversity. It well understands that current major food market trends such as global fast food, national foods that cross country boundaries (for example, Chinese and Mexican food), and purely national foods might require continued organizational evolution, which, in turn, means maintaining a flexible workforce.

Such flexibility is achieved by careful recruitment and training of managers. Unilever's managers constantly watch for young, bright local university graduates and scientists. Recruits go through in-house training programs on a continuing basis, maintaining contact with their peer cohorts around the world. Job rotation across product groups and countries and use of third-country nationals in high-level executive positions in country subsidiaries further cement informal transnational network ties across various country units. Unilever also uses international working groups to handle specific tasks and issues. Twice a year international conferences bring together managers from all over the world to listen to management plans and to meet and renew old friendships.

need to establish criteria that are especially relevant for choosing a foreign director, such as close ties to local government, considerable experience in economic planning, or years of top management experience running a global company in a related industry. U.S. directors' liability laws can result in non-U.S. citizens being reluctant to serve. Scheduling meetings is another difficulty. A foreign director must fly to the United States for one- or two-day meetings several times a year.

Just as U.S. companies need Europeans and Asians to add a fresh perspective, Asian family-owned firms similarly need Western multinationals and their managers to bring in professional management techniques and a taste for open communication and meritocracy. Of course, as Asian firms begin to launch factories and sales offices across Europe and the Americas, Western contacts help them find their way. Cultural clashes abound, however, particularly in the contrast between the Asian emphasis on personal relationships in business and the Western preference for legal contracts and agreements.

Sources: "Globalizing the Company with Foreign Board Members," *Business International*, March 4, 1991; "Asia's Family Empires Change Their Tactics for a Shrinking World," *Wall Street Journal*, April 19, 1995.

In the pharmaceutical industry, Schering-Plough reorganized its U.S. and global marketing divisions into two major customer groups: primary care physicians and specialists. Each group was in charge of certain drugs, based on who most likely understood the need for such drugs and had the power to prescribe them. Thus, the specialist group handled drugs to treat hepatitis C, Crohn's disease, brain tumors, and cardiovascular disease. Further, international pharmaceutical sales were subdivided by geography, with one subgroup in charge of Japan, Latin America, and the Far East and the other subgroup having responsibility for Europe, Canada, Africa, and the Middle East. The United States had its own domestic marketing division.[14]

GENERAL MOTORS: REDUCING U.S. CONTROL

General Motors' decentralizing authority comes from Detroit. GM set up European headquarters in Zurich. The heads of sales at its major product divisions in Europe—Opel (Germany), Vauxhall (UK), and Saab—all report to the European sales chief based in Zurich. Similarly, the heads of production and product development at the three product divisions report directly to Europe's COO in Zurich. Zurich coordinates European business, planning, and operations, with some division of tasks between national and European headquarters. Zurich focuses on Europe-wide planning and strategy, environmental matters, personnel, and relations with the EU in Brussels and other European capitals.[15]

The GM example refers to organization only in Europe. When considering global operations, designing an organizational structure becomes even more difficult. This can be gauged by considering Toyota's global operations, as shown in Figure 6-5. Toyota has significant high-volume manufacturing operations in North America, Europe, and Asia; the heart of its operations is in Japan. Each location is a major source of exports. As a result, Toyota's organizational structure needs not only to manage and coordinate global manufacturing and supply chains, but also to link these sources of product with upstream global R&D and product development and with many downstream global markets, subsidiaries, and distributors across the continents.

Figure 6-5   Toyota's Global Manufacturing Organization

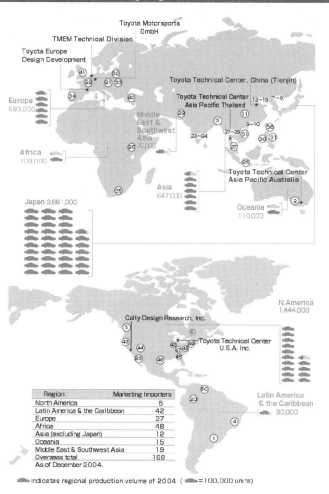

Region	Marketing Importers
North America	5
Latin America & the Caribbean	42
Europe	27
Africa	48
Asia (excluding Japan)	12
Oceania	15
Middle East & Southwest Asia	19
Overseas total	168
As of December 2004.	

indicates regional production volume of 2004 (=100,000 units)

Source: Toyota Motor Corporation web site; company worldwide organization (http://www.toyota.co.jp/en/about_toyota/manufacturing/worldwide.html); accessed April 27, 2005.

SHELL: RELYING ON MATRIX ORGANIZATION

The companies of the Royal Dutch/Shell Group, whose scenario planning was discussed earlier, also adopted a matrix structure, with the additional innovation of the matrix involving three dimensions: regions, industry sectors, and functions. Shell's several hundred operating companies, which are autonomous, draw on global resources of the "service" companies, including regional, sectoral, and functional management.

Shell has nine service companies providing specialized advice and services and consisting of executives who have considerable operating experience in the field. Thus, an operating company could call on experts in petroleum exploration techniques, in financial management, or in chemical plant management. The service companies include trading companies dealing in oil, chemicals, and coal.

The three dimensions of the service companies include five regional coordinators who monitor the profits of the operating companies and approve investments and six business sectors that consist of upstream oil and gas and downstream oil, including marketing, natural gas, chemicals, coal, and metals. Sectoral panels supervise strategy for national, regional, and worldwide lines of business. Further, nine specialized functional departments exist: finance, legal affairs, materials, planning, public affairs, research, safety and environment, information systems, and human resources and organization. The CEO of each operating company must draw up the annual plan, however, calling on any of the service companies for whatever assistance is needed. The quality and experience of the service companies are what make the system work. A drawback, though, is the vast quantity of information that flows to headquarters. All in all, Shell believes that the gains from giving autonomy to operating companies provide a compensatory quick-response capability.[16]

Another example of matrix organization is the Radisson hotel chain, which is segmented by market and geographic area. The geographic segment focuses on North and South America, Europe, and Asia and the Pacific; the market segments include business travel, leisure travel, and group travel. The matrix structure leads to teams that can focus global resources on specific local properties.

PHILIPS: GLOBAL PRODUCT DIVISIONS

Philips, the Dutch electronics multinational, also stressed quick local responses and a customer orientation as it reorganized for global operations.[17] Philips reduced local subsidiary autonomy to focus on three core global product divisions: consumer electronics, electronic components, and IT/communications. National subsidiary autonomy was reduced to allow a global manufacturing strategy to be formulated for each product division. Today the importance of the product line is stressed by bringing product division directors on board. At the same time, central control allows for rationalized manufacturing on a global scale for each product line in order to gain economies of scale.

How can such a system not stifle local subsidiaries? Philips wants to be imaginative in creating new products and asks for input from key markets for this task. At the same time, central control is needed to prevent the creation of different national products for each market. Philips has located "competence centers" in crucial markets—car electronics in Germany and domestic appliances in Italy, for example. Also, the company uses multidisciplinary teams with expertise in development, design, manufacturing, and sales, thus keeping in mind technical and manufacturing considerations. The global organization was always a crucial factor in making reorganization decisions; but the contribution of national organizations was considered vital for making decisions about local sales and distribution, as well as for dealing with national regulations and developing relationships with government representatives.

Philips takes care to balance the opposing demands of centralization and local responsiveness over the stages of a product's life cycle. In the early stage, product launch is centrally coordinated in Europe, the United States, and Japan, while centralized manufacturing and standardization reduce costs. In the maturity phase, local subsidiaries play a larger role, tailoring local marketing, possibly including some product modifications. In the decline phase, emphasis shifts to centralized manufacturing and cost saving. Local subsidiaries make the greatest contribution and have the greatest autonomy in choosing distribution channels, which Philips believes must be adapted to local conditions. The powerful distribution and dealer networks built by local subsidiaries become a key competitive advantage in Philips' global strategy.

Reorganization at Square D Company, AGCO Corporation, and Ciba-Geigy

Square D Company is an example of the role of organizational structure in mediating headquarters and regional interests. Square D manufactures electrical products in over 100 factories, including 31 outside the United States. Traditionally, international responsibility had been based at U.S. headquarters. The work was divided between the vice presidents for international marketing and international manufacturing. U.S. products were sold overseas, foreign subsidiaries had little authority, and communication with the United States was infrequent.

To implement a global strategy, the electrical group was divided into three business units: distribution equipment, power equipment, and controls. At the same time, five regional divisions were created: the United States, Asia and the Pacific, Canada, Europe, and Latin America. The result was a product/region matrix with the following structure:

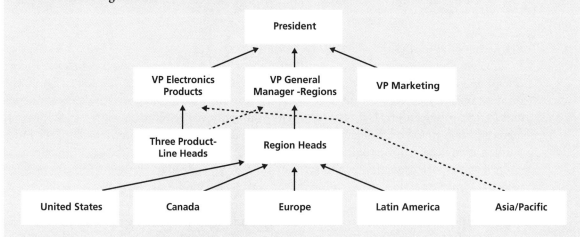

The matrix consists of product-line heads and regional managers, except for Asia/Pacific, which reports directly to a vice president of marketing because of Square D's limited manufacturing presence in Asia. Quar-

An important element in developing new products is the R&D lab. As firms try to decide whether to customize products for individual markets, they also must decide how to organize the R&D function. If R&D is centralized, organizational procedures must allow product customization requests to come in from the various subsidiaries, with a way to prioritize such requests and respond in a timely manner. One approach is to appoint a business executive to serve as liaison between subsidiaries and the central R&D lab, channeling and prioritizing customization requests. Then the actual development can be carried out at the central lab or at regional sites, serving specific clusters of markets. Such ventures also require the formation of virtual teams that are established on a project basis, using communication networks, e-mail, and videoconferencing to allow for exchange of information and debate on major issues.[18]

terly meetings are held in the United States with the product-line and regional heads as well as with domestic managers. Communications are emphasized via a quarterly videotape and an in-house magazine distributed worldwide.

The benefits from this reorganization include the following:

- Greater regional autonomy with profit and loss responsibility
- Timely relay of market information about electrical standards, priorities for each market, and feedback on demand trends and competition—all to benefit manufacturing worldwide
- Ability to design a global product effectively and economically; the smooth flow of information from around the world helps determine global product requirements and allows pooling of manufacturing and engineering capabilities
- An emphasis on cooperation and global line responsibilities, fostering a global corporate culture

Ciba-Geigy presents an alternative approach to using regional managers. The company is divided into 14 major worldwide product lines and 34 profit centers. If a country has only one product subsidiary, that division reports directly to the worldwide product division manager, who, in turn, reports to an executive committee member responsible for that product line. When countries have multiple product divisions, however, they are supervised by a regional manager, who reports to an executive committee member who has responsibility for a geographic area. Ciba-Geigy has three broad geographic areas: Europe, the Americas, and Asia/Australia. Thus, executive committee members have both product and geographic responsibilities. The company's regional managers oversee local responsibilities including legal, personnel, quality and security, management development, and performance measurement. The regional managers also represent the company in interaction with local governments, unions, and the media. Regional manager and local product division managers are jointly responsible for profits. Bonuses for regional managers are based on a combination of local country profits and worldwide profits, as well as division profits in cases where the regional manager has local product division responsibility.

Another example is AGCO Corporation, which designs, manufactures, and distributes agricultural equipment. It moved to a new matrix management structure, motivated by the need to focus on specific brands in specific geographic areas while also giving more authority and responsibility to functional heads, thus creating more control. The matrix was also intended to foster greater cooperation worldwide. It allows the company to develop top management by giving managers an opportunity to gain hands-on international experience in an operating positions.

Sources: "Square D Unites Managers to Compete Globally," *Business International*, September 21, 1987; "The Role of the Country Manager," *Business Europe*, March 27, 1995; "AGCO Announces New Organization Structure as Part of Succession Planning," PR Newswire European, February 12, 2004.

Organizational flexibility will be the necessary ingredient as organizations change to meet the challenges of a global economy and new forms of competition from knowledge-rich and Internet-based companies. Organizing to harness knowledge from around the world is the critical challenge. Building and using knowledge bases; motivating people to contribute to and use shared knowledge; and fostering interaction among virtual organizational units and teams that channel specific forms of knowledge about customers, business processes, and products—those are all part of the new organizational structures.

ORGANIZATIONAL RESPONSES TO ASIAN AND LATIN AMERICAN MARKETS

GE has 12 major lines of business in Asia; but unlike many Asian conglomerates that cross-sub-sidize their disparate lines of business, GE insists that each line of business be independent. In practice, this means that GE has a manager for each country. That manager can give a common face to all of GE's businesses in a country. However, the CM at GE works in a matrix context, with each line of business evaluated on how well it contributes to the global profits of that line of business and to the country unit's profits. Another critical element of GE's Asian focus is the rotation of managers across GE's various Asian country units. Human resources is a scarce and limiting factor, and the executives bring varied experience but a common GE perspective to each business to which they are assigned.[19]

Sometimes a company's situation and strategic need may dictate that it stop using mostly local managers and bring in more expatriates. For example, as China began to move to GSM-based cellular phones, Motorola saw its phone division sales drop precipitously. Because it did not have a GSM switch to sell with its phones, it lost out to competitors who could offer a complete turnkey system. To reverse the trend, Motorola brought back senior level expatriates, replacing some high-level local managers. Motorola also began to sell older models at steep discounts so it could compete with traditional landline phones, increase its cellular market share, and hold off competitors to give it time to upgrade its technologies. That involved licensing a local Chinese company, Da Tang, to produce CDMA switches, a new U.S. technology intended to replace the GSM standard that was becoming widespread in China. Recently, Motorola launched new technologies allowing connectivity among CDMA200 1X and Wi-Fi networks. By 2004, China represented 9 percent (nearly $3 billion) of Motorola's worldwide sales.[20]

A similar matrix structure is used by DuPont in South America. Responding to the formation of Mercosur, DuPont has integrated its South American operations, with headquarters outside of Sao Paulo, Brazil, where all product-line managers are typically based. Each manager also has responsibility for a country in Mercosur and for smaller markets outside Mercosur. Such regional integration allows for the specialization of products by plants located in different countries with between-plant transfers of goods to meet various customer needs.

An interesting issue in organizations where matrix structures exist and where CMs work closely with several product-line managers is how to measure performance. Budgets can be set and performance against budget can be used as a means of evaluation. Beyond financial targets, CMs are responsible for soft variables such as handling government relations, maintaining corporate culture, and nurturing managers in their areas. Each region and each country may find it necessary to develop specific measures adapted to its needs and to its culture.[21]

Given the importance of organizational structure fitting with a firm's global business strategy, the structure will likely change as markets evolve and a company's strategy changes. Such organizational evolution can be seen in advertising agencies in China. Their initial customers, foreign multinationals in China, found that they needed to expand their operations beyond the three largest cities of Beijing, Shanghai, and Guangzhou into smaller provincial capitals such as Fujian. The multinationals needed advertising and communication services in these smaller, less well-known cities because they found themselves competing with larger local firms who were also attempting to establish their brands in these smaller markets. Such brand competition requires not only advertising, but also direct sales, sales promotion, and an integrated communications strategy.

For the advertising agencies, both multinationals and local Chinese companies were important customers; local Chinese companies began to account for about half of all advertising spending. With continued growth, China was forecasted to become the second largest advertising market in the world by 2010, from about $14.5 billion in 2003. This meant that advertising agencies had to expand beyond the three biggest cities into several smaller ones, providing advertising services, increasing their knowledge of local issues, and adding local clients to their customer base. This is a complex and difficult task to implement.

Not surprisingly, Ogilvy & Mather China, one of the largest foreign advertising agencies in China, sought to speed up this organizational expansion. It acquired a majority control of Fujian Effort, a large independent Chinese agency in Fuzhou, the capital of Fujian province. While this acquisition-based expansion met clients' needs, it also emphasized issues of corporate culture. Ogilvy had to grapple with merging the culture of Fujian Effort, a closely held Chinese company, with its own multinational advertising culture.[22]

Organizational Culture and Organizational Structure

As illustrated in the example of Ogilvy in China, as a firm develops its international business organization, besides having to create a formal organizational structure (assigning roles, responsibilities, authority, accountability, and reporting relationships), it must also concern itself with spreading the organizational culture. As Schein notes, organizational culture is deeply embedded in a group through its history and experiences and is embodied in the way in which the organization approaches problem solving.[23]

A firm's or group's organizational culture consists of processes and values that all group members share. They agree that those values and processes, because they have been successful in the past, should continue to be used to solve problems in the future. The organizational culture determines how members are accepted by the group; how power is gained, exercised, and lost in the group; and how rewards and sanctions will be used by the group to motivate or deter certain behaviors. Such cultures can vary even within a large organization, with subcultures developing around functional roles, geographic or regional locales, professions, business units, etc. Thus, within a large U.S. organization, the marketing culture is likely to be distinct from the organizational culture of an engineering and product development unit or a manufacturing site. Such differences are exacerbated when the firm expands overseas to set up an international business organization. Many, if not most, employees in its overseas international business subsidiaries are likely to be local nationals or third-country nationals. In those cases, the company's organizational culture needs to be communicated and established; further, it needs to coexist with the national culture.

For example, U.S. firms often use individual sales quotas by territory. Receiving commissions based on sales performance and exceeding quotas can form a large (sometimes the biggest) share of total compensation. Salespeople may be given considerable autonomy to plan their sales calls and may report back to the head office once a week or less, communicating remotely and acting with a high degree of independence. Cold calling may be required; and salespeople may be expected to be highly productive, optimizing their time while in the field. Such behaviors are consistent with the broader U.S. culture that stresses individualism, material success, performance measurement, risk taking, and independence. However, such practices may be difficult to transfer to more traditional cultures where salespeople feel more comfortable being paid principally with salary, prefer close supervision and direction from sales managers, and are reluctant to initiate sales calls on clients to whom they have not been introduced or with whom they have no previous connection.

This suggests that the solution may lie in helping to socialize foreign salespeople gradually to the company's dominant organizational culture, beginning with careful recruitment to select individuals who may be a better fit with the company's values and processes. At the same time, the company should expect to adapt its processes to the changed environment and to the local culture while still maintaining its core values and core ethical stance.

THE ROLE OF HEADQUARTERS

A constant theme running through the various attempts at creating an organizational structure appropriate for global strategy is the role the parent company headquarters should take. Corporate headquarters can play three roles in its dealings with subsidiaries around the world: controller, coach, or orchestrator.[24]

A controller gives considerable autonomy to subsidiaries and uses measurements, such as profits by a small business unit, to determine when to intervene. This is classic management by exception.

The coach also decentralizes authority to subsidiaries but is available to provide support and advice, somewhat along the lines of the Shell example described previously. This means that the coach will intervene when necessary, attempting to strike the right balance between decentralization and central control.

The orchestrator is an interventionist with central control and responsibility for activities such as manufacturing, R&D, and finance. Subsidiary managers, therefore, have less autonomy. This style may be appropriate for industries for which global integration is important and investment needs are large, as in oil, steel, mining, and financial services.

In addition, headquarters can play two other temporary roles: surgeon and architect. When major upheavals threaten a firm and its industry, the company may have to be restructured, with many units divested, product lines dropped, and workers laid off. The other extreme is restructuring through acquisitions, as in the case of Sony, which reacted to the failure of the Betamax video format by deciding to emphasize "software," that is, music and film production. This restructuring has led Sony to acquire U.S. record companies and film studios. This phase also requires strong central direction from the architect, who reshapes the company according to a global vision before returning to the mode of coach or orchestrator.

Company roles should be consistent with the nature of businesses within the global firm. The degree of synergy between the various lines of business in a firm, the level of risk facing the firm, and the intensity of competition determine which headquarters style is appropriate. (See Table 6-4.)

Table 6-4 Role of Headquarters			
	Controller	Coach	Orchestrator
Synergy	Little or none	Medium	High
Risk	Low	Medium	High
Competition	Stable	Open	Intense

Source: M. Goold and A. Campbell, *Strategies and Styles,* United Kingdom: Ashridge Management Centre, 1989.

Table 6-5	Types of Information Error			
Type of Ignorance	Type I Error	Type II Error	Type III Error	Type IV Error
Pluralistic (reality consists of two or more independent elements)	Management does not recognize the need to adapt existing strategies to local context of individual markets.	Management implements strategic decisions, ignoring objections of the firm's alliance partner, who is likely to be knowledgeable about the local environment.	Management does not enter a market because there are too many government regulations … when demand is not large enough to support a new competitor.	Management does not correctly assess market potential because of low per capita income … when there are a large number of people per household.
Probabilistic (certainty does not exist and probability—likelihood of outcome—suffices to govern practice)	Managers argue that the global market is not attractive due to the need to adapt to foreign markets.	Managers ignore suggestion of subsidiary management that local economic conditions may prevent the accomplishment of stated company goals.	Managers expect to compete successfully in a country because there are only local competitors.	Managers conduct a survey to collect data on consumers in developing countries without making appropriate modifications to research techniques.

Sources: From Table 1 of Michael Harvey and Milorad M. Novicevic, "Staffing Global Marketing Positions: What We Don't Know Can Make a Difference," *Journal of World Business*, Volume 35, Issue 1, 2000, pages 80–94; Random House Unabridged Dictionary © 1997 by Random House, Inc., on Infoplease (http://www.infoplease.com/ipd/A0604422.html); accessed May 17, 2005.

If a company's lines of business are such that both high and low risk are present, the task of headquarters becomes blurred. For a high-risk business, headquarters may have to play the role of orchestrator; for a low-risk business, a controller role is more appropriate. Unless the company restructures so that only one kind of business line profile prevails, the firm must live with multiple roles. This implies that no one organizational structure is appropriate for a global firm with many lines of business. This is the reason that large global firms seem to be constantly changing their organizational structure. As the profiles of the various lines of business change, new organizational structures are necessary.

Whatever the organizational structure, its success depends on the people filling the various positions created by the organizational structure. Difficulties arise because global organizations are often headed by expatriates who are proven executives with success in their home countries. As they move to new and distinct foreign markets, they are likely to bring with them assumptions and processes that may be wrong or inadequate for the new markets they are entering. Misapprehension or ignorance can wreck havoc on the formulation and execution of a business strategy. Harvey and Novicevic suggest that such problems can be countered with careful staffing, where the firm combines expatriate with "in-patriate" (host country nationals relocated to headquarters) management.[25] Such a staffing policy would allow the multinational firm to integrate missing context-specific knowledge and avoid the types of mistakes included in Table 6-5. This approach would be particularly important in developing countries where the cultural distance is large.

The Country Manager (CM)

A key element in the growing multinational company is the country manager (CM).[26] What does the CM do? The CM is often given local profit center responsibility, is responsible for multiple functional areas, and is the liaison with regional and headquarters management. Expected to be as much an entrepreneur as a manager, the CM seeks to increase local autonomy.

Factors changing the role of a CM include, for example, demands for greater global integration, of R&D and manufacturing. Other factors include the subordination of national interests, the rise of product-based global organizations and global customers, and regional integration policies such as the EU and NAFTA. How do those forces impact the CM? They tend to reduce the CM's local authority to implement global and regional policies in the national sphere. The CM's main focus becomes local sales and distribution, along with local planning, forecasting and budgeting, financial management and control, personnel and labor relations (including training local managers), and government relations. Public relations is another responsibility of the CM, particularly representing the parent company in meetings with local trade and industry officials and in community relations. However, the CM's autonomy may depend on the importance of the local subsidiary, typically determined by the subsidiary's size, age, and experience; total sales revenues and market position; overall performance; and the ability and effectiveness of local management. The cultural distance of the local subsidiary from its parent is also relevant.

CMs can draw on their local roots to build businesses. For example, Richardson Hindustan's CMs were able to highlight the role of natural herbs used to formulate Vicks VapoRub cold medicine. That appealed to Indian consumers because they could see connections to the age-old Indian Ayurvedic system of medicine that also draws on native herbs and plants. At the same time, the parent company's transnational approach allows CMs to learn from local solutions and apply them in other national markets; for example, the success to be had from year-round advertising or from using traditional distribution systems in emerging markets.[27]

As was suggested previously, multinationals constantly change their organizational structure as environmental change and daily operations disclose weaknesses in the way the firm is organized. Organizational fads exist, such as companies following competitors reorganization from one based on product lines to an organization that is based on geographic areas. Perhaps the best example of this is the rush to develop matrix organizations that proved too difficult to manage. McKinsey studied 43 American consumer goods companies to see if organizational changes could be linked to international success.[28] He found that superior international growth in sales and profits seemed to be linked to several traits:

- Centralized international decision making except in new product development
- Requirement that top management have international experience
- Use of videoconferencing and e-mail to link international managers
- Successful integration of international acquisitions
- Multiple product managers in a country reporting to a CM, as shown in the Ciba-Geigy example discussed earlier

The Informal Organization

Regardless of which organizational structure is chosen, the central problem is that organizational structure is static while the environment is dynamic. How can a multinational preserve strategic and organizational flexibility? The answer is to go beyond the formal organization. Beyond organizational structure, the firm must focus on communication channels, interpersonal relationships, and changing individual perceptions. The goal should be to let the informal organization bloom. Overall, an environment of intense competition, overcapacity, and technological change means that companies will succeed because of their clarity of corporate purpose, effective management processes, and ability to develop people. Instead of sweeping strategic visions, employees who believe in what the company is trying to achieve are more likely to move a company to success.[29]

FORMING INDUSTRY WEBS: GOING BEYOND A COMPANY'S ORGANIZATIONAL BOUNDARIES

Another facet of organizational structure is how a company is organized to deal with outsiders. As companies begin to work closely with entities such as suppliers and competitors, a network approach is becoming more common. Such network linkages go beyond purely commercial links; they encompass a larger relationship wherein the two partners attempt to share resources and to harmonize competitive strategies for competitive advantage. Such networks can include key suppliers and customers; competitors; and entities such as governments, unions, universities, research institutes, and trade associations.

Such networks are particularly interesting in technology-based industries where companies form a web without any formal agreement. Instead, the web is built around a common technological standard. Coalescing around a technological standard reduces risk because there is greater assurance of larger market size. In addition, the web of informal linkages allows individual firms to focus their strategy and to concentrate on relatively narrow segments of the value chain. Because the technological standard reduces risk, the web shapers, who set the standard, have the option of keeping the standard to themselves (that is, creating a proprietary standard as Apple attempted to do with the Macintosh). The trade-off is whether to increase the size of the web by freely giving away the standard or to attempt to capture profits while reducing the size of the web.

Implementation and Organization

A global strategy makes it inevitable that some intervention by headquarters will be necessary, ranging from informing to persuading, then coordinating and approving, and culminating in directing.[30] As headquarters moves from informing to directing, it is taking greater control and lessening autonomy at the subsidiary.

Headquarters' involvement may vary from country to country, with greater intervention occurring in regions experiencing troubles. A global company needs strong local managers, but managers need experience to become strong. Some product strategy issues and business activities can be left safely to subsidiary managers. Indeed, companies should seek to create areas where such autonomy is fostered.

The extent to which foreign subsidiaries are allowed to practice greater or lesser independence in designing local business strategies is affected by:[31]

• The subsidiary's past relationship with headquarters; for example, how much the subsidiary trusts headquarters, whether the subsidiary believes it is dependent on headquarters, whether the subsidiary believes it is part of the parent organization, how the subsidiary participates in setting local market objectives, and how much cooperation exists between the business manager and headquarters' business organization.
• Industry conditions; namely, whether the subsidiary is in a local market characterized by market turbulence and market concentration and whether the global industry is characterized by technological turbulence. Subsidiaries may have more autonomy when the local market is turbulent. Also, subsidiaries are more likely to follow headquarters' direction when the local market is concentrated and when there is considerable technological turbulence worldwide.

• Economic and cultural distance. Subsidiaries will have more autonomy when there is greater economic and cultural distance between the local market and the parent country.

Regional Headquarters: A Halfway House

Decentralization in terms of the division of labor between corporate headquarters and the units in foreign markets has been presented. Frequently, however, as a firm's business in a region such as Europe or Latin America grows larger, the business becomes important enough to warrant separate attention. This can lead to the establishment of a new level in the organization between corporate headquarters and the foreign markets; that is, a regional headquarters. A **regional headquarters** is not necessarily located within the region, although it usually is for larger regions such as Europe. Many U.S. companies, for example, have their Latin American headquarters in Coral Gables, Florida, truly a halfway point between corporate headquarters and country operations. Regardless of location, however, regional headquarters gives undivided attention to the affairs of the region.

Almost all of the world's major computer companies find it necessary to have a regional headquarters in Asia for the important Asia/Pacific market. Firms such as Apple, Unisys, and Hewlett-Packard are based in Hong Kong. AT&T is in Singapore, IBM is in Tokyo, and ICL is in Australia.

Conclusions about Organizational Structure

From the preceding discussion, three generalizations can be made about organizational structure:

• The structure must be tailored to the situation and needs of the individual firm. No standard model exists.
• Changing conditions require the firm to adapt; as a result, organizational structures are in almost continual evolution.
• Perhaps the most important conclusion, though, is that firms are now recognizing that organizational structure can never be a complete and satisfactory means of coordinating their international operations.

Accordingly, they are trying to incorporate the product, geographic, and functional dimensions into their decision making without changing their organizational structure. In other words, other approaches besides organizational structure can be used to coordinate international business.

Stopford and Wells studied structural changes but noted that "management skills" were more important than the formal organization structure.[32] In a later study, Bartlett found that many successful firms did not worry about structural change, but focused attention on the individual tasks they were facing. "Instead of joining the quest for the ideal structure, they looked at the connection between environment, strategy, and the 'way of managing.' " Hedlund found the same to be true for Swedish multinationals. Instead of introducing matrix structures, they complemented their simple organization forms by making changes in information systems, budgeting, rotation of personnel, etc.[33]

As subsidiaries mature, they also evolve and develop different roles. Taggart has suggested that such evolution can result in four subsidiary configurations: as a confederation, as a strategic "auxiliary," as an autarchy, and as a detached unit. Birkinshaw also focuses on such evolution, with the path changing from that of being a sales subsidiary, to local sales and manufacturing, to a regional hub, and then to a global organization with a world product mandate.[34]

These evolutionary changes and what Bartlett calls the "way of managing" include a variety of approaches that can best be considered as control devices.

Controlling International Business

Companies operate internationally to attain certain corporate goals. The purpose of control is to direct operations to achieve desired objectives. Considered this way, control is the essence of management, consisting of establishing standards, measuring performance against the standards, and then suggesting and implementing corrective action for deviation from standards and plans.

Control is inextricably related to the previous topics—planning and organization—which are prerequisites of control systems. Planning involves setting standards and goals, the first step in the control process. The organization of a firm establishes the hierarchy, the division of labor, and the communication channels for management control. Furthermore, the degree of decentralization affects the control task. General control principles are as valid internationally as they are domestically. Special problems arise from different environments in which the operations occur. Communication gaps—distance between a firm's different markets and differences in language, nationality, and culture—are the major causes of difficulty. Problems also arise from differences in financial and monetary environments. For example, government supervision, exchange controls, and differing rates of inflation limit a firm's ability to control transfer prices, remittances, and logistics; that is, limit where it will buy and sell internationally.

Special Measurement Techniques

In addition to regular reporting, specialized techniques exist for evaluating performance. One of the most noteworthy is the company audit.

The corporate audit is a methodical examination of the total marketing effort, often by some outside expert. Such an audit may be done by global managers for each market every few years. Certainly, the audit would add to management's understanding of the firm's foreign business, helping management improve the business. An audit is especially useful when a firm is changing its involvement in a country. At a higher level, an audit may be made of the total international business of a firm.

Organization

The purpose of organization is to facilitate management control. The organizational structure shows the lines of authority, the hierarchy of control. Going beyond organizational structure, a study by Doz and Prahalad emphasizes organizational context as a means of maintaining strategic control.[35] By organizational context, they mean that administrative mechanisms exist (apart from changing the organizational structure) that allow headquarters to maintain control in changing environments and circumstances. Table 6-6 gives an overview of these administrative mechanisms. Doz and Prahalad's argument is that headquarters must maintain strategic control if international operations are to be optimized. To achieve this, organizational context (the administrative mechanisms) is more effective than structural change. Dow, for example, refuses to create a written organizational chart because it would de-emphasize the nonstructural methods the company uses to deal with competing strategic imperatives.

For example, in executive placement, it may be necessary to consider the propensity of individual managers to take a headquarters/business perspective versus a subsidiary/market perspective. Reporting relationships may be created to encourage greater or lesser local autonomy. Management accounting and reward systems may be used to enforce a strong national profit

Table 6-6 Administrative Mechanisms for Strategic Control		
Data Management Mechanisms	**Managers' Management Mechanisms**	**Conflict Resolution Mechanisms**
Information systems	Choice of key managers	Decision responsibility requirements
Measurement systems	Career paths	Integrators
Resource allocation	Reward and penalty systems	Business teams
Strategic planning	Management development	Coordination committees
Budgeting process	Patterns of socialization	Task forces
		Issue resolution process

Source: Adapted from Yves L. Doz and C. K. Prahalad, "Headquarters' Influence and Strategic Control in MNCs," *Sloan Management Review,* Fall 1981, page 16.

center mentality or to create an international perspective. Membership in critical committees may be adjusted to recognize either global or foreign national concerns. Critical functional staff groups may be centralized at headquarters or attached to local operating units. Table 6-7 provides additional positive and negative control mechanisms.

Budget

The budget is the basic control technique used by most multinationals. The control offered by the budget is essentially negative; it may prevent excessive expenditure, but it does not ensure that goals will be reached. Furthermore, if the foreign subsidiary is substantially independent financially, control from headquarters can be difficult. In that case, the administrative mechanisms mentioned by Doz and Prahalad become especially important.

Subsidiaries as Profit Centers

One way to minimize the control burden on corporate headquarters is to have each subsidiary operate as a profit center. Profit centers can take on varying degrees of responsibility. With a high degree of delegation, the subsidiary handles most control problems. Headquarters may enter the scene only when profits are unsatisfactory. Most U.S. companies operate their foreign subsidiaries as profit centers, but with differing degrees of decentralization.

The profit center approach to controlling subsidiaries has several advantages. It maximizes the use of local knowledge and on-the-spot decision making and minimizes the frictions of absentee management. It is good for subsidiary morale because local management likes to "run its own shop."

On the negative side, local management, evaluated on short-term profitability, may act in ways that endanger long-term profits. Autonomous subsidiaries are difficult to integrate into a coherent international operation. Therefore, a high degree of decentralization is most feasible when the subsidiaries are self-contained in buying and selling and have minimal reliance on the corporation for other inputs.

Information Systems for Control

Information is needed to plan, assess performance against plans, and monitor changes in the competitive and client environment. A company's planning and organizational structure deter-

Table 6-7   Control Mechanisms for Joint Ventures

Positive	Negative
Ability to make decisions	Board
Ability to design:	Executive committee
Planning process	Approval required for:
Appropriate requests	Specific decisions
Policies and procedures	Plans and budgets
Ability to set objectives for joint venture general manager (JVGM)	Appropriation requests
Bonus of JVGM tied to parent results	Nomination of JVGM
Ability to decide on future promotion of JVGM (and other joint venture managers)	Screening/No objection of parent before
JVGM's participation in parent's worldwide meetings	ideas are discussed with joint
Relations with JVGM; phone calls, meetings, visits	venture partner
Contracts:	
Management	
Technology transfer	
Marketing	
Supplier	
Participation in planning or budgeting process	
Parent organizational structure	
Reporting structure	
Staffing	
Training programs	
Staff services	
Feedback; strategy/plan budgets, appropriation requests	
Staffing parent with someone with joint venture experience	
Informal meetings with other parent	

Source: Adapted from J. L. Schaan, "Parent Control and Joint Venture Success: The Case of Mexico," cited in J. M. Geringer and L. Herbert, "Control and Performance of International Joint Ventures," *Journal of International Business Studies,* Volume 20, Issue 2, Summer 1989.

mine what information is gathered and how it will be channeled through the organization. The amount of information collected can be enormous. (The topic of IT is presented in Chapter 5.)

Without information, global corporations cannot be integrated efficiently. Mattel, a U.S. toy company, is a good example. Toy sales are concentrated around the Christmas season, with 60 percent of sales occurring between late September and mid-December. Toy makers must stock sufficient quantities of the best-selling toys in order to do well. Mattel produces most of its toys in plants in the Far East and needs to be able to change production plans to take advantage of new sales forecasts, which are based on sales figures. That is, if a certain toy sells out in early November, Mattel needs to know this so it can increase production in Hong Kong, then ship the toy where demand is greatest. Equally important, if a toy is not selling well, the company needs to know so it can stop production. Otherwise, the company may have to write off inventory.

Mattel also needs to receive updated figures on toy inventory at its warehouses around the world so it can shift excess inventory from slow-selling areas to high-demand markets. This requires a global computer and communication system that can track production of several thousand toys, inventories at warehouses in various countries, and all retail stock. Mattel built a global information system linking headquarters with distribution centers and its Far Eastern plants. Now the company knows what finished goods are due from which plant on a daily basis and where inventory is located. This allows for "better alignment of the production schedule, market forecast, and real orders." Another benefit is that engineers can quickly exchange product specifications with plants, reducing the time it takes for an idea about a toy to become a finished product.

The global information system allows Mattel to update inventory, production schedules, and engineering specifications in a day, as opposed to between 7 and 30 days formerly. In addition, the system allows Mattel to reduce inventories significantly. Without this system, global strategy and its implementation would remain a dream.

Once such networks are in place, they can be used for other purposes. Communication through e-mail and videoconferencing allows for closer coordination of international business, making both local autonomy and centralized coordination achievable. Such systems also allow for close monitoring and the exchange of information about competitors from around the world, which can be invaluable in determining competitive response.

Summary

The basic elements of a business plan include the environment and the company situation in each market, the firm's objectives, and the strategy and tactics that will help the firm achieve its objectives.

Plans have a short-range and a long-range component. They should be developed for each foreign market and within the context of a global plan, integrating the domestic and foreign markets as well as other areas of activity, such as manufacturing, technology planning, and R&D.

A comprehensive operating plan is necessary to help a firm achieve its short-term objectives. The plan should include elements such as detailed sales and market share targets, planned new distribution outlets, brand awareness goals, plans for new product introduction, test-marketing plans, and other research activities. A planning calendar typically requires reconciliation of national plans with headquarters' goals. Once headquarters accepts the plan, budgetary targets are derived and become the basis for managerial action and evaluation.

Broad company-wide plans must be adapted to individual markets. Local participation is necessary, and additional information gathering and analysis will ensure a plan that is better adapted to individual market realities.

Long-range planning deals with uncertainty. The focus is on developing scenarios in basic areas such as technology, market growth, competitive change, and a firm's resources. The goal is to be prepared for contingencies and to be alert for major opportunities.

Responding to competitive moves is another essential aspect of planning. This is contingency planning, with a firm deciding how it will react if the competition cuts prices, launches a new product, or strikes up a strategic alliance.

Paradoxically, the best way to counter competition may be through a strategic alliance with another competitor. Such alliances reduce risk, save time, provide access to technology and markets, and even secure supply sources. The main question is whether it is better to have a competitor as a partner. Generally, for a strategic alliance to work well, the competitor must possess a complementary asset.

Planning cannot work without a well-designed organization structure to implement the plans. The basic choice is between centralization and decentralization; in some cases, manufacturing may be centralized, with technology development, product adaptation, and sales decentralized.

Multinational organizations can be structured along geographic, product, or functional lines. The chosen structure may then evolve to a matrix organization. As the environment changes, organizational structure also must change.

Examples of companies such as Reynolds Metals, Unilever, General Motors, Square D Company, Royal Dutch/Shell, the Salim Group, and Philips show that there is no one way to structure an international organization. The examples also show that firms change their structure over time.

A central issue is the role that headquarters should play. One approach is to view headquarters as controller, coach, or orchestrator. In addition, when major changes are occurring in the corporate environment, headquarters may play the role of surgeon or architect.

Further, headquarters' style must be consistent with the nature of the firm. Firms may be grouped according to three criteria: synergy between lines of business, level of risk, and intensity of competition facing the firm.

Headquarters can affect the quality of implementation by taking a stance that ranges from informing to persuading, coordinating, approving, and directing subsidiary actions. Headquarters must decide how much autonomy to grant subsidiaries. In some cases, it may want to direct new product development while using persuasion in the area of pricing.

Control is necessary to monitor progress against plans and budgets. The chief control tasks are establishing performance standards, measuring performance against standards, and taking corrective action in the case of deviations. Audits are useful in looking at the performance of foreign markets.

Global information systems are a necessary component of international planning. A wide variety of information can be gathered and, if usefully organized, can help a firm increase sales and manage global factories and inventories, ultimately giving the firm a competitive edge.

Questions and Research

6.1 What basic elements should be included in a company's international business plan?

6.2 What distinguishes a short-range plan from a long-range plan? What sort of activities are appropriate for inclusion in a short-range plan?

6.3 What elements would you include in a firm's operating plans for international markets?

6.4 What is the appropriate relationship between a national subsidiary's business plans and headquarters' broad goals?

6.5 Why should headquarters' broad plans be uniquely adapted to individual country markets?

6.6 Why should future scenarios be incorporated in a firm's long-range business plan?

6.7 How does competition affect international business planning?

6.8 Why would a firm consider forming a partnership with a competitor?

6.9 Analyze the tire and pharmaceutical industries as examples of strategic alliance formation. What general principles emerge from your analysis?

6.10- How is a firm's organizational structure relevant to its international planning?

6.11 Explain this statement: Organizational structure is essentially a choice between head-quarters' centralization and local autonomy.

6.12 What are the merits of choosing functions, products, and geographic areas as the basis for organizational structure?

6.13 Compare the organizational structures chosen by Reynolds Metals, Unilever, General Motors, Square D Company, Royal Dutch/Shell, the Salim Group, and Philips. Explain why each organization has chosen a different path for its organizational structure. Is there an ideal structure? Explain.

6.14 How can headquarters influence the implementation of plans? Under what conditions will headquarters be more or less directive?

6.15 What is control? How is control related to multinational planning?

6.16 What are some measurements that could be useful in controlling a multinational subsidiary?

6.18 What are the components of a global information system? How do such systems fit in with international planning?

6.19 Explain how Mattel's global information system gives it a competitive edge in the global toy industry.

Endnotes

1 Chae, Myung-su and John S. Hill. "Determinants and Benefits of Global Strategic Marketing Planning Formality," *International Marketing Review*, Volume 17, Issue 6, 2000, pages 538–562.

2 Leclair, Debbie Thorne. "Marketing Planning and The Policy Environment in The European Union," *International Marketing Review*, Volume 17, Issue 3, 2000, pages 193–215.

3 "Chairman of Aventis justifies decision to merge with Sanofi," *Les Echos*, June 14, 2004.

"Pfizer gains final approval to buy Pharmacia," *New York Times*, April 15, 2003.

"In Huge Drug Merger, Sandoz and Ciba-Geigy Plan to Join Forces," *Wall Street Journal*, March 7, 1996.

"Multibillion-Dollar Creation of a Drug Colossus," *Wall Street Journal*, March 8, 1996.

4 Ohmae, Kenichi. "The Global Logic of Strategic Alliances," *Harvard Business Review*, March–April 1989.

5 Dyer, Jeffrey H., Prashant Kale, and Harbir Singh. "How to Make Strategic Alliances Work." *Sloan Management Review*, Summer 2001, pages 37–43; Porter, M. E. and Mark Fuller, "Coalitions and Global Strategy" in *Competition in Global Industries*, M. Porter, ed., 1986, Boston: Harvard Business School Press.

6 Speier, Cheri, Michael G. Harvey, Jonathan Palmer. "Virtual Management of Global Marketing Relationships," *Journal of World Business,* Volume 33, Issue 3, 1998, pages 263–276.

7 Vorhies, Douglas W. and Neil A. Morgan. "A Configuration Theory Assessment of Marketing Organization Fit with Business Strategy and Its Relationship with Marketing Performance," *Journal of Marketing,* Issue 67, January 2003, pages 100–115.

8 See Bartlett, Christopher, Sumantra B. Ghoshal, and Julian Birkinshaw. *Transnational Management,* 4th Edition, 2004, New York: McGraw-Hill; Prahalad, C. K. and Yves Doz, *The Multinational Mission,* 1988, New York: The Free Press.

9 Bartlett, Christopher and Sumantra Ghoshal. "Managing across Borders: New Strategic Requirements,"

Sloan Management Review, Summer 1987.

10 "AGCO Announces New Organisation Structure as Part of Succession Planning," *PR Newswire European*, February 12, 2004.

11 Quelch, John. "Does Globalization Have Staying Power," *Marketing Management*, March–April 2002.

12 Bartlett, Christopher, Sumantra B. Ghoshal, and Julian Birkinshaw. *Transnational Management,* 4th Edition, 2004, New York: McGraw-Hill; Bartlett, C. and S. Ghoshal, "Organizing for Worldwide Effectiveness: The Transnational Solution," *California Management Review,* 1988.

13 Maljiers, Floris A. "Inside Unilever: The Evolving Transnational Company," *Harvard Business Review,* September–October 1992.

14 "Schering-Plough Reorganizes," *Pharmaceutical Executive*, August 2003.

15 "GM Plans Major Overhaul of Business in Europe," *Wall Street Journal,* June 17, 2004, Section A, page 3.

16 "Shell: A Global Management Model," *Management Europe*, March 13, 1989.

17 "Philips: Thinking Global, Acting Local," *Management Europe,* April 10, 1989.

18 "Issues for the European CEO (4): New Products," *Business Europe,* February 12, 1997.

19 "GE's Asian Units: Rugged Individuals," *Crossboarder Monitor,* November 5, 1997.

20 "Comeback Kid in China," Business China, May 25, 1998; Motorola, *2005 Corporate Profile* (http://www.motorola.com/mot/doc/5/5332_MotDoc.pdf); accessed April 27, 2005.

21 "Mercosur: The Right Fit," *Business Latin America,* September 7, 1998.

22 "Ogilvy Builds China Presence beyond Three Largest Cities," *Wall Street Journal,* June 17, 2004, section B, page 4.

23 Schein, Edgar. *Organizational Culture and Leadership,* 1988, San Francisco: Jossey-Bass.

24 Goold, M. and A. Campbell. *Strategies and Styles,* 1989, United Kingdom: Ashridge Management Centre.

25 Harvey, Michael and M. M. Novicevic, "Staffing Global Marketing Positions: What We Don't Know Can Make a Difference," *Journal of World Business,* Volume 35, Issue 1, 2000, pages 80–94.

26 Quelch, John A. "The New Country Managers," *McKinsey Quarterly,* Number 4, 1992, pages 155–165; Quelch, John A. and Helen Bloom, "The Return of the Country Manager," *McKinsey Quarterly,* Number 2, 1996, pages 30–43.

27 Das, Gurcharan. "Local Memoirs of a Global Manager," *Harvard Business Review,* March–April 1993, pages 38–47.

28 "Study Sees U.S. Businesses Stumbling on the Road toward Globalization," *Wall Street Journal,* March 22, 1993.

29 Bartlett, Christopher and Sumantra Ghoshal. "Changing the Role of Top Management: Beyond Strategy to Purpose," *Harvard Business Review,* November–December 1994.

30 Quelch, John and Edward Hoff. "Customizing Global Marketing," *Harvard Business Review,* Volume 64, Issue 3, May–June 1986, pages 59–68.

31 Hewett, K., M. S. Roth, and K. Roth. "Conditions Influencing Headquarters and Foreign Subsidiary Roles in Marketing Activities and Their Effects on Performance," *Journal of International Business Studies,* 2003, Volume 34, Issue 6, pages 567–585.

32 Stopford, John and Louis T. Wells, Jr. *Managing the Multinational Enterprise,* 1972, New York: Basic Books.

33 Bartlett, Christopher A. "Multinational Organization: Where to After the Structural Stages?" Cambridge, MA: Harvard Business School, 1981; Hedlund, Gunnar, "The Evolution of the Mother-Daughter Structure in Swedish Multinationals," *Journal of International Business Studies,* Fall 1984, Volume 15, Issue 2, pages 109–123.

34 Birkinshaw, Julian and Neil Hood, editors. *Multinational Corporate Evolution and Subsidiary Development,* 1998, London: Macmillan; Birkinshaw, Julian and Neil Hood, "Multinational Subsidiary Evolution: Capability and Charter Change in Foreign Owned Subsidiary Companies," *Academy of Management Review,* Volume 23, 1998, pages 773–795.

35 Doz, Yves L. and C. K. Prahalad. "Headquarters' Influence and Strategic Control in MNCs," *Sloan Management Review,* Fall 1981, pages 15–29.

Further Readings

Bartlett, Christopher A., Sumantra Ghoshal, and Julian Birkinshaw. *Transnational Management: Text, Cases, and Readings In Cross-Border Management,* 4th Edition, 2004, Boston: McGraw-Hill.

Bhagat, Rabi S., Ben L. Kedia, Paula D. Harveston, and Harry C. Triandis. "Cultural Variations in the Cross-Border Transfer of Organizational Knowledge: An Integrative Framework," *Academy of Management Review,* April 2002, Volume 27, Issue 2, pages 204–221.

Daniels, John D., Lee H. Radebaugh, and Daniel P. Sullivan. *International Business,* 10th Edition, 2004, Upper Saddle River, NJ : Prentice Hall.

Deresky, Helen. *International Management: Managing Across Border and Cultures,* 5th Edition, 2006, Upper Saddle River, N.J.: Pearson Prentice Hall.

Emmott, Bill. "Japan Inc., RIP," *Wall Street Journal,* March 10, 2005, page A.16

Francesco, Anne Marie and Barry A. Gold. *International Organizational Behavior,* 2nd Edition, 2004, Upper Saddle River, NJ: Prentice Hall.

Geppert, Mike. "Multinational Companies are Not 'Stateless' Enterprises," *Organization,* March 2005, Volume 12, Issue 2, pages 302–306.

Ghoshal, Sumantra and Lynda Gratton. "Integrating the Enterprise," *MIT Sloan Management Review,* Fall 2002, Volume 44, Issue 1, pages 31–38.

Harvey, Michael and M. M. Novicevic. "Staffing Global Marketing Positions: What We Don't Know Can Make a Difference," *Journal of World Business,* Volume 35, Issue 1, 2000, pages 80–94.

Harvey, Michael G., Milorad M. Novicevic, and Cheri Speier. "An Innovative Global Management Staffing System: A Competency-based Perspective," *Human Resource Management,* Winter 2000, Volume 39, Issue 4, pages 381–394.

Konopaske, Robert and John M. Ivancevich. *Global Management and Organizational Behavior,* 2004, Boston: McGraw Hill.

Leclair, Debbie Thorne. "Marketing Planning and The Policy Environment in The European Union," *International Marketing Review,* Volume 17, Issue 3, 2000, pages 193–215.

Mintzberg, Henry and Joseph Lampel. "Do MBAs make better CEOs? Sorry, Dubya, it ain't necessarily so," *Fortune,* February 19, 2001, Volume 143, Issue 4, page 244; Chae, Myung-su and John S. Hill, "Determinants and Benefits of Global Strategic Marketing Planning Formality," *International Marketing Review*, Volume 17, Issue 6, 2000, pages 538–562.

Paul, Herbert. "Creating a Global Mindset," *Thunderbird International Business Review,* March–April 2000, Volume 42, Issue 2, pages 187–200.

Pfeffer, Jeffrey and Robert I. Sutton. *The Knowing-doing Gap: How Smart Companies Turn Knowledge into Action,* 2000, Boston: Harvard Business School Press.

Phatak, Arvind V., Rabi S. Bhagat, and Roger Kashlak. *International Management: Managing in a Diverse and Dynamic Global Environment,* 2005, Boston: Mc-Graw-Hill.

Quelch, John. "Does Globalization Have Staying Power," *Marketing Management,* March–April 2002.

Rowsell-Jones, Andrew and Mark McDonald. "Giving Global Strategies Local Flavor," *Optimize,* April 2005, Volume 4, Issue 4, pages 52–57.

Schoemaker, Paul J. H. "Scenario Planning: A Tool for Strategic Thinking," *Sloan Management Review,* Winter 1995, pages 25–40.

Speier, Cheri, Michael G. Harvey, and Jonathan Palmer. "Virtual Management of Global Marketing Relationships," *Journal of World Business,* Volume 33, Issue 3, 1998, pages 263–276.

de la Torre, Jose, Yves L. Doz, and Timothy Devinney. *Managing the Global Corporation: Case Studies in Strategy and Management,* 2nd Edition, 2001, Boston: McGraw Hill.

Townsend, Peter and Len Cairns, "Developing the Global Manager Using a Capability Framework," *Management Learning,* September 2003, Volume 34, Issue 3, pages 313–327.

Wind, Yoram and Vijay Mahajan. "Convergence Marketing," *Journal of Interactive Marketing,* Spring 2002, Volume 16, Issue 2, pages 64–79.

CHAPTER 7

Ethics and International Business

Learning Objectives

Events over the past five years have highlighted dramatic instances of firms' unethical, irresponsible, and illegal activities. This behavior is not good for the firms; their constituents, who include customers and stockholders; or the public at large. This chapter explores how ethical standards should govern global business. It discusses ethical principles and how they affect the development of moral standards. The chapter then discusses the variety of ethical dilemmas that affect international marketing and ways corporations have attempted to resolve them, using numerous examples.

The main goals of this chapter are to

1 Identify recent instances of unethical behavior and the consequences of that behavior.

2 Describe ways in which industries are responding to the call to halt irresponsible activities undertaken by upper-level managers and industry leaders.

3 Present laws and legal actions taken by various governments to legislate ethical behavior.

4 Identify efforts under way by international agencies to address the need for morally responsible behavior.

5 Discuss the positive long-term impact of good corporate citizenship.

The Effect of Ethical Behavior on Global Business

Consider the following instances:

- A firm increases its sales of cigarettes in countries such as Indonesia because of growing restrictions and liability issues placed on them in markets such as the United States.[1]
- Pharmaceutical firms have rarely focused R&D dollars on developing drugs to fight diseases such as malaria, a disease that kills millions of children around the world, as such diseases are not prevalent in the firms' principal markets in Europe and the United States; Sanofi has offered to sell at cost on a nonprofit basis a new antimalarial drug in a late stage of development; Novartis has similarly started selling its antimalarial drug on a nonprofit basis in poor countries.[2]
- A firm markets its Internet gambling services to U.S. citizens and fights attempts to regulate such activities, taking its case to the WTO.[3]
- The European Commission began investigating Apple after receiving complaints from consumers that downloading songs from the iTunes music service in the U.K. was more expensive than in other parts of Europe;[4]
- Activists accuse toy and clothing manufacturers of sourcing their products from suppliers who do not respect labor rights and protest against such practices (those protests have a possible negative effect on the manufacturers' reputations and brands); independent agencies are asked to audit and certify the manufacturing practices of toy firms such as Mattel.[5]
- In the United States, there are many well-documented cases of unethical behavior on the part of individuals and corporations that led to the Sarbanes-Oxley Act of 2002, as well as the antifraud actions being pursued by the European Commission, the OECD, and the International Federation of Accountants. Names such as Enron, Adelphi Communications, Parmalat, Nortel Networks, Ahold NV, and WorldCom are forever associated with unethical, unscrupulous, and illegal behavior.

As the above examples suggest, ethical dilemmas abound in international marketing. This chapter explores these dilemmas and suggests approaches for companies interested in practicing ethical international marketing.

The Environmental Investigation Agency has noted that Indonesia is losing an area of forest the size of Switzerland every year. The Indonesian government estimates that illegal logging costs $3 billion a year in lost revenue in addition to environmental damage. A problem is the corrupt army, police, and bureaucracy that abet illegal timber trade. China is a major market for Indonesian timber, but the country does not assume responsibility for the illegal logging and cutting down of forests in Indonesia.[6]

Should international marketing managers focus just on making a profit, let governments regulate their behavior, and practice compliance with the letter of the law? This is an extension of the classic free-market Friedman position—that the job of business is to make a profit. However, there are several reasons why international businesses should be concerned with ethics.

All firms need to worry about their legitimacy. Corporations are granted permission by society to operate with legal limited liability, to raise capital, etc.; and if they do not behave responsibly, their existence might be threatened.

Multinational corporations (MNCs) have more power compared to local firms, local consumers, and perhaps local governmental authorities; they also have accumulated more knowledge about products, markets, consumer behavior, and societal consequences of their actions. Therefore, multinationals must be careful to use this power ethically.

Culture and local context influence local values and local moral standards. MNCs may find that they have to balance conflicting local values and corporate values. They must judge, then, when to adapt to local standards and when to hold on to their moral standards—which may be Western, but they consider to be universal.

Another issue is one of agency. MNCs have a multitude of executives and employees carrying out actions on behalf of the corporation. Corporations need to ensure that abstract and laudable moral standards they hold are implemented by their employees in all markets.

Economic ideology may also play a part in affecting the ethical standards of a firm. Capitalism elevates the role of consumption, wealth accumulation, and the right to private property. This, in turn, colors how firms in a capitalist system view their social responsibility and affects how much they believe they should concern themselves with social justice, environmental pollution, and the like. Capitalism also assumes perfect competition and the lack thereof may lead to a higher level of unethical behavior. (There are no or few competitors who can gain from being more ethical, and collusion is possible when an oligopoly exists.) In such a situation, governmental regulation to promote competition and antitrust regulations may be a necessary complement to gradually enhancing ethical behavior.

Therefore, firms must make a diligent effort to understand moral principles from which to draw ethical standards. Those standards will govern their behavior and help them bridge the gap between profit-oriented actions and greater corporate social responsibility.

Developing Ethical Standards

Corporations need to be ethical. Corporations are a creation of society and are allowed to exist, to carry on business, to bear limited liability, and to be granted legal protection in areas such as contract law, all at the sufferance of society. In return, society expects corporations to keep societal interests in mind when conducting business. In a sense, business exists in cooperation with society and cannot survive for the long term if it practices continual unethical behavior. Such unethical behavior hurts society, consumers, suppliers, workers, and the general social welfare (for example, the consequences of pollution). Unethical behavior will result in a gradual erosion of society's acceptance of and patience with the corporation. It is in the long-term self-interest of the corporation to practice ethical behavior. Firms have to obey the law, and legal compliance may be seen as satisfying society's expectations of ethical behavior. In many cases, however, legal compliance represents a bare minimum, a floor for ethical behavior. Hence, firms need to explore and establish for themselves the ethical standards that will govern their behavior. Questions typically arise over what is ethical behavior and how far ethics must govern corporate behavior. Developing ethical standards is a gradual process—one corporations can develop over time through a process of learning, dialogue, and reflection with their workers and customers, with other businesses, and with other societal institutions.

In judging whether corporate actions meet an ethical standard, firms may need to assess legal compliance in light of their own ethical standards. A firm that is in compliance with the law may decide that it does not need to concern itself further with ethics. However, in the international arena, local laws may be at odds with universally accepted moral principles—apartheid laws in South Africa being an egregious example. Hence, firms seeking to develop and uphold ethical standards may find it necessary to go beyond legal compliance and assess whether their actions meet ethical standards. Firms may want to pay particular attention to the consequences of their actions and how the outcomes of their actions affect various individuals and groups. (This perspective is further explored in the next section in a discussion of rights and justice as moral principles governing ethical actions.)

To conduct business activities in an ethical manner, a firm needs to develop moral standards that will serve as a foundation for all of their behavior. Several moral principles can help shape ethical standards for a corporation. Those principles include utilitarianism, justice, human rights, and caring for others.

Utilitarianism and concerns with rights and justice stem from the two dominant schools of thought in ethics—teleological and deontological theories. Utilitarianism stems from teleological roots, while deontological thinking yields the "rights" approach. The teleological school focuses on ends, choosing actions that maximize good and minimize harm for most people. In contrast, the deontological school emphasizes means and the fact that people are entitled to be treated as ends in themselves. Therefore, actions may not transgress a person's basic rights; hence, the results are less important than respecting individual rights.[7] These approaches are presented next.[8]

Utilitarianism

Utilitarianism judges behavior in terms of the costs and benefits to society; it suggests choosing actions that result in the greatest net benefit or the lowest net cost. Such judgment also results in efficient behavior, in using resources efficiently. Implementing utilitarianism means being able to measure costs and benefits. The measurement may be subjective in that the benefit of a meal or a job may have different values for different people; hence, two people may not agree on the precise cost and benefit of an action. Some of the most important aspects of life (quality of life, for example) are also the most difficult to measure. Another difficulty involves trade-offs; that is, how much of a certain cost to accept in return for other benefits. Further, the costs may fall disproportionately on certain segments of society while the benefits accrue to other (distinct) segments of society. Utilitarianism does not easily accommodate the impact of these costs on a segment that may be disadvantaged. That is, the distribution of costs and benefits is not a paramount consideration under the utilitarian perspective. The eventual distribution of costs and benefits that results may conflict with the notion of an individual's rights and with the concept of justice for an individual or group. Hence, moral principles built on rights and on justice are equally important.

Rights and Justice

Theories based on rights and justice have many roots. Immanuel Kant's *categorical imperative* is a useful starting point, stating that people should not be treated as means, but as ends. This means that people are beings whose existence as free, rational individuals should be promoted, that everyone should be treated as a free person equal to everyone else.[9] The possibility arises, however, that individual rights will conflict. In such cases, society must decide whose rights take precedence. Hence, justice and fairness become important in determining ethical behavior.

Reference was made earlier to evaluating trade-offs under the utilitarian perspective and the possibility that some segment of society may be burdened with costs while the benefits accrue to other segments. Bringing justice into the perspective helps reassess actions. A *distributive justice* approach can be used, the goal being to achieve a fair distribution of society's benefits and burdens. Under this approach, people who are similar in relation to the issue being considered (for example, those experiencing a job loss) should be granted similar benefits and bear similar burdens. An alternative view is *compensatory justice*, which holds that justice involves compensating people for wrong done to them or for loss suffered.

A complicating factor is the weight given to need, ability, and effort when assessing the justness of distributive outcomes. Capitalism assumes that the benefits an individual receives should be proportional to his or her contribution. Socialism, in contrast, is biased towards needs and distributes benefits according to need, while expecting people to work according to their ability. This can offend an individual's sense of fairness, as there may be little relation between work and reward and little freedom to choose what kind of work one might want to do.

John Rawls has attempted to develop a theory of justice that takes into account equality, needs, ability and effort, minimum standards of living, and preservation of freedom.[10] He asserts that the distribution of benefits and burdens in a society is just:

1. If everyone has the same degree of liberty; that is, one's liberties are protected from infringement by others—the Principle of Equal Liberty.
2. If there are inequalities in society, efforts are made to improve the position of the most needy members of society—the Difference Principle.
3. If everyone has the same opportunity to qualify for the most privileged positions in society's institutions—the Principle of Fair Equality of Opportunity.

Caring for Others

One characteristic of the ethical principles discussed thus far is that they are impartial; they do not take into account specific individuals. However, most individuals assess their acts partly in terms of the impact their acts have on people they know—their family; friends; coworkers; neighbors; community; even city, state, and nation. The question arises, should individuals show special consideration for those with whom they have a close relationship; that is, parents, children, spouses, relatives, and close friends? Is showing favoritism ethical? Cultural differences may play a part here, with cultures that favor collectivism over individualism; for example, accepting and requiring special consideration for others with whom one has a close relationship.

Integrative Social Contracts and Hypernorms

As suggested in the previous discussion, cultural differences can be a source of ethical conflicts because of the underlying multiple value systems. An effort to reconcile such conflicts is Donaldson and Dunfee's **Integrative Social Contracts** theory and their **hypernorms** approach.[11] They suggest that in the context of most local cultures, managers can apply ethical standards derived from the local context, principally from domestic firms, industries, professional associations, and other organizations. However, there will be instances when hypernorms take precedence. Hypernorms are manifest, universal norms that represent principles so fundamental to human existence that they are reflected in a convergence of religious, philosophical, and cultural beliefs.[12] These norms represent standards that are in some sense universal, most likely negative injunctions against murder, deceit, torture, oppression, and tyranny.[13] An example of a hypernorm, suggested by Donaldson and Dunfee, is informing employees about dangerous

Beyond Compliance

In light of widespread, well-documented lapses in corporate ethical behavior at the outset of the twenty-first century, more and more firms and nonprofits are coming to realize that it is necessary to manage and conduct corporate affairs "beyond mere compliance" with legal norms. That is, as defined by Marcus and Kaiser:

> In the continuum of ethics (political consciousness) law, this gap where the law ends or does not yet speak to regulate conduct is the area "beyond compliance." For corporations to function in an ethically responsible manner, business managers must recognize that the technical limits of law do not set a moral floor for behavior. Operating beyond compliance requires recognition that, though some moral obligations to others may not be codified, yet that does not make their observance any less imperative.

> Managing beyond compliance requires the members of an organization to progress beyond the at-any-cost corporate culture of previous decades. It will require a move beyond the gamesmanship of hyper-technical parsing and the what-can-be-gotten-away-with mentality by business managers, their attorneys, accountants and other professionals guiding and advising the corporation.[14]

Furthermore, given legal decisions that have traced corporate liability back two, three, or more decades, managing beyond compliance is a pragmatic stance for twenty first-century corporations. As Marcus and Kaiser stated:

> The advantages of such progressive leadership will be myriad. The risk that unethical behavior

health hazards, a universal ethical standard that should override any local practice that contradicts this ethical injunction.

Given these different approaches to developing moral principles, how should a firm incorporate such principles as it seeks to develop its own ethical standards? One approach might be to accept that different ethical principles have arisen because of drawbacks in one of the approaches. Thus, a pragmatic approach may require drawing on the implications of all of these theories as specific policies and actions are tested. Further, discussion of the ethicality of a firm's policies and actions in light of the various principles is necessary to arrive at reasoned moral judgments that are shared across a firm, thus helping to derive moral standards.

In the international arena, why does unethical behavior happen? Job pressures, lack of personal ethics, flawed corporate culture and leadership, a complaisant government and national culture, poor governance processes, lack of sanctions, ease of using intermediaries and hiding one's tracks, large stakes (size of orders, profits)—all of those can create a breeding ground for unethical behavior. Hence, internal discussion is essential to help develop an individual's ethical outlook, since the ethical standards of a firm are nothing but the collective acting out of the ethical beliefs of all of the employees of the firm. Thus, examining and debating ethical principles can result in individuals with a shared ethical outlook and a firm with high moral standards underpinning collective ethical actions. Such a discussion might embrace the following typology shown in Figure 7-1.

poses to the vitality and perpetuity of a company cannot be overestimated. Pushing the legal envelope into arguably unethical territory at various stages in the process or levels in the entity invariably produces a cumulative end result well outside of the legal obligations of compliance. This approach was the cause of many of the financial disasters that beset some of the largest and oldest US firms in the beginning of this century. Further, given that the law is continually evolving, mere compliance with the letter of the law can be dangerous. Unless a company has its finger on the precise pulse of where the law is going, it can get stung by mere compliance, particularly where personal harm is caused by corporate action or inaction. Tobacco companies did not violate any legal regulation when they failed to warn the public of the known health risks posed by cigarettes. Nonetheless, they now face billions of dollars in punitive damage judgments for their negligence. Companies that dispose of toxic waste in water or soil in a manner that causes personal injury or property damage can be held legally liable for such harm regardless of the legality of the original dumping. Examples abound of situations where a company's activities result in financial liability that far exceeds the cost-benefit calculation factored into corporate decision making.

There is also an apparent trend toward conferring legal reward for companies operating beyond compliance. Principles of organizational accountability impose indirect vicarious liability on a corporation for the actions of its agents (managers, employees). Increasingly organizations are held accountable for the actions of their agents whether management knew of the misdeeds or not. To alleviate some of the harshness of such strict liability on the entity, some statutes and court decisions have recognized that a company's financial damages may be mitigated to the extent that the organization affirmatively attempted to prevent the illicit behavior—that is, to the extent that it operated the entity beyond the bare floor of legal compliance.[15]

Figure 7-1 Developing Ethical Standards

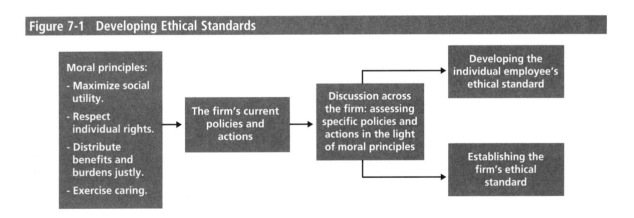

Source: Adapted and developed from Figure 2.1, Manuel Velasquez, *Business Ethics*, 5th Edition, Prentice-Hall, 2002, page 131.

In the next section, a variety of ethical dilemmas that face the international firm and that apply the methodology outlined in Figure 7-1 are presented to illustrate how they can be used to develop ethical standards.

Types of Ethical Conflicts

To understand the range of ethical conflicts that may arise when MNCs conduct international business activities, it is useful to consider the marketing value chain and assess where conflicts may occur at each step of the chain. (See Table 7-1.)

Global Strategy and Competing for Market Share

Part of global strategy is deciding which markets to compete in, then developing strategies and actions to win market share in those markets. An ethical problem arises when bribery is used to win business and market share and to influence public officials, co-opt consumer agencies, and consumer rights watchdogs.

For example, Monsanto agreed to pay fines of $1.5 million to settle bribery charges. The company had made $750,000 in payoffs to Indonesian officials to get permission to sell its genetically modified seeds (permission that it ultimately did not receive).[16] The bribes were paid by local executives and lobbyists working for Monsanto but were apparently done without the knowledge of Monsanto's top management. Upon learning about the transgression, Monsanto voluntarily informed U.S. authorities and accepted sanctions, though prosecutors did attribute the occurrence of the bribes to careless oversight by the company. In another example, the U.S. firm Fidelity National Financial was accused by its Taiwanese competitor of paying bribes through its Alltel Information Services subsidiary (which it had recently acquired) to secure software contracts worth around $176 million.[17] (See Figure 7-2.)

The example of Alltel provides some insight into the gradual process by which large-scale bribery unfolds. The sales effort in question began in January 2001, and major contracts were closed only in September and October 2004. During this lengthy period, there were changes in top management at the client firm, a suspension of the initial contract (leading to pressure to obtain reinstatement), the authorization of illegal payments, and the trail of evidence needed to establish illegal behavior.

Clearly, such bribery and corruption do have indirect costs, such as unfair competition, misallocation of resources, inefficiency, the long-term impact on slowing growth, and reduced entrepreneurial drive. If seen as pervasive and arbitrary, bribery and corruption can reduce the motivation to set up business and enter new markets. How should firms respond? Doh and others have suggested a gamut of activities. They range from avoiding such markets to changing entry mode (using joint ventures, licensing, arms length distribution), developing and adhering to corporate codes of conduct against bribery (a concern being that local firms might refuse to join such an agreement, thus gaining a temporary advantage), and being thoroughly trained and educated about bribery. As well, the firm could develop laws and agreements governing such behavior.[18]

It is useful to see how the principles and methodology in developing ethical standards can be applied to specific corporate actions. Consider the common problem of bribery in international markets described previously. Bribes can be paid to facilitate routine transactions, such as obtaining expedited customs clearance of goods that have been legally imported, or to be chosen over a competitor to receive, for example, a sizable government contract.

• The first kind of bribe, grease payments, may be seen as maximizing social utility. It preserves jobs and speeds the transit of scarce goods to customers, though it may favor the rights of the individual receiving the bribe over others. It also somewhat distorts the distribution of bene-

Table 7-1   Ethical Conflicts in the Value Chain

Value Chain Activity	Example
Global strategy: competing for market share	Bribery to obtain contracts
International marketing research	Testing new drugs in emerging markets
New product and service development development	Ignoring low-income segments and populations in new product
Global manufacturing; supply chain and logistics and linkage to international marketing	Supply chain manufacturing outsourcing partners who exploit local labor, negatively affecting the reputation of the company
International pricing	Price discrimination across markets
Global branding	Accusations that brands charge premium prices, create barriers to entry, shut out local competitors, and create cultural homogeneity
International distribution	Exclusive distributors that raise prices and reduce competition
Staffing international marketing positions; control and incentive systems	Hiring family members to fill supervisory positions
International advertising	Inappropriate appeals that clash with cultural values
Multiple stakeholders and societal consequences	SUVs and their impact on global warming

Figure 7-2   Anatomy of a Bribe—Fidelity National and the China Construction Bank

2001
June	Alltel Information Services (AIS) and Grace & Digital Information Technology (GDIT) agree to help sell Fidelity National Financial (FNF) software to China Construction Bank (CCB).
July	CCB and AIS sign an interim software licensing agreement.
December	CCB and AIS sign a long-term licensing agreement.

2002
January	The chairman of CCB is fired and replaced; the contracts with AIS are suspended.
March	AIC terminates its agreement with GDIT.
May	AIS hosts the new CCB chairman and others to a golf outing at Pebble Beach.

2003
April	FNF takes over AIS and renames it Fidelity Information Services.
September	CCB agrees to license FNF's software.

2004
October	Fidelity announces that CCB will use its software to process loans.

2005
March	The CCB chairman resigns for "personal reasons."

Source: "Suit Alleges US Firm Paid Bribes for China Contracts," Wall Street Journal, March 21, 2005.

fits in favor of the person receiving the bribe. It burdens society with the additional costs of the bribe, especially when they are passed on to customers or shareholders. Grease payments probably have little positive impact on the principle of caring for others; though in many emerging markets, government jobs may be handed as favors to close relatives and friends of senior political figures. A firm might judge grease payments to be justifiable on the grounds of greatest social benefits at minimum social costs with little (hence, acceptable) injury to social justice and individual rights. In another firm, the same discussion could come down on the side of branding such bribes as unethical on the grounds that social justice should take precedence over any additional net benefit that society might receive.

• However, in the case of the bribe to obtain business over a competitor, the same application of the moral principles of utilitarianism, rights, social justice, and hypernorms might result in most firms agreeing that such bribes are unethical and unjustifiable. The key point is that firms need moral principles and a reasoned discussion in order to judge their policies and actions and to arrive at ethical standards that are acceptable to them—policies they can abide by and implement.

Legal Regulation and Compliance

National and supranational laws and regulations may clarify what constitutes minimal ethical behavior and may constrain the range of legal actions that a firm can undertake in its international operations. As stated in Chapter 4, attempts to forge supranational laws governing business conduct are counter to traditional legal notions and respect for national sovereignty. **National sovereignty** means that a country can conduct its own affairs without interference from other governments or the laws of any other country. Thus, when the EU was formed, individual European nations had to agree to accept European laws and pass enabling legislation to mirror those laws. The alternative is to create voluntary associations such as the OECD, the UN, and the WTO and to voluntarily agree to accept and abide by their rules and guidelines, such as those against bribery and corruption.

The UN, as part of its **Global Compact**, announced in June 2004, "Businesses should work against corruption in all its forms, including extortion and bribery." The UN Convention against Corruption stresses that corruption is damaging to national economic growth. It has recommended codes of conduct for public officials, transparency of public procurement, the prevention of bribery to influence public officials, and generalized anticorruption crime-fighting efforts. While the UN stops short of policing efforts, it does recommend the sanctioning of such unethical behavior. Transparency International, a supranational NGO that seeks to eradicate corruption in international trade and business, similarly notes in its "Business Principles for Countering Bribery" that

The enterprise shall prohibit bribery in any form whether direct or indirect.... The enterprise shall commit to implementation of a Programme to counter bribery.[19]

U.S. Law

The Foreign Corrupt Practices Act (FCPA) specifically bans payments to gain business, though it does allow facilitating payments. "The difficulty in allowing some level of bribery is that it may become a slippery slope leading to larger and more frequent payments. Hence, corporations may prefer to ban all such payments. For example, Sealed Air Corporation (manufacturer of Bubble Wrap® cushioning and other packaging products) has developed a **code of conduct**, sections of which are provided below.

Sealed Air Corporation has a reputation for conducting its business on a highly ethical level. It is important that we continue this record of integrity in the future.

Each and every employee of the Company and its subsidiaries throughout the world is responsible for the maintenance of our fine reputation. We expect that each employee will support the Company's principles of business ethics and behave in a manner consistent with these high standards. No employee in a supervisory position has the authority to instruct a subordinate to violate the ethical guidelines of the Company.

Each of our employees is expected to comply with the law, but our standard of business ethics goes beyond compliance with law. No list of rules can substitute for the exercise by anyone who represents our Company of basic morality, common decency, high ethical standards and respect for the law. If an employee is in doubt about the acceptability of a particular course of action, the following test should be applied: Assuming full public disclosure of the action, would both the employee and the Company feel comfortable from a moral, ethical and legal standpoint? If the answer is "Yes," then the action is very probably consistent with our corporate philosophy. If not, then the action should be reviewed with the employee's manager or with the Company's Law Department before proceeding.

Our products and services will be sold on their merits. We will compete vigorously and fairly in the markets we serve. We will afford our competitors the degree of respect that we expect them to afford us. We will not enter into illegal arrangements nor engage in illegal concerted activities with our competitors or with others. . . .

Sealed Air requires its employees to comply fully with anti-corruption laws in the United States and similar laws in other countries. Sealed Air forbids its employees to make or offer illegal bribes or kickbacks intended to secure favored treatment for the Company from customers, suppliers, domestic or foreign government officials or others. This rule also applies to the use of intermediaries to make such payments.[20]

Sealed Air's Code of Conduct is clear in stating the company's explicit ethical standard that "goes beyond compliance with law." It further suggests an easy-to-understand generalizable test: "Assuming full public disclosure of the action, would both the employee and the Company feel comfortable from a moral, ethical and legal standpoint?" Such unequivocal and clear statements from top management help create a climate of regard for ethical standards and a strong desire to comply with them. Such a commitment is the necessary first step to developing ethical standards that pervade a company.

International Research

A particular issue with international research, particularly in emerging markets, is that a firm or its agencies may be working with research samples and with underlying populations whose members may be less informed, less educated, and less powerful when compared with the foreign firm. Hence, ethical standards dictate that a firm insist that permission of the research subject, informed consent, confidentiality, and restrictions on using and sharing information gathered from research be in place before the research begins. As in the home country, a firm needs to be especially attentive when using children as subjects for its international research effort. Pharmaceutical drug testing in emerging markets is an example of the kinds of ethical issues that firms need to take into account when conducting international market research, as discussed below.

DRUG TESTING IN EMERGING MARKETS

Before they can be certified by the FDA and other drug certification agencies worldwide for use in treating ill patients, newly developed drugs require extensive testing for toxicity, effectiveness, side effects, and interactions with other drugs. Drug companies have begun testing new drugs among populations in countries such as India, Africa, and Eastern Europe. The attraction for researchers is a larger pool of patients to draw from who have not received much medical treatment involving new drugs ("drug-naïve") as well as the low costs of administering the drug trials. For instance, Covance, one of the world's largest drug development service companies, has considerably expanded its clinical trials services in Central and Eastern Europe. To find potential recruits for its new drug studies, Covance draws on a population of over 470 million people in 20 countries in this region. In return, the countries and their health-care systems gain access to advanced medical treatments and new drugs under development. The drug companies and Covance clients benefit from "high patient recruitment rates and excellent data quality." The Central European region also has well-trained medical investigators; and the drug trials can be done at a low cost, which may explain the five-fold increase in clinical trials in the Czech Republic, Poland, and Hungary over the past ten years. Another attraction is the "high incidence of many of the diseases most targeted by the pharmaceutical industry"; for example, Bulgaria has one of the highest rates of cardiovascular disease and strokes.[21]

Ethical conflicts can arise when the only access to health care for low-income patients is through participation in such clinical trials. Some of the difficulties of conducting these trials include recruiting patients for whom English is not a native language. Their understanding of English is often limited. In such a case, questions can be raised about their giving informed consent when signing a liability release in English. In India and other countries with a patriarchal bent, women may be pressured by male relatives to sign releases and enter new drug trials. To be sensitive to possible exploitation, the contract research organization should use local and regional ethics committees at the hospitals and local facilities to evaluate patient recruitment practices and the proposed features of the clinical trials. Joseph Herring, president of Covance, notes that certain principles govern such collaboration, with the most important principle being the dictum "Aspire to a good that is greater than the individual or the group."[22]

One such drug trial on a new AIDS-prevention remedy was abruptly halted in Cameroon on the grounds that drug trial participants were not being fairly treated. A nonprofit public health organization, Family Health International (FHI), was conducting a study on the efficacy of an AIDS antiviral drug, Viread, also known as tenofovir. At a high risk for AIDS, the people in the study were from the five countries of Ghana, Nigeria, Malawi, Cameroon, and Cambodia. The drug was being supplied free by Gilead Sciences. If the drug tests were successful. Gilead planned to make Viread available at cost to poor countries.

The Cameroon study had recruited 400 women, including prostitutes at a high risk of contracting the AIDS virus. As is customary in drug trials, half the patients in the study were randomly assigned to receive a placebo pill, while the other half received a daily dose of tenofovir.

The participants received monthly health exams, including liver and kidney function exams to test for drug toxicity. The women had given informed consent and in the presence of a multilingual patient advocate, had received advice about practicing safe sex. The study had been approved by Cameroon's National Ethics Committee and by FHI's own review board. If a patient in the trial contracted AIDS, he or she was to be referred to a Cameroon AIDS treatment program for antiviral drugs. However, a French AIDS activist group, Act Up-Paris, managed to get the study halted on the grounds that the patients in the trial were "utilized as veritable guinea pigs" in an attempt to promote the drug's commercial prospects. In turn, the New York-based AIDS activist group Treatment Action decried Act Up-Paris's actions as "ethical imperialism." The five-country study had been funded by the Bill and Melinda Gates Foundation with a grant of $6.5 million. Act Up-Paris's protests had also halted the study in Cambodia. A similar study was being carried out in the United States to test the efficacy of the drug in AIDS prevention among gay men in Atlanta and San Francisco.[23]

New Product Development (NPD)

New product development (NPD) for foreign markets usually involves product adaptation and segment identification. Firms have to decide how to adapt their products, which segments they will adapt products for, and whether to develop entirely new products for those markets and segments. Given the fact that large portions of the developing world are poor, affordability is an issue; keeping affordability in mind, firms have to consider whether to adapt products. In emerging markets, firms should be attentive to the impact on the user—in terms of health, welfare, and value. The oft-held view is that low-end products are commodities with limited profit prospects. While low-margin products sold in sufficiently high volumes may yield adequate returns on investment, firms may be concerned that entry into such segments runs counter to their chosen strategy of concentrating on highly differentiated niche products sold at high prices for high profit margins.

Product development focusing on the needs of low-income populations can be a controversial choice within a firm. Making such a choice has particular significance in the global pharmaceutical industry. Diseases such as AIDS and malaria are scourges that have a huge affect in Africa, in India, and in other tropical countries—with lives lost and debilitating effects on the ability to work.[24] A well-known example is Merck's work on a drug for river blindness in the highlands of Africa.[25] This disease affects about 20 million people, primarily poor, in remote parts of Africa. The disease is transmitted by black flies whose habitat is swift-flowing water. Merck spent over $100 million of its R&D funds on developing a potential treatment for this disease, but would not be able to market it commercially given the low purchasing power of the affected population. They decided to make their treatment for river blindness, ivermectin, available free of charge for distribution by numerous agencies, including the UN.[26]

Merck's development and subsequent donation of a treatment for river blindness is an example of **Global Public Good (GPG)**.[27] The World Bank defines GPGs as "commodities, resources, services and systems of rules or policy regimes with substantial cross-border externalities that are important for development and poverty reduction, and that can be produced in sufficient supply only through cooperation and collective action by developed and developing countries." With regard to pharmaceutical drugs—given the paucity of drug development efforts directed toward affordable drugs for diseases such as river blindness—private philanthropies have often stepped up their efforts. For example, in 1999, the Global Alliance for

Vaccines and Immunization (GAVI) donated over $750 million to promote the development of vaccines. GAVI gave an equal amount again in 2004 to help develop vaccines against malaria, AIDS, tuberculosis, and other diseases (yellow fever, influenza, and hepatitis).

Segmentation and the Poor

Market segmentation focuses on identifying segments that are sizable and fast-growing, that offer profit opportunities, and that are relatively less intensely competitive. For firms, this has generally translated into seeking niche markets and selling higher-priced, value-added products and services. Low-end products are avoided because they offer slim margins, are volume-driven, and are likely to become commodity businesses. Yet most of the world's consumers are poor, and global marketers must confront the issue of selling to the world's poor.

In his book *The Fortune at the Bottom of the Pyramid*, C. K. Prahalad emphasizes that profits are possible in this segment.[28] By practicing what he terms "inclusive capitalism," companies can do well financially and develop new sources of value. He notes that in much of India and China, single-use packages account for the bulk of sales. For example, 60 percent of the value of all shampoo sold in India is in single-serve packages that sell for about a penny apiece. The product is profitable for global multinationals such as Unilever and Procter & Gamble, as well as for a myriad of small local firms.

Another example of market segmentation is that of providing subsistence farmers in rural villages with access to PCs, allowing them to track weather, source agricultural inputs at competitive prices, and track commodity price fluctuations so they can market their crops at fair prices and retain a reasonable share of the profits. To develop such PC kiosks, companies have to innovate along several dimensions, including developing the following:
• Rugged PCs
• Back-up power supply to manage power outages
• Solar panels to provide inexpensive energy
• Satellite-based telephone hookup to allow Internet access

What is interesting is that potential entrants into such markets are not creating just "single-serve" equivalents of their standard products, but are creating innovative solutions that can serve as a platform for additional products capable of being marketed globally.[29] As companies strive to manufacture affordable products, they may rethink design, feature sets, functionality, materials, and the like, resulting in price-performance breakthroughs that can serve as powerful entry points in challenging incumbents in developed markets. As an example, Prahalad refers to an effort in India to develop a car for under $3,000 to cater to India's vast numbers of lower-middle class consumers (the recently poor). While such cars may lack many of the features demanded by consumers in Germany or Japan, they will be built utilizing significantly lower-priced parts and subsystems, which will inevitably affect the global market and competition in the auto parts industry. It is entirely possible that nascent car companies in India and China will develop significant competitive advantages in products, logistics, and service capabilities, gradually enabling them to compete successfully in the advanced nation markets.[30] What is noteworthy is that a firm's ethical impulse not to marginalize low-income consumers can lead to its enhanced long-term global competitiveness—another example of "managing beyond compliance."

Global Manufacturing and the Supply Chain

Mattel (see the discussion in Chapter 5) and other toy companies manufacture the bulk of their toys in China and other Asian countries. By doing so, they can take advantage of low-cost labor and an efficient logistics system that allows them to raise or lower procurement quantities as demand evolves in the United States and Europe. It allows them to rapidly design and manufacture new toys in response to competitors' successes. It also allows them to quickly adapt their toys to changing tastes among their primary market—children and parents. Thus, overseas manufacturing is critical to the toy companies' global procurement strategy. Further, linkages between their global manufacturing and global marketing help preserve international competitiveness. These companies have come under attack from public interest groups for not paying enough attention to the welfare of their overseas workers, particularly when those workers are employed by subcontractors in China, Vietnam, and elsewhere. In response, Mattel has developed a set of Good Manufacturing Practices (GMP) that govern their overseas manufacturing practices and provides an overarching ethical framework for such decisions. The elements of their GMP are listed below.

Mattel Good Manufacturing Practices (GMP) Highlights

(The firm must comply with local laws as a minimum standard.)

1. **Management Systems.** Facilities must have systems in place to address labor, social, environmental, health and safety issues.
2. **Wages and Working Hours.** Employees must be paid for all hours worked. Wages for regular and overtime work must be compensated at the legally mandated rates and all overtime must be voluntary.
3. **Age Requirements.** All employees must meet the minimum age for employment as specified by country and Mattel requirements.
4. **Forced Labor.** Employees must be employed of their own free will. Forced or prison labor must not be used to manufacture, assemble, or distribute any Mattel products.
5. **Discrimination.** The facility must have policies on hiring, promotion, employee rights, and disciplinary practices that address discrimination.
6. **Freedom of Expression and Association.** Each employee must have the right to associate, or not to associate, with any legally sanctioned organization.
7. **Living Conditions.** Dormitories and canteens must be safe, sanitary, and meet the basic needs of employees.
8. **Workplace Safety.** The facility must have programs in place to address health and safety issues that exist in the workplace.
9. **Health.** First aid and medical treatment must be available to all employees.
10. **Emergency Planning.** The facility must have programs and systems in place for dealing with emergencies such as fires, spills, and natural disasters.
11. **Environmental Protection.** Facilities must have environmental programs in place to minimize their impact on the environment.

Source: Mattel Inc.'s Corporate Social Responsibility Report, 2004, page 18
(http://www.mattel.com/about_us/Corp_Responsibility/csr_final.pdf).

To obtain widespread adoption of its GMP principles, Mattel has to be persuasive in motivating its suppliers to implement such practices and must be willing to accept the higher procurement costs that follow. Mattel can feel comfortable knowing it is following ethical principles in its procurement only when its far-flung supply network can be swayed to adopt such principles themselves. Mattel's actions, if successful, could burnish its reputation in the eyes of parents and children. Setting a high ethical standard within its supplier network will also raise the bar for the rest of the industry. They will become aware of Mattel's sourcing principles and may be expected to follow similar ethical principles. One possible consequence is the betterment of working conditions worldwide for workers in similar factories in a variety of industries beyond toys and apparel.

Pricing

A generalized problem is one of high prices relative to incomes in specific markets. An extreme example is the cost of the AIDS "cocktail" of drugs, which arrests the progress of AIDS and allows patients to attain a semblance of normalcy. But this course of treatment averages over $10,000 a year (far beyond the reach of most Africans) and Africa has one of the highest rates of AIDS infections. One response has been the development of copycat drugs by Indian pharmaceutical companies, which are sold for less than one-tenth the price of regular drugs. This development was made possible because India recognized process patents only until 2005, allowing Indian firms to legally manufacture similar drugs using noninfringing processes, thus underpricing Western competitors in the markets of Africa.

Other pricing problems may include price fixing, unfair discounts, discriminatory discounts, and premium pricing in poor neighborhoods (such as offering high-interest payroll loans). All of those practices are possible because of a lack of competition, allowing the foreign firm to exercise market power through pricing control. Another factor is the desire to maximize profits from the higher margins that result from higher prices, without much concern for affordability. In the long run, those practices can be self-defeating, as the higher prices create an umbrella that allows for the emergence of competitors who can develop and offer products suited to local needs at affordable prices.

Global Branding

Corporations develop global brands as one of the bases for product differentiation in the global marketplace. The intent is for consumers to learn to trust the brand and purchase it with confidence that the company behind the brand will deliver quality and value. Firms build brands by extensive advertising and promotion. Extensive investment in a brand is often rewarded with premium prices and brand loyalty, resulting in repeat purchases and higher long-term income. Brand loyalty also translates into increased sales volume and sustainable market share, creating a barrier to entry.

However, these very qualities of a global brand—namely, premium prices, barriers to entry, and brand loyalty—are also held against the company and the brand. These factors are sometimes seen as negative consequences that prevent smaller local companies from competing and winning market share. The argument is that brands delude customers into believing that consuming certain brands provides a superior lifestyle. Furthermore, the emotional attachment to a brand promotes a "vapid lifestyle" and an increasingly consumerist economy, in the eyes of some. Brand power is also seen as allowing companies behind the brand to use low-cost labor in developing economies, to ignore workers' rights, and to use materials and create consumption habits (for example, the SUV) that are harmful to the environment.[31] The No Logo movement, which first gained prominence in the U.K. and Europe, is the foremost proponent of such an argument, blaming global brands for creating cultural homogeneity and creating "a Barbie world for adults."[32]

Local policy makers and international executives both need to consider whether strong global brands crowd out local brands (for shelf space and mind space); also whether global brands represent a battle between unequals (between large global brand companies and smaller, underfinanced competitors from developing countries). At the same time, a company that makes massive investments in building and sustaining global brands is likely to want to safeguard its reputation with vigor and avoid unethical actions, whether it is selling shoddy quality and dangerous products, harming the environment, or exploiting workers in poor countries. The company has to worry that consumers will take their business elsewhere it if it undertakes such actions. Enlightened, long-term self-interest may, in fact, motivate a company with a global brand to behave more ethically, if only because it is more in the global limelight.

ETHICAL BEHAVIOR AND BRAND VALUE

A company with a strong brand has to worry that its brand reputation and strength will be hurt because of perceived or real ethical missteps. A brand is powerful and profitable precisely because consumers develop a preference for and choose to purchase a brand. Repeat purchases by brand-loyal customers provide the underpinning for brand equity and recurring income and profits. However, brand strength can also be a magnet for activists, who see corporations as the root of many of society's ills. Activists are quick to target major brands, utilizing antisocial behavior. For example, Gap is held responsible by some activists for exploitative labor practices undertaken by its network of global suppliers. Unilever is accused of contributing to overfishing and depleting fishery stocks worldwide because of its global procurement of fish. The danger is that consumers will remember such accusations, whether founded or not, and drop their preference for the brand, sapping the brand's ability to be successfully marketed internationally.

A company can respond to such threats by inculcating values across the firm, subscribed to by all employees, which are consonant with its customers' values. For example, Gap can (and did) show its concern for fair labor practices by developing and auditing fair labor standards for all of its suppliers, then making clear to all of its global consumers that its garments are procured only from suppliers who adhere to the company's global code for treatment of labor. Its Social Responsibility Report summarized the results of over 8,500 visits to its 3,000 supplier factories in 50 countries. These visits led Gap to revoke its approval of 136 factories and also led to its rejection of contract manufacturing bids from many more factories for serious violations of minimum wage, safety, environmental, and other standards (such as use of underage laborers).[33]

A company following Gap's path should be careful to ensure that its public pronouncements on values are reflected in its behavior; that is, all of its employees understand and implement the company's values through their actions, in choosing suppliers, and in continuing to do business with them. In analogous fashion, Unilever responded to accusations that it contributed to overfishing by joining with the Worldwide Fund (WWF) to form the Marine Stewardship Council (MSC). The MSC certifies well-managed fisheries and preserves surrounding ecosystems as being compliant with environmentally sound practices. There are similar organizations for other industries, such as fair-trade coffee and eco-friendly wood.

When thinking about values, companies also need to distinguish between values that are central to the company's core businesses and values that may be somewhat peripheral. Companies need to ensure that they closely monitor values that are crucial to their business. In the case of Gap, this clearly points to the need to monitor suppliers who provide the company with clothing and other fashion accessories.

Where peripheral issues are concerned, a company's actions may have less impact on the outcomes; hence, the company may be better served by working with industry groups and broader initiatives, as in the example of De Beers' condemnation of conflict diamonds.[34] **Conflict diamonds** are diamonds that are sold to raise resources to purchase weapons and prolong conflict. These diamonds come from mines in areas held by rebel armies and by warring nations. De Beers, along with other diamond-producing-industry companies, diamond-consuming nations, and other interested parties have worked together under the auspices of the UN in a set of talks known as the Kimberley Process. The goal has been to halt trade in conflict diamonds.

International Distribution

The issue here is restraint of trade, with undue pressure put on channels to prevent discounting. Firms may argue that discounting undercuts their value-based strategy. In response to such channel and pricing control, smuggling and gray markets emerge. **Gray markets** arise when goods destined for a particular geographic market are diverted to other markets, often through unauthorized distribution channels (sometimes through smuggling), to meet the needs of the alternative markets. Prices are often below those set in official distribution channels. Gray markets exist in markets as diverse as automobiles, brand-name apparel, cosmetics, and electronic consumer goods. Some of the consequences of gray market emergence include dilution of exclusivity, free riders, damage to channel relations, undermining pricing strategy, creating liability risk, and possibly damaging reputations.[35]

For example, Kubota tractors destined for the U.S. market are specifically designed to meet OSHA standards and other safety regulations. Kubota found that some of its tractors sold in the Japanese market were refurbished and then resold in the United States. With inadequate warranties, the tractors were not compliant with U.S. safety regulations. This activity has serious consequences for Kubota's brand equity and customer satisfaction—and possibly product liability. But the underlying reason is price. A segment of the market is willing to accept flawed warranties and compromised safety standards in return for gray-market tractors at lower prices. Companies faced with gray-market competition have to be willing to develop solutions that balance their profit interests with those of emerging price-conscious customer segments.

Global Promotion

A general problem in global promotion is a lack of cultural sensitivity that results in offending local mores and values. An example is the controversial series of Benetton clothing ads that featured interviews with convicted killers. The campaign was called "We, on Death Row." With respect to this and other campaigns, Benetton believes that "campaigns are not only a means of communication but an expression of our time."

Beyond the themes and content of ad campaigns, other treacherous areas are false advertising, advertising to children, and not respecting religious and other cultural values. A larger question is the power of advertising to influence consumption, a point referred to earlier as part of the No Logo movement. One can indeed question the long-term consequences of advertising that promotes consumption at the cost of ever-increasing indebtedness and personal bankruptcy. But it would be difficult for a marketing executive to question whether promoting conspicuous consumption and a throwaway culture is ethically suspect.

Multiple Stakeholders and Societal Consequences

As corporations move beyond a narrow focus on customers and shareholders as paramount, other stakeholders such as employees, the government, and society at large begin to matter.[36] Considering multiple stakeholders suggests that businesses should be managed with the long-term well-being of all stakeholders in mind. From that perspective, factors such as the good of society, the needs and rights of workers, the need to preserve jobs, and the need to train youth for jobs later in life are *all* seen as equally important relative to profits. Table 7-2 shows the reciprocal nature of interests between the firm and its multiple stakeholders. Thus, the utilitarian perspective with multiple stakeholders might well justify a reduction of profits to preserve long-term worker welfare.

An example of the impact of multiple stakeholders is the Green movement and the growing demand that firms pay attention to the environmental pollution consequences of their actions. Customers and the public at large are more aware of and pay attention to recyclability, the nature of packaging used, and the problem of electronic waste. For instance, the EU has regulations in place requiring firms to be responsible for recycling end-of-life products that they manufacture. Green seals of approval, now common, are a factor that influences consumers' buying behavior. An example of the kind of dilemma created by weighing consumer demand and acting environmentally responsible is presented in the next section.

Ford Motor Company solicited input from insurance companies for the design of its autos. The reason for this seemingly unlikely pairing is that Ford wanted to design cars that would be less expensive to repair when they were involved in accidents. Ford thought that doing this could result in less expensive insurance premiums for its customers, which it could use in promoting its cars.[37]

Table 7-2 The Firm and Stakeholders Reciprocity

Constituent	Threat to Constituent	Threat to Company
Shareholders	Investment—expectation of economic success	Source of capital resources
Employees	Wages, benefits, and job security	Skills, labor, and loyalty
Customers	Reliable, affordable, quality products and services	Revenues to keep the firm profitable
Business Partners	Potential economic success	Dependent on partners for business operations
Community	Tax base and economic/social benefit to the community and its members	Right to build facilities and to operate in an environment conducive to a productive and competent workforce

Source: Adapted from A. Marcus and S. Kaiser, *Managing Beyond Compliance*, Garfield Heights, OH: NorthCoast Publishers, 2006.

The Ethical Nature of Promoting Large SUVs

Cars emit carbon dioxide, which is thought to contribute to global warming. Such emissions can be reduced when fewer people purchase large SUVs, which are generally fuel-inefficient vehicles. CAFE (corporate average fuel economy) rules are set at only 20.7 miles per gallon for SUVs as compared to 27.5 mph for full-size cars.[38] Hence, SUVS have come under attack as making the United States more dependent on imported oil, as well as for their poor safety record. The industry, by manufacturing and promoting more fuel-efficient cars and trucks, could help reduce dependence on energy imports. Should car companies, therefore, promote fuel-efficient cars and encourage the public to buy them at the expense of pricier, more profitable, large, fuel-guzzling SUVs?[39] In Canada, the answer has been a resounding "yes." Canadian automobile companies signed an agreement with the Canadian government, agreeing to reduce greenhouse gas emissions by 17 percent over five years, which would involve using fuel-saving technologies and alternative fuels such as ethanol, clean diesel, and biodiesel.

Prioritizing Values

When there are multiple stakeholders, corporations need guidance as to how to prioritize values. A puzzle for corporations is that there are many worthy causes and constituencies. A firm's consumers and its shareholders might ask what it is doing about global warming, terrorism, governmental corruption, and poverty, among other issues. An automobile company might well argue that its products have little to do with terrorism, governmental corruption, and poverty. The company may go on to state that it is working on reducing emissions and is devoting funds to research to develop an engine that is clean-burning, thus helping to reduce global warming. In rebuttal, activists might point out that the company imports thousands of containers full of parts every year and that its manufacturing processes in other countries, coupled with these shipments, contribute to pollution and global warming. The company may find out that it markets its cars in countries with high levels of corruption and that its dealer network in those countries resorts to questionable business practices in fleet sales to government agencies. It may discover that its factories hire employees whose families live in substandard housing and are unable to find good schools for their children, who are thus growing up poorly educated. Through such a discovery process, firms will gradually realize that their very prominence makes them the target of consumers and activists who hold them responsible for and expect them to ameliorate societal ills.

A recent effort, the Copenhagen Consensus, is an example of how firms might prioritize their social responsibilities.[40] The Copenhagen Consensus project has attempted to (1) rank some of society's major problems and (2) prioritize the problems based on the costs and benefits of developing solutions, then ranking the solutions based on what results in the greatest benefit for the least cost. (See Table 7-3.) This is an example of the utilitarian approach to ethical dilemmas.

To analyze the costs and benefits of solutions to each of the major problems, the project assembles nine of the world's leading economists, including four Nobel laureates. This approach accepts the fact that resources are scarce and that society does not have unlimited resources to tackle all of society's problems at once. Therefore, is it better to spend marginal resources on promoting primary education, reducing global warming, or fighting the spread of communicable diseases? The Copenhagen Consensus attempts to come up with answers to that sort of question and in the process, develops and gains acceptance for its methodology of making trade-offs between "causes." Firms that are similarly pulled in different directions could well employ pri-

Table 7-3	The Copenhagen Consensus "Top-Ten Problems"	
1. Climate change	6. Governance and corruption
2. Communicable diseases	7. Malnutrition and hunger
3. Conflicts	8. Population and migration
4. Education	9. Sanitation and water
5. Financial instability	10. Subsidies and trade barriers

oritizing methodologies to focus first on issues and values that affect the core of their business.[41]

This review of ethical issues that arise in international business has attempted to be wide-ranging. There are no absolute, single answers to ethical conflicts that arise in international business. However, firms must be prepared with a set of ethical standards that are agreed to by all employees. The firms and their employees can then apply those ethical standards to help resolve ethical conflicts in an honorable manner.

Summary

Ethical dilemmas abound in international business, ranging from the advisability of developing products for low-income consumers to price discrimination across countries.

Because they are societal institutions that exist with the permission of the various societies and markets they serve, firms need to act ethically across international markets.

Firms also have to consider cultural differences and how they may reflect different ethical standards. Firms need to factor those differences into their own behavior.

Several moral principles are useful in arriving at ethical standards. These moral principles include utilitarianism, theories of rights and justice, Kant's categorical imperative, the notion of caring for significant others, and the Integrative Social Contracts theory.

In addition, a recent perspective includes the notion of "managing beyond compliance": the recognition that a gap exists where the law ends or does not yet speak to regulate corporate conduct. Operating beyond compliance means that although some moral obligations to others may not be codified, that fact does not make their observance any less imperative.

To develop ethical standards, a firm must apply the moral principles to its policies and actions, discuss them among the its employees, and then arrive at its (mutually agreed and enforceable) ethical standards. At the same time, individual employees should use the moral principles and discussion of the firm's policies and actions to develop their own ethical standards.

Ethical dilemmas pervade a firm's international marketing value chain.

Major problems include bribery to compete for business and market share, market research, development of new products for low-income segments of the population, assurance that subcontractors manufacturing products marketed globally adhere to working standards that safeguard worker welfare, and act as a deterrent towards international price discrimination. Other potential problems extend to the perceived consequences of global branding and the backlash against global brands as contributing to high prices and a consumerist culture, problems in international distribution and advertising, and pressures from multiple stakeholders (the Green lobby, for example) over the environmental consequences of a firm's products and marketing.

Firms need some guidance on how to prioritize the values of multiple stakeholders. The Copenhagen Consensus project offers one example of how such priorities can be set.

Questions and Research

7.1 How can concerns over ethical behavior affect global business practices? Provide examples.

7.2 Why should a firm be concerned about ethics in international activities?

7.3 What are some fundamental moral principles that are relevant to assessing global business actions?

7.4 How can a firm connect moral principles to the development of ethical standards that would govern its international activities?

7.5 Describe some ethical conflicts that can arise along the value chain.

7.6 How can ethical standards help overcome problems associated with bribery and corruption in international markets?

7.7 Discuss Sealed Air Corporation's Code of Conduct discussed in the text. How can such codes of conduct be implemented? How can other firms learn from Sealed Air Corporation?

7.8 How do ethical issues affect the clinical testing of new pharmaceutical drugs in emerging markets?

7.9 How can firms develop successful business models to use in offering products and services for the poorest segments of the population in emerging markets? Why is it ethical for firms to concern themselves with "the bottom of the pyramid"?

7.10 How can a multinational firm be affected by unethical manufacturing practices among its suppliers? How has Mattel handled such conflicts?

7.11 How can unethical behavior affect brand equity and brand value? How have firms such as Gap and Unilever addressed such ethical concerns? What can be learned from them?

7.12 How does the presence of multiple stakeholders affect conduct? Focus on the issue of reducing environmental pollution globally to discuss how the green lobby affects global business practices.

7.13 Multiple stakeholders may have different goals that conflict with each other. How can a firm prioritize multiple conflicting goals as it attempts to practice ethical behavior?

7.14 Discuss the concept of GPGs in the context of developing new drugs for treating illnesses found primarily in poor emerging nations whose populations cannot afford the cost of new pharmaceutical drugs, even when proven highly effective. What broad lessons are learned from such an example for the practice of global business?

Endnotes

1 "Cigarette Deal Sets Market Rolling," *Financial Times*, March 16, 2005, page 30.

2 "Affordable Drug to Treat Malaria 'Ready Next Year,' " *Financial Times,* April 8, 2005, page 6; "Sanofi to Sell Cheap Malaria Drug: French Company Decides Against Patent Protection, Reducing Number of Deaths," *Wall Street Journal,* April 8, 2005, page B3.

3 "House of Cards: The WTO and Online Gambling," *The Economist,* November 20, 2004, Volume 373, Issue 8402, page 82.

4 "EC Launches iTunes Pricing Investigation," *Guardian*, February 24, 2005.

5 "Independent Monitor Completes Follow-Up Audit of Mattel Facilities and Suppliers in China and Mexico," *Yahoo! Finance*, December 17, 2004.

6 "Tackling Wood-Nappers: Illegal Logging in Indonesia," *The Economist*, May 7, 2005, Volume 375, Issue 8425, page 63.

7 Adapted from Marcus, A. and S. Kaiser, *Managing Beyond Compliance*, 2006, Garfield Heights, OH: NorthCoast Publishers.

8 This section draws on Velasquez, Manuel, *Business Ethics*, 5th Edition, 2002, Upper Saddle River, NJ: Prentice Hall.

9 Velasquez, Manuel. *Business Ethics*, 5th Edition, 2002, Upper Saddle River, NJ: Prentice Hall, pages 97-99.

10 Rawls, John. *A Theory of Justice,* 1999, Harvard Press; Velasquez, Manuel, *Business Ethics,* 5th Edition, 2002, Upper Saddle River, NJ: Prentice Hall, pages 116-120.

11 Donaldson, T. and T. W. Dunfee. "Towards a Unified Conception of Business Ethics: Integrative Social Contracts Theory," *Academy of Management Review*, Volume 19, 1994, pages 252-284.

12 Donaldson, T. and T. W. Dunfee. "Towards a Unified Conception of Business Ethics: Integrative Social Contracts Theory," *Academy of Management Review*, Volume 19, 1994, page 265.

13 Spicer, A., T. W. Dunfee, and W. J. Bailey. "Does National Context Matter in Ethical Decision Making? An Empirical Test of Integrative Social Contracts Theory," *Academy of Management Journal*, Volume 47, Issue 4, 2004, pages 610-620.

14 Marcus, A. and S. Kaiser. *Managing Beyond Compliance: The Ethical and Legal Dimensions of Corporate Responsibility,* 2006, Garfield Heights, OH: NorthCoast Publishers, page vi.

15 Marcus, A. and S. Kaiser. *Managing Beyond Compliance: The Ethical and Legal Dimensions of Corporate Responsibility,* 2005, Garfield Heights, OH: NorthCoast Publishers, pages vi-vii.

16 "Seed Money: In Indonesia, Tangle of Bribes Creates Trouble for Monsanto," *Wall Street Journal,* April 5, 2005, page A1.

17 "Suit Alleges US Firm Paid Bribes for China Contracts," *Wall Street Journal*, March 21, 2005.

18 Doh, Jonathan P., Peter Rodriguez, K. Uhlenbruck, J. Collins, and L. Eden. "Coping with Corruption in Foreign Markets," *Academy of Management Executive*, Volume 17, Issue 3, 2003, pages 114-129.

19 Transparency International, *Business Principles for Countering Bribery,* 2003.

20 Sealed Air Corporation Code of Conduct (http://www.sealedair.com/corp/conduct.html); accessed April 7, 2005.

21 Vrabevski, Milan. "Clinical Trials in Bulgaria, Parts 1 and 2," *European Pharmaceutical Contractor (EPC) Magazine,* Summer 2002 and Autumn 2002.

22 Herring, Joseph L. "A Winning Prescription for Drug Development Outsourcing," *European Pharma-*

ceutical Contractor, Autumn 2004.

23 "Cameroon Halts AIDS Study," *Wall Street Journal,* February 8, 2005, page D7.

24 "The Menace of AIDS," *The Economist*, July 8, 2002; "Four Horsemen of The Apocalypse," *The Economist*, Volume 367, Issue 8322, May 3, 2003, page 85.

25 "Merck Corporation and the Cure for River Blindness: Case 5-3, page 132 in LaRue Tone Hosmer, *The Ethics of Management*, 4th Edition, 2003, Boston: McGraw-Hill.

26 World Development Report, 2000/2001, Box 10.1, page 182, Washington, DC: The World Bank, 2001.

27 Kaul, Inge, Pedro Conceicao, Katell Le Goulven, and Ronald U. Mendoza, eds. *Providing Global Public Goods,* 2003, New York: Oxford University Press; Kaul, Inge, Isabelle Grunberg, and Marc Stern, *Global Public Goods—International Public Cooperation in the 21st Century,* 1999, New York: Oxford University Press.

28 Prahalad, C. K. "The Fortune at the Bottom of the Pyramid—Eradicating Poverty through Profits," *Financial Times,* 2004, Upper Saddle River, NJ: Prentice Hall.

29 Wind, Yoram and Vijay Mahajan. "Convergence Marketing: Strategies for Reaching the New Hybrid Consumer," *Financial Times*, 2002, Upper Saddle River, NJ: Prentice Hall.

30 Prahalad, C. K. "Why Selling to the Poor Makes for Good Business," *Fortune*, Volume 150, Issue 10, November 15, 2004, pages 70-73.

31 "The Case for Brands," *The Economist*, Volume 360, Issue 8238, September 2001, page 9.

32 Klein, Naomi. *No Logo: Taking Aim at Brand Bullies*, 2000, New York: Picador USA.

33 The Gap, Incorporated, *2003 Social Responsibility Report* (http://www.gapinc.com/social_resp/social_resp.htm); accessed May 14, 2005.

34 Allen, James and James Root. "The New Brand Tax," *Wall Street Journal*, September 7, 2004, Section B, page 2.

35 Antia, K. D., Mark Bergen, and Shantanu Dutta. "Competing with Gray Markets," *Sloan Management Review*, Volume 46, Issue 1, Fall 2004, pages 63-70.

36 Garriga, Elisabet and Domenec Mele. "Corporate Social Responsibility Theories: Mapping the Territory," *Journal of Business Ethics*, Volume 53, 2004, pages 51-71.

37 "Ford Designed Mustang to be More Insurance Friendly," *USA Today*, Tuesday, August 9, 2005, Section B, page 1.

38 "Roadroller: Sport-utility Vehicles," *The Economist*, Volume 366, Issue 8307, January 18, 2003, page 62.

39 "Greening of The Boardroom—Socially Conscious Investors Get Results on Global Warming," *Boston Globe*, March 31, 2005, page E1; "Car Makers Reach Canadian Accord to Cut Emissions," *Wall Street Journal,* April 5, 2005, page B1.

40 Copenhagen Consensus (http://www.copenhagenconsensus.com); accessed June 15, 2005.

41 Lomborg, Bjorn. "Prioritizing the World's To-Do List," *Fortune*, Volume 149, Issue 10, May 17, 2004, pages 60-62.

Further Readings

Donaldson, T. and T. W. Dunfee. "Towards A Unified Conception of Business Ethics: Integrative Social Contracts Theory," *Academy of Management Review,* Volume 19, 1994, pages 252-284.

Garriga, Elisabet and Domenec Mele. "Corporate Social Responsibility Theories: Mapping the Territory," *Journal of Business Ethics*, Volume 53, 2004, pages 51-71.

Machan, Tibor R., ed. *Business Ethics in the Global Market*, 1999, Stanford, CA: Hoover Institution Press.

Marcus, A. and S. Kaiser. *Managing Beyond Compliance: The Ethical and Legal Dimensions of Corporate Responsibility,* 2006, Garfield Heights, OH: NorthCoast Publishers.

Rawls, John. *A Theory of Justice,* 2005, Cambridge, MA: Belknap Press.

Review of Business, Special Issue: *Global Regulatory and Financial Reporting Reform and the Convergence of Accounting and Auditing Standards: The Time Has Come,* Volume 26, Issue 2, Spring 2005.

Spicer, A., T. W. Dunfee, and W. J. Bailey. "Does National Context Matter in Ethical Decision Making? An Empirical Test of Integrative Social Contracts Theory," *Academy of Management Journal,* Volume 47, Issue 4, 2004, pages 610-620.

U.S. Dept. of Commerce, International Trade Administration. *Business Ethics: A Guide to Responsible Business Enterprise in Emerging Markets,* 2003, Washington DC: Government Printing Office.

Velasquez, Manuel. *Business Ethics,* 6th Edition, 2006, Upper Saddle River, NJ: Prentice Hall.

Wartick, Steven L. and Donna J. Wood. *International Business and Society,* 1998, Malden, MA: Blackwell Business Publishers.

Recommended Web Sites

Business Ethics (http://www.business-ethics.com), especially "100 Best Corporate Citizens for 200x" (select 2000-2005) (http://www.business-ethics.com/whats_new/100best_2005.html) and Resources for Educators (http://www.business-ethics.com/For-Educators.htm).

Business Ethics, Canada (http://www.businessethics.ca).

Corporate Ethics (Washington Post—http://www.washingtonpost.com/wp-dyn/business/specials/corporateethics).

Corporate Fraud Task Force (U.S. Government, Office of Deputy General, U.S. Department of Justice)—(http://www.usdoj.gov/dag/cftf). For specific cases, see the Significant Criminal Cases and Charging Documents web page—(http://www.usdoj.gov/dag/cftf/cases.htm).

Corporate Social Responsibility (http://www.csrwire.com).

E-Business Ethics (Colorado State) (http://www.e-businessethics.com); play the Gray Matters game (developed by Lockheed Martin)

GLOSSARY

-A-

aesthetics the prevalent ideas in a culture concerning beauty and good taste, as expressed in the arts and the appreciation of color and form

autarky national self-sufficiency

-B-

balance-of-payments referring to summary statements of all economic transactions between one country and all other countries over a period of time, usually one year

bimodal income distribution referring to a country in which most people are below the per capita income figure with a small wealthy group above it (that is, no middle class)

-C-

caste a type of detailed, rigid social organization

categorical imperative Immanuel Kant's theory stating that people should not be treated as means, but as ends

change agents those that cause or effect change

civil (code) law law that is based on an extensive and, presumably, comprehensive set of laws organized by subject matter into a code

class groupings a type of loose, flexible social organization

code of conduct nonlegislated guidelines that an organization decides to follow

commercial infrastructure the availability and quality of supporting services such as banks and financial institutions, advertising agencies, distribution channels, and marketing research organizations

commercial policy government regulations that have a bearing on foreign trade

common law tradition-oriented law in that the interpretation of what the law means on a given subject is heavily influenced by previous court decisions as well as by usage and custom

common market a grouping of nations that seeks to standardize or harmonize all government regulations affecting trade

common territory a homeland; a neighborhood, a suburb, a city, or even a tribal grouping

comparative advantage an economic theory used to explain the ability of a country to produce better and cheaper goods than another country

compensatory justice an approach stating that justice involves compensating people for wrong done to them or for loss suffered

conflict diamonds diamonds that are sold to raise resources to purchase weapons and prolong conflict

consultation in the context of the WTO's use of the term, a principle that allows a forum for nations to compromise over trade disagreements rather than resort to arbitrary trade-restricting actions

content music, videos, e-mail, telephony, and information that drive people to want an Internet connection

COR Export Trade Certificate of Review; a special certificate that provides a U.S. firm or a group of companies with immunity from antitrust suits regarding export activities specified in the document

culture a total pattern of behavior that is shared by a group of people, is consistent and compatible in its components, and is a learned behavior

customs union similar to a free-trade area in that it has no tariffs on trade among members; it has the more ambitious requirement that members also have a uniform tariff on trade with nonmembers

-D-

database marketing analyzing and using knowledge about customers and potential customers to develop products and business strategies

data mining analysis of data to identify patterns for predictive purposes

distributive justice an approach whose goal is to achieve a fair distribution of society's benefits and burdens

dumping selling products below the cost of manufacture or selling for a lower price abroad than at home

-E-

ethics the science or study of morality in human conduct

European Union (EU) as of May 1, 2005, the economic amalgamation of 25 European nations

exchange control government regulation of foreign exchange transactions

export trading company (ETC) a service firm that provides expertise and assistance to other firms in moving products and services around the globe

-F-

foreign business management the organization, planning, and control of global business activities

-G-

geographic proximity referring to the fact that countries that are neighbors are typically better trading partners than countries that are distant from each other

global business management the act of coordinating business activities in multiple markets in the face of global competition

Global Compact a voluntary international corporate citizenship network initiated by the UN that states, "Businesses should work against corruption in all its forms, including extortion and bribery."

Global Public Good (GPG) "commodities, resources, services and systems of rules or policy regimes with substantial cross-border externalities that are important for development and poverty reduction, and that can be produced in sufficient supply only through cooperation and collective action by developed and developing countries," as defined by the World Bank

gray markets refer to goods destined for a particular geographic market but diverted to other markets, often through unauthorized distribution channels (sometimes through smuggling), to meet the needs of the alternative markets

gross national income (GNI) a measure of the total domestic and foreign value created by residents

-H-

hypernorms manifest, universal norms that represent principles so fundamental to human existence that they are reflected in a convergence of religious, philosophical, and cultural beliefs

-I-

infrastructure external facilities and services of an economy, including paved roads, railroads, energy supplies, and other communication and transport services

Integrative Social Contracts a theory stating that in the context of most local cultures, managers can apply ethical standards derived from the local context, principally from domestic firms, industries, professional associations, and other organizations

intellectual property (IP) thoughts and ideas that are turned into paintings, music, software, and architectural designs and the processes used to create products

intellectual property protection (IPP) methods such as registration of trademarks and patents used to protect a firm's intellectual property

International Monetary Fund (IMF) an organization that acts as a forum for monetary and fiscal discussions that affect the world economy and that supplies financial assistance (loans) and technical assistance (economic consultants)

Islamic law Shari'a; law of the religion of Islam

-K-

kinship the social organization or structure of a group; the way people relate to other people

-L-

legal environment a nation's laws and regulations pertaining to business

-M-

market size a consideration with regard to present markets and potential markets when a firm is examining world markets

material culture the tools and artifacts in a society, excluding physical things found in nature unless they undergo some technological transformation

matrix organization an organizational structure that makes use of dual rather than a single chain of command, lateral (dual) decision making, and a chain of command that fosters conflict management and a balance of power

multinational corporation (MNC) the company manufactures and markets its products or services in several countries.

-N-

national sovereignty the right of a country to conduct its own affairs without interference from other governments or the laws of any other country

natural resources a nation's actual and potential forms of wealth supplied by nature as well as its land area, topography, and climate

nondiscrimination in the context of the WTO's use of the term, a principle that calls for each contracting party to grant all other parties the same rate of import duty

non-tariff barriers (NTBs) trade barriers that include customs documentation requirements, marks of origin, food and drug laws, labeling laws, antidumping laws, "buy national" policies, and subsidies

-P-

per capita income statistics most often used to describe a country economically; calculated as the total value of goods created divided by the total population of a geographic area

political environment when referring to international business, any national or international political factor that can affect its operations

product life cycle the consumption pattern or sales trend for a class of products

-Q-

quota a quantitative limit on trade of good or services

-R-

regional headquarters an organizational level between corporate headquarters and the foreign markets

regionalism economic cooperation within regions

religion an organized system of belief in a supernatural power or powers that control human destiny; helps explain why people behave as they do

repatriate to send home

resale price maintenance (RPM) the effect of rules imposed by a manufacturer on wholesale or retail resellers of its own products to prevent them from competing too fiercely on price and thus driving profits down from the reselling activity

risk-based multistage production sequencing allows for development of production plans for the manufacturing process based on predictability or stability of demand

-S-

special interest group a kind of social grouping that may be religious, occupational, recreational, or political

strategic alliance a relationship formed by two or more organizations to increase the performance of the companies

sustainable economic development policies and programs designed to help developing countries by paying for or subsidizing the use of environmentally sound practices to reach economic goals

-T-

tariff a tax on internationally traded goods and services

tariff factory a company's establishment of local assembly operations to get around the tariff barriers of protected markets

technology the techniques or methods of making and using that which surrounds us

topography the surface features of a country's land, including rivers, lakes, forests, deserts, and mountains

transfer pricing the price at which intercompany transfers take place

-U-

United Nations Conference on Trade and Development (UNCTAD) a permanent organ of the United Nations General Assembly; its goal is to further the development of emerging nations

urbanization the number of people living in cities rather than rural locations

utilitarianism a moral principle that helps shape ethical standards for a corporation; behavior is judged in terms of the costs and benefits to society; actions that are chosen should result in the greatest net benefit or the lowest net cost

-W-

World Bank an institution whose goal is to promote economic growth, to provide loans for infrastructure development, and to improve the living conditions of the world's population

World Trade Organization (WTO) an international body dealing with the rules of trade between nations

INDEX

About NorthCoast Publishers

NorthCoast Publishers is a **Business Administration Publisher**, serving the Higher Education curriculum in the fields of International Business, Marketing, Management, and Entrepreneurial Studies.

"Quality publications at an affordable price" is our mantra. Thus, our publications will feature:

- a lower, more affordable price point than the competition;
- a fully supportive website for each product that acts as a "Portal" for the discipline and offers more educational substance and dialogic alternatives than the competition;
- an attractive, two-color design – primarily in paperback – with a full battery of teaching aids.
- the offering of modularized, "Custom" versions of our publications to those audiences comprised of 200 or more students that wish to use selected portions of our products.

The firm also provides close customer contact, offering hands-on editorial services, development of interactive software, securing of copyright clearances, timely manuscript editing and quality final production. This nimbleness and responsiveness extends to advanced and innovative marketing techniques – again, making use of the Web and electronic commerce.

We look forward to your participation in this exciting new endeavor and we would welcome any questions or suggestions you might have of us. Contact us at www.NorthCoastPub.com.

Sincerely,

Roger L. Williams   Robert H. Vaughn
Publisher   Vice-president, Operations

To find out about our new books, special offers and much more,
access our website at www.northcoastpub.com

From the authors of **this** book.
International Marketing, 9th (11\05)
Authors: Terpstra, Vern; University of Michigan,
Sarathy, Ravi; Northeastern University,
Russow, Lloyd; Philadelphia University
ISBN 1933583-177, 580 pp., paperback; $99.00

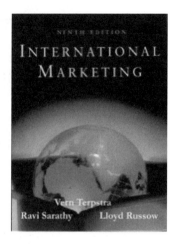

This is a Basic Text for courses in International Marketing and International Business. Relevant case studies are included for each section of the text. The Ninth Edition of this popular text has been completely revised, reflecting current developments in the field and the imperatives of dealing with an increasingly Globalized Economy. Drawing upon the extensive and unparalleled international marketing experience of its authors (one of whom is new to the Ninth Edition), *International Marketing* takes a comprehensive look at the environment, problems and practices of today's international marketing arena. This text gives students a real-world taste of this dynamic field, preparing them for entry into the marketing workplace of the 21st Century. Chapters on "Information Technology", and "Ethics", in particular, have been moved to the front section of the book, reflecting the widespread and pervasive impact of newer technologies and ethical questions on the marketing field.

Strategies in Entrepreneurial Finance (11\05)
Author: Stoller, Greg; Boston College
ISBN 1933583-118, 320 pp., paperback; $85.00

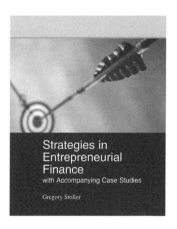

Strategies in Entrepreneurial Finance provides an in-depth casebook on the strategies required to build a company as viewed through the lens of entrepreneurial finance. It uses fourteen selected, original case studies describing the trials and successes encountered by real people as they started out as small business entrepreneurs. To add a real-world perspective to the cases and to round out the learning, the casebook also includes several sections that contain a multitude of qualitative and quantitative approaches and examples.

Globalization and International Business
Authors: He, Xiaohong; Quinnipiac University, *et. al.*
ISBN 1933583-428, paperback; Approx. 370 pgs., Preliminary ed 02/06; $92.00

Dr. He and her associates bring a wealth of real world international business experience, as well as years of college teaching to this exciting introductory textbook.. This groundbreaking work stands out in three respects from its competitors: 1.) it is *multi-disciplinary* and integrative in focus; 2.) truly international, it examines the issues from the point-of-view of both developed western countries and less developed nations; 3.) international business activities are placed within the context of history and globalization. Thus, there is ample detail on historical development, forms of government, social responsibility, and (importantly), *ethics*.

**Managing Beyond Compliance: The Ethical and Legal
Dimensions of Corporate Responsibility** (12\05)
Authors: Marcus, Alfred; University of Minnesota
Kaiser, Sheryl; Loyola College
ISBN 1933583-290, 420 pp., paperback; $77.00

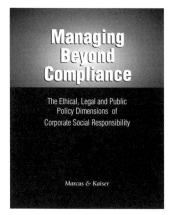

A thoughtful, contemporary treatise on Business Ethics, this text will provide a breath of fresh air for those professors wishing to combine current
strands of thought in business ethics and corporate social responsibility. The
text takes the position that the ethical dimension of business goes beyond
business policy and regulation; it shapes and informs law and public policy.
Rarely, however is the ethical dimension perfectly reflected in law; thus,
"Managing Beyond Compliance" is a necessity.

Essentials Financial Accounting, I (6\05)
Author: Carter, C.P.; Univ. of Massachusetts
ISBN 1933583002, 320 pp., paperback; $65.00

The students' need to know about "resources and their sources" is the foundation for the presentation of
the material. Each topic presented in the text is examined in terms of how it affects a company's resources
(assets) and sources of resources (liabilities and stockholder equity). Once the effects of events have been
examined, the text turns to journal entries in discussing the usual material in financial accounting.
Accounting for business events through *debits* and *credits* is an important part of the text – as is a thorough
coverage of the accounting cycle.

Order card

Book	ISBN	Price	Qty	Total
International Marketing, 9th	1933583177	99.00	_____	$_____
Entrepreneurial Finance	1933583118	85.00	_____	$_____
Globalization & International Bus	1933583428	92.00	_____	$_____
Managing Beyond Compliance:	1933583290	77.00	_____	$_____
Financial Accounting, vol I	1933583002	65.00	_____	$_____
Global Environment of Business	1933583185	52.00	_____	$_____
			Sub Total	$_____
		Shipping and Handling $7.00 x Qty		$_____
		Ohio Tax 8%		$_____
		Total		$_____

**Or order on-line at www.northcoastpub.com
Call us toll free 866-537-0323**

Global Environment. Business (8\05)
Authors: Terpstra, Vern; University of Michigan
Sarathy, Ravil Northeastern University
Russow, Lloyd; Philadelphia University
ISBN 1933583185, 302 pp., paperback; $52.00

This brief text gives students a real-world taste of this dynamic field, preparing them for entry into the global workplace of the 21st Century. "Information Technology", in particular, is featured — reflecting the widespread and pervasive impact of newer technologies on the field of international business.

_____

_____

_____

_____

NORTHCOAST PUBLISHERS INC
5063 TURNEY RD
GARFIELD HEIGHTS OH 44125